FROM PLAIN FARE
TO FUSION FOOD

FROM PLAIN FARE
TO FUSION FOOD

BRITISH DIET FROM THE
1890s TO THE 1990s

Derek J. Oddy

THE BOYDELL PRESS

First published 2003

Published by The Boydell Press
An imprint of Boydell & Brewer Ltd
PO Box 9, Woodbridge, Suffolk IP12 3DF, UK
and of Boydell & Brewer Inc.
PO Box 41026, Rochester, NY 14604–4126, USA
website: www.boydell.co.uk

ISBN 0 85115 934 6

A catalogue record for this book is available from the British Library

Library of Congress Cataloging-in-Publication Data
Oddy, Derek J.
From plain fare to fusion food : British diet from the 1890s to the
1990s / Derek J. Oddy.
p. cm.
Includes bibliographical references and index.
ISBN 0-85115-934-6 (Hardback : alk. paper)
1. Diet – Great Britain – History. 2. Food habits – Great
Britain – History. I. Title.
TX360.G7 O33 2003
394.1'0941 – dc21
2002153717

Typeset by Keystroke, Jacaranda Lodge, Wolverhampton
Printed in Great Britain by
Athenaeum Press Ltd, Gateshead, Tyne & Wear.

CONTENTS

List of illustrations   vi
Preface   ix
Abbreviations   xiii

1   Plain fare: diet during industrialization   1

2   Food supply, shops and food safety, 1890 to 1914   11

3   Nutrition, environment and health before 1914   41

4   The Great War and its aftermath, 1914 to 1921: discontent on the food front   71

5   Food and food technology in the interwar years   95

6   The question of malnutrition between the wars   113

7   The Second World War: the myth of a planned diet, 1939 to 1950   133

8   The revival of choice: food technology, retailing and eating in postwar Britain   169

9   Food consumption, nutrition and health since the Second World War   201

10   Overview: change in the twentieth century   224

Appendices   236
Bibliography   248
Index   263

ILLUSTRATIONS

Plates

2.1	Indigestion	33
4.1	Alimentary intelligence	73
4.2	Be sure to send Oxo	79
4.3	Food queues in the First World War	80
4.4	The great uncontrolled	85
5.1	The new knowledge of nutrition	99
5.2	Stop me & buy one	108
6.1	The Empire Christmas Pudding, 1928	118
6.2	The fish-and-chip shop, 1931	121
7.1	Vitbe brown bread	141
7.2	Sorry! No more of this	145
7.3	Grow your own food	152
7.4	Meals without meat	156
8.1	The Fish Finger, 1955	175
8.2	Self-service shopping	179
8.3	Electrolux fridge/freezer	187

Figures

9.1	Daily energy intake per head in Great Britain, 1970 to 1999	222
10.1	Energy sources of the British diet, 1795 to 1999	226

Tables

3.1	Annual average trends in infant mortality, 1891 to 1915	48
3.2	Infant mortality rate in Bradford, 1911, by rateable values of housing	48
3.3	Child mortality in England from the 1870s to the First World War	49
3.4	Weekly food consumption per head in family budget surveys, 1890 to 1913	56
3.5	Weekly food consumption per head arranged by income levels	59

3.6	Weekly food consumption per head of working-class men and women, 1894	62
3.7	Daily nutrient intake per head calculated from family budget surveys, 1890 to 1913	64
3.8	Daily nutrient intake per head arranged by income levels	66
3.9	Daily nutrient intake per head of working-class men and women, 1894	66
3.10	Daily nutrient intake per head in casual labourers' and paupers' families, 1909 to 1912	67
3.11	Weekly food consumption per head in servant-keeping families in York, 1901	69
3.12	Daily nutrient intake per head in servant-keeping families in York, 1901	69
4.1	Civilian food rations per head per week, 1917 to 1920	87
5.1	Supply of canned foods in Britain, 1924 to 1935	97
6.1	Estimates of Britain's food supply expressed as weekly food consumption per head of the population, 1920 to 1938	114
6.2	Estimates of Britain's food supply expressed as daily nutrient intake available per head of population, 1920 to 1938	114
6.3	Weekly food consumption per head in Scottish urban working-class families, 1928 to 1933	119
6.4	Daily nutrient intake per head in Scottish urban working-class families, 1928 to 1933	120
6.5	Weekly food consumption per head shown by dietary surveys in the 1930s	128
6.6	Daily nutrient intake per head shown by dietary surveys in the 1930s	129
7.1	Orr's 'Iron Ration' per day	137
7.2	Daily nutrient analysis of Orr's 'Iron Ration'	137
7.3	Weekly food consumption per diet head in London between February and July 1940	142
7.4	Weekly food consumption per diet head in London between February and May 1941	142
7.5	Daily nutrient intake per diet head in London in 1940	143
7.6	Daily nutrient intake per diet head in London in 1941	143
7.7	Weekly food rations per head in the two World Wars	149
7.8	Weekly food consumption per head of the population, 1937 to 1950	150
7.9	Daily nutrient intake per head of the population, 1937 to 1950	151
7.10	Outbreaks of food-poisoning in England and Wales, 1939 to 1944	161

7.11 Numbers of children having school meals and milk
      in England and Wales during the Second World War   163
7.12 Nutritional improvement in prewar Special Areas
      during the Second World War   165
8.1   Change in household structure in Great Britain, 1961
      to 2000   183
8.2   Changing leisure patterns in Great Britain, 1950 to
      1959   184
8.3   The frozen-food market in Britain, 1990   190
9.1   Weekly household food consumption in Great Britain,
      1945 to 2000   202
9.2   Daily nutrient intake in Great Britain, 1945 to 2000   207
9.3   Notifiable diseases: food-poisoning, 1983 to 1999   214
9.4   Weekly consumption per head of food and drink
      eaten outside the home, 1994 to 1999   217
9.5   Daily nutrient intake per head of food and drink
      eaten outside the home, 1995 to 1999   219
9.6   Daily nutrient intake per head of food eaten out,
      by income and gender, 1999   220
9.7   Daily nutrient intake per head of the population in
      Great Britain, 1970 to 1999   221
9.8   Percentage of population aged 16 to 64 defined as
      obese in England, 1980 to 1998   221
10.1 Percentage of total food supplies produced in the
      United Kingdom   225

PREFACE

This study of food and nutrition in the twentieth century begins in the 1890s, even though it can be argued that the ethos of the nineteenth century persisted beyond 1900 and at least until 1914. The history of diet, however, is better explained by the concept of a 'long' twentieth century, the start of which was marked by new technology and increasing commercialization of the food market during the 1880s and 1890s. By then the urban environment of late Victorian society was largely complete. Its major aspects remained unchanged from the 1890s to the 1920s, or even the early 1930s in some parts of Britain. The 1890s have attracted much interest in view of the social investigations in London and York by Charles Booth and B. S. Rowntree which revealed the social problems accumulated by more than a century of rapid population growth and urbanization. Although their work and that of other social investigators who followed them drew attention to the housing, employment and nutrition of the very poor, the view of Britain presented by these inquiries ignored the improvements in living conditions during the late nineteenth century. Undoubtedly the majority of the population had benefited to some extent from an advance in the standard of living. Nevertheless, as far as nutritionists and physiologists in the first half of the twentieth century were concerned, the image created by the social investigators of a society in which there was widespread malnutrition – or, strictly speaking, under-nutrition – was valid and still a matter of concern when further improvements in both housing and employment had taken place.

When *The Englishman's Food* was first published on the eve of the Second World War, 'the gravely deficient "poverty diet" of England which persisted throughout the 'thirties' was still a contemporary problem. Its origins 'dated from about 1890 and was responsible in the last decade of the nineteenth century for a marked deficiency in the physique and physical efficiency of much of the community'.[1] Any history of diet must examine that assessment and incorporate it into the account of what people in Britain were eating and the nutritional value of their food. Between the 1890s and the Second World War this requires the examination of family budget surveys. These investigations have

---

[1] J. C. Drummond and Anne Wilbraham, *The Englishman's Food*, revised edn (1957), p. 389

ix

shortcomings in terms of their size, design, purpose, and their coverage both in time and place. Nevertheless, they are indispensable sources of information; indeed, they provide the only quantitative evidence of what ordinary people ate. When Dr Hamill was sent to Geneva in 1937 as the United Kingdom's representative at the League of Nations' Conference of National Nutrition Committees, he had to admit that no official statistics as to the food consumed in the United Kingdom were compiled or published. He could only draw attention to the family budget inquiries that had been collected, even though civil servants at home in Britain were currently denigrating them as 'propaganda'.

The overall theme in planning this book has been to focus on what food entered the British diet and the circumstances in which it was produced, processed, supplied and eaten. Where evidence allows, a nutritional analysis has been introduced in order to evaluate the diet's contribution to health and physical development. Chapter 1 outlines how the traditional diet had been modified by industrial and urban changes in the nineteenth century. Chapter 2 therefore begins the study of diet in the twentieth century in detail by examining the supply, production, retailing and catering provisions of the food market before 1914, followed in Chapter 3 with evidence for food consumption and the nutritional value of the diet. This pattern is repeated for the interwar and postwar years, with the two World Wars, 1914–18 and 1939–45, forming natural divisions. Both wars brought about expediencies in the allocation of food but neither disrupted the long-term pattern of food consumption in Britain. Instead, if there is an overall pattern to the twentieth century from the point of view of food consumption, it should be to consider the period from the 1890s to the 1960s as one of stability – the final era of plain fare. A wider choice, better quality, fresher foods were the parameters that encompassed the expectations held by most people. However, from the 1970s until the end of the twentieth century change has been marked, not only in technology and processing but also in social patterns and behaviour, culminating in the adoption and adaptation of ethnic cuisines. In the 1990s, the shelves of supermarkets, the menus of cafés and the spread of their tables and chairs on to the pavements in British towns show how Britain has become a fusion-food culture.

It seems appropriate, as the twenty-first century opens, to look back at the dietary history of the preceding hundred years. However, there are certain difficulties attendant upon any history that stops almost at the present day. First, the nature of the sources change over the time covered and their analysis must reflect the problems inherent in writing 'contemporary' history when official records are still closed. Second, examining people's diet may give rise to a number of preconceptions in the reader's mind. The inspiration for many readers will be *The Englishman's Food*, although, with its revised version dating from as long ago as 1957, the need for a longer view of the twentieth century is obvious. Dorothy Hollingsworth, who had the greatest admiration for Jack Drummond, used his papers in revising *The Englishman's Food* and writing her supplementary chapter, but neither her experiences at the Ministry of Agriculture, Fisheries and Food nor access to official papers allowed a balanced picture to emerge.[2] A far more important account of the twentieth century appears in John Burnett's *Plenty and Want*, although his latest edition ended its survey in 1985 in the middle of a period of marked change.[3]

Any plan to write must involve exclusions. Bibliographers should note that this is not a cookery book – there are plenty of them in bookshops and in some cases they masquerade as history. There are thus no recipes except for one or two wartime perversions of peacetime food. There is almost nothing on various minority interests in food – vegetarianism is barely mentioned, there is almost no reference to food allergies or food fads and even 'organic food' is largely ignored. This is a study of mainstream food consumption that does not explore these matters in any detail.

The research that has gone into this book originated in the Department of Nutrition at Queen Elizabeth College in the 1960s. Professor John Yudkin was interested in a multi-disciplinary approach to nutrition and introduced his nutrition undergraduates to lectures by Theo Barker and other social scientists. In addition, inspired by the possibility that social science might offer something to life sciences which allowed a better understanding of the context in which they operated, John Yudkin raised the funds to create a Social Nutrition Research Unit at Queen Elizabeth College, headed by John McKenzie in the early 1960s. Working there brought me in contact with a number of immensely stimulating people – Professor John Yudkin, John McKenzie, Arnold Bender, Pamela Mumford, Derek Miller, Mike Stock, Anne Nicolson, Mollie Copping (who had worked with Dame Harriet Chick in the 1920s), Liz Evans and Catherine Geissler. The Historians and Nutritionists Seminar, which began at Queen Elizabeth College in the 1960s and ran until 1999, had a lifespan matching the research that has contributed to the writing of this book. The Seminar brought together Theo Barker, John Burnett, Ted Collins, Peter Mathias, Richard Perren and Edith Whetham among historians and John Yudkin, Arnold Bender, Derek Miller and Catherine Geissler among the nutritionists, with contributions from a number of other scholars who have produced

---

[2] The republication of *The Englishman's Food* by Pimlico Books in 1991 missed the opportunity for it to be revised.

[3] John Burnett, *Plenty and Want. A Social History of Food in England from 1815 to the Present Day*, 3rd edn (1989).

seminal work in the history of food. Its existence was a lifeline for the academic study of the history of food and diet in Britain. A number of papers given at the Seminar have already been published.[4] Since 1989 this research into the history of food has developed through wider European contacts into the International Commission for Research into European Food History (ICREFH), which originated at Münster in 1989 due to the efforts of Professor Hans-Jürgen Teuteberg. ICREFH has met regularly since then and produced books arising from its biennial symposia organized at Brunel University by Professor John Burnett; at Wageningen by Dr Adel den Hartog; at the Alimentarium, Vevey, by Dr Martin Schärer; at the Rowett Research Institute, Aberdeen by Professor Alexander Fenton (Edinburgh), at Tampere by Professor Marjatta Hietala, and at Alden Biesen by Professor Peter Scholliers (Free University, Brussels).[5] ICREFH's symposia have stimulated research for some aspects of this book.

Finally, my thanks are due to many people who have helped me over the years, in particular, at the British Library, the Public Record Office and the Rowett Research Institute where Lorna Daly carried out much painstaking sorting and recording of the surviving material for nutritional analysis. I am grateful to the Advertising Archives, the British Library, the Public Record Office, Birds Eye Walls Ltd, *The Chemist and Druggist* and Sainsbury's Archives for permission to reproduce the illustrations. Financial support for this research was received from the Social Science Research Council and its successor, the Economic and Social Research Council; I am grateful to Dr David Allen and Dr John Malin for their interest in this research and the administrative support of these grants. More recently The Leverhulme Trust awarded me an Emeritus Fellowship to study diet and nutrition in Britain from 1890 to 1990 which has help me to complete this book. Lastly, my wife Judy has been my greatest support as critic and proofreader. She has saved me from many errors; those that remain in the text are my responsibility alone.

London,
February 2002

[4] D. J. Oddy and D. S. Miller, eds, *The Making of the Modern British Diet* (1976); D. J. Oddy and D. S. Miller, eds, *Diet and Health in Modern Britain* (1985); Catherine Geissler and D. J. Oddy, eds, *Food, Diet and Economic Change Past and Present* (Leicester, 1993).
[5] ICREFH's website at: http://www.vub.ac.be/SGES/ICREFH.html lists its publications.

ABBREVIATIONS

AR	*Annual Report*
BBC	British Broadcasting Corporation
BFJ	*British Food Journal*
BMA	British Medical Association
BMI	Body Mass Index
BMJ	*British Medical Journal*
Bn	Billion (as one thousand million)
BSE	Bovine Spongiform Encephalopathy
CAP	Common Agricultural Policy
CCR	Committee of Civil Research
CHO	Carbohydrate
CJD	Creutzfeld Jacob Disease
CMO	Chief Medical Officer
COMA	Committee on Medical Aspects of Food policy
CSO	Central Statistical Office
CWS	Co-operative Wholsesale Society
cwt	Hundredweight (the long hundredweight of 112lb.)
DC	Departmental Committee
DDT	Dichlorodiphenyltrichloroethane
DEFRA	Department of the Environment, Food and Rural Affairs
DSIR	Department of Scientific and Industrial Research
EAC	Economic Advisory Council
EMB	Empire Marketing Board
HMSO	His [or Her] Majesty's Stationery Office
ICREFH	International Commission for Research into European Food History
I-DCPD	Inter-Departmental Committee on Physical Deterioration
kcal	Kilocalories
kj	Kilojoules
lb.	Pounds (avoirdupois)
LGB	Local Government Board
M	Million(s)
MAF	Ministry of Agriculture and Fisheries
MAFF	Ministry of Agriculture, Fisheries and Food
ml	Millilitres
MMC	Monopolies and Mergers Commission
MOHs	Medical Officers of Health

MRC	Medical Research Council (Medical Research Committee before 1920)
NAO	National Audit Office
ONS	Office for National Statistics
oz.	Ounces
PP	Parliamentary Papers
PRO	Public Record Office
RFI	Retail Food Index
RNI	Reference Nutrient Intake
RPM	Resale Price Maintenance
SC	Select Committee
WAAF	Women's Auxiliary Air Force
YMCA	Young Men's Christian Association

Units of measurement

The units of measurement used for money, length, weight and volume are contemporary. Imperial measure is used before 1971. The metric system is used after 1971 and for the nutritional analyses.

Older measures, such as the quartern loaf, have been retained in the text while they were still in common use. The quartern loaf (originally a quarter-peck loaf weighing 4lb. 5½oz.) weighed 4lb. in the early twentieth century. A boll of flour was 140lb. (or half a sack).

1

PLAIN FARE

Diet during industrialization

The industrial and urban development of Britain in the eighteenth and nineteenth centuries was accompanied by major changes in the food of the people. Until the second half of the nineteenth century, the principal determinant of food consumption was the state of domestic agriculture. Before the development of a large-scale international trade in foodstuffs, the population depended on a limited range of food materials available on a markedly seasonal basis. Dietary patterns were determined by the extent to which traditional methods allowed foodstuffs to be preserved. Thus the predominant food material on the eve of the Industrial Revolution was bread made from either wheat, barley or oats, surpluses of which were processed to produce beer and spirits. Animal food – bacon or pickled meat, fish, butter and, to a lesser extent, cheese – was preserved by the liberal use of salt. Green vegetables were seasonal in supply, as were pulses, roots or bulbs such as onions, though the latter were capable of storage for some time. Nevertheless, every year brought the 'hungry gap' of the late winter and early spring when supplies of vegetables were exhausted, a pattern which had not been entirely eradicated in country districts before war was declared in 1914.

The consolidation of landholdings and changes in agricultural techniques of the eighteenth and early nineteenth centuries turned many country-dwellers into a rural proletariat dependent on wage-labour as the principal source of income and with little access to land of their own on which to produce food. Rural society, as a self-sustaining ecosystem, was in a terminal phase. For most of the nineteenth century only the vestiges of a peasant economy remained, largely confined to the more remote upland or marshland regions. Change was at its most extreme where industrial development in textiles, metal production and engineering created an urban society dependent almost entirely upon the marketplace for food supplies. As the nineteenth century progressed, reliance on the marketplace grew, not only with the expansion of industrial towns but also to meet the needs of the semi-rural but commercialized communities of miners, fishermen, and shipbuilders, and the various crafts and trades of market towns.

High prices of foodstuffs and food riots during the period of the Napolconic Wars reflected the stresses that rapid population growth placed on the market. Prior to the railways there were limitations to the long-distance movement of foodstuffs. The widespread adulteration of commodities such as bread, tea and beer, which continued throughout the nineteenth century, indicated that the food supply was barely adequate to meet the demands of the growing population. For the majority of the population, the cost and narrow range of food materials limited the diet both in quantity and variety and also made it vulnerable to interruptions in supply. Nevertheless, there were no great dearths during the Industrial Revolution, even though high prices around 1840 led to the decade later acquiring the epithet the 'Hungry Forties'. The one major crisis resulting from the potato blight was confined principally to Ireland. In Britain, the failure of the potato crop in 1846–7 was restricted to the Western Highlands of Scotland, where the potato had achieved an importance almost as great as in the Irish diet. The resulting food shortage was prevented from becoming a famine by the hasty improvisations of the Highland Relief Board. A later food crisis in Lancashire in the early 1860s, during the Cotton Famine, resulted from the lack of purchasing power rather than a failure in food supply, and this was also contained by the extensive use of charitable relief.[1]

Food prices began to fall from the 1820s due at first to improved productivity in domestic agriculture but, later, as free trade policies were adopted and transport facilities improved, food from the New World and other newly productive regions began to reach Europe. Growing industrial and commercial employment and the creation of an urban domestic environment reduced ties with the land, which further increased dependence upon commercial sources of food supply. Domestic sources of food production declined rapidly as an urban lifestyle was adopted. Supplies of milk, potatoes, vegetables, pigs and chickens to agricultural labourers' homes were all reduced by changes in the organization of land. Their loss, or the reduction in their contribution to the diet, remained a major grievance in rural areas until the end of the nineteenth century.

Dietary and culinary traditions in Britain before 1900

For the majority of the population, housing, income and hours of work were major constraints upon the cooking and serving of food, so that to be concerned with meals reflected leisure, wealth and the availability of domestic labour. During the period of industrialization, arrangements such as the timing of meals and the style of menus changed as signifi-

---

[1] D. J. Oddy, 'Urban famine in nineteenth-century Britain; The effect of the Lancashire cotton famine on working-class diet and health', *Economic History Review*, 2nd ser., Vol. XXXVI, 1 (February 1983).

cantly as did many other aspects of people's lives. Longer hours and increased regularity of work, the separation of workplace from home and, later in the nineteenth century, the widespread attendance of children at school, all influenced patterns of eating and drinking.

Before industrial and urban lifestyles became widespread in the nineteenth century, dietary habits had varied markedly by region and social class. In southern England, the emphasis on 'wheaten bread, strong beer, and butcher's meat' curbed the variety of meals and reduced the importance of cookery skills. For the poor it was generally accepted that 'bread makes the principal part of the food of all poor families and almost the whole of the food of . . . large families'.[2] Many meals were made up of bread and tea alone, while the general demand for white wheaten bread meant that barley and oatmeal used as porridge or 'hasty pudding' were in decline as early as the late eighteenth century. Moreover, the price of fuel in southern England was already forcing poor people to buy bread from the baker rather than bake it themselves. Potatoes were more commonly eaten in the north and west of Britain. Sir Frederic Eden contrasted the southern diet of tea twice a day, best wheaten bread and a little bacon with that of the north of England: 'In point of expense, their general diet as much exceeds, as, in point of nutrition, it falls short of, the north country fare of milk, potatoes, barley bread and hasty-pudding.'[3] Eden's north country fare was similar to Scotland's oatmeal porridge, potatoes and milk or cheese, with kale the ever-present vegetable. Both in Scotland and the north of England, the practice of farm servants living in was widespread during the nineteenth century, which meant that many ate at the farmer's table, though 'boarding out' became more common at times when food was dear.

From the early years of the nineteenth century, the domestic economy of the agricultural family in southern England was under pressure. It depended upon having sufficient funds to obtain a pig from a farmer below market price, obtaining credit to buy flour by the sack, and having 'sufficient garden ground for planting a good patch of potatoes'.[4] Domestic brewing required families to use at least a bushel of malt every month to obtain 28 gallons of small beer, and the cost of materials and fuel (plus the cost of the equipment for young men setting up their own families) meant that during the nineteenth century brewing as well as baking began to decline in many rural areas. 'How wasteful, and indeed how shameful for a labourer's wife to go to the baker's shop', thundered

---

[2] Reverend David Davies, *The Case of Labourers in Husbandry* (Bath and London, 1795), p. 21.
[3] Sir Frederic M. Eden, *The State of the Poor*, vol. I (1797, facsimile edn, 1966), p. 14.
[4] Davies, *Labourers in Husbandry*, p. 23.

William Cobbett,[5] but the decline in traditional self-sufficiency continued, and from the mid-nineteenth century only pockets of resistance to shop products remained. Cooking and meal preparation became more modest in rural districts as the nineteenth century progressed and this was mirrored in the newly urbanized areas by the disappearance of home-made soups, broths and pottages where these had formerly been traditional. Indeed, the fact that people were satisfied to eat bread with cold meat or cheese and beer as regular everyday fare in much of England may well have been the principal factor limiting the growth of culinary arts in Britain. Family budget evidence for the first half of the nineteenth century suggests that bread was 'the staff of life'. People ate a pound or more of bread per day with other foods only gradually coming into use. Potatoes and sugar were relative rarities at the beginning of the nineteenth century but became normal items of diet as the century progressed. Similarly, meat and fats (whether from meat or dairy produce) were eaten only in small amounts but gradually grew in importance as incomes increased. Oatmeal was a food of declining significance during the nineteenth century even though it remained important in parts of northern England and Scotland. Energy intakes were some 2,000 to 2,300 calories per head.[6] Protein and fat intakes were low and carbohydrate intake was high. In areas where milk and cheese were only a small part of the diet calcium levels were extremely low.

Meal patterns

Eating three meals a day had become the accepted pattern everywhere in Britain as early as the eighteenth century. Even menus in workhouses, hospitals and schools confirmed the general arrangement of three meals a day.[7] For most people, the main meal was a midday dinner eaten at home, though there were groups of workers such as farm labourers, shepherds, carters, miners and fishermen whose tasks normally took them away from their families at that time. The midday dinner was remarkably flexible in terms of its timing and arrangements. Urban artisans ate at midday, as travellers frequently did at inns, but among the better-off classes in town and country alike, dinner was usually later at two or three o'clock.

[5] William Cobbett, *Cottage Economy* (1822), p. 82.
[6] See D. J. Oddy, 'Food, drink and nutrition', in F. M. L. Thompson, ed., *The Cambridge Social History of Britain 1750–1950, Volume 2, People and their Environment* (Cambridge, 1990).
[7] Isolated exceptions were those Oxford colleges that retained the medieval habit of dining at eleven and supping at six. See James Woodforde, *The Diary of a Country Parson 1758–1802*, selected and edited by John Beresford (Oxford, 1978), p. 51.

At table 'English service' was still general until after the Napoleonic Wars, so that for a family dinner 'Boiled Rabbits Smothered with Onions, French Beans stewed, Apple Pudding, Pease, Leg of Grass Lamb roasted' might all appear on the table together. Occasionally, a 'remove' dish would be brought to the table to replace another, in which case it would frequently be an opportunity for a soup or fish dish to be replaced by poultry or game, but generally people chose what dishes they wanted while the rest of the food stood cooling. Sometimes salads and a dessert were available from a sideboard.[8] Within twenty years or so of the Battle of Waterloo, however, the French pattern of serving meals in successive courses became fashionable, though popular works such as *The Family Oracle of Health* (1824) still recommended the simpler, traditional eating practices. French dishes, French service by courses at dinner and, above all, French chefs became the dominant influence among leading families and the London clubs. Alexis Soyer, chef at the Reform Club between 1839 and 1851, epitomized this transformation. Not only did soup and fish now act as a first course and precede the second course of meat dishes, but the coupling of entrées with the older English practice of 'removes' gave a progression to meals which culminated in the menus suggested by Mrs Beeton from 1861 onwards.[9] At the same time, nineteenth-century mealtimes began to change. Professor John Burnett has drawn attention to Queen Victoria's preference for eating late in the evening: among the fashionable, social emulation rapidly converted dinner to an evening meal from the 1840s onwards, counterbalanced by the development of 'English breakfast' eaten at eight or nine in the morning. Such patterns were well fitted to the activities of landed estates and country house parties, but they also suited the mercantile, professional and industrial middle classes whose business activities were becoming separated from their places of residence. In consequence, supper disappeared except in the form of a late snack or drink. The long gap between the two principal meals of the day came to be filled by a light lunch at one or two o'clock and, in fashionable houses from the 1840s, by afternoon tea.

During the 1870s or 1880s a further refinement in eating habits was the introduction of service *à la russe*, in which courses, instead of containing a number of dishes, were reduced to one or two only. The recognized order of the meal familiar in the twentieth century – soup, fish, entrée, roast, dessert – became standardized in its varying degrees of complexity. Once established, this combination of evening dinner and service *à la russe* created a distinction in eating habits between the

---

[8] Mrs Charlotte Mason, *The Ladies' Assistant*, 6th edn (1787), gives examples of meals with 'Two Courses'.

[9] For the best account of these changes see Burnett, *Plenty and Want*, chs 4 and 9.

middle class who adopted these patterns and the working class who continued to regard dinner as a midday meal to be eaten at home if at all possible. These differences persisted well into the twentieth century. If the male head of a working-class family could not eat at home during a working day, it was quite likely that his wife and children would eat only a meatless meal. Sunday dinner was regarded as the highlight of the week, symbolized by the cooking of the main purchase of butcher's meat. Only in the event of severe privation was the attempt to maintain the status of the Sunday dinner abandoned.

One variation which bestrode the social class barriers was the 'high tea', originating on Sunday evenings and normally eaten by the middle classes without the attendance of servants. High tea retained many of the characteristics of the suppers formerly eaten in the English style but from the 1880s onwards, the 'faster' members of society reacted against its formlessness in favour of Sunday evening dinner parties.[10] Among the working classes, however, the popularity of high tea increased, particularly in northern England and Scotland as the 'meat tea'. It encompassed the diverse needs of children returning after school and the male wage earner coming home from work. Among the poorer classes it could be no more than the cooking of a bloater or herring, but on excursions or on holidays it might become the occasion for eating fish and chips, a dish which, it has been claimed, originated in Oldham in the 1860s.[11] Whatever variation the form of the high tea took, the essential feature was the extension of a meal based predominantly on bread, butter and tea by the inclusion of some kind of fish or meat usually cooked in a frying-pan. Thus, by the end of the nineteenth century, it had become accepted as the norm that those who could ate three cooked meals a day and those who could not yet afford to do so aspired to this pattern of eating.

Supplying the urban consumer

Prior to the transformation of Britain into an urban society, the customary structure of food markets had been for farmers to dispose of their produce via auctions or wholesale in market towns. However, the urban growth of the nineteenth century and the transport facilities provided by railways led to the trade in food becoming increasingly long

---

[10] R. C. K. Ensor, *England 1870–1914* (Oxford, 1936), p. 143, was moved to term this 'hedonism'.

[11] W. H. Chaloner, 'Trends in fish consumption', in T. C. Barker, J. C. McKenzie and J. Yudkin, eds, *Our Changing Fare* (1966), pp. 109–10; J. K. Walton, *Fish and Chips and the British Working Class, 1870–1940* (Leicester, 1992), pp. 25–8.

distance in character from the 1860s onwards. Traditionally, food processing took place locally: butchers made their own sausages and pies, bakers their own biscuits and cakes. From the mid-nineteenth century onwards, supplying food to consumers in the expanding towns created endless problems of transport, storage and distribution for wholesalers. As towns grew, the advance of bricks and mortar on to farmland made the retention of links with the countryside for town dwellers more and more difficult to maintain. Moreover, the local area of country around any British town provided very little of its food supply other than some seasonal fresh meat, poultry, eggs, fruit and vegetables. More significantly, the urban diet in the later nineteenth century came to depend to a considerable extent not so much on the countryside as on foodstuffs being processed on an industrial scale in the towns themselves. Thus millers, bakers, brewers and distillers were among the first to apply mass-production techniques to food and to locate themselves in ports and urban centres of population. Another food industrially produced was margarine, though the shops that sold it tried to discount the artificiality of its origins by calling themselves 'dairies'. Otherwise, improvements in the variety and availability of foodstuffs for the urban housewife resulted largely from the major retailing chains that grew up in the later years of the nineteenth century. None of them was national in coverage, though the Co-operative Wholesale Society, formed in 1863, became the supplier on a national scale to the various local retail co-operative societies. These commercial factors pointed to a decline in home-produced foods during the decades before 1914,[12] though the food market still reflected regional and local differences and seasonality of food supplies remained strong.

Technologies to support the growing scale of the food-supply system before the early twentieth century were not extensive. Refrigeration and cold storage were still new and the supply of artificial ice was insufficient for needs in high summer. Until the closing years of the nineteenth century, the use of natural ice was the only means of reducing the temperature of food either as a preservative or to enhance its presentation at the table. Underground ice houses, or some form of well-insulated buildings, had existed on a number of great estates since the seventeenth century and the ice trade from East Anglia to London was well established by the early 1800s.[13] The ice trade expanded substantially as the nineteenth century progressed with imports from the USA, notably from Wenham Lake near Boston, and Norway. Iceboxes, lined with tin or zinc,

---

[12] D. J. Oddy, 'The working-class diet 1886–1914'. University of London Ph.D. thesis 1971 (unpublished), pp. 80–3.
[13] See W. H. Chaloner, 'Trends in fish consumption', in Barker *et al.*, *Our Changing Fare*, p. 105.

came into use in upper-class kitchens from the 1840s onwards since ice could be bought from street vendors. During the 1850s, ice chests, with an upper compartment for storing ice, below which food was placed, were patented. These cupboards became known as refrigerators.[14] Their use was limited to upper- and middle-class families but they enabled mid-Victorian dinner parties to begin serving sorbets, ice-cream and iced puddings. The popularity of these dishes led to attempts to make artificial ice, or at least to make ice go further. Mixing ice with saltpetre or salt lowered its temperature and improved its capabilities for freezing food. Churn freezers, invented in the USA around 1864, were imported soon afterwards,[15] and the demand for ice grew dramatically in the third quarter of the nineteenth century. By then, the natural ice trade relied in the main upon imports from Scandinavia, which undercut the price of Wenham Lake ice from the USA. The ice trade slowed once cold-storage refrigeration machinery was developed but at its peak over 0.5M tons were imported in 1899.[16]

Specialist food processors and manufacturers emerged during the third quarter of the nineteenth century. Despite the widespread adulteration of some foods, those supplied by food manufacturers established some limited standards of quality.[17] This was reinforced by the branding of goods after the Trade Marks Act was passed in 1875. Much of the growth in food processing was based upon cheap sugar as a means of preservation. From the 1870s onwards the fruit harvest became linked to factory production of jams, pickles and relishes. Coupled with imported fruits, cheap sugar led to the large-scale manufacture of marmalade, lemon curd and table jellies. Imported dried fruits were the raw materials for mincemeat and seasonal products, such as Christmas puddings.[18] Towards the end of the nineteenth century, the grocers' and provision merchants' windows began to fill up with packets, jars and, to a lesser

---

[14] Maggie Black, *Food and Cooking in 19th Century Britain: History and Recipes*, Historic Buildings and Monuments Commission for England (1985), p. 16. Robert David, 'The demise of the Anglo-Norwegian ice trade', *Business History*, 37, 3 (July 1995), p. 63, cites ice safe prices in the 1907 Army and Navy Stores catalogue between £4 to £12 each, though the cheapest was only £1 4s 6d (£1.23).

[15] Black, *Food and Cooking*, p. 17.

[16] Richard Perren, *The Meat Trade in Britain 1840–1914* (1978), pp. 181–2. See also Elizabeth David, *Harvest of the Cold Months* (1994), for an extensive discussion of the supply and use of natural ice. There was a difference in quality between the imported 'crystal ice' which was suitable for table decorations and locally produced 'rough ice' which, like the early artificial ice, tended to be opaque and was therefore less valued.

[17] See Burnett, *Plenty and Want*, ch. 10.

[18] C. Singer, E. J. Holmyard, A. R. Hall and T. I. Williams, *A History of Technology*, Vol. V (Oxford, 1958), ch. 2, pp. 37–8.

extent, tins. It was becoming cheaper to buy many items from the shop rather than make them at home. Packets of custard powder, egg powder and shredded suet became normal materials in middle-class kitchens.[19] The consumption of tea, used widely in Britain by the 1870s, was increasing and the switch away from green China teas to black teas from India and Ceylon drunk with milk occurred between 1876 and 1896.[20] Packets of Van Houten cocoa and those of Fry's, Cadbury's and Rowntree's were gradually becoming popular as technology improved their product and as manufacturers began extensive advertising of their products.[21] The development of condensed milk in Switzerland in the 1860s brought imports of the Milkmaid brand from the Anglo-Swiss Condensed Milk Company and a similar product from Henri Nestlé from the late 1870s. Nestlé had turned to the production of 'infant cereal' in 1868 and 'Nestlé's Bread and Milk Flour' was sold in Britain before 1870, often under the name 'Lacteous Farina', and promoted frequently via scientific or professional journals, much as were the products of the burgeoning patent medicine industry.[22] When the tins of infant food and condensed milk appeared on the shelves of the food retailers, it was an indication of the extent to which commercial sources were beginning to dominate the food market.

The mobility of the population suggests one further aspect of food and eating in late nineteenth century Britain. The Great Exhibition of 1851 began an age of commercial entertainment. With this came an unprecedented growth of catering for business travellers and tourists alike, together with the provision of eating places for commercial travellers, salesmen, and the daily influx of the professional and commercial classes into town centres. Not only were there the street vendors noted by Henry Mayhew but by the late 1870s, London's Post Office Directory listed 400 dining-rooms and 300 refreshment rooms, while the temperance movement had opened 100 coffee public houses.[23]

---

[19] T. A. B. Corley, 'Nutrition, technology and the growth of the British biscuit industry, 1820–1900', in Oddy and Miller, *Modern British Diet*, p. 23.

[20] P. Mathias, 'The British tea trade in the nineteenth century', in Oddy and Miller, *Modern British Diet*, p. 92.

[21] J. Othick, 'The cocoa and chocolate industry in the nineteenth century', in Oddy and Miller, *Modern British Diet*, p. 82; See also Francis Goodall, 'Marketing consumer products before 1914: Rowntree's and Elect Cocoa', in R. P. T. Davenport-Hines, ed., *Markets and Bagmen: Studies in the History of Marketing and British Industrial Performance 1830–1939* (1986), ch. 2.

[22] See Albert Pfiffner, *Henri Nestlé from Pharmacist's Assistant to Founder of the World's Largest Food Company* (translated from the German by David Pulman) (Vevey, Switzerland, 1995). The Anglo-Swiss Condensed Milk Company and Nestlé amalgamated in 1905.

[23] D. J. Richardson, 'J. Lyons and Co. Ltd: caterers and food manufacturers, 1891–1939', in Oddy and Miller, *Modern British Diet*, pp. 162–3.

The travelling public required food also. Stage-coaches had always picked up and delivered their passengers at inns and taverns, and the railways also had to consider providing food for passengers. The existence in many towns of station hotels dating from the second half of the nineteenth century is evidence of the needs of the travelling public, as was the building of refreshment rooms in stations and the provision of dining-cars in trains.[24]

Britain entered the twentieth century with a population of 36M people, mainly town dwellers, who obtained the bulk of their food from shops. Population growth remained high until 1914. This meant a sustained pressure on food supplies and in consequence a significant proportion of food was still adulterated. With advances in international trade, the sources of much of the nation's food lay overseas. Yet despite the advances in food preservation and processing, the diet of the working people who formed the majority of the population was surprisingly limited in variety. Although prejudices played a part in constraining people's choice of foods, in a low-wage economy it was undoubtedly the cost of food that was the principal factor in the restricted nature of the British diet at the beginning of the twentieth century.

[24] T. C. Barker and C. I. Savage, *An Economic History of Transport in Britain*, 3rd edn (1974), p. 99.

2

FOOD SUPPLY, SHOPS AND FOOD SAFETY, 1890 TO 1914

Until 1914, there was a general belief that people in towns were fed by the countryside. It was obvious to contemporaries that the countryside was engaged in agriculture, though its larger estates still provided opportunities for rural pastimes such as hunting and shooting which reflected past relationships between men of property and the land. However, towards the end of the nineteenth century, the countryside was no longer the centre of political power it had once been and, as the urban population grew, the countryside no longer had the capacity to feed the towns. From 1860 onwards, the adoption of a free trade policy meant that the urban demand for cheap food had defeated the landed interests that had sought to maintain the countryside as the towns' principal source of supply for commodities such as bread-grains, meat and vegetables. The advocates of cheap food – the industrialists and urban middle classes – were eager to import foodstuffs from abroad if that was cheaper than producing food at home. Britain's trading capacities, both commercial and maritime, made this possible. During the second half of the nineteenth century imports of principal foodstuffs grew and from the 1870s agriculture began a decline that lasted for some 60 years. Cereal-producing areas of southeastern England, particularly those on heavy clay soils, were depressed from 1879 as grain prices fell. Although under free trade agriculture was subject to market forces, the government could not completely ignore its plight. The creation of the Board of Agriculture in 1889 was as far as the state went in unifying various countryside interests.[1] From 1885 to 1914, price falls extended into livestock and dairy produce.[2] By 1913, 53 per cent of cultivated land was under grass.[3] Few people gave much thought to the effects of a free trade policy upon the food supply until the question

[1] Sir John Winnifrith, *The Ministry of Agriculture, Fisheries and Food* (1962), pp. 23–4. The Board of Agriculture for Scotland was created by the Small Landholders (Scotland) Act, 1911 and, according to *The British Imperial Calendar*, began to operate in 1913.
[2] R. Perren, 'The landlord and agricultural transformation 1870–1900', in P. J. Perry, ed., *British Agriculture 1875–1914* (1973), p. 109.
[3] S. Pollard, *The Development of the British Economy 1914–1967*, 2nd edn (1969), p. 8.

was raised in the context of the growing militarism of the Edwardian years. In 1905, the Royal Commission on the Supply of Food and Raw Materials in Time of War presented an assessment that showed the extent to which the sources of Britain's food had changed.[4] Approximately 80 per cent of the grain for bread was imported and 45 per cent of meat came from abroad.[5] One wholly imported food that had grown in significance in the British diet during the late nineteenth century was sugar. Before the First World War, total retained imports rose to just under 39M hundredweight (cwt) in 1913. Allowing for industrial use, annual sugar consumption was the equivalent of about 51lb. per head from 1894 to 1908 rising to 55lb. per head in 1913, which meant the British were eating around a pound of sugar per head per week. This emphasized the strategic concept upon which free trade in food depended: in time of war, the Royal Navy would be able to protect Britain's trade routes; it would not be possible to starve the country out in the event of a European war.

Food processing

Bread

Bread, still the principal foodstuff for many, underwent many changes. The fundamental reason was the alteration of commercial flour brought about by roller-mills introduced during the late 1870s.[6] The earliest roller-mill in Britain had been built at Glasgow in 1872, but that established by Radford at Liverpool in 1878 began the general conversion of milling practices, which was accomplished within the next few years. As extraction techniques developed, a multiplicity of grades of flour appeared, often to the confusion of the older baker, who previously knew only 'straights', and 'whites' or 'supers'. One worried craftsman wrote to the *Baker's Record*:

> I feel puzzled why the flour works so soft and sticky the last few years. A few years ago, when millers began to talk about the new roller process flour, I thought we should get such good flour; but, to my disappointment, it is not near so good now as it used to be. I am using half patent and half brewer's yeast, which I have done for many years – the same kind of flour, principally

[4] *Report of the Royal Commission on the Supply of Food and Raw Materials in Time of War*, Parliamentary Papers (PP) 1905 (Cd.2643), XXXIX.
[5] W. H. B. Court, *British Economic History 1870–1914, Commentary and Documents* (Cambridge, 1965), pp. 189–90.
[6] Drummond, *Englishman's Food*, p. 297.

town whites and households – and yet can't get the same good bread as I used to do.

Although the *Bakers' Record* partly answered the question by observing that London bread 'is of an inferior quality, and it cannot be denied that to save a shilling in buying, much poor flour is used',[7] it failed to point out that lower extraction rates produced a soft flour, low in gluten, from which it was difficult to make good bread using traditional methods. It was some time before bakers were agreed on the change. 'Competent bakers say the flour standards have been lowered, and that it is now necessary to buy a higher market standard to obtain results which a lower one formerly gave,' concluded a writer in another trade journal, 'there is far too much low grade made, being the residue of an over large patent extraction, and of numerous intermediary grades.'[8]

The increasing reliance on American wheats further modified the type of flour available that the baker could afford to use:

Previous to 1880, old wheat was the rule rather than the exception; and there is a vast difference between old wheat and new in its working quality. Some of the older bakers here may remember the time when a good deal of Irish flour came into the market, and they may remember, too, what splendid flour it was. It was made from two and three-year old wheat, and consequently was thoroughly matured and made grand flour. Now, we dare say it would be almost impossible to get a sample of one-year-old wheat. It is all a matter of price. We used to reckon long ago that it put 1s.6d on a boll of wheat to carry it for a year. Supposing flour is made of two-year-old wheat, that means 4s.6d on a bag of flour; if three-year-old wheat, it means 6s.9d. You can see then how, in the race for cheapness, old wheat became a memory. Wheat is cut down and rushed to market, from the market to the mill; from the mill to the baker's trough, in an amazing short space of time, and this must have given to modern bakers a set of problems that their fathers knew nothing about.[9]

As a result of these changes, bread for the middle-class and suburban trade began to be made from 'whites' or 'supers' or 'patents', and this led to a rise in the standard of the household loaf. However, in working-class districts, where competition was severe and profit margins extremely slender, '"ordinary Bakers", which at best makes only an indifferent loaf', continued to be used. By the early years of the twentieth century the residual nature of much of this flour brought the comment not that London bread was bland and tasteless but rather that 'the flour

[7] 18 February 1888, p. 6; 3 March 1888, p. 4.
[8] *Baker and Confectioner*, 4 January 1907, pp. 18–19.
[9] *Baker and Confectioner*, 28 April 1899, p. 368.

used being of such low quality ... the bread was strong and rank flavoured'.[10]

Almost as fundamental to the baker's craft as the composition of his flour was his oven. Internally fired side-flue ovens remained generally in use into the 1880s having required only slight modification to avoid prosecution under the Smoke Nuisance Act, 1853. Nevill's London bakehouses had used hot-air ovens, externally heated by steam pipes, since the 1850s and these, and the external-flue coke-fired ovens used by the Civil Service Bread Company from the late 1870s, were suitable only for the large-trade bread factories. From the 1890s, more and more small firms attempted to meet the competition of the factory bakers by modernization, although as late as 1906 a trade paper found it surprising that so many of the older ovens were still in existence. The saving of fuel, the absence of fumes in the bakehouse, a more even and easily altered temperature, with the added advantage of continuous baking, were all reasons why steam ovens grew in numbers.[11]

The last two decades of the nineteenth century also saw mechanization affecting the time-honoured and laborious preparation of the dough. Until well after the mid-nineteenth century, a day-long process of fermentation and kneading by hand was typical throughout the country.[12] Attempts were made from 1860 onwards to popularize dough-mixing machines, but the dependence upon manual labour to operate them limited their use. Power-driven machinery started to appear in the 1870s, and became more generally known after annual exhibitions began in 1882.[13] While the older hand methods remained in use in country districts, by the mid-1890s a wide range of semi-mechanized systems had been adopted in the towns,[14] aided by progress in controlling the fermentation processes. Sour bread due to poor fermentation was common until the 1890s, since no tables of temperatures and durations for 'setting the sponge' were published until 1888.[15] Even as late as 1907, a lecturer at the National Bakery School could say that 'working by "rule of thumb" is dying, we are ready to admit, but very slowly'.[16] Yeast also became the subject of considerable improvement through the interest taken in using the by-products of the brewing and distilling industries. Specific yeast foods began to be marketed during the 1880s. This made it possible for the fermentation processes to

[10] *Baker and Confectioner*, 4 January 1907, pp. 18–19.
[11] *Baker's Quarterly Magazine*, March–June 1906, p. 16.
[12] *Baker and Confectioner*, 25 June 1897, p. 570.
[13] *Baker and Confectioner*, 25 June 1897, p. 571.
[14] *Baker and Confectioner*, 13 July 1894, pp. 30–1.
[15] *Baker's Record*, 15 September 1888, p. 5.
[16] *Baker and Confectioner*, 13 September 1907, pp. 260–1.

be greatly reduced. By 1897 the 'gold medal recipe' involved only four hours from start to finish, compared with the fourteen hours of preparation and two and a half hours to three hours of baking required by earlier recipes. Yet this long process was still normal in Scottish bakeries, and an even longer recipe prevailed in Ireland.[17] Until the early 1890s it seemed 'there was even a strong antipathy to the dough-kneader, for it was generally believed that there could be no dough made equal to that made by hand',[18] but the trade felt that a sharp rise in quality and appearance, ascribed to the effect of competitions and exhibitions, had taken place by 1904. Technical classes at the Borough Polytechnic in London, and in Glasgow, Liverpool, Manchester and Belfast were in operation by 1906, and their popularity was due to a general feeling that 'scientific knowledge has come out closely into touch with practical requirements'.[19]

Despite this activity in baking technology, the quality of bread before 1914 was very variable. In respectable suburbs, the trade reflected new techniques:

Bread has improved greatly during recent years; partly owing to an improved grist in the milling of flour; partly to the quick, straight dough processes adopted; partly to the high baking temperatures and short periods in the ovens; partly to better machinery and better sanitary conditions under which the work is concluded.[20]

Glimpses of a different kind of loaf emerge from the poorer working-class districts. A sample from Manchester's 'slum districts' was said to have a 'dull greyish colour and somewhat coarse, sodden looking texture'.[21] In London, where poor grade flour was normally used in working-class districts, 'the loaves were often sour and contained some marvellous holes'.[22] Imported wheat and poor-quality flour caused problems for many traditional bakers. Wet, poorly risen, flavourless loaves were common complaints, and in the warmer months, outbreaks of 'rope' – a bacterial infection of bread (*Bacillus mesentericus*) –

---

[17] *Baker and Confectioner*, 25 September 1897, pp. 569–572; 25 March 1898, pp. 254–8.
[18] *Baker and Confectioner*, 30 August 1912, pp. 147–8.
[19] *Baker and Confectioner*, 14 October 1904, pp. 323–4.
[20] *Baker's Magazine*, April 1907, p. 68.
[21] *Baker's Magazine*, April 1907, p. 62. The comment on colour is surprising since one innovation of the decade had been the introduction of flour bleaching, which had become widespread very quickly. See the *Baker and Confectioner*, 15 April 1904, pp. 327–8 and 18 June 1907, pp. 49–50.
[22] *Baker and Confectioner*, 15 January 1909, p. 47.

occurred frequently up to 1914.[23] Such bread was usually disposed of through 'undercutters' and street vendors in poor districts.

Everywhere, though, there was an increase in purchasing shop goods from bakers and a decline in the use of bakers' ovens for baking meals by the public. The gradual disappearance of public baking – the practice of cooking the Sunday dinner in a baker's oven – was no doubt due to the greater number of kitchen ranges fitted in cottages before 1914 and especially to the introduction of gas stoves in urban areas where domestic gas supplies were available. In addition to bread, biscuit factories, having mechanized biscuit production successfully in the mid-nineteenth century, began large-scale production of slab cake in the 1890s, which the retail chains sold cheaply. By 1914, there were few areas where home-baking of household bread had survived and bread, cakes and biscuits were predominantly 'shop goods'.[24]

Meat

In the meat trade technical change was turning the butcher into a meat retailer, even if he dealt solely in home-bred and home-killed meat, though the widespread sale of foreign frozen meat made that unlikely. Public health concerns with satisfactory conditions of slaughter reinforced this trend. By 1910, a survey of the meat trade made this point clear:

> In speaking of the small meat-purveyor's shop, we have assumed that there will be no slaughterhouse attached. The tendency everywhere at the present day is towards large abattoirs, and it may be assumed that in a few years' time private slaughterhouses will be entirely abolished. Abattoirs play an important part in the hygiene of the country and are the only perfect means by which the distribution of diseased meat may be avoided.[25]

The decline of the private slaughterhouse in London was evident from the London County Council's licensing system. In 1889, the number licensed was 692. Ten years later, there were 411, and in 1908 only 273; this trend reflected the fall in the numbers of applications for licences.[26] Similarly, by 1909, 30 per cent of Manchester's meat was killed in

[23] *Baker and Confectioner*, 15 January 1909, p. 47; *Baker's Quarterly Magazine*, June–September 1906, p. 70.
[24] *Baker and Confectioner*, 26 June 1914, p. 569.
[25] G. R. Leighton and L. M. Douglas, *The Meat Industry and Meat Inspection*, 5 vols (1910), Vol. III, p. 485.
[26] *Meat Trades Journal*, 4 August 1910, p. 144.

abattoirs, 60 per cent was imported either alive or as carcasses, and only 10 per cent was killed in private slaughterhouses.[27]

As far as considerations of taste were concerned, one undoubted change was the tendency to reject fat meat. Even in 1880, when the first consignment of frozen meat arrived in the *Strathleven*, the only part of the cargo that was difficult to sell was some large fat carcasses of mutton. By the 1890s Irish bacon was in demand for the same reason: 'The demand for English bacon is gradually diminishing. It is too fat to suit the taste of London consumers.'[28] A similar situation prevailed in other large industrial centres; Lancashire cotton operatives, it was said, had 'no appetite for fat meat'. In country districts, however, the preference for fat meat, whether mutton or pork, remained strong until the First World War.[29] The size of the joint was also probably declining, though there is little evidence on this point. In noting that the trade had seen a reduction in the carcass weight of mutton favoured by butchers from 64lb. in 1882 to 48–52lb. in 1912, Critchell and Raymond wrote:

> The tendency for the favourite weight of sheep to grow steadily less and less is largely due to the insistent demand of the lower classes for more variety on their table. The small joint sells first because the wife of the English artisan and labourer is not skilled in making tasty dishes out of cold meat.[30]

As a result, lamb began to replace mutton in public favour, both in size of joint and for its taste. The change in marketing and retailing that had been brought in with the frozen meat trade affected the flavour of the meat. Clearly the taste of well-hung English meat was stronger than when 'in the "Colonial" or "cutting" trade' meat was rushed into the shop to be cut up 'hard and bright'. For the butcher, this was necessary to avoid the unsightly 'drip' or the development of slime on the meat that had retarded the trade in frozen beef. However, the resulting toughness and lack of flavour made mutton less attractive than the New Zealand Canterbury lamb which had become ubiquitous by 1914.

Thus the development of refrigeration in the last quarter of the nineteenth century brought about significant change in the supply of meat. Initially, due to the technical limitations of the early refrigeration systems, most imports came across the Atlantic from North America. The earliest cargo of mutton from New Zealand was landed in 1882.

[27] *Report of the Departmental Committee on Combinations in the Meat Trade*, PP 1909 (Cd.4643), XV, Q.4742.

[28] *The Scotsman*, 24 September 1894, p. 9.

[29] J. T. Critchell and J. Raymond, *A History of the Frozen Meat Trade* (1912), pp. 221–3.

[30] Ibid., p. 107.

Meat from South America began to arrive from 1883 onwards, but the trade remained somewhat irregular until 1895. Although T. C. and J. Eastman of New York are generally credited with transporting the first consignment of chilled meat across the Atlantic in October 1875,[31] the pioneers of retailing frozen food in Britain appear to have been John Bell and Sons of London and Glasgow. Already established as multiple retail butchers for some half a century, they opened their first frozen-meat shop in 1879. When they amalgamated with Eastman's in January 1889, Bell's had 330 frozen-meat shops.[32]

The frozen-meat trade passed rapidly through an experimental phase during which both retailers and consumers resisted its introduction. Butchers who remained in the fresh home-killed trade derided those who adopted frozen meat as 'hard-beef smashers'. Before 1914, most meat from the Southern Hemisphere was frozen to –9° to –12°C (10–15°F) as distinct from meat chilled to –1° to –2°C (28–30°F), which remained soft and required no thawing before sale.[33] Critchell and Raymond described chilled and frozen meat as taking up 'a commanding position in Smithfield supplies' during the 1890s, despite the shortage of cold storage facilities in London.[34] There was a rush to form ice companies in the 1880s and 1890s. Even so, during hot weather in 1894, ships possessing refrigeration plants were kept in London to supplement storage facilities on shore.[35] The expansion of cold storage capacity followed the formation of a number of specialist firms to meet the shortage.[36] Between 1888 and 1908, storage capacity in London increased from 300,000 carcass units (of 56lb. or 25.4kg) to 2.73M units. In Britain as a whole frozen storage capacity increased from 1M to 12.7M carcass units over the same period. The success of the frozen-meat trade was ensured by the introduction of the Contagious Diseases Acts (1878, 1884 and 1896), which restricted livestock traffic from areas infected with various animal diseases. By 1892, the Board of Agriculture and Fisheries had made prohibition orders forbidding imports from France, Belgium, the Netherlands, Denmark, Sweden, Spain and Portugal. Further exclusions were placed on Norwegian, Canadian and Irish livestock, and extended to the Argentine and USA in

[31] Ibid., pp. 24–6; see also Perren, *The Meat Trade in Britain*.
[32] Critchell and Raymond, *Frozen Meat Trade*, pp. 209–10.
[33] Leighton and Douglas, *Meat Industry and Meat Inspection*, Vol. II, p. 448.
[34] Critchell and Raymond, *Frozen Meat Trade*, p. 191.
[35] *Meat Trades Journal*, 28 June 1894, p. 140.
[36] For example, Union Cold Storage Company and the London Central Markets Cold Storage Company. See Leighton and Douglas, *Meat Industry and Meat Inspection*, Vol. II, pp. 446–8. David, *Harvest of the Cold Months*, Table 2, p. 55, indicates that sixty artificial ice companies were formed between 1880 and 1900. United Carlo Gatti, Stevenson & Slater Ltd was probably the largest ice producer.

1903.[37] By the early 1890s, most London West End butchers had refrigerators[38] and the importance of refrigeration became clear to the major meat-importing firms. Before 1900, James Nelson and Sons Ltd, Eastman's Ltd, the River Plate Fresh Meat Co Ltd, W. and R. Fletcher Ltd and the London Central Meat Co Ltd had begun to develop chains of shops retailing frozen meat to the urban population, notably in the industrial midlands and the north of England.

Fish

Technical change in fishing methods facilitated an increase in supply rather than changing the nature of the catch. Until the mid-nineteenth century the mainstay of the fishmongers' trade was prime-quality fish which had been taken from the line and kept alive until it reached the market. With speedier traffic on land and the use of ice, trawling began to expand from the 1840s onwards. Trawling was a method of fishing known for centuries but, by suffocating a large part of the catch, produced dead fish of little value, much of which went to waste.[39] Sailing vessels were of limited effectiveness as trawlers but by the 1880s specifically designed steam-engined fishing vessels were in use. In 1911, over 3,000 power-driven vessels formed the bulk of the deep-sea fleet. As the capacity of fishing vessels increased voyages were extended if fish could be kept in ice.[40] The effects of more intensive fishing became apparent in the 1890s: catches began to fall off in size and smaller fish were more noticeable among them. In 1893 the Select Committee on Sea Fisheries found 'there was a decided diminution in the average size of flat fish caught in the North Sea, especially plaice, and that the total quantity of fish landed had only been maintained by a large increase in the catching power'. This, they concluded, 'must be attributed to over-fishing by trawlers in certain localities'.[41] By 1900 the evidence before the Select Committee on the Sea Fisheries Bill was plainer still. Their report found 'that it is proved beyond doubt that there is a very serious diminution in the supply of certain kinds of flat fish, particularly in the North Sea' and 'that one of the causes of this diminution of supply is undoubtedly the

[37] *Departmental Committee on the Meat Trade.* See Appendix IV for a list of the orders made.
[38] *Report from the Select Committee on Marking Foreign Meat*, PP 1893–94, XII, Question 3148 (to Mr J. J. Thompson, Managing Director of Eastman's Ltd).
[39] *Report of the Royal Commission on Trawl Net and Beam Trawl Fishing*, PP 1884–85 (C. 4328), XVI, QQ.8639, 11,140.
[40] *Report to the Board of Trade on the System of Deep Sea Trawl Fishing*, PP 1883, XVIII.
[41] *Report from the Select Committee on Sea Fisheries*, PP 1893–94, XV, iii–iv.

destruction of immature fish'.[42] However no minimum size limits for fish caught by British vessels were introduced. With landings rising sharply after 1901, the problems of how to sell 'trawl rubbish' assumed greater proportions. Coalfish (saithe), catfish, dogfish (flake), monks and similar kinds of fish were usually 'either passed off as a substitute for the more widely known varieties, or else sold under some fancy name'.[43] The consumer clearly did not take to them by either name or appearance, but was seldom able to distinguish them when substitution took place. The solution lay in presenting the fish in an unrecognizable form, and the technique of filleting began to spread rapidly during the first years of the twentieth century. The practice probably developed locally where landings of catfish and coalfish were heavy.

Filleting was developed on the East Coast of Scotland. W. S. Eunson, a fish-curer of Aberdeen, was advertising 'The Eunson Fish Fillet' to the trade by 1906, and in a series of articles on fish-curing for the *Fish Trades Gazette* laid claim to having popularized filleted catfish and coalfish in Glasgow.[44] The effect of the innovation was noted in the Fishery Board for Scotland's Report for 1905:

> Gurnards, cat-fish, and anglers, are, so far, of little importance as contributors to the food supply, although in recent years the demand for these and other so-called coarse fish has greatly increased. Within the last two seasons, moreover, this demand has been accelerated by curers subjecting such fish to the filleting process before putting them into the hands of the consumer. Thus not only has the variety of fish been rendered indistinguishable, but the form in which they were presented for consumption has given little trouble in cooking.[45]

By 1910 it had become a very widespread practice:

> enormous quantities of catfish, big Icelandic haddocks, and cod are now filleted in Hull for the inland markets, and sold as 'filleted haddock'. When the fish has been sliced it is placed in a solution of salt and pyroligneous acid (a coal-tar derivate), which dyes it a golden brown.[46]

Filleting was undoubtedly popular among working-class families, whose acceptance of fish was limited by strict considerations of time and

---

[42] *Report of the Select Committee on the Sea Fisheries Bill*, PP 1900, VIII.

[43] *Fish Trades Gazette*, 7 May 1910, p. 21.

[44] *Fish Trades Gazette*, 6 January 1906, p. 22, 'Fishcuring up-to-date', and various subsequent issues.

[45] *Twenty-fourth Annual Report of the Fishery Board for Scotland*, PP 1906 (Cd.2986), XVII, xxvii.

[46] *Fish Trades Gazette*, 2 April 1910, p. 14.

money. The cost of fuel and fat, the time and skill required in preparing the fish for the pan and the high proportion of waste were all factors limiting fish consumption.

By contrast to the success of the frozen-meat trade, the freezing of fish was generally a failure before 1914. Fishing vessels used ice to store fish for up to about a fortnight while at sea but, when landed, the fish was generally unfit to be frozen. Even if perfect-looking fish could be produced (and the pioneers of the process experienced difficulties in preventing frozen fish from acquiring a yellow staining of the skin), a trade paper reported that the resulting product was so rank as to be inedible.[47] Proposals to import frozen fish directly from New Zealand to Manchester in 1904 came to nothing and it was a novelty when a shipment of frozen Canadian halibut was delivered to Grimsby in good condition in December 1913.[48]

Milk

The market in dairy produce underwent significant structural change between 1890 and 1913. Sales of milk in liquid form had increased considerably from some 491M gallons in 1890 to around 788M gallons in 1908, a rise of 60 per cent.[49] Since there is no evidence of rising milk yield before 1914 and the number of cows and heifers rose by only 10 per cent, the output of milk products in the form of butter and cheese must have declined. The rapid rise in butter imports during the 1890s confirms this, especially since there was little change in retail prices.[50] The liquid milk trade before 1914 was:

> almost entirely the result of changes in the dietary of the people and of the rapid growth of towns and cities during the last century. The spread of the consumption of tea, coffee and cocoa as popular beverages, the increasing use of cow's milk for feeding infants and the need of light and easily assimilated foods on the part of urban populations have contributed to its expansion and progress. Within the last forty years alone, the consumption of fresh milk has almost doubled.[51]

[47] *Fish Trades Gazette*, 7 May 1904, p. 24.

[48] *Annual Report on Sea Fisheries for 1913*, PP 1914 (Cd.7449), XXX, 24.

[49] R. H. Rew, 'An inquiry into the statistics of the production and consumption of milk and milk products in Great Britain', *Journal of the Royal Statistical Society*, LV (1892), pp. 244–78; *The Agricultural Output of Great Britain*, PP 1912–13 (Cd.6277), X.

[50] *Report of an Enquiry by the Board of Trade into Working-Class Rents and Retail Prices*, PP 1913 (Cd.6955), LXVI, p. xliv.

[51] Linlithgow Committee, *Interim Report on Milk and Milk Products*, PP 1923 (Cmd.1854), IX, para. 14.

Consumption of milk grew despite its poor quality. Many farmers did not bother to cool milk, while farm water supplies were seldom adequate for this purpose.[52] Nor did the railways provide refrigerated or cooled trucks for the carriage of milk. The bulk of the milk reaching Finsbury in 1903 was untreated and already twelve to eighteen hours old when it completed its journey.[53] Since some was later resold by larger trade organizations to small shopkeepers, much of the milk on sale in the borough was over twenty-four hours old. As a result preservatives, notably formalin, were found in milk on a wide scale, particularly at the weekend when demand was greatest.[54] In south London the position was similar:

> Dr Priestly, medical officer of health for Lambeth, has stated that much of the milk consumed in the poorer quarters is three or four days old, and probably Lambeth is not the only district in which this state of affairs exists. The milk has passed through the hands of three or four dealers by each of whom a dose of some preservative has been added in order to prevent the actual onset of decomposition.[55]

In 1901, a committee of the Board of Agriculture reported that 50 per cent of London's dairymen used preservatives in milk.[56] Pasteurization and sterilization processes became more popular after 1900, as the distance milk travelled to market increased, though 'not with the primary object of destroying any disease germs which might be present, but to postpone souring and so add a few hours to its life'.[57] B. S. Rowntree remarked on the sediment 'so often seen in English milk',[58] since milk sold from open containers in shops was frequently contaminated. Milk was a commodity that was beginning to travel considerable distances to urban markets, in many cases from country areas hitherto devoted primarily to the making of butter and cheese. Within living memory of townsmen in 1914 most 'milk drunk in the towns was produced either in the town itself or within a few miles of it'.[59] But 'town dairy' milksheds were in rapid decline and the spread of building was threatening many

---

[52] *Report of the Departmental Committee on Preservatives and Colouring Matter in Food*, PP 1901 (Cd.833), XXXIV, QQ.3951–3.
[53] G. Newman, *Report on the Milk Supply of Finsbury* (1903), p. 8.
[54] Newman, *Milk Supply of Finsbury*, pp. 34–5.
[55] *Report of the Inter-Departmental Committee on Physical Deterioration, Evidence*, PP 1904 (Cd.2210), XXXII, Q.1267.
[56] *D. C. on Preservatives and Colouring Matter*, para. 18.
[57] *Second Interim Report of the Committee on the Production and Distribution of Milk*, PP 1917–18 (Cd.8886), XVI, para. 23.
[58] B. S. Rowntree, *Poverty: A Study of Town Life* (1901), Appendix F., p. 391.
[59] R. L. Cohen, *The History of Milk Prices* (Oxford, 1936), p. 17.

'suburban farms'.[60] Wholesale contractors were buying milk from farms between 50 and 150 miles from London, yet cooling and refrigerated transport was rare in the liquid milk trade.[61] In consequence, much milk, if not actually adulterated by the addition of water, contained substances claimed to act as preservatives. The amount of liquid milk converted to condensed milk is not known, though retained imports of condensed milk rose from 0.52M cwt in 1894 to 1.25M cwt in 1913. Supplies rose from 1.5 lb. per head per year in 1894 to almost 3.1 lb. per head twenty years later. Although much condensed milk was used commercially by the bakery and confectionery trades, as well as cafés and restaurants, especially during the summer months, public health reformers associated its use in poor working-class districts with epidemic diarrhoea among infants.[62]

Cheese

As the market for liquid milk expanded, so the supply available for cheese-making declined. Before 1914, cheese-making in Britain remained largely a farmhouse industry disposing of its produce through markets such as the Chester, Whitchurch, Nantwich, Kilmarnock and Frome cheese fairs.[63] The demand from towns outstripped this supply, especially in view of the seasonal availability of milk. However, from the 1890s onwards, attempts to cut costs in cheese-making, the impact of new knowledge of bacteriology and changes in taste all began to alter conditions of cheese production. Before 1914, factory cheese was regarded as inferior because its flavour was affected by the staleness of milk supplies to the factories, much of which had frequently failed to find other markets.[64] Although factory production of cheese made little progress in England before the First World War,[65] its effect on the quality and flavour of cheese in the shops was increasingly noticeable due to the growth of imports from North America in the late nineteenth century. From 1900 to 1914, imported cheeses amounted to around 2.5M cwt per year of which Canada supplied approximately half in the form of factory-produced Cheddar-type cheese. The North Atlantic

[60] *Report of the Travelling Commission of Enquiry into the Cost of Production of Milk*, PP 1919 (Cmd.233), XXV, 435, para. 14.

[61] *D. C. on Preservatives and Colouring Matter*, QQ, 3951–3.

[62] G. Newman, *The Control of the Milk Supply* (1904), p. 13.

[63] Cohen, *History of Milk Prices*, p. 43; *The Times*, 29 September 1913, 12a.

[64] Valerie E. Cheke, *The Story of Cheese-making in Britain* (1959), p. 245.

[65] In *The History of Milk Prices* (p. 43), Ruth Cohen suggested that factory cheese comprised only 10 per cent of total output in 1907–8.

trade benefited from a short-duration voyage, which did not require refrigeration, but as cold storage capacity at sea expanded, producers from further afield entered the trade. By 1910 to 1914, New Zealand supplied up to a-quarter of all imports.[66] Standardized factory cheese had some effect on British cheese-making. During the 1890s, Ayrshire dairy producers attempted to learn Canadian methods. Better control of milk temperatures and more accurate measurement of the amounts of rennet used as starters gave a more uniform process. In addition, by the late 1890s there was much investigation of ripening processes which Babcock and Russell in America had found to be the result of enzyme action.[67] The effect of research generally was towards shortening the ripening processes. Hard-pressed cheeses (such as Cheddar and Cheshire) were most affected by these changes which produced a milder and softer textured cheese than before. Dr F. Lloyd, engaged in research into Somerset cheese-making in the 1890s, was surprised to find that:

> so many variations existed in the making and relative ripening speeds of the Cheddar cheese; Some was now being made which would mature for market in three months, instead of the minimum 12 months at one time considered essential if fit to eat. Also the texture of the cheese now preferred had to be close instead of 'open and holey', showing that there had been a change in public taste, apart from the differences in the quality of the cheese made.[68]

The pressure from cheese-makers towards shorter-ripening cheese became overwhelming. Costs of skilled labour and the risks attendant on successful ripening encouraged more and more farmers to look for a rapid turnover from the sale of underripe or early ripening cheeses. In turn this began to change consumer preferences for cheese. As more and more imported cheese entered the country under conditions of cold storage, and with farmers selling to cheese factors as soon as possible, the bulk of cheese sold in the country was in an underripe state. There seems little doubt that this cheese became accepted and 'soon preferred by the majority of consumers'.[69] The completeness of this change was noted after the First World War:

[66] Cohen, *History of Milk Prices*, p. 36. The American trade fell off after the McKinley Tariff, 1890. Imports of New Zealand cheese for 1910 to 1914 reached 537,000 cwt (27,280 metric tons), almost double that from the Netherlands (270,000 cwt or 13,717 metric tons). There was a marked reduction in Canadian imports from 1.71M cwt (86,872 metric tons) in 1905–9 to 1.37M cwt (69,600 metric tons) in 1910 to 1914.

[67] C. Singer, E. J. Holmyard, A. R. Hall and T. I. Williams, *A History of Technology* (Oxford, 1958), Vol. V, pp. 33–5.

[68] Cheke, *Cheese-making*, p. 209.

[69] Ibid., p. 233.

In colliery districts, or in any district where heavy manual labour is common, early ripening cheeses are mainly sold, as, for instance, in the mining districts in the north-west where Cheshire and Lancashire cheeses are sold almost straight from the press, and similarly in South Wales as regards Caerphilly cheese. At one time, a considerable quantity of Cheshire cheese came to London, but since the alteration in type from a long keeping to an early ripening cheese of greater acidity, which took place some 30 years ago in response to a specific demand from the north, the London market for Cheshire cheese has declined.[70]

By the interwar period, the demand for very old cheese was said to be insignificant,[71] but the disappearance of the slow-matured cheese did not occur without some protest before 1914.

Fats

Poor-quality butter, heavily salted and with added water, was common in towns during the late nineteenth century. English farm supplies tended to be erratic and variable in quality.[72] Butter seldom kept well, particularly in summer when it was in most plentiful supply, unless heavily salted. Since only Irish salt butter could be expected to be edible up to six months after being made, the bulk of it was consigned to the winter trade in English and Welsh industrial districts.[73] Irish salt butter was known to contain as much as 20 to 25 per cent water through the use of hot brine solutions,[74] and its fat content might be under 70 per cent.[75] 'Milk-blended butter' first appeared in 1900, afterwards becoming widely used in Ireland as a method of increasing the water content of butter. Undoubtedly, until butter substitutes began to compete with the poorer quality butters, much butter reached the consumer in a poor state through deficient keeping qualities and careless storage. As acceptable substitutes appeared on the market, grocers were forced to take greater care in retailing. It was, however, the rapidly growing import trade of

---

[70] Linlithgow Committee, *Interim Report on Milk*, para. 169.

[71] Ministry of Agriculture and Fisheries (Economic Series No.22), *Dairy Produce Marketing Report*, 1930, p. 130.

[72] *Report from the Select Committee on Food Products Adulteration, 1894–96*, PP 1896, IX.

[73] *S.C. on Adulteration*; evidence of P. Hickey, 1895, QQ.721, 723, and R. Hickey, 1895, Q.2219.

[74] *S.C. on Adulteration*, PP 1894, XII, QQ.2065–6, 2215.

[75] O. Hehner and A. Angell, *Butter: Its Analysis and Adulterations*, 2nd edn (1877), Table II, pp. 77–80.

cheap butter from Denmark, Australia, Russia and New Zealand that limited the consumption of margarine and butter substitutes.[76]

Butterine, well established as the name for butter substitutes, was replaced by 'margarine' through the efforts of Irish MPs seeking to protect the Cork butter industry.[77] In the Margarine Act, 1887, margarine was defined as 'substances, whether compounds or otherwise, prepared in imitation of butter, and whether mixed with butter or not'. It was to be clearly labelled as margarine in the shop and was to be wrapped in paper or a bag bearing the word 'margarine'; moreover, the customer was to be told by the retailer that it was margarine and not butter that he or she was buying. By the beginning of the twentieth century, margarine had changed greatly since the 1870s when, as 'oleo' obtained from beef fat, it was similar to lard, if well refined. During the late 1870s and 1880s 'oleo' formed only some 50 to 60 per cent of butterine, with the balance made up of churned milk, 5 per cent or so of strong flavoured butter, some vegetable oils (groundnut, sesame, cottonseed) and colouring matter.[78] It remained a technically imperfect substitute for butter and of variable quality. The introduction of the Storch process in the 1890s was a major technical step forward. By using bacterial cultures known as 'starters', a flavour almost identical to butter was produced in vegetable fats. From 1898, the rising prices of animal fats and consequent fears that the industry might fall into the hands of the American meat firms stimulated further research into the use of vegetable oils. The low melting point of vegetable oils created problems of texture for margarine manufacturers and it was not until about 1906 that this was overcome by hydrogenation to 'harden' them.[79] Between 1908 and 1914 this process led to an improved margarine which, particularly when wrapped in branded half-pound packets, gained wider acceptance.

Eggs

A novel food entering the diet in the twentieth century was the new-laid egg. Eggs had not been marketed to any extent in the nineteenth century, and the taste for them was still of recent origin:

---

[76] Cohen, *History of Milk Prices*, p. 29.

[77] *Hansard*, Third Series, Vol. 318, 1325.

[78] *Report from the Select Committee on the Butter Substitutes Bill*, PP 1887, IX; evidence of Sir Frederick Abel, QQ.3, 6, 7, 54, 93.

[79] See R. Moller (Otto Monsted Ltd), 'The making and marketing of nut margarine', *Grocery*, February 1914, pp. 73–4.

Twenty years ago, the vast majority of persons, as we then wrote, had never tasted a really new-laid egg, and did not know what it was like: now many thousands do, and are willing to pay for it.[80]

This, in 1902, was how recently the market appeared to have developed. Apart from the months from April to June, the market generally had only 'fresh' or 'preserved' eggs to offer. Many so-called fresh eggs were imported, and varied greatly in price and quality.[81] Eggs reputedly fresh from Denmark or Germany might well include re-exports of Russian origin. Essentially these (and those from Egyptian and colonial sources) were 'eggs which have travelled 2,000 to 3,000 miles, and consequently are from three to six weeks old at least',[82] so that housewives buying 'in the ordinary manner' commonly found two or three unusable eggs per dozen.[83] No wonder that, in William Cobbett's words, preserved eggs were 'things to run from not after'.[84] Russian eggs were generally the cheapest and often the stalest, 'being almost putrid when sold in England and chiefly used in manufactures, for which, at a low price, they answer perfectly'[85] – an interesting comment on the level of acceptability in the pre-1914 food market. Even English farm eggs were notoriously variable in quality due to haphazard collection and marketing. Cold storage had no impact on the egg trade in Britain before 1918, and as late as the 1920s, a Ministry of Agriculture Report described English farm eggs from early summer to November as 'dangerous stuff to deal with',[86] because the inclusion of stale or partly incubated eggs was still common. Early in the 1890s, a trade paper classed British farm eggs as frequently worse than imported produce.[87] The knowledge that prices would rise during the later months of the year was an important factor, leading farmers to delay sending eggs to market and yet to offer them for sale as fresh or even new-laid. In many counties it appeared that eggs were sent to wholesalers at only weekly or fortnightly intervals. Most English eggs were therefore two to three weeks old by the time they reached the consumer, and some deterioration in condition was inevitable.

The factors affecting the growing demand for eggs were generally agreed by writers before 1914. Urbanization, they noted, was a major

[80] L. Wright, *The New Book of Poultry* (1902), p. 166.

[81] *Encyclopaedia Britannica*, 11th edn, 1910–11, Vol. XXII, p. 220.

[82] E. Brown, 'The British egg supply', *Journal of the Royal Agricultural Society of England* 61 (1900), p. 618.

[83] E. Brown, *British Poultry Husbandry* (1930), p. 216.

[84] Quoted in Brown, 'The British egg supply', p. 238.

[85] *Encyclopaedia Britannica*, 11th edn, 1910–11, Vol. XXII, p. 220.

[86] Ministry of Agriculture and Fisheries (Economic Series No. 10), *Report on Egg Marketing in England and Wales*, 1926, p. 22.

[87] *Provision Trades Gazette*, July 1891, p. 10.

factor in the increase. For many people town life implied not so much a changed environment as changed activities. The increase in commercial occupations provided a greater number of people, at least among the lower-middle classes, with more sedentary occupations. A growing interest in eggs as food appears to have been part of a movement towards the eating of lighter food, of which sedentary activity may have been only partly the reason. 'Cycling alone has done much', suggested one writer seeking to explain the taste for new-laid eggs. 'The dietetic value of eggs is appreciated as it was not before, and the relish for such light food is extending.'[88] However, any change must be seen in perspective against the consumption of preserved eggs. Before the First World War, the 'new-laid' and 'fresh' egg trade was still remarkably seasonal in character, and many housewives bought eggs in periods of plenty for preserving against the shortage between early August and the end of February. Preserving them had some limitations on the usefulness of the egg: 'the shell always becomes weak, and almost invariably explodes when the egg is boiled',[89] so that new-laid eggs remained at high prices beyond the reach of working-class pockets for most of the year. Equally seasonal was the demand for preserved eggs between Michaelmas and Christmas, which in London and the south retained their popularity for some years even after the First World War.[90] Kept in dry salt it was said that eggs 'do fairly even for boiling up to six or eight months'. Other methods recommended were to smear the shells with butter or a mixture of olive oil and beeswax, but the majority of preserved eggs were kept in a salt or lime solution, or else water-glass (silicate of soda solution).[91]

Fruit and vegetables

The market for fruit and vegetables was highly seasonal in nature and largely unaffected by technological advances. Most vegetables were locally grown, though the range available was somewhat restricted and some imports – principally potatoes and onions from European suppliers – were necessary. Otherwise, vegetables were available only in season: carrots, onions and root vegetables from the late summer onwards with cabbage, sprouts and similar greens for the winter. Fruit was similar in its availability, with soft fruit in the summer and hard fruit, such as apples and pears, in the autumn. Fruits grown under glass, such as grapes and peaches, were sold at prices that made them part of

---

[88] Wright, *New Book of Poultry*, p. 167.
[89] *Grocery*, December 1899, p. 758.
[90] MAF, *Egg Marketing Report*, p. 120.
[91] Wright, *New Book of Poultry*, p. 46.

a luxury trade centred largely on London, where melons and pineapples were also high-priced rarities.[92] The lack of cold storage in Britain and the exceptionally perishable nature of fruit kept prices high but an international trade in fruit was developing before 1914. From the 1890s, Californian peaches and pears began arriving in London in ships fitted with cool chambers but the greatest benefit was to the trade in apples. Tasmanian apples arriving in the spring, were followed by European fruit in the summer and autumn, and American and Canadian apples in the winter.[93] Thus began the process of eliminating seasonality, which took almost a century to complete. Imported apples, bananas and oranges became cheap enough to enter urban working-class diets occasionally. Outside the large urban centres of population fruit other than that produced in gardens was scarce. Flora Thompson recorded that 'small, sour oranges' were the only fruit the greengrocer sold to village people in the countryside of the 1880s.[94] However, by the end of the nineteenth century the trade in bananas was expanding rapidly. Bananas from the Canaries, Tenerife and Madeira were picked under-ripe and the period of the voyage used for ripening. Experimental use of refrigeration during the 1890s to bring West Indian fruit to London was unsuccessful, but a subsidized trade from Jamaica commenced in 1901.[95] As imports increased, prices fell. Bananas came within working-class horizons and grew rapidly in popularity. In 1899 a trade paper reported 'the street men have been selling perfect specimens at 1d. each or 1s a dozen fingers'. In Ireland, in the same year; prices were generally at '2d per finger, which is prohibitive to popular sale'.[96] Although in 1905 the Fruit Industry Committee wrote of 'the extraordinary growth of the taste for fruit on the part of the public', its belief 'that fruit is becoming more and more a regular article of food, for all classes' was based on the evidence of Sir William Thiselton Dyer, Director of the Royal Botanic Gardens at Kew, whose knowledge of fruit consumption apparently depended on the refuse left on his paths.[97] One estimate put

---

[92] *Report of the Departmental Committee on the Fruit Industry of Great Britain*, PP 1905 (Cd.2589), XX, para. 68; also *Fruit, Flower and Vegetable Trades' Journal*, 13 December 1913, pp. 955–6.

[93] *The Greengrocer, Fruiterer and Market Gardener*, 29 April 1896, quoting correspondence in *The Times*.

[94] F. Thompson, *Larkrise to Candleford* (Oxford, 1954), p. 120.

[95] P. N. Davies, *Fyffes and the Banana: Musa Sapientum: A Centenary History 1888–1988* (1990), pp. 71–7, and ch. 6. Joseph Chamberlain, the Colonial Secretary, offered the senior partner of the Elder Dempster Line, Alfred Jones, a subsidy to offset the decline in Jamaican sugar exports.

[96] *Fruit Grower Fruiterer Florist and Market Gardener*, 23 March 1899, p. 181; 8 June 1899, p. 364.

[97] *DC on the Fruit Industry*, para. 7; also Q.307.

consumption at nine bananas per head per year in 1900–4, rising to twenty in 1909–13, at which level bananas were still not 'a regular article of food'.[98]

There was, however, some change in the general attitude towards fruit-eating. The Drummonds noted that though fears 'that fruit caused fevers' had begun to disappear – possibly as early as the end of the eighteenth century[99] – nevertheless the 'age-old belief that fruit and vegetables are bad for children' lingered on almost to the end of the Victorian period.[100] The prejudice against unusual fruit in Flora Thompson's childhood during the 1880s was shown when tomatoes first appeared in her village.[101] By the late nineteenth century, Pavy's *Treatise on Food* compromised with the older viewpoint by allowing that an orange 'in the ripe state is so little likely to occasion disorder as to be admissible under almost every condition both of sickness and of health'. Regarding most other fruit, Pavy expressed extreme caution: 'in a raw state the apple must not be looked upon as easy of digestion', while cherries and plums were 'more apt than most other fruits to produce disorder of the bowels'.[102] Certainly 'summer diarrhoeas' were still attributed to the 'corrupting influence' of fruit well into the twentieth century.

The regulation of food quality

The Census in 1911 revealed that the population was still increasing at more than 1 per cent per annum. In those circumstances, enlarging the food supply and extending the shelf life of the more perishable items was important for wholesalers and retailers throughout the food market.

---

[98] Barker et al., *Our Changing Fare*, pp. 77, 128.

[99] Drummond, *Englishman's Food*, p. 77.

[100] Ibid., pp. 235, 379. See also Rowntree's standard diet which allowed no vegetables except potatoes, and a little vegetable broth for children. Rowntree, *Poverty*, pp. 99–102.

[101] Thompson, *Larkrise*, pp. 122–3. The travelling greengrocer was reluctant to sell the child a tomato: '"Love-apples me dear. Love-apples, they be, though some hignorant folks be a callin' 'em tommytoes. But you don't want any o' they – nasty sour things, they be, as only gentry can eat. You have a nice sweet orange wi' your penny."' Upon Laura's insistence to try one there was popular concern: 'Such daring created a sensation among the onlookers. "Don't 'ee go tryin' to eat it, now," one woman urged. "It'll only make 'ee sick. I know because I had one of the nasty horrid things at our Minnie's." And nasty horrid things tomatoes remained in the popular estimation for years; though most people today would prefer them as they were then, with the real tomato flavour pronounced, to the watery insipidity of our larger smoother tomato.'

[102] F. W. Pavy, *A Treatise on Food and Dietetics*, 2nd edn (1875), pp. 301, 303–7.

Thus chemical preservatives, such as borax or formalin, were used extensively in foodstuffs to extend shelf life.[103] The opportunities for adulteration and the use of additives and improvers was irresistible, and there were some notable instances when consumers' health was seriously affected as producers cut corners. In 1900, the use of glucose contaminated with arsenic in the brewing of beer in Lancashire and Staffordshire led to 6,000 cases of food poisoning, of whom seventy died.[104] The establishment of the Royal Commission on Arsenical Poisoning, 1903, focused public awareness on the low production standards of food and drink, and concern was heightened still further by the publication of Upton Sinclair's novel *The Jungle* in 1906, though canning was used for only a minority of foodstuffs.[105]

The practice of adulteration became increasingly subject to regulation in the early years of the twentieth century. The professional development of public analysts in the last quarter of the nineteenth century gave governments the confidence to investigate food production in a more systematic matter. The Sale of Food and Drugs Act had been passed in 1875[106] but later legislation in 1899 expected all areas of Britain to have Medical Officers of Health and Public Analysts in post. Their impact before 1914 was limited to trying to avoid the grosser forms of contamination of food and food premises, and the nature of their work may be followed in the pages of *The British Food Journal* from its foundation in 1899. Its circulation made it almost an in-house journal for public analysts, which meant that principally it contained law reports of offences under the 1875 Sale of Food and Drugs Act, and the Act that replaced it in 1899. Other legislation, such as the Margarine Act, 1887, provided case reports of interest to its readership. For example, high prices of dairy produce encouraged the production of butter substitutes, often known by shopkeepers as 'compound' or 'bosch butter'.[107] In 1896 the Select Committee on Food Products Adulteration concluded that 'of late years much butter has been put upon the market which contains a proportion of water greatly in excess of that which would naturally be found in it, the difference having been fraudulently added to increase the weight'.[108] 'Milk-blended butter' probably

---

[103] See *D. C. on Preservatives and Colouring Matter*.

[104] M. Pyke, *Townsman's Food* (1952), p. 188.

[105] For the effect upon the trade in tinned meat, see *The Grocers' Journal*, 28 July 1906, pp. 11–12.

[106] Earlier legislation – the Adulteration of Foods Act, 1860 and the Adulteration of Food, Drink, and Drugs Act, 1872 – was permissive and thus limited in its effectiveness.

[107] The name was derived from 's-Hertogenbosch in The Netherlands, a centre of margarine production and the adulteration of butter with treacle or syrup.

[108] *S.C. on Food Products Adulteration*, PP 1896, IX, 508.

contained in excess of 25 per cent water. Its popularity was assured by a High Court decision in 1902 in favour of Messrs Pearks, Gunston and Tee, which ruled that it was not covered by the 1887 Margarine Act. The public analysts achieved a remedy in the 1907 Margarine Act, which set an upper limit of 24 per cent water content for milk-blended butter and 16 per cent for butter and margarine.

However, it must not be assumed that risk of prosecution was an adequate deterrent to adulteration. The successful prosecutions under the 1887 Act began to give some idea of the extent of the misrepresentation of food in shops in poor districts. Prosecutions at both retail and wholesale level continued unabated until 1914, frequently with margarine being directly substituted for butter without any attempt at blending. Some adulteration of milk also persisted up to the First World War. By 1908, 'heavy adulteration', that is, the direct addition of water, was said to have practically disappeared and to have been replaced by 'toning', a process through which the major London contractors reduced the quality of the milk to the minimum standard required by the 1901 regulations.[109] It became increasingly difficult for the Medical Officers of Health to obtain convictions:

> The detection of adulteration is becoming more and more difficult, and is due, in the first place, to the astuteness of the vendors of the adulterated articles, and in the second to the more highly scientific means now practised.

One public analyst felt: 'it would be difficult to induce a herd of cows properly fed and in healthy condition, to yield milk of so low a quality as would correspond to the minimum standard.'[110] Between 1899 and 1914, *The British Food Journal*'s pages highlighted the provisions of the new food legislation, cases of adulteration, discussed the composition of foods, and reported on production and preservation techniques, particularly the canning process, that led to new developments in the British diet. In summary, its pages provided a record of the law's attempts in the early twentieth century to eliminate the imperfections of the urban food supply system.

Notwithstanding the legislation at the end of the nineteenth century, improvements in food quality remained a matter of concern to some Britons. Calls for dietary reform reflected this disquiet and led to a lengthy debate about the value of bread.[111] Food supplements, such as cod-liver oil, malt and beef extracts, came on the market to satisfy those

---

[109] *Thirty-Eighth Annual Report of the Local Government Board*, PP 1909 (Cd.4786), XXVIII, lxxxvii–lxxxviii.
[110] *Forty-Second A.R. of the L.G.B.*, PP 1913 (Cd.6982), XXXI, lxvi.
[111] Burnett, *Plenty and Want*, pp. 236–7.

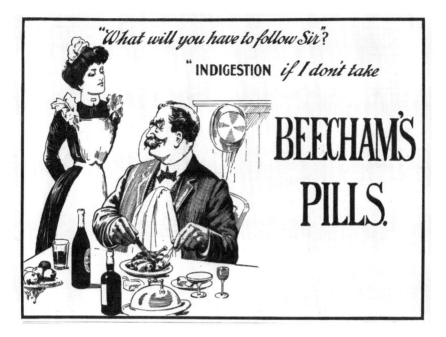

Plate 2.1 In the early twentieth century the recognized way to health was by hearty eating. One penalty was dyspepsia, the fear of which led to a widespread use of patent medicines. (Image courtesy of The Advertising Archives)

who perceived themselves inadequately nourished by their normal diet. Concern regarding the quality of food was probably implicit in the Victorians' interest in their digestion, especially their anxiety over dyspepsia and constipation. The proliferation of pills, or American 'compressed tablets', claiming digestive properties – however dubious or dangerous their assertions might be – found ready buyers right up to the First World War. Beecham's Pills 'Worth a Guinea a Box' offered relief from 'All Bilious & Nervous Disorders such as Sick Headache, Constipation, Weak Stomach, Impaired Digestion, Disordered Liver and Female Ailments'. Beecham's advertisements claimed sales of 6M boxes a year before the end of the nineteenth century.[112] Carter's Liver Pills, Eno's 'Fruit Salt', Holloway's Ointment and American products (such as Wyeth's Peptonic Tablets, Kepler Oil and Malt, and Burroughs' Beef & Iron Wine) sold by Burroughs Wellcome were all designed to exploit the

---

[112] For example, see advertisement in *Good Things Made Said and Done for every Home & Household*, 34th edn (Leeds, 1896).

market for digestive problems. Kepler Malt Extract, for example, claimed to be 'extensively prescribed on account of its dietetic value and digestibility'. From the 1890s many 'pharmaceutical' products contained 'morphia' or cocaine.[113] Other strange-sounding preparations such as Freeman's Syrup of Phosphorus claimed to be 'equal to ten doses of cod-liver oil' in restoring appetite and to be suitable for the treatment of 'Indigestion, Constipation, Loss of Energy' in revitalizing and 'restoring the failing functions of life'.[114] The dubious nature of these claims went unchallenged, and the market for pills and patent medicines remained highly profitable for the major producers of trademarked goods.[115]

Food retailing

Against this background of changing technology and quality, food retailing underwent a transformation from small-scale businesses based on personal service to large-scale enterprises. Indeed, at the very beginning of the twentieth century, the independent grocer's survival seemed in doubt. In an editorial called 'The passing of the grocer', *The Times* saw the small shop as being threatened by multiple-branch retailers and co-operative societies alike.[116] Even so, by their very numbers, small-scale retail shops were still by far the commonest places in which the British bought their food. The corner shop varied considerably in scale and status: some, but not all, occupied large specialist premises; most were not exclusively food retail outlets. Moreover, businesses of any kind were far from permanent: the small shop was easy to open in the front room of any terraced house; it was even easier to close down. Nevertheless, the shop gave many a family the hope of social advancement and there were always thousands ready to take the risk.

Early in the twentieth century, just prior to the First World War, it may well have been the case that Britain was oversupplied with food shops. Besides the countless small traders, estimates for 1910 suggest that there were 114 multiple-shop firms in the grocery and provisions trade selling through some 2,870 branches between them. The meat trade encompassed twenty-three multiples with 3,828 branches, the bread and flour confectionery trade included twenty-one firms with 451

---

[113] R. R. James, *Henry Wellcome* (1994), p. 92.
[114] See advertisement in *Good Things Made Said and Done*.
[115] James, *Wellcome*. See pp. 292–3 for Burroughs Wellcome's defence of its trademark 'Tabloid' between 1900 and 1903.
[116] *The Times*, 18 August 1902, cited in Michael J. Winstanley, *The Shopkeeper's World 1830–1914* (Manchester, 1983), p. 120.

branches, while chocolate and sugar confectionery added another ten firms with 308 branches. Milk supply involved twenty multiples with 324 branches.[117] In addition, by 1913 the retail co-operative societies claimed almost 2.9M members in working-class areas.[118] Competition, if one can believe the trade press, had reached a point where the small retailer felt it was 'excessive' and 'unfair' to honourable tradesman. This state of affairs was the outcome of nineteenth-century developments in the British economy which, through the growth of wholesale trade in food, had fundamentally altered earlier patterns of retailing.

Imports of tea, bacon, and especially the new 'artificial' food – margarine – came to market in a way which began to blur the older distinctions between grocer and provision merchant. Providing outlets for these foodstuffs throughout the growing working-class urban areas during the late nineteenth and early twentieth centuries was the function of the multiple-unit retailers. The aggressive marketing of foods such as tea and margarine was fundamental to the growth of the multiple chains of retailers between the 1870s and the First World War. Lipton's, the International Tea Company, the Home and Colonial Stores, Maypole Dairies, Meadow's, Pearks and so on in England, and Massey's, Templeton's, Cochrane's and Galbraith's in Scotland, caused a dramatic change in food-retailing practices. The expanding market for margarine in working-class areas from 1909 onwards was a key to the growth of retail chains such as Maypole Dairies[119] and the multiples that sold the products of the Dutch firms, Jurgens' and Van den Bergh's.[120] By 1912, Jurgens' supplied Home and Colonial Stores and several small regional chains, while Van den Burgh's supplied Lipton's, Pearks' and Meadow's (including Keeloma).

The creation of new products by food manufacturers provided customers with further attractions. From the 1880s onwards, patented flours such as Allinson's, Hovis and Daren appeared, and loaves of brown bread based upon them and other flours, such as the 'Malt Loaf', were bought for their 'health food' attributes.[121] The years from the 1890s to 1914 saw the introduction of breakfast cereals, most of which were imported from North America. These included the US products Quaker Oats, Puffed Wheat and Grape Nuts, and from Canada, Force

---

[117] W. Hamish Fraser, *The Coming of the Mass Market 1850–1914* (1981), Table 9.1, based on J. B. Jefferys, *Retail Trading in Britain 1850–1950* (Cambridge, 1954).
[118] Fraser, *Coming of the Mass Market*, p. 124,
[119] Maypole's margarine was supplied principally by Otto Monsted, a Danish company with a factory at Southall, Middlesex.
[120] See C. Wilson, *The History of Unilever*, Vol. II (1954), ch. VII.
[121] See E. J. T. Collins, 'The "consumer revolution" and the growth of factory foods: changing patterns of bread and cereal-eating in Britain in the twentieth century', in Oddy and Miller, *Modern British Diet*, particularly pp. 28–31.

Wheat Flakes and Shredded Wheat. British breakfast cereals such as John Bull existed, but, like the imported foods, their market was limited, largely by advertising that stressed their 'natural' or 'biologic' importance in the diet.[122] Such foods typified the marked increase in proprietary branded foods that occurred around the turn of the century. Pre-packed tea and packaged biscuits from Huntley and Palmer, Peek Frean, Carr or Macfarlane Laing and McVitie were becoming national brands through extensive advertising. The switch to fruit-growing in former arable areas created a jam industry with Chivers at Histon, Cambridge (1874), Wilkin's at Tiptree in Essex (1885), as well as other firms such as Crosse and Blackwell, Wood Brothers in Kent, and Beach and Sons at Pershore in Worcestershire.[123] The growing market for Keiller's marmalade was sufficient for it to be produced in both Dundee and London from 1879 onwards.[124] Brands were important to demonstrate quality, as shown by Rowntree's Elect cocoa and Cadbury Brothers' confectionery. Two of Cadbury's current best lines pre-date the First World War: Dairy Milk was launched in 1905 and Bournville plain chocolate in 1908.

The wide variety of manufactured food products coming to the shops illustrated the changes in the diet. Among the better-off, 'plain fare' apparently no longer satisfied people's tastes. The 'Table Delicacies and Dainties' packed in glass bottles, jars and moulds with 'hermetically sealed' lids or screw caps provided the novelties of the late Victorian and Edwardian tables of the middle classes. Potted meats, chicken, tongue, sardines, lobster, herring roes, prawns, peeled shrimps and meat pastes, fish pastes and jams enlivened tea and supper tables or picnic hampers. Soups, pâtés, salad creams and chutney frequently echoed Britain's Imperial role – Royal Naval Chutney, Col. Skinner's Chutney and Major Gray's Sweet Sliced Mango Chutney. Lemon squash or lime juice cordial, pickled or spiced fruits, Tomato Catsup by Gordon & Dilworth and Pan Yan Pickle could be bought not only from provision merchants but also from major London stores, whence they could even be posted to expatriates in places as disparate as Abyssinia and Zanzibar.[125]

The kitchens of the middle-class homes in the new dormitory suburbs[126] where these relishes were consumed were more extensively

---

[122] Collins, 'The "consumer revolution"', in Oddy and Miller, *Modern British Diet*, pp. 31–3.

[123] Angeliki Torode, 'Trends in fruit consumption', in Barker *et al.*, *Our Changing Fare*, pp. 122–4.

[124] W. M. Mathew, *Keiller's of Dundee. The Rise of the Marmalade Dynasty 1800–1879* (Dundee, 1998), p. 95.

[125] See *Yesterday's Shopping, Gamages General Catalogue 1914* (Ware, 1994).

[126] See D. J. Olsen, *The Growth of Victorian London* (Harmondsworth, 1979), ch. 5, 'The villa and the new suburb'.

equipped than those of the mid-nineteenth century. Sets of enamelled pots and pans, kettles, egg poachers, fish kettles, roasting dishes, fish fryers and preserving pans were essential items but various gadgets to mince, slice, extract or press were also on the market. Gas cookers led to the introduction of newer, thinner pots and pans. Middle-class areas of towns generally had gas supplied, and gas cookers became common in the decade before 1914. Gas began to spread into working-class areas from the 1890s once the pre-paid meter had been invented but, on the whole, it was in the newer areas commonly described as 'improved artisans' dwellings' that it was to be found.[127] Cooking in working-class housing built in the late nineteenth century was generally done on coal-fired ranges, usually with an oven built in at the side of the grate, and sometimes a water-heating facility. Despite the fact that most of the newer houses had gas supplied, few had electricity and then only for lighting. One item of domestic technology seldom found was the refrigerator. There were 'ice safes' in the 1907 Army and Navy Stores catalogue but Gamages offered no refrigerators powered by either gas or electricity in 1914. Low-temperature technology for the domestic preservation of food was uncommon before the First World War.

By 1914, the retail market for food comprised three sectors. There were the retail co-operative societies backed by the Co-operative Wholesale Society (CWS), the multiples in both general foodstuffs and specialist trades such as meat (Dewhurst's) and bread (Bilslands of Glasgow) and the independent retailers ranging from Fortnum and Mason's in Piccadilly to small corner shops. The latter were predominant by their very numbers, their claims to personal service, and their practice of delivering goods ordered by customers to their homes. Personal service had become the essential characteristic of the grocery trade insofar as it retained the notion that the grocer's original function had been to break bulk. The shopman's skill in merchandising lay in cutting, slicing, weighing and packing food exactly to the customer's order. The initial threat to the grocer and provision merchant's existence came from the standardization and pre-packaging of commodities such as tea, margarine and (but outside the food trade) soap. This gave an incentive to the wholesaler to control quality and to introduce product differentiation. Well before the end of the nineteenth century, branded food products were subject to extensive advertising in newspapers, on billboards in town streets, and on the platforms of railway stations. The development of food technology in the nineteenth century for the manufacture of cakes, biscuits, breakfast cereals, pies, patent foods of varying kinds and soft drinks created products for the food retailer in

---

[127] H. J. Dyos, *Victorian Suburb: Study of the Growth of Camberwell* (Leicester, 1961), p. 148.

which the wholesaler's price became more significant than the skills of the shopkeeper's counter hands. Indeed, in the densely inhabited urban areas where many working-class customers were concentrated, the food retailer's risk was minimal if he kept to cash sales. Thomas Lipton could open a store a month in the 1880s by putting down a week's rent on the premises and buying goods on a month's credit.[128] However, in the poorest districts shopkeeping was an insecure business as people bought only a limited range of food items and turned to the 'undercutters' and street stalls selling low-quality goods when in need.

Commercial catering

From the end of the 1880s there was a marked increase in catering facilities. Urban life not only meant business and commerce but also leisure. Chains of dining-rooms began to be established in London and some spread into the major provincial cities. The temperance catering movement had been in difficulties in the 1880s but out of it grew two London chains whose main business lay in providing midday meals of a limited kind. Lockharts operated fifty coffee rooms by 1893, while Pearce and Plenty ran twenty dining-rooms with the motto 'Quality, Economy, Despatch'. These were the fast-food outlets of the 1890s but other chains began to emerge, some of which operated better class restaurants. Mass catering was provided by the Aerated Bread Company (ABC) which operated sixty cafés in the early 1890s and the Express Dairy's 'milk and bun' shops. Lyons' first teashop opened in 1894 and, as others followed, rapidly grew into a standardized chain providing light refreshments. Their quality and cleanliness made them popular with women shopping or working in the new field of office employment as typists. In response, Pearce and Plenty developed The British Tea Table, and Lockharts their Ideal Restaurants. Lyons' success led the company to sell its tea and cakes over the counter in its teashops and to extend its trade into restaurants in the West End and the City. It opened the Trocadero in Piccadilly in 1896 and its first Lyons' Corner House in 1909. It also began to develop teashops in the provinces.[129]

The most widespread outlets of commercial catering were undoubtedly the fish-and-chip shop and the public house. By 1914, fish-and-chip shops were almost universal in Britain: 'hardly any market town or

---

[128] P. Mathias, *Retailing Revolution. A History of Multiple Retailing in the Food Trades Based upon the Allied Suppliers Group of Companies* (1967), pp. 40, 50–2 and ch. 6.

[129] D. J. Richardson, 'J. Lyons and Co Ltd: caterers and food manufacturers, 1894–1939', in Oddy and Miller, *Modern British Diet*, pp. 161–9.

substantial village is without at least one fish-and-chip shop' or else, possibly, a mobile van selling fish and chips.[130] Even areas that had little waged work for women outside the home generally supported a fish-and-chip shop. Most were small-scale operations, either single outlets or, less likely, shops with one or two branches, though a few small chains of fish-and-chip shops existed before 1914. A substantial number were run by women, and the general view that entry costs were low meant that fish-and-chip shops were seen as a lucrative venture for 'penny capitalists'.

Even more common than the fish-and-chip shop was the public house. In 1896, there was one pub to every 168 people in Manchester, every 176 in Sheffield, every 215 in Birmingham and every 279 in Liverpool. Leeds with 345 people per pub and London with 393 were less well endowed with drinking places.[131] Pubs were meeting places and recreation centres, and many were still focal points of the Victorian transport system. Since pubs were at the heart of male society, there were concentrations of pubs around army barracks in garrison towns and in ports and dockyards. Consumption per head of both beer and spirits had reached a peak in 1875–66.[132] At that time over thirty-four gallons per head of beer and almost 1.5 gallons of spirits per head were consumed annually. A gradual decline followed, apart from the late 1890s, until 1905 to 1914, when beer consumption was around twenty-eight to thirty gallons per head and spirits approximately 0.9 to 1.0 gallon per head per year.[133] These statistics were open to question but the levels of consumption were such that drink was often the largest item of expenditure in working-class families. Charles Booth believed that as much as one-quarter of working-class earnings was spent on drink, and B. S. Rowntree – who carried out a census of activity at a number of public houses – estimated that in York at the turn of the century it might be one-sixth.[134] Booth's map of London's pubs showed how heavily they were concentrated in working-class areas and how estates of fashionable housing, such as the Bedford

[130] Walton, *Fish and Chips and the British Working Class*, pp. 37, 148.
[131] Brian Harrison, 'Pubs', in H. J. Dyos and Michael Wolff, eds, *The Victorian City Images and Realities, Vol. I Past and Present and Numbers of People* (1976), p. 162.
[132] Beer and spirits are energy sources not to be ignored: beer provides around 200kcal per pint, wine about 480–500kcal per bottle and spirits over 200kcal per 100ml.
[133] A. E. Dingle, 'Drink and working-class living standards in Britain, 1870–1914', in Oddy and Miller, *Modern British Diet*, pp. 117–18. A more recent estimate of beer consumption in the late 1870s has put it as high as 40.5 gallons per head. See T. R. Gourvish and R. G. Wilson, *The British Brewing Industry, 1830–1980* (Cambridge, 1994), Table 2.3.
[134] Dingle, in Oddy and Miller, *Modern British Diet*, p. 120. See also Rowntree, *Poverty*, Supplementary chapter (a), 'Public-houses and clubs'.

estate in Bloomsbury, did not permit them. In better-off areas, grocers' licences catered for drinking at home. Specialist firms, such as Gilbey's wine-shops, developed for the off-licence trade. Refreshment house licences allowed alcoholic beverages to be sold with midday meals in business districts.[135] The temperance movement, despite all its propaganda against drunkenness, made little progress in reducing the consumption of alcoholic beverages, though a movement for public house reform was generated in the late 1890s. The reformers sought to improve conditions in public houses by promoting the sale of food and non-alcoholic drinks, improving the buildings and restricting the number of licences to sell alcoholic drinks.[136] For the bulk of the working classes in late Victorian and Edwardian times, however, the pub, even in its unreformed guise, provided an escape from overcrowded houses and a poor domestic environment.

[135] Harrison, 'Pubs', in Dyos and Wolff, *Victorian City*, pp. 166–8. Gladstone introduced refreshment house licences in 1860 and grocers' licences in 1861. See John Burnett, *Liquid Pleasures. A Social History of Drinks in Modern Britain* (1999), p. 149.
[136] Robert Thorne, 'The public house reform movement', in Oddy and Miller, *Diet and Health in Modern Britain*, pp. 231–54.

3

NUTRITION, ENVIRONMENT AND HEALTH BEFORE 1914

The science of nutrition had become an important weapon for socially aware people in British society at the beginning of the twentieth century. At one end of the political spectrum were those concerned with imperial defence whose interests lay in the health and strength of the British soldier. At the other end were public health reformers investigating the 'social problem' for whom the social costs of urban–industrial society were to be found in terms of mortality and morbidity among women and children. Both were interested in physical standards and looked for guidance to the sciences of physiology and nutrition. Nutrition was still imperfectly understood. 'Until 1900 energy dominated the science of nutrition', wrote Professor V. H. Mottram[1] and prior to the First World War, all dietaries emphasized the importance of the energy value of foods eaten. It had been known for much of the second half of the nineteenth century that food was composed of carbohydrates, proteins (or proteids as they were then termed) and fats. The energy required for daily needs had been estimated by Lyon Playfair as early as 1865, and later work by Pettenkofer and Voit in Munich, Rubner in Berlin and Atwater in the USA had made little difference to the view that adult males required between 2,700 and 4,500kcal per day according to the amount of physical effort their work required.[2] By the beginning of the twentieth century these estimates were used by various authorities to limit the amount of food provided by institutional diets. In Britain, B. S. Rowntree was familiar with Atwater's work and used it in his study of workhouse diets. Institutional diets frequently ignored people's normal choices of food in favour of some combination of foods that expressed a social or moral prescription; for example, it was common for workhouse diets to allow adults no sugar or butter to prevent gratifying the inmates' taste.[3] Besides, from the point of view of economy,

---

[1] V. H. Mottram, *Human Nutrition*, 2nd edn (1963), p. 15.
[2] W. O. Atwater, *Methods and Results of Investigations on the Chemistry and Economy of Food* (Washington, DC, 1895).
[3] See Rowntree, *Poverty*, ch. IV; Dr Edward Smith's recommendations in 1867 called for inmates' diets to be agreeable and as near normal as possible. See *Report to the Poor Law Board on the Uniformity of Workhouse Dietaries*, PP 1867, LX.

energy was obtainable far more cheaply from cereals if served as bread or porridge. For people at work, particularly when engaged in moderate or heavy manual work, animal food was thought to be essential. By 1900, protein was known to be an important component of the diet in building muscle as well as a source of energy. The minimum amount required was thought to be 100g per day but 'in the better diets' protein intakes of 130 to 150g were deemed necessary for moderate work. It was therefore generally accepted that a high-protein diet was necessary for health. Despite this belief, reports of experimental diets based on 25 to 36g of protein a day led Professor Chittenden of Yale, an American physiologist, to propose a low-protein diet for general consumption, though he recognized the prevailing opinion was that 'by hearty eating lies the road to health and strength'.[4]

Rubner's work had shown that 1g of protein produced 4.1kcal, the same as 1g of carbohydrate, and 1g of fat yielded 9.3kcal, so physiologists began to construct dietaries for the poor in which fat and carbohydrate were interchangeable as sources of energy. The substitution of one for the other was merely a question of cost. By the twentieth century it was recognized that carbohydrate in the form of sugar was a cheap form of energy compared with that obtained from animal fats, for while the cheapest margarine provided 450kcal for a penny, sugar provided almost 900kcal.[5] The availability of cheap energy from sugar was accepted as one of the advantages of free trade but, despite this, Sir Michael Hicks-Beach imposed a duty on it in his 1901 budget to help pay for the cost of the Boer War. He chose sugar since it was an 'article of universal consumption which is very cheap'.[6] The construction of dietaries which were very high in carbohydrates had limits. In Edinburgh: 'It is generally found that when the amount of carbohydrates exceeds about 500 or 600g, the digestive organs begin to be disturbed.'[7]

---

[4] R. H. Chittenden, *Physiological Economy of Nutrition* (1904), pp. 472–3. In reviewing Chittenden's *Physiological Economy of Nutrition*, the *British Medical Journal* took pleasure in belittling B. S. Rowntree's investigations in York for his acceptance of the need for a high-protein diet. See *BMJ*, 1906, I, 400. Chittenden modified his recommendations in *The Nutrition of Man* (1907) to allow a 70kg (11st) man 60g protein a day, though this did not prevent a further attack on low-protein diets from appearing in Sir James Crichton Browne, *Parcimony* [sic] *in Nutrition* (1909), particularly ch. 2.

[5] These figures are based on margarine at 8d and sugar at 2d per pound. See D. N. Paton, J. C. Dunlop and E. Inglis, *On the Dietaries of the Labouring Classes of the City of Edinburgh* (Edinburgh, 1901), p. 9, for the use of such calculations (though beware their arithmetical error).

[6] J. F. Rees, *A Short Fiscal and Financial History of England 1815–1918* (1921), pp. 181–4. Hicks-Beach also imposed a tax on imported bread-grains in 1902 which lasted for only one year. The sugar tax had been abolished in 1874.

[7] Paton *et al.*, *Dietaries of the Labouring Classes*, p. 9.

Although it was known that foods contained various minerals their role was not understood. Similarly, there were no explanations for the presence of rickets, anaemia and scurvy, though these diseases were known to occur when diets were deficient. All were commonly found among the poorer sections of society. Rickets, known as 'a disease of poverty and darkness', affected the bones of children whose diets were limited in milk, cream, butter and eggs. Chlorosis or 'green sickness' was a form of anaemia that was common before the First World War among young women shopworkers and those in domestic service.[8] Infantile scurvy occurred not among the poor, as did rickets, but among the middle-classes who had adopted patent baby foods or the over-enthusiastic boiling of cows' milk in place of breast milk.[9] The work begun at Cambridge in 1906 and published in 1912 by F. G. Hopkins had no immediate impact.[10] Thus 'accessory food factors', as vitamins were termed originally, minerals and fibre formed no part of the pre-1914 knowledge of nutrition. In consequence, medical evidence given to the series of inquiries into health made by the state that followed the National Conference on Infant Mortality in 1906 lacked clarity and coherence. Witnesses struggled to express empirically what they did not understand conceptually. Physical appearance had to express nutritional status: 'Hard, dry, "staring" hair,' wrote a Scottish school medical officer, 'is just as much a sign of defective nutrition in the child as in the animals in the farmyard.'[11] Otherwise, there could only be a retreat into moralizing: 'Improper food and hurried methods of eating account for much malnutrition.'[12] This ignored what Drummond later summed up as 'by far the most important cause, semi-starvation due to sheer poverty'.[13] Thus the 'countless substances other than protein, carbo-hydrates, and fats' that Hopkins was already envisaging as 'well nigh as essential as are the basal constituents of the diet' provided no measure by which the poor physical development and ill-health of people could be assessed.

The importance of the interaction between nutrition and the physical environment as a factor affecting the health of large sectors of the urban working class cannot be overstated. After the First World War the link

---

[8] See the Introduction to Medical Research Council, Special Report Series, No.157, Helen M. M. Mackay, *Nutritional Anaemia in Infancy*, 1931.
[9] For milk and milk substitutes in the feeding of infants and children, see Drummond, *Englishman's Food*, pp. 373–9.
[10] F. G. Hopkins, *Journal of Physiology*, 44, (1912), p. 425.
[11] Education (Scotland) Department, *First Report on the Medical Inspection of School Children in Scotland* (1913), para. 81.
[12] M. E. Bulkley, *The Feeding of School Children* (1914), p. 172.
[13] Drummond, *Englishman's Food*, p. 405.

was sometimes questioned. M'Gonigle and Kirby, for example, noted that:

> environment is not the only factor so operative, and possibly not the most important one. Most medical officers who served in France during the Great War were impressed by the healthiness of the troops who lived, often for long periods, under environmental conditions which, even at their best, could only be described as unsatisfactory.[14]

That may indeed have been true for men living on full Army rations, and it would not be dissimilar from the conclusion reached by many social investigators before 1914, who commented favourably on the health and strength of the male labourer. The urban environment, however, was inhabited not only by adult males in their twenties and thirties but also by women and children, and was the setting for births and child-rearing. Although public health administration in the last five years or so before 1914 received a new impetus in the hands of medical officers such as Sir Arthur Newsholme at the Local Government Board and George Newman at the Board of Education, the attack on the poor environment of inner urban districts could not change inadequate diets. Both Newsholme and Newman were convinced environmentalists. Writing on the health of the schoolchild as school medical inspections were introduced, Newman expressed the effects of the urban environment in a single sentence. 'At the best, however, and in anything like the social and economic conditions which now prevail, the work which the Local Education Authority can do in directly preventing and reme-dying the evils of malnutrition has somewhat definite limits.'[15] With this expression of the inadequacy of pre-1914 social policy to influence social conditions in mind, it should be evident that the connexion between environment and diet was essential to understanding the view that malnutrition was widespread.

Working-class housing before 1914

Among the divisive influences at work in society in the late nineteenth century was a sense of separation due in part to the physical segregation of the classes that resulted from suburban development.[16] Although

---

[14] G. C. M. M'Gonigle and J. Kirby, *Poverty and Public Health* (1936), pp. 143–9.
[15] Board of Education, *Annual Report of the Chief Medical Officer for 1910*, PP 1911 (Cd.5925), XVII, para. 314.
[16] H. Pelling, *A History of British Trade Unionism* (Harmondsworth, 1963), pp. 90–1.

middle-class families had begun to move away from the central districts of towns into the new suburbs, the working classes did not generally benefit from the suburban housing which was being created. In areas of inner London some one-third or more of the population lived two or more in a room.[17] This was not solely a metropolitan problem; in the northeast, Lancashire and the Midlands, large and small towns alike exhibited high percentages of overcrowding.[18] The 1911 Census showed that almost one-fifth (19.4 per cent) of the population were 'poorly housed' in that they lived in households with fewer than four rooms, while almost 9 per cent were stated to be overcrowded by the Registrar General's definition of more than two persons per room.[19] In inner London, much of this was due to the occupation of former middle-class dwellings by several working-class families. This accentuated sanitary problems: in Shoreditch in 1910, it was commonly found that 'rooms intended to be used as bedrooms or parlours have now to serve for the entire accommodation of a whole family'. Such conditions facilitated the spread of disease and the continuance of a high infant mortality.[20] Similar conditions existed in some Scottish towns where there was a long tradition of one- or two-room dwellings. The Physical Deterioration Committee were told that 76 per cent of the population in the North Canongate ward of Edinburgh lived in one- or two-roomed dwellings which, besides the parents, often accommodated seven, eight or nine children.[21]

Casual labour, short-time working, low wages or defective supply of housing were undoubtedly interrelated factors in the apparent immobility of the working-class population.[22] Even well-paid workers appear to have accepted the urban environment as normal by not choosing to move from poor housing in town centres. In Middlesborough, a relatively new town largely created in the second half of the nineteenth century, men earning good wages lived in houses with inadequate bedroom space, frequently lacking provision for food storage, and served by a pail-closet sanitation system.[23] Similar apparent indifference

[17] Details quoted in *45th A.R. of the L.G.B. Supplement: Report on Child Mortality*, PP 1917–18 (Cd.8496), XVI, Section XI, pp. 70–1.

[18] *45th A.R. of the L.G.B. Child Mortality Report*, pp. 70–1.

[19] *Census of England and Wales, 1911. General Report*, 1917 (Cd.8491), Table LXVII.

[20] *42nd A.R. of the L.G.B. Supplement. Second Report on Infant Mortality*, PP 1913 (Cd.6909), XXXII, pp. 70–1.

[21] *Report of the Inter-Departmental Committee on Physical Deterioration*, PP 1904 (Cd.2175), XXXII, para. 112.

[22] M'Gonigle and Kirby, *Poverty and Public Health*, ch. 7, noted the detrimental effect of rehousing on family budgets.

[23] *45th A.R. of the L.G.B. Child Mortality Report*, pp. 57–60.

to the domestic environment was common in the industrial towns of Lancashire and the northeast.

The inadequacy of domestic water supplies was an integral part of the problem since it was only from the mid-1880s that piped water on constant supply was becoming available. In 1886, under half the houses in London received water on a constant supply basis, and although 86 per cent of houses had been reached ten years later, it was not until 1906 that the system was almost complete.[24] Where multi-occupancy of houses was widespread, not every family received a separate supply of water. Health visitors noted this as contributing not only to the general dirtiness of homes but in the reduction of household activities to a minimum.[25] Shortage of water limited the amount of cooking the housewife was able to do, and was associated with the storage of food, especially milk, in dirty containers.[26] Although multi-occupancy was less of a problem in the provinces than in the central districts of London, industrial demands for water frequently restricted the availability of domestic supplies. In some towns, as in Crewe and St Helens, local authorities relied mainly on industrial surpluses for domestic supplies,[27] and poor sanitation in Lancashire generally resulted, at least in part, from this cause:

> Until recent years the midden privy was practically universal in the county. No doubt this was due in the first instance, to the scarcity of water supply for domestic purposes, and to the great demand for pure water for the local manufactures.[28]

Nevertheless, the majority of urban areas had a piped water system, though in rural areas progress had been much slower. In 1914 only 38 per cent of rural parishes in England and Wales had any partially piped system of water supply.[29] Within the decade before 1914 many areas began to convert their sanitation and scavenging systems. However, the improvement achieved was perhaps limited, since in Stoke-on-Trent, for

[24] *16th A.R. of the L.G.B.*, PP 1887 (C. 5131), XXXVI, cxlvi; *26th A.R. of the L.G.B.*, PP 1897 (C. 8583), XXXVI, clxii; *36th A.R. of the L.G.B.*, PP 1907 (Cd.3665), XXVI, xcvii.

[25] *42nd A.R. of the L.G.B. Second Report on Infant Mortality*, p. 72.

[26] Medical Officer of Health for Burslem, quoted in *39th A.R. of the L.G.B. Supplement. Report on Infant Mortality*, PP 1910 (Cd.5263), XXXIX, p. 104.

[27] See W.H. Chaloner, *Social and Economic Development of Crewe, 1730–1923* (1950), and T.C. Barker and J.R. Harris, *A Merseyside Town in the Industrial Revolution* (1959).

[28] *43rd A.R. of the L.G.B. Supplement. Third Report on Infant Mortality (Lancashire)*, PP 1914 (Cd.7511), XXXIX, p. 6.

[29] *Return on Water Undertakings (England and Wales)*, PP 1914, LXXIX, p. 543.

example, 'in some districts privies or pail closets remain in a large proportion of the total streets, although most of the houses in each street was supplied by water-closets. Consequently noxious effluvia and the plague of flies persist.' Conditions such as this came to light due to the disquiet about infant mortality that developed from 1906 onwards. Greater knowledge about working-class homes was obtained, mainly through the gradual application of the Notification of Births Act, 1907,[30] in conjunction with the Midwives Act, 1902.[31] Only after the Housing and Town Planning Act, 1909[32] did simplifying the procedure for closing insanitary property lead to any widespread attempt to improve housing.

Overcrowded conditions were not only found in the older central areas of towns. Where industry had created semi-urban conditions in the counties there could also be an inadequate housing supply, poor living conditions and yet apparent indifference to the situation. In Durham, where the 'free house' system of colliery-owned property prevailed, this was particularly noticeable:

> The Durham miners earn good wages, but they live in houses grossly inferior to the average workman's house in other areas, with terrible results in regard to the welfare of their wives and children.[33]

Thus improvements in the economic position of wage-earners due to rising wages or falling prices had little effect in raising the standard of living due to the stronger hold of environmental conditions on working-class life. 'It is significant,' wrote Sir Arthur Newsholme in 1913, 'that prior to the last decade the average infant mortality in England and Wales failed to decline, not withstanding steady improvement in the average economic condition of wage-earners during this period.'[34] The high levels of infant mortality shown in Table 3.1 illustrate the problem. The negative impact of overcrowding and inadequate housing on family life was somewhat mitigated by improving medical facilities which reduced the effect of disease. Newsholme, commenting on the increased hospitalization of the sick, pointed out that such action by the state was akin to the provision of supplementary housing at a time of domestic crisis.[35] The correlation between poor housing conditions and high

---

[30] 7 Edw. 7, c.40. It was not universally in force, however, until after the 1915 Notification of Births (Extension) Act (5 and 6 Geo.5, c.64).
[31] 2 Edw. 7, c.17.
[32] 9 Edw. 7, c.44.
[33] *45th A.R. of the L.G.B. Child Mortality Report*, p. 69.
[34] *42nd A.R. of the L.G.B.: Second Report on Infant Mortality*, p. 74.
[35] A. Newsholme, *Fifty Years in Public Health* (1935), p. 305.

Table 3.1 Annual average trends in infant mortality, 1891 to 1915

Quinquennial periods	England and Wales deaths (0–1)/1000 live births	Scotland deaths (0–1)/1000 live births
1891–1895	151	126
1896–1900	156	125
1901–1905	138	120
1906–1910	117	112
1911–1915	110	113

Source: Calculated from B. R. Mitchell and Ph. Deane, *Abstract of Historical Statistics* (Cambridge, 1962), ch. 1.

Table 3.2 Infant mortality rate in Bradford, 1911, by rateable values of housing

Rateable values (£)	Number of infant deaths	Infant mortality rate (deaths/000 live births)
6 and under	397	163
6 to 8	202	128
8 to 12	117	123
> 12	49	88

Source: L.G.B. Second Report on Infant Mortality, p. 85.

infant mortality is illustrated in Table 3.2 by the example from Bradford. However, while it was frequently assumed that poor housing conditions and poverty coincided, this was not always true. Some poor housing was occupied by 'clerks and employees above the rank of labourers'[36] and poor housing was felt to be a significant factor in explaining the prevalence of diphtheria in Enfield, a still new suburban area, in 1909.[37]

In general, bad housing was inseparable from poor diet but insofar as infant mortality represented the combination of poor nutrition and poor hygiene, identifying under-nutrition among infants in Edwardian Britain is difficult. A more specific indicator of poor nutrition may be found in the child mortality rate among those aged between 1 and 4 years. The recognition of this as a measure of malnutrition was introduced by the World Health Organization (WHO) in the 1960s for use in aid programmes in parts of the world where monitoring of health by clinical

[36] *42nd A.R. of the L.G.B. Second Report on Infant Mortality*, p. 73.
[37] *39th A.R. of the L.G.B. Report of the Medical Officer*, PP 1910 (Cd.5312), XXXIX, p. 9.

studies was deficient. Malnutrition, or more specifically under-nutrition, is assumed to be present if the child mortality rate is greater than ten per thousand.[38] This may be applied to analyse the vital statistics of past societies for which clinical assessments of health are not available. Before the First World War, the child mortality rate in Britain was much higher than the WHO standard, which suggests under-nutrition was prevalent. Table 3.3 shows that although child mortality in England and Wales fell from over thirty-one per thousand in the 1870s, it remained in excess of eighteen per thousand during the first decade of the twentieth century. There is no more powerful indicator that under-nutrition was widespread. Thus under-nutrition, ill-health and poor environmental conditions combined to constrain eating as a cultural experience for many people before the First World War.

Table 3.3 Child mortality in England from the 1870s to the First World War

Decade	Child population (1–4 years) (M)	Annual average number of deaths (1–4 years) (000s)	Child mortality rate (Deaths per 000)
1871–1880	2.576	80	31.2
1881–1890	2.783	75	27.0
1891–1900	2.857	69	24.3
1901–1910	2.991	55	18.4

Source: Derived from the *Census Reports of England and Wales*.

The impact of environment on the diet

Inadequate facilities for food storage were almost always a condition of poor housing standards. It was a particular problem where large houses had degenerated into multiple-occupancy. In Shoreditch, the health visitor's report for 1910 noted that:

> In one or two-roomed homes where the only storage for food is a cupboard in the recess by the side of the fire, it is extremely difficult, and sometimes almost impossible, to keep milk in a fit state for an infant's food, especially in the summer. In this connection, I may point out that there was proper pantry accommodation in only two of the 37 homes where the . . . deaths from summer diarrhoea had occurred.[39]

[38] World Health Organization, Technical Report Series, 1966, No.340.
[39] Quoted in *42nd A.R. of the L.G.B. Second Report on Infant Mortality*, p. 72.

In working-class dwellings in Burnley: 'Usually there is no place for the storage of food, including milk, other than a small cupboard placed at the side of the kitchen fireplace, and possessing no means of ventilation to the outside air.' In Lancashire towns there was said to be 'a general absence of proper food cupboards',[40] while at Burslem a lady sanitary inspector noted that when provision was made, housewives continued to keep milk in the cupboard by the fire. Food storage problems, as much as poverty, led working-class families to buy food in small quantities: 'Even when means permit it is impossible to economize by buying in larger quantities if there is no fit and proper place in which to store the food.'[41]

Meal patterns within the family are important determinants both of choice of food and the amount consumed. Diets with very low fat content limited the housewife's manner of cooking and making meals,[42] quite apart from any restriction imposed by lack of facilities or knowledge. In the towns, perhaps particularly in London where some areas of large houses had degenerated into multi-occupancy, families frequently lacked cooking facilities which meant 'the culinary art, if practised at all, is reduced to its crudest form of expression'.[43] Mrs Pember Reeves, who was an experienced visitor of poor homes in south London, agreed that 'In houses where no gas is laid on, the gas-stove cannot take the place of the missing oven, and it is extraordinary how many one-roomed dwellings are without an oven.'[44] Even in the country Rowntree noted that good ovens were exceptional so that bread was seldom home-baked. Newer houses had ovens too small for a large baking and were therefore wasteful of fuel.[45]

Factors of this kind made meal preparation drudgery and the diet monotonous. Among poor London families Mrs Pember Reeves concluded: 'The diet where there are several children is obviously chosen for its cheapness, and is of the filling, stodgy kind. There is not enough of anything but bread. There is no variety. Nothing is considered except money.'[46] At Corsley, in Wiltshire, Maud Davies noted agricultural labourers' families in which 'the wife cooks only once or twice a week during the winter. She cooks oftener in summer when potatoes are more

[40] 43rd A.R. of the L.G.B. Third Report on Infant Mortality, p. 15.
[41] 42nd A.R. of the L.G.B. Second Report on Infant Mortality, p. 72.
[42] S. Davidson and R. Passmore, Human Nutrition and Dietetics, 6th edn (Edinburgh, 1969), pp. 88, 241, suggested a practicable minimum of about 20 per cent fat.
[43] I-DCPD, para. 227.
[44] Magdalen S. P. Reeves, Round About a Pound a Week (1915), p. 111.
[45] B. S. Rowntree and M. Kendall, How the Labourer Lives (1913), p. 40.
[46] Reeves, Round About a Pound, p. 103.

plentiful.'[47] It was exceptional to find a woman who, like 'Mrs T has been a cook and takes pride in her cooking and housekeeping. She cooks every day.'[48] Among the overcrowded London families Mrs Reeves found no similar example; in her experience 'the Lambeth woman has no joy in cooking for its own sake'.[49]

The eating of food, therefore, was seldom a social occasion. Social investigators reported that among Liverpool dock labourers' families:

> The custom of entertaining friends by inviting them to share a meal does not seem much in vogue in homes of this class. Indeed it would appear, perhaps owing to the unattractive character of most of the food consumed, that eating is regarded much less as one of the pleasures of life than among those who pride themselves upon their more intellectual interests. 'Women wouldn't thank you for a cup of tea,' said one housewife wonderingly, when asked if she never had a friend to tea.[50]

The funeral was a possible exception. In Middlesborough, Lady Florence Bell noted:

> A funeral indeed is one of the principal social opportunities in the class we are describing. 'A slow walk and a cup of tea' it is sometimes called, and the busy preparations in the house for a day or two before, the baking, the cleaning, the turning out, are undoubtedly often tinged with the excitement and anticipation of an entertainer.[51]

Otherwise the normal week's menu showed little variation:

> To boil a neck (of mutton) with pot herbs on Sunday, and make a stew of 'pieces' on Wednesday, often finishes all that has to be done with meat. The intermediate dinners will ring the changes on cold neck, suet pudding, perhaps fried fish or cheap sausages, and rice or potatoes. Breakfast and tea, with the exception of the husband's relishes, consist of tea, and bread spread with butter, jam, or margarine.[52]

In Scotland, there was often less variety still in the midday meal when the family ate together at home:

---

[47] Maud F. Davies, *Life in an English Village* (1909), p. 211.
[48] Ibid., p. 214.
[49] Reeves, *Round About a Pound*, p. 112.
[50] Liverpool Economic and Statistical Society, *How the Casual Labourer Lives* (Liverpool, 1909), p. xxiv.
[51] Lady Florence Bell, *At the Works: A Study of a Manufacturing Town* (1907), p. 119.
[52] Reeves, *Round About a Pound*, p. 111.

There is very little variety in the dinners provided. Where the mother is at home 'broth' is the staple dish. It is generally made with ½ lb of boiling beef, 1d of leeks, carrots and turnips, and ½d of barley. The meat is eaten with the potatoes as a second course. If the family are economising ¼ lb of beef, with 1d bone or parings, will be used; and there is no second course.[53]

The monotony of the diet was an important factor in determining total food consumption. When the food from animal sources in the diet was reduced, the consumption of starchy foods was in turn restricted. Rowntree recorded a family in Essex who, 'though they never felt actually hungry after their dinner, they were never "completely satisfied like", except on Sundays'.[54] If food was insufficiently palatable, people found it difficult to eat enough to satisfy the body's needs.[55] For this reason, however limited in amount food from animal sources was in the working-class diet, it served as a vehicle to enable larger amounts of carbohydrate foods to be consumed. Thus meat, in Rowntree's words, was often 'a flavouring rather than a substantial course'.[56] Mrs. Reeves also understood the role of palatable foods: 'The tiny amounts of tea, dripping, butter, jam, sugar, and greens, may be regarded rather in the light of condiments than of food.'[57] These small amounts were essential to make the semblance of a meal. For example, for midday dinner, potatoes

are an invariable item. Greens may go, butter may go, meat may diminish almost to vanishing-point, before potatoes are affected. When potatoes do not appear for dinner, their place will be taken by suet pudding, which will mean that there is no gravy or dripping to eat with them. Treacle; or – as the shop round the corner calls it – 'golden syrup', will probably be eaten with the pudding, and the two together will form a midday meal for the mother and children in a working man's family.[58]

This illustrates the complementary nature of foods: some form of fat or sugar was essential to accompany the main, largely starchy, component of a meal. Sugar acted as a substitute for food from animal sources and thus determined the type of starchy cereal food eaten. In the country, Rowntree noted that to overcome the shortage of animal fats dumplings

[53] Dundee Social Union, *Report on Housing and Industrial Conditions and Medical Inspection of School Children* (Dundee, 1905), p. 31.
[54] Rowntree and Kendall, *How the Labourer Lives*, pp. 39–40, 240.
[55] J. Yudkin, 'Patterns and trends in carbohydrate consumption and their relation to disease', *Proc. Nutr. Soc.* 23, p. 149.
[56] Rowntree and Kendall, *How the Labourer Lives*, p. 308.
[57] Reeves, *Round About a Pound*, p. 103.
[58] Ibid., p. 98.

were made with a little lard, suet or dripping and a very few currants. Even in 'better-off families' there was:

> a good deal of pastry consumed. Some housewives make nearly half the flour into pastry. This might seem an extravagance; but it must be remembered that the pastry is extremely plain and extremely solid. It is usually regarded by the worker as more satisfying than bread; and it saves butter.[59]

Both Booth in London and Paton in Edinburgh found that among the poorer families meal patterns were irregular and social standards broke down – presumably due in part to the environment but, possibly, also reflecting the difficulties of managing with limited food materials. 'Remains of food are always about,' wrote Booth,[60] 'there is perhaps no cupboard – probably part of a loaf is on the table with a little butter and a much-used knife, or a teapot, an unwashed cup or two and a cracked plate.' With a family of growing children usually eating at different times from the husband, the strain on resources and meal patterns was increased: 'the children drink tea five or six-times a-day, and get a piece of bread whenever they ask for it.'[61] For the housewife under pressure, bread served as a convenience food to meet the children's hunger without actually making a meal:

> Bread, however, is their chief food. It is cheap; they like it; it comes into the house ready cooked; it is always at hand, and needs no plate and spoon. Spread with a scraping of butter, jam, or margarine, according to the length of purse of the mother, they never, tire of it as long as they are in their ordinary state of health. They receive it into their hands, and can please themselves as to where and how they eat it. It makes the sole article in the menu for two meals in the day. Dinner may consist of anything from the joint on Sunday to boiled rice on Friday. Potatoes will play a great part as a rule, at dinner, but breakfast and tea will be bread.[62]

This quotation makes a further point relevant to food intake, that of the distribution of food within the family. There is very little direct

---

[59] Rowntree and Kendall, *How the Labourer Lives*, pp. 39–40, 240.
[60] Booth, *Life and Labour*, 2nd ser., Vol. 5 (1903), p. 326.
[61] Paton, *et al.*, *Dietaries of the Labouring Classes*, p. 17. The report on case VII of the survey reads: 'The children "have 'pieces' whenever they ask for them", says the Dietary Study-book, and Mrs B. "would be ashamed to have it otherwise."' This was a large family with differing meal times, though obviously the mother prided herself on never denying the needs of hunger in her children. Miss Bulkley agreed that 'In the poorest homes there are frequently no fixed meal times; the children are given "a piece" when they are hungry, and this is often eaten in the street or on the doorstep.' *Feeding of School Children*, p. 172.
[62] Reeves, *Round About a Pound*, pp. 97–8.

evidence from the beginning of the twentieth century to support the general assumption that the man, as breadwinner, was entitled to as much food as would satisfy him, especially when he was engaged in manual labour. High-status food such as meat and fish was largely consumed by him for his dinner or as 'relishes' for his supper. This consumption pattern was long-standing. Dr Edward Smith had regarded it as typical as early as 1863:

> The meat or the bacon, when the whole quantity is small, as 2 lb. to 4 lb., is commonly cooked for this (Sunday) dinner, and all partake of it. What is left is reserved for the husband, who either takes a little portion with him for his dinner daily, or eats it at home; and it is remarkable that this is not only acquiesced in by the wife, but felt by her to be right, and even necessary for the maintenance of the family. The remark was constantly made to me, 'that the husband wins the bread, and must have the best food'. If the family be thrifty, the husband will have a morsel of meat or bacon daily throughout the week, but in other instances the whole is consumed in the first two, three or four days. The important practical fact is however well established, that the labourer eats meat and bacon almost daily, while his wife and children may eat it but once a week, and that both himself and his household believe that course to be necessary, to enable him to perform his labour.[63]

Charles Booth implied a similar distribution of food within the family when he wrote, 'a good deal of bread is eaten and tea drunk especially by the women and children',[64] and the pattern in London did not change within the following twenty years. Mrs Reeves found that 'meat is bought for men, and the chief expenditure is made in preparation for Sunday's dinner, when the man is at home. It is eaten cold by him the next day.' The man also, in her estimate, consumed the entire purchase of bacon and half of all the fish bought.[65] The view of one witness before the Committee on Physical Deterioration that 'if the mother does do any cooking it is only for the father' begins to make sense when viewed in this light.[66]

Food consumption

A more precise assessment of the diet may be obtained by quantifying data derived from family budgets. From the late 1880s until the outbreak

---

[63] *Sixth Report of the Medical Officer to the Committee of the Privy Council*, PP 1864, XXVIII, Appendix 6, p. 249.

[64] Booth, *Life and Labour*, 2nd ser., Vol. 5, p. 327.

[65] Reeves, *Round About a Pound*, pp. 97, 103.

[66] I-DCPD, para. 290.

of war in 1914 there is an almost continuous run of family budget inquiries, all of which contain much information on food consumption. Inspired by the work of Le Play on the Continent, the social survey flourished in Britain at a time when no large-scale state investigations were considered feasible or indeed proper. The family budget survey was the means of recording the life of the people in detail. It was undertaken for a number of reasons the principal of which was the sense of social concern about the nature of poverty and, necessarily, the diet of the working classes. There was a growing awareness that the wealth gained by Victorian society had not been shared with the working classes; indeed, that poverty in society had not been eliminated. There was also concern that working-class living conditions should be improved which followed from the acceptance of the germ theory of disease. There were, moreover, two anxieties of an economic nature: first, that foreign competition required a speeding up and intensification of effort in the workplace to meet the new industrial power of the USA and Germany; and second, as the century came to an end, the view that the health and strength of the working classes was an important resource upon which the future of Britain's imperial strength depended. This last point became of greater significance during the first decade of the twentieth century as international alliances indicated the likelihood that war might break out in Europe.

Knowledge of the diet was essential from any of these viewpoints, since before 1914 it was commonplace for weekly food expenditure to take 60 to 70 per cent of a working-class family's income.[67] The proportion was highest in rural districts, particularly in the more remote parts of Britain where payment of wages in cash was still not yet universal. Food expenditure fell below 60 per cent of income in some urban areas – even below 50 per cent among the better-off skilled men in London who took part in the urban workmen's 1904 survey – but a weighting of 60 for food was retained in the first Cost of Living Index of 1913. The largest item of expenditure was meat which took between 25 and 32 per cent of the family's food budget, followed by 20 to 25 per cent spent on bread and flour – though this varied according to the region. It was lower in the northeast of England where home-baking was still practised and in Scotland where oatmeal remained an important food in regular use. Bread remained the principal food for families at all income levels of the working class up to and during the First World War as shown in Table 3.4 (See Appendix A1 for a fuller range of foods). Starchy foods, namely bread and potatoes, produced much of the energy in the diet, though sugar was also important. Jam and sweet spreads,

[67] See D. J. Oddy, 'The working-class diet, 1886–1914', University of London Ph.D. thesis, 1971, Tables 50–75.

Table 3.4 Weekly food consumption per head in family budget surveys, 1890 to 1913

Survey	Date	Bread	Potatoes	Sugar	Cereals	Fats	Meat	Milk
		(lb.)	(lb.)	(oz.)	(oz.)	(oz.)	(lb.)	(pt.)
Board of Trade	1887	7.5	1.6	15	3.7	4.9	1.4	1.5
Booth	1889	6.5	2.1	12	1.5	3.9	1.6	1.4
Economy Club	1891–94	7.0	1.1	15	1.7	5.7	1.4	1.3
Oliver	1894	5.5	3.6	16	5.4	5.2	3.2	1.6
Schulze	1895	7.4	2.3	17	3.6	10.1	1.2	1.6
Mean		*6.7*	*2.1*	*15*	*3.1*	*5.2*	*1.8*	*1.5*
Rowntree	1899–1901	6.8	2.0	15	1.7	5.2	1.5	1.5
Paton	1900	4.7	1.2	13	6.4	4.2	1.2	1.6
England (rural)	1902	7.2	3.9	16	1.7	5.4	1.1	0.8
Scotland (rural)	1904	4.2	4.7	13	35.7	4.9	0.7	3.7
Ireland	1904	3.5	7.0	9	21.7	3.0	0.6	3.2
UK (urban)	1904	6.7	2.9	16	4.7	8.1	1.3	1.7
Mean		*6.6*	*3.1*	*16*	*6.2*	*7.7*	*1.3*	*1.8*
Dundee	1906	5.4	2.8	13	10.1	4.9	0.5	2.9
Bell	1906	9.7	1.8	21	0	7.2	1.0	0.6
Davies	1906	5.6	n.k.	13	0.7	7.4	1.6	0.8
Women	1910	7.1	3.0	21	2.0	9.6	1.8	2.4
Rowntree	1912–13	7.1	2.0	12	1.2	5.7	0.7	0.8
Lindsay	1913	5.1	2.8	15	6.2	5.7	1.5	2.0
Mean		*6.1*	*2.6*	*14*	*4.2*	*6.0*	*1.5*	*1.4*

such as honey or treacle, were eaten regularly. The variation in cereal consumption – mainly oatmeal, though some rice was eaten – from a few ounces per head in England to six to ten ounces in Scottish towns and as much as thirty-five ounces per head in Scottish rural areas is most marked. The importance of these foods meant that 60 to 70 per cent of the energy value of the diets in these surveys came from carbohydrates.

Animal products entered working-class diets in only limited amounts. In spite of the large cash outlay, meat consumption ranged between 0.75lb. and 1.5lb. per head per week, while less than a quarter of a pound of cheese per head was eaten. Not all surveys recorded fish, since its availability in rural areas of England and Ireland was limited. In towns, the use of fish ranged from one to ten ounces per head per week. Milk consumption was broadly linked to the amount of cereal consumed, ranging from between 0.6 and 1.7 pts per head per week in English urban surveys to 2pts per head in Scottish and Irish towns and as much as 3.7 pts per head in rural areas. Fats played only a small part in the diet. Even taking butter, margarine, lard and dripping together, the amount eaten ranged between four and eight ounces per head. Most surveys recorded the use of eggs within the range from a half to two eggs per week. The eating of fruit and vegetables varied. In some rural areas, surprisingly, there was no mention of fruit and vegetables, which implied that they were either home-grown or else not available. In either case, these foods were highly seasonal in their contribution to the diet. Consumption of vegetables also varied markedly by region.

The impact of Charles Booth's and B. S. Rowntree's investigations, coupled with the concern over low physical standards raised by the difficulties of recruitment of men for the South African War (1899–1902), led to several inquiries. Investigations into the lives of English rural labourers in 1902, and Scottish and Irish rural labourers in 1904 were followed by the collection of evidence from 1,944 families of urban workmen throughout the United Kingdom. Despite the claim by Sir Henry Campbell-Bannerman that almost 30 per cent of the population was underfed, no wage census or monitoring of food consumption was introduced as part of these investigations, though strategic concerns over the food supply led to the Royal Commission of 1905.[68] The 1904 inquiry by the Board of Trade was significant not merely due to its size and the fact that it was specifically an inquiry into food consumption but because its results were used later as the basis for the first Cost of Living Index in 1913.[69] The average diet still contained a large amount of bread (6.7lb.) and potatoes (2.9lb.). Amounts of sugar, meat and milk were similar to other surveys of the period. Many of the Board of Trade's respondents were the better-off, skilled craftsmen among trade unionists and it is interesting to note that their families consumed vegetables, fruit, jam, fish, eggs and cheese much like the middle-class families recorded by Rowntree.

Historians have regarded the last quarter of the nineteenth century as a period in which the standard of living rose and significant improvements in real wages occurred.[70] It has therefore been assumed that this was a period of dietary change. The Drummonds thought the changes began with a fall in the consumption of bread and flour in the late nineteenth century. Dietary change they explained was:

> related to a rising standard of living for the falling curve representing bread and flour is complementary to the rising curve for sugar and sweetmeats. It is

---

[68] Oddy, 'Working-class diet, 1886–1914', p. 363.

[69] *Report of an Enquiry by the Board of Trade into the Earnings and Hours of Labour of Workpeople of the United Kingdom*, PP 1912–13 (Cd.6053), CVIII.

[70] See R. Floud and D. McCloskey, *The Economic History of Britain since 1700*, Vol.2 (Cambridge, 1981), and authorities cited in D. J. Oddy, 'Working-class diets in late nineteenth-century Britain', *Economic History Review*, 2nd. ser., Vol. XXIII, 2 (1970), pp. 314–23.

also related to a rise in the consumption of meat. These relationships reflect the fact that bread is the staple food of poverty and that people eat much less of it when they can afford to buy meat and to indulge in the type of dish with which sugar is eaten.[71]

As a model for dietary change, their views are undoubtedly correct in general terms but fit the period 1890 to 1914 somewhat imperfectly. There is no evidence from working-class families to suggest that any increase in meat consumption took place. Similarly, the increase in the amount of sugar consumed was much smaller than might be expected. It is not surprising, therefore, that there is no evidence that bread and flour consumption (expressed in bread-equivalent terms) declined.

Food consumption and incomes

Each survey comprised families of different income levels, so that variations in purchasing behaviour and eating patterns are obscured by the means shown in Table 3.4. Grouping individual families from the different surveys by income bands allows a perspective on consumption behaviour to emerge. Table 3.5 shows the weekly food consumption for 122 families in the 1890s arranged by incomes as well as means from the larger inquiry in 1904 into the food consumption of urban workmen. The income bands in the first part of the table reflect the poverty line debate of the 1890s in view of Rowntree's estimate that the poverty line was 21s 8d per week. Income bands in the 1904 inquiry differed but in both parts of Table 3.5 30s per week is a significant point in dietary terms dividing better-off families from poorer ones. What both sections of the table indicate is the effect of income on purchases of food. Working-class families bought more food when they had more money. This was not confined to high-status foods of animal origin such as meat and milk but occurred also for bread and potatoes, which were starchy, everyday foods.

The adequacy of the amounts of food provided by working-class diets can be tested in two ways. The first is by the empirical observations of contemporary observers. Charles Booth, for example, believed that the lowest income groups, or ' "very poor" – are at all times more or less "in want". They are ill-nourished and poorly clad.'[72] While this represented only a small proportion of the working classes, the wages paid for unskilled labour in general were, in Rowntree's words, *insufficient to provide food, shelter and clothing, adequate to maintain a family of*

---

[71] Drummond, *Englishman's Food*, p. 299.
[72] Booth, *Life and Labour*, I, p. 131.

Table 3.5 Weekly food consumption per head arranged by income levels

Income	Number	Bread	Potatoes	Sugar	Cereals	Fats	Meat	Milk
(sh/week)		(lb.)	(lb.)	(oz.)	(oz.)	(oz.)	(lb.)	(pt.)
Surveys in the 1890s								
A: <18	27	5.5	1.1	11	2.0	3.9	0.9	1.0
B: 18–21	17	6.5	1.6	16	1.7	4.4	1.2	1.2
C: 21–30	38	7.2	1.6	14	3.2	4.7	1.5	1.2
D: >30	35	7.3	2.4	17	3.9	7.1	1.7	2.1
Middle class	5	3.0	2.9	23	3.2	12.1	3.2	5.4
Urban workmen's inquiry 1904								
<25	261	6.4	2.5	14	5.7	6.7	1.0	1.2
25–30	289	6.8	2.9	16	5.4	7.9	1.2	1.6
30–35	416	6.7	2.9	16	6.2	8.6	1.4	2.0
35–40	382	6.8	2.9	18	5.4	9.1	1.4	2.1
>40	506	7.1	3.0	19	5.7	10.6	1.5	2.1
Mean	*1,944*	*6.8*	*2.8*	*17*	*5.7*	*8.6*	*1.3*	*1.8*

moderate size in a state of bare physical efficiency'. This meant that 'every labourer who has as many as three children must pass through a time, probably lasting for about ten years, when he will be in a state of "primary" poverty; in other words, when he and his family will be underfed'.[73] Booth, however, felt that 'regular standard earnings'[74] marked a difference in social status within the ranks of unskilled labourers. Regular earnings of between 21s and 30s per week meant that life was 'more than any other, representative of the "way we live now"'. As a result:

> Meals are more regular. For dinner, meat and vegetables are demanded every day. Bacon, eggs and fish find their place at other times. Puddings and tarts are not uncommon, and bread ceases to be the staff of life. Skill in cookery becomes very important, and though capable of much improvement, it is on the whole not amiss. In this class no one goes short of food.

However, by basing these conclusions on such a wide income range, Charles Booth partly contradicted his own concept of the existence of a 'line of poverty' for a family with three or four children at about 24s per week.[75] The improvement that Booth found in social standards as meal

---

[73] Rowntree, *Poverty*, pp. 133–5. Rowntree's italics.
[74] Booth, *Life and Labour*, I, p. 50.
[75] Booth, *Life and Labour*, 2nd ser., Vol. V, pp. 321–5, 329.

patterns developed was hardly reflected in nutritional status. The arrangement of the 1890s diets by income levels in Table 3.5 shows that not until income exceeded 30s per week was it possible for the level of bread consumption to be maintained with increased consumption of all other more palatable foods. The extent to which animal food entered the diet as income rose may also be seen. The food consumption of families with over 30s per week shows that by comparison with the 21–30s per week group, 75 per cent more milk and 51 per cent more fats were consumed. Bread consumption hardly changed at all but certainly did not fall as the Drummonds' model predicted.

Given that the distribution of food within the family followed the general pattern customary in the nineteenth century, it is impossible to see how the diverse physiological needs of a manual worker, his wife and growing children could be met adequately. The inference that can be drawn from the writings of Edward Smith, Charles Booth or Seebohm Rowntree – firsthand observers of the working-class home – is that under these conditions women and children were undernourished. Rowntree's summary of the situation was:

> We *see* that many a labourer, who has a wife and three or four children, is healthy and a good worker, although he earns only a pound a week. What we *do not* see is that in order to give him enough food, mother and children habitually go short, for the mother knows that all depends upon the wages of her husband.[76]

This distribution of food within the family appeared to be the normal behaviour implicit in working-class culture; it was reinforced by patterns of food choice which were largely limited by social convention and habit. Whether or not the need was for more energy, social emulation required that more meat or dairy produce be bought as income rose. When A.L. Bowley evaluated conditions in towns in 1913, he modified Rowntree's method by adopting a 'New Standard' diet which included meat, since 'in fact, a workman would sacrifice part of the defined necessaries in favour of a meat diet'.[77] Thus advice to the poor on how to improve their diet was of little avail: working-class families showed little interest in increasing their intake of vegetable proteins.[78] Dunlop, commenting on the diets of Edinburgh labourers,

[76] Rowntree, *Poverty*, p. 135, n. 1.
[77] A. L. Bowley and A. R. Burnett-Hurst, *Livelihood and Poverty* (1915), p. 80. In his measurement of the poverty line Rowntree had constructed a standard diet which deliberately omitted meat as being both too expensive and unnecessary for poor families.
[78] Paton *et al.*, *Dietaries of the Labouring Classes*, p. 87.

wrote: 'There is a relatively great use of more expensive foods, such as beef, milk, and eggs, and a relatively small use of some cheaper food, such as oatmeal, peas and barley.' Dunlop's prescription that 'in the dietaries of the poorer classes the fats should be cut down as much as possible, and the energy should, as far as digestion will allow, be supplied in carbohydrates' was not popular.[79] The obsession with the energy cost of the diet ignored the palatability of the foods involved and their acceptability within the family. Rowntree noted the implications of middle-class demands for 'economy' by the working classes: 'It means that a wise mother, when she is tempted to buy her children a penny-worth of cheap oranges will devote the penny to flour instead.'[80] It remained for Mrs Reeves to comment somewhat tartly upon the reality of middle-class dietary advice within a working-class environment:

> There are those who, if they happen to read these weekly menus, will criticise with deep feeling the selection of the materials from which they are composed. It is not necessary to pretend that they are the absolute best that could be done, even upon that money. It is quite likely that someone who had strength, wisdom, and vitality, who did not live that life in those tiny, crowded rooms, in that lack of light and air, who was not bowed down with worry, but was herself economically independent of the man who earned the money, could lay out his few shillings with a better eye to scientific food value. It is quite as likely, however, that the man who earned the money would entirely refuse the scientific food, and demand his old tasty kippers and meat. It is he who has to be satisfied in the long run, and if he desires pickles, pickles there will be. The fact that there is not enough money to buy good healthy house-room means that appetites are jaded, and that food which would be nutritious and valuable, and would be eaten greedily by people who lived in the open air, seems tasteless and sickly to those who have slept four in a bed in a room 10 feet by 12 feet.[81]

Since family budgets were obtained for the whole household, individual food consumption cannot be known. Standardizing the diet per head necessarily conceals individual differences in food consumption. For this reason, Dr Thomas Oliver's survey of individual diets in 1894 provided a unique opportunity to make some comparison, however limited in numbers, between sexes. Table 3.6 shows the weekly diets of twenty-one men and six women. The men were mostly married with families but four of the women were breadwinners because a husband or father was dead or out of work. These four were all employed as lead workers. The two remaining diets were of unmarried

[79] Ibid., pp. 9, 73.
[80] Rowntree and Kendall, *How the Labourer Lives*, p. 312.
[81] Reeves, *Round About a Pound*, p. 131.

Table 3.6 Weekly food consumption per head of working-class men and women, 1894

	Number of studies	Bread	Potatoes	Sugar	Fats	Meat	Milk
		(lb.)	(lb.)	(oz.)	(oz.)	(lb.)	(pt.)
Men	21	3.4	4.6	15	5	4.1	2.2
Women	6	3.3	1.4	21	6	1.0	0

cotton-workers. The difference in food consumption relates to the habit of men eating a main meal of meat, or bacon or fish and potatoes, while the women limited their meals to bread and butter and tea.

Even if the contrast was not normally so extreme as Oliver's survey suggested, the result of such a marked imbalance in the distribution of food within the family must have affected the health of women and children. Rowntree noted that among the poorer families in York 'Extraordinary expenditure, such as the purchase of a piece of furniture, is met by reducing the sum spent on food. As a rule, in such cases it is the wife and sometimes the children who have to forego a portion of their food.'[82] It was clear that 'women and children suffer from underfeeding to a much greater extent than the men. It is tacitly agreed that the man must have a certain minimum of food in order that he may be able to perform the muscular work demanded of him.'[83] Under-nutrition may well have contributed to the lethargic behaviour noted in the home by both Booth[84] and Mrs Reeves: 'All of these women seemed to have lost any spark of humour or desire for different surroundings. The same surroundings with a little more money, a little more security, and a little less to do, was about the best their imaginations could grasp.'[85]

Children were more evidently affected. The Physical Deterioration Committee devoted a considerable section of its *Report* to school-children, concluding that 'a large number of children habitually attend school ill-fed'.[86] The impact of even such a general statement as this caused a further inquiry the following year in which considerable attention was paid to the effect on children of the irregularity of diet from one day to another.[87] Some evidence, indeed, suggested that children existed in what might be termed a low-intake equilibrium. In the view of one witness:

[82] Rowntree, *Poverty*, pp. 54–5.
[83] Rowntree and Kendall, *How the Labourer Lives*, p. 309.
[84] Booth, *Life and Labour*, 2nd ser., Vol. 5, p. 326.
[85] Reeves, *Round About a Pound*, p. 91.
[86] I-DCPD, para. 353.
[87] *Report of the Inter-Departmental Committee on Medical Inspection and Feeding*

children who are chronically underfed and ill-nourished are not necessarily hungry. He says that underfed children have small stomachs, 'slum stomachs' he calls them, and perverted appetites; they refuse plain nutritious food; prefer stale food, and crave for condiments, pickles, and highly seasoned articles, such as liver and onions and black puddings. He has great difficulty to educate the children to eat simple nutritious food, such as fish or rice pudding.[88]

The somewhat limited Education (Provision of Meals) Act, 1906 resulted from these inquiries, but did not fundamentally change the situation. By 1911 to 1912 only 41 per cent of local education authorities provided any school meals, though children's weight loss in school holidays proved their value.[89]

Nutritional analysis of family budget data

The second test of the adequacy of working-class diets is by subjecting the evidence from family budget surveys to nutritional analysis. The results are set out in Table 3.7 (see also Appendix A2), which shows that the typical diets of the 1890s and early 1900s yielded around 2,100kcal (8,790kj) a day from some 380g of carbohydrate, 70g of protein and 60g of fat. Proteins, provided by the animal products eaten, made up 10 to 12 per cent of the energy value, but the fat content was low and supplied only 19 to 28 per cent of the energy in the diet. Under the circumstances of life before the First World War there was a distinct possibility that such diets were deficient in vitamin A (retinol) and vitamin D. The contemporary comments on schoolchildren's health in poor urban areas seem to confirm that vitamin deficiency was extensive. Minor disorders of eyes, roughness of skin, 'dry, thin, and short or wispy' hair[90] and the presence of rickets and anaemia in Britain before 1914 point to poor diets with insufficient food of animal origin during children's growth periods.

There is no obvious trend towards rising energy intakes, though the highest energy values were obtained from urban rather than rural diets. However, families in oatmeal-eating rural areas in Scotland had higher energy intakes than those in English rural areas or the poorer diets in

---

of *Children attending Public Elementary Schools*, PP 1906 (Cd.2779), XLVII, para. 233.

[88] *I-DC on Med. Insp. and Feeding of Children*, para. 288.

[89] Bulkley, *Feeding of School Children*, pp. 49–54, and ch. V.

[90] I-DCPD, Q.450.

Table 3.7 Daily nutrient intake per head calculated from family budget surveys, 1890 to 1913

Survey	Date	Energy value		Protein	Fat	CHO	Iron	Calcium
		(kcal)	(kj)	(g)	(g)	(g)	(mg)	(g)
Board of Trade	1887	2,240	9,372	59	57	372	10.3	0.31
Booth	1889	2,020	8,452	61	57	315	10.6	0.28
Economy Club	1891–94	2,091	8,749	54	60	335	9.1	0.27
Oliver	1894	2,799	11,711	93	114	366	15.5	0.50
Schulze	1895	2,454	10,268	61	75	384	10.9	0.36
Mean		*2,321*	*9,710*	*66*	*73*	*354*	*11.3*	*0.34*
Rowntree	1899–1901	2,069	8,657	57	59	328	10.1	0.31
Paton	1900	1,784	7,464	54	52	276	10.1	0.38
England (rural)	1902	2,148	8,987	51	55	362	9.2	0.28
Scotland (rural)	1904	2,365	9,895	67	59	391	13.3	0.62
Ireland	1904	2,150	8,996	58	40	390	13.3	0.48
UK (urban)	1904	2,443	10,222	67	74	378	12.3	0.47
Mean		*2,160*	*9,037*	*59*	*57*	*354*	*11.4*	*0.42*
Dundee	1906	1,968	8,234	54	41	345	10.2	0.58
Bell	1906	2,443	10,222	54	56	431	9.3	0.19
Davies	1906	1,790	7,489	49	69	243	7.2	0.30
Women	1910	2,551	10,673	73	79	383	13.1	0.63
Rowntree	1912–13	1,889	7,904	46	38	340	9.4	0.27
Lindsay	1913	2,131	8,916	64	62	330	11.2	0.58
Mean		*2,129*	*8,906*	*57*	*58*	*345*	*10.1*	*0.43*
Mean	*1887–1913*	*2,203*	*9,218*	*60*	*62*	*351*	*10.9*	*0.40*

Scottish towns such as Edinburgh, Dundee and Glasgow where bread-eating had taken hold.[91] The low intakes of protein and fat and high intakes of carbohydrate confirm that there was relatively little food of animal origin in these diets. Protein intakes were generally within the range 50 to 70g per head per day and fat intakes from 40 to 80g per day. These diets also yielded low levels of calcium, ranging from 0.2g to 0.6g per day and an awareness of this lay behind the campaign to encourage the drinking of milk, which began in the interwar years and continued

---

[91] For more detailed comparison see D. J. Oddy, 'The paradox of diet and health: England and Scotland in the nineteenth and twentieth centuries', in A. Fenton, ed., *Order and Disorder: The Health Implications of Eating and Drinking in the Nineteenth and Twentieth Centuries* (Phantassie, East Lothian, 2000), pp. 45–63.

until the 1970s. The other essential mineral identified by the nutrient analysis, iron, showed a marked variation in daily intakes ranging from 7mg to 13mg. Some of the lowest intakes were found in rural areas in England where there was least variety in the diet. Iron deficiency is associated with anaemia – a recognized nutritional problem during the early twentieth century.

Some evidence of regional variation in the diet may be obtained from the largest survey of the period – the 1904 inquiry into urban workmen's diet – which had sufficient numbers to allow regional means to be formulated. The highest energy values were found in Ireland, Scotland and London, all of which exceeded 2,500kcal (10,460kj) per day. They were offset by the north of England and the Midlands, both of which had energy values under 2,400kcal (10,040kj) and the rest of England (mainly southern and southwestern districts) with under 2,200kcal (9,200kj) per day. The differences could be accounted for by the fact that more potatoes were eaten in Ireland, more oatmeal and milk in Scotland, and more meat in London than anywhere else. Sugar and fat consumption was highest in the north of England. In none of the areas was there any sign of a reduction in bread or potato consumption.

The adequacy of the diets shown in Table 3.7 in nutrient terms is highlighted by their rearrangement by levels of income in Table 3.8. There is no doubt about the paucity of the diets in the lowest income groups. Families below Rowntree's poverty line of 21s 8d had severely restricted diets and were undernourished by any standards. However, the gap between them and families in the 21 to 30s per week group was small. In fact, since 21 to 30s per week typified the incomes received by the bulk of the semi-skilled workers, the routine clerical workers and even some of the skilled artisan classes, it is surprising that they too experienced a restricted diet of just over 2,100kcal (8,800kj) per day. When incomes rose above 30s per week, the energy value of the diet rose by 400 kcal to over 2,500kcal (10,460kj) per day. Above that income level evidence of malnutrition was unlikely to be seen. It follows that Rowntree's poverty line at 21s 8d per week was not significant as the level of family income below which nutritional status was inadequate, nor was it applicable to only a limited sector of the working classes. There is also a general similarity between the 1904 diets and those in the 1890s; the differences (as far as income groups can be aligned) was no more than a small shift from carbohydrate to fat in the source of the energy value of the diet. The reason for this change may be seen in Table 3.5. The 30 to 35s per week group ate 66 per cent more milk, 40 per cent more meat, and 28 per cent more fats but only 5 per cent more bread than those in the under 25s group. These food increments were the basis for the increase in fat shown in the 1904 diets in Table 3.8. However, they did not change the basic composition of the diet, in which bread and potatoes remained the dietary staples.

Table 3.8 Daily nutrient intake per head arranged by income levels

Income (sh.week)	Number	Energy value		Protein	Fat	CHO	Iron	Calcium
		(kcal)	(kj)	(g)	(g)	(g)	(mg)	(g)
Surveys in the 1890s								
A: <18	27	1,578	6,602	42	40	262	7.4	0.22
B: 18–21	17	1,964	8,217	51	50	369	9.0	0.27
C: 21–30	38	2,113	8,841	58	58	340	10.2	0.28
D: >30	35	2,521	10,548	68	75	393	12.3	0.41
Middle class	5	3,256	13,623	98	131	420	15.5	0.95
Urban workmen's inquiry 1904								
<25	261	2,129	8,908	56	59	343	10.5	0.37
25–30	289	2,409	10,079	64	71	379	11.8	0.45
30–35	416	2,549	10,665	71	80	388	13.1	0.53
35–40	382	2,637	11,033	73	84	398	13.4	0.56
>40	506	2,832	11,849	76	92	423	14.2	0.58
Mean	*1,944*	*2,511*	*10,507*	*68*	*77*	*386*	*12.6*	*0.50*

Table 3.9 Daily nutrient intake per head of working-class men and women, 1894

	Energy value		Protein	Fat	CHO	Iron	Calcium
	(kcal)	(kj)	(g)	(g)	(g)	(mg)	(g)
Men	3,321	13,895	114	146	387	19.0	0.69
Women	1,870	7,824	48	51	310	7.9	0.18

Professor Oliver's insight into individual diets confirms the inadequacy of women's diets, as the nutritional analysis in Table 3.9 shows. The energy intake of the men's diet was over 3,300kcal but women obtained only 1,870kcal. Women obtained less than half the protein intake of the men and little more than one-third of the men's fat intake. Iron and calcium intakes by women were both low, 7.9mg of iron being barely more than half and 0.18g calcium only a quarter of modern recommended intakes.[92] The difference between the nutrient intakes of

---

[92] See Reference Nutrient Intakes (RNIs) in Table 1.5, Department of Health, *Dietary Reference Values for Food Energy and Nutrients for the United Kingdom* (1991).

the men and women reinforces the fact that while almost all men ate one main meal of meat, bacon or fish and potatoes, the women sustained themselves on bread and butter and tea three times a day.

As the Edwardian period ended, questions remained unanswered as to whether the working-class diet was improving. Some surveys collected between 1904 and 1910 had shown energy values of between 2,300 to 2,500kcal (9,625 to 10,460kj) per day. However, the two final surveys of the pre-1914 period – Rowntree and Kendall into English rural labourers' families and Lindsay into Glasgow urban families – both carefully executed inquiries, suggested that energy values of these diets were still in the 1,900 to 2,100kcal (7,950 to 8,790kj) per day range. Yet none of the surveys in Table 3.8 plumbed the lowest depths of society among the casual labourers or paupers on outdoor relief, where even more restricted diets were to be found. Table 3.10 shows three surveys from Liverpool, Norwich and Lambeth where food consumption was very low.[93] These are examples of families who did not have enough bread and potatoes for their needs and in consequence the daily nutrient intakes show energy values as low as 1,200kcal (5,020kj) in London and less than 1,700kcal (7,110kj) in the provincial towns. The levels of nutrient intakes suggest that families restricted to such a diet for any length of time were severely undernourished.

Table 3.10 Daily nutrient intake per head in casual labourers' and paupers' families, 1909 to 1912

Survey	Number	Energy value		Protein	Fat	CHO	Iron	Calcium
		(kcal)	(kj)	(g)	(g)	(g)	(mg)	(g)
Liverpool (1909)	31	1,675	7,008	48	42	277	9.3	0.20
Norwich (1910)	8	1,670	6,987	37	35	301	8.2	0.22
Lambeth (1912)	11	1,190	4,979	29	27	207	6.0	0.15
Mean	*50*	*1,570*	*6,569*	*42*	*38*	*265*	*8.4*	*0.19*

[93] See Liverpool Economic and Statistical Society, *How the Casual Labourer Lives* (Liverpool, 1909); *The Destitute of Norwich and How They Live* (Norwich, 1910); and Reeves, *Round About a Pound*, 1913.

Diet in servant-keeping households

A great deal has been written about the menus and eating habits of the middle classes in Britain. In *Plenty and Want*, Professor Burnett's chapter on 'High living' surveys the development of the daily menu among those who had sufficient income – generally in excess of £300 per year – to be part of the servant-keeping classes before 1914.[94] The clearest quantitative evidence of the diets of the middle classes at the beginning of the twentieth century comes from Rowntree whose book *Poverty* included the food expenditure of six servant-keeping families but not their annual incomes. Their average weekly expenditure on food ranged from £1 3s 6d for three adults to £3 19s 7d for six adults and three children.[95] The effect of having more money to spend on food may be seen in the prices paid and the purchase of more meat and milk. The poorer families in the 1890s family budgets paid 5d or 6d per pound for beef while the servant-keeping families paid 9d or 10d, some of which undoubtedly went on better cuts. Other foods bought such as mutton, bacon and fish showed similar price differentials when compared to prices paid by working-class families, though pork (7d per pound), dripping (4d to 5d per pound) and milk (2d per pint) showed no variation in price. Servant-keeping families paid for palatability and style, as seen in their purchases of lump sugar, Hovis flour, coffee, glacé cherries and patent breakfast food, but most significantly by their greater expenditure on milk, fruit (bananas, oranges, grapes and a pineapple) and vegetables. Having servants certainly meant the purchase of foods requiring more home preparation – yeast for home-baking, neck of mutton for soups and stews, fish for fish cakes, jelly 'squares', flour for teacakes (though even in Yorkshire – the last bastion of home-baking – some teacakes were bought from shops).

In Table 3.11 the major difference between these middle-class diets and those of working-class families is in the higher consumption of milk, meat and sugar, though less bread was eaten.[96] With the exception of budget 24, the nutrient analysis in Table 3.12 indicates higher energy values and higher intakes of each nutrient shown than working-class families.[97] Intakes of calcium and iron were higher than modern

[94] Burnett, *Plenty and Want*, ch. 10.

[95] Rowntree, *Poverty*, p. 253.

[96] Food consumption figures may differ from those given in *Poverty* due to the standardization applied by the computer food category programme.

[97] Rowntree's own calculations given in *Poverty* were based on Atwater's American food tables of the 1890s and do not correspond to the nutrient analysis based on R. A. McCance and E. M. Widdowson, *The Composition of Foods*. MRC Special Report Series No.297 (1960).

Table 3.11 Weekly food consumption per head in servant-keeping families in York, 1901

Budget	Bread (lb.)	Potatoes (lb.)	Sugar (oz.)	Cereals (oz.)	Fats (oz.)	Meat (lb.)	Milk (pt.)
19	4.0	3.1	15.1	0.0	13.1	3.2	7.7
21	3.5	4.2	25.4	5.4	20.7	4.2	4.0
22	2.5	2.4	20.0	3.0	10.1	2.8	5.8
23	2.7	2.8	35.6	0.0	7.2	4.4	4.7
24	2.2	2.1	18.8	7.4	9.4	1.2	4.7
Mean	3.0	2.9	23.0	3.2	12.1	3.2	5.4

Table 3.12 Daily nutrient intake per head in servant-keeping families in York, 1901

Budget	Energy value (kcal)	(kj)	Protein (g)	Fat (g)	CHO (g)	Iron (mg)	Calcium (g)
19	3,398	14,217	107	147	411	17.2	1.08
21	4,264	17,841	122	208	478	21.7	1.06
22	2,856	11,950	83	130	339	12.0	0.87
23	3,607	15,092	115	138	476	19.3	0.86
24	2,155	9,017	61	81	296	13.8	0.82
Mean	3,256	13,623	98	131	420	15.5	0.95

recommended levels.[98] In these diets, 12 per cent of the energy came from protein, 36 per cent from fats while only half (51.7 per cent) was obtained from carbohydrate; in some families this fell to as low as 45 per cent. These characteristics – more energy from fatty foods and a reduction in the importance of carbohydrates – were not apparent in working-class diets until much later in the twentieth century.

[98] See Department of Health, *Dietary Reference Values*, Table 1.5, in which RNIs for calcium are equivalent to 0.7g, an increase on levels recommended in the Department of Health and Social Security, *Recommended Intakes of Nutrients for the United Kingdom* (1969). Recommended daily intakes of iron for adults range between 9mg and 15mg.

Summary

The evidence from almost 2,500 budgets of working-class families over the period from the 1890s to 1914 indicates that inadequate diets extended more widely among unskilled workers than mere casual labourers earning a pound a week or less who were the principal target of social investigators. Whatever objections there may be to assessing diets per head, the conclusion is inescapable that, with an income below 30s per week and the normal number of growing children for the period before the First World War, families might well obtain only 2,000 to 2,200kcal (8,370 to 9,200kj) and 50 to 60g of protein per head per day. This nutritional analysis provides quantitative evidence in support of the contention by Drummond that malnutrition was widespread in Britain before the First World War.[99] Rearranging the evidence by income levels suggests that malnutrition occurred at income levels up to 30s a week in the 1890s and 25s a week in the 1904 survey. Given the unequal distribution of food between men and women, the British family – at least those among the working classes with low incomes – appears to be one in which the adult male ate and drank to the point of becoming stout; his wife, through under-eating, inclined to illness and experienced hardship in pregnancy; while the children's shortage of food, particularly at puberty, meant boys suffered restricted growth, and girls, whose growth was similarly inhibited, were likely to experience illnesses such as anaemia. Despite this prognosis, those working-class adults who survived the toll of infancy and childhood were relatively healthy, hardy and able to cope with a life of hardship and heavy physical exertion, subject to their life expectancy at birth being only the mid-forties for males and upper-forties for females. For the young adult males in the population, their physical stamina was tested at sea and in the trenches between 1914 and 1918.

[99] Professor Roderick Floud and his co-authors accept urbanization as a negative factor on the heights of young male adults. See R. Floud, K. Wachter and A. Gregory, *Height, Health and History. Nutritional Status in the United Kingdom, 1750–1980* (Cambridge, 1990), p. 224. Insofar as height represents completed physical development, the downward trend in heights in the nineteenth century reflects the fact that the physical development of the British population cannot be linked to real wage trends or theoretical improvements in the standard of living. Floud *et al.* categorize the period 1850 to 1914 as one of recovery and improvement in physical development, and hence nutritional status. Given their sources, this applies only to young adult males. Their generalization does not provide evidence of any improvement which reduced the existing physical gradient between the social classes.

4

THE GREAT WAR AND ITS AFTERMATH, 1914 TO 1921

Discontent on the food front

The effects on diet of the Great War differed considerably from prewar expectations, since neither the length of the conflict nor the effectiveness of the submarine campaign against merchant shipping had been envisaged by politicians and civil servants. For the first two years of hostilities against the Central Powers there were bumper harvests, and supplies were sustained by normal trade conditions. However, in view of the fact that the greater part of Britain's foodstuffs was imported, the lack of planning was a hazardous strategy, particularly since the supply of 'the very narrow range of staples eaten by the working classes' (i.e. bread, sugar, lard, cheese, bacon, condensed milk and meat) was at risk:

> The British Isles produced only one-fifth of the wheat, two-fifths of the butter and cheese, three-fifths of the meat and bacon, and none of the sugar that they required. Only in respect of fish, potatoes, and milk were they self-sufficient, and even the consumption of liquid milk was eked out by importation of condensed varieties.[1]

The lack of intervention by Walter Runciman, President of the Board of Trade from 1914 to 1916, to control food supplies was consistent with his 'Free Trade' principles and the Liberal government's general philosophy, but it prevented any coherent food policy from developing. The regulation of the food market therefore occurred in an *ad hoc* manner: the Home Secretary effected control of the sugar trade on 7 August 1914, by establishing a Royal Commission;[2] from October 1914, the War Office requisitioned large imports of meat, especially frozen meat, to ensure the army's needs were met. In January 1915, there were five committees discussing various aspects of food supply, including,

---

[1] F. H. Coller, *A State Trading Venture* (Oxford, 1925), p. 1.
[2] *First (Interim) Report of the Royal Commission on Sugar Supply*, PP 1917–18 (Cd.8728), XVIII, 635; see W. H. Beveridge, *British Food Control* (Oxford, 1928), pp. 5–9, 22–9, for an account of Runciman's resistance to state trading.

nominally, a Cabinet Committee on Food Supplies.[3] From February 1915, when the German naval command adopted unrestricted attacks on merchant shipping, the growing success of German submarines and the increasing demands upon British shipping forced change.[4] By 1917, U-boats had sunk 2M tons of Britain's merchant fleet. However, with one-third of Britain's ships engaged in supplying the armed forces abroad and one-fifth on loan to the Allies, only one-third was available for the home supply trade, including food.[5] Since the maintenance of imports was of paramount concern, the Board of Agriculture appointed a Royal Commission on Wheat Supplies in October 1916, but it was not until the beginning of 1917 that a Food Production Department was established to stimulate output at home.[6] As the food distribution crisis developed, one of the first acts of Lloyd George's new coalition government upon taking office was to create a Ministry of Food. It operated from December 1916 to March 1921 and was headed not by a Minister of Food but by a 'Food Controller', the first of whom, until June 1917, was Lord Devonport, followed by Lord Rhondda until July 1918.[7] The Ministry of Food had a strange history. It began by attempting to operate a non-intervention policy but eventually had to accept control of the distribution of food through a rationing scheme. In essence, it was a trading venture – as were the wartime Royal Commissions that had preceded it – rather than a policy department, while the War Cabinet's desire to concentrate on producing the materials of war at home meant that it had little time or interest for any social or redistributive function in connexion with food. Thus the idea behind the Ministry of Food was that it should help maintain war production and prevent unrest at home.

Food supply in a free market, 1914 to 1917

In August 1914, the message politicians and press offered to the civilian population was 'business as usual'. Beyond its propaganda value, this patently was not what happened in the food market. Importers invoked the war-risks clauses in their contracts and freight rates soared. People immediately rushed to buy food and hoard it, particularly sugar, that

---

[3] L. M. Barnett, *British Food Policy During the First World War* (1985), pp. 21–2; Beveridge, *British Food Control*, p. 7, suggests that the Committee on Food Supplies 'found little to do' and ceased to function after February 1915.

[4] See Barnett, *British Food Policy*, pp. 2–3, 41; J. R. Marrack, *Food and Planning* (1946), ch. VII.

[5] Marrack, *Food and Planning*, p. 164.

[6] Ibid., pp. 164–5; Pollard, *British Economy*, 1914–67, p. 43.

[7] When Lord Rhondda died in July 1918, Mr J. R. Clynes, his deputy, became Food Controller.

MINISTRY
OF
FOOD
CONTROL

ALIMENTARY INTELLIGENCE.

Mr. Punch. "DO YOU CONTROL FOOD HERE?"
Commissionaire. "WELL, SIR, 'CONTROL' IS PERHAPS RATHER A STRONG WORD. BUT
WE GIVE HINTS TO HOUSEHOLDERS, AND WE ISSUE 'GRAVE WARNINGS.'"
[Mr. Punch, however, is glad to note that more drastic regulations are about to be enforced.]

Plate 4.1 This cartoon reflects the anomalous position of Lord Devonport (formerly Sir Hudson Kearley of Kearley and Tonge, wholesale grocers) who, as Food Controller between December 1916 and May 1917, had insufficient powers to enforce any food policies. (Reproduced by permission of the British Library, Shelfmark 5270)

'essential' food, which in peacetime had been supplied largely from German and Austrian sugar-beet. Sugar prices increased by 80 per cent in the first week of the war to around 3¼d per pound but fell back again somewhat when the initial rush to hoard subsided. The quartern loaf of bread, the principal item of the diet for the working classes, which had cost about 5¾d before the war began, jumped in price, reaching 8¼d in May 1915 and 11½d by June 1917. In the first week of the war the price of bacon retailing at 1s 4d per pound rose to 1s 10d for those working-class customers buying by the quarter-pound. Working-class families were also most affected by the rising price of meat. Between July and October 1914, beef prices increased by 16 per cent. Home-produced fresh meat rose least, but lower quality beef, particularly imported frozen meat, rose 30 per cent in price since the armed services' requirements were bought from this category. From November 1914, a tax of 3d per pound was placed on tea in the first wartime budget. Such price rises, at a time when the working classes spent 60 per cent of their income on food, were a matter of great concern and the government's failure to fix food prices became a major source of labour dissatis-faction. Full employment and wage rises brought some relief after the initial months of disruption and distress but, ironically, the families of reservists called to the colours in 1914 were worst hit by the admin-istrative muddles which left wives without money and short of milk for infants. In the East End of London, Sylvia Pankhurst opened 'Cost Price Restaurants' for women and children facing relief by the Poor Law.[8] For low-income families the rising price of food was a continual problem; in September 1915, Mr McKenna's budget raised taxes on tea, coffee and cocoa, but the heaviest increase was on sugar duty, which rose from 1s 10d to 9s 4d per cwt. The effect was to restrict consumption as the retail price of sugar reached 6d per pound in 1917.[9] By mid-1917 the average price of all foods was double that of 1914.[10]

Although great difficulties in food distribution were experienced during the later stages of the war, Britain was never subject to the shortages experienced by civilian populations in central Europe in 1918. Even at the end of the war, when 'bodies of workmen like to call

[8] E. S. Pankhurst, *The Home Front* (1932), pp. 43–5.

[9] J. F. Rees, *A Short Fiscal and Financial History of England 1815–1918* (1921), pp. 213–19. At this price, cheap sugar as a source of energy was a myth. One penny spent on sugar at 6d per pound would produce only 300kcal, while a penny spent on margarine at 10d per pound would yield 360kcal. McKenna raised duties on tea, coffee, cocoa and sugar again in his 1916 budget. In the last wartime budget, Mr Bonar Law made a further increase in the duty on sugar.

[10] Barnett, *British Food Policy*, pp. 36–7, and Appendix 3, *Percentage Increase in Retail Food Prices, United Kingdom*.

themselves Soviets',[11] food shortages did not cause severe privation. The 'breadstuffs policy' – which meant that bread would not be rationed – required the energy needs of the population to be met so that output could be maintained. Thus land producing potatoes or wheat yielded more energy than if it was used as grazing land for meat. This food production strategy was adopted by the government following the *Report on the Food Supply of the United Kingdom* by the Royal Society's Physiology (War) Committee.[12] However, the potato crop in 1916 was poor, being some 25 per cent below normal. When bad weather handicapped the sowing of autumn wheat, a sense of approaching crisis in the home food supply was generated. Mr Asquith's government was forced to consider appointing a Food Controller against the background of an acute shortage of farm labourers and other agricultural workers, since conscription in 1916 accentuated the loss of men who had volunteered earlier. The passing of the Corn Production Act, 1917, which stimulated the ploughing up of grassland, brought price stability back to cereal farming.[13]

Sources of discontent, 1915 to 1917

Rising prices became a focus for discontent, which gave rise to a mood of uncertainty about the security of food supplies. The sinking of the *Lusitania* in May 1915 was followed by anti-German riots in Liverpool, London and other towns. A German restaurant in London was attacked and some looting from bakers' shops occurred. Special constables were posted to protect food shops but troops were called out in the East End of London.[14] Quite early in the war, the need to increase industrial output led the government to seek improvements in working conditions and to limit time and money spent on drinking alcoholic beverages. A Central Control Board (Liquor Traffic) was established in 1915. David Lloyd George viewed drink as 'our greatest enemy'. Even more strongly, the Bishop of London proclaimed that 'men who drank at home were murdering the men in the trenches'. These outbursts

---

[11] Public Record Office (PRO), MAF60/113. Special Cabinet Papers 1915–1919. Memorandum by Sir Alfred Mond, First Commissioner of Works.
[12] Board of Trade, *The Food Supply of the United Kingdom*. A Report drawn up by a Committee of the Royal Society, PP 1916 (Cd.8421), IX. This was the sole example of scientific advice being influential in the war in connexion with food and nutrition. See Marrack, *Food and Planning*, pp. 174–8, though this view is discounted by Dr Margaret Barnett. See Barnett, *British Food Policy*, p. 111.
[13] Coller, *State Trading Adventure*, pp. 9–13.
[14] Mrs C. S. Peel, *How We Lived Then 1914–1918* (1929), pp. 34–8; Pankhurst, *Home Front*, pp. 193 5.

encouraged temperance and prohibitionist activists to try to limit the consumption of alcoholic beverages; in 1916, brandy required a doctor's prescription. During 1917, however, resistance by working men had almost reached a 'no drink, no work' stage.[15] Although best known for the restrictions imposed on licensing hours and, in the later stages of the war, for limitations imposed upon the output of beer by the brewers, the Central Control Board also had a canteen committee. There were few industrial canteens providing meals at work before 1914 but, as work on munitions expanded, the government required the provision of meals and places to eat them, and the need was increased further by the growing employment of women munitions workers. By 1918, industrial canteens served one million meals a day.[16] An attempt was made in the later part of the war to widen the practice of communal eating by the introduction of subsidized restaurants or 'national kitchens'. The first of them, in May 1917, were known as 'communal kitchens'. Some provided only the facility to carry away cooked foods but others offered the opportunity to eat food on the premises, though their locations and facilities made them unattractive to any but the poorer classes.[17] In any case, many people had no prewar experience of eating outside their homes. 'The truth of the matter was that there was no demand for National Kitchens, and that they had no reasonable chance of success,' wrote Mr Clemesha, the Food Controller in the north-west of England:

> the working man would have his meals at home so long as he could, and would not take his wife and family out to an 'eating house' except as a last resort. The clerk and the typist might go to a café, or to a restaurant, where a light meal was provided at a cheap rate, but the working man either took his dinner with him to work in a tin or basket, or went home to eat it in the bosom of his family. The fried fish shop he knew, the cold supper bar where he could buy tripe or 'trotters' he was acquainted with, but a restaurant was not in his line.[18]

Although wartime full employment meant more money in working-class homes, shortages due to problems of food distribution and restrictions on alcoholic drinks became important aspects of the under-lying social discontent that simmered throughout 1916. In October, the Board of Trade formed a Food Department under William Beveridge. Its

---

[15] Peel, *How We Lived Then*, pp. 63–65.

[16] Sir Noel Curtis-Bennett, *The Food of the People, being The History of Industrial Feeding* (1949), p. 227. His figure is based on E. L. Collis and M. Greenwood, *The Health of the Industrial Worker* (1921).

[17] Barnett, *British Food Policy*, p. 151.

[18] H. W. Clemesha, *Food Control in the North-West Division* (Manchester, 1922), p. 31.

initial operations, such as a 'Meatless Day' in restaurants, were inept. This was accentuated by the 'Eat Less Meat' economy campaign run by the War Savings Committee towards the end of 1916. Dissatisfaction became more openly evident in 1917, by which time patriotic appeals requesting restraint in the consumption of food had worn thin.[19] Letters to the press complained that German prisoners of war were fed better than British civilians. The spring of 1917 brought new food orders by the Food Controller, which further incensed the civilian population. Government regulation flour was required to have an 81 per cent extraction rate and the bread baked from it to contain 10 per cent of flour from cereals other than wheat. Moreover, the resulting 'war bread' was to be stale – more than twelve hours old – when sold, in order to reduce its palatability. The manufacture and sale of 'light pastries, muffins, crumpets, and teacakes' was prohibited, as was the use of sugar in scones. Meatless days and potato-less days were to be observed each week in public dining-rooms, hotels and restaurants. For meals served between 3 p.m. and 6 p.m. only 2oz. of bread, cake or biscuits was permitted, while bread and sugar were 'rationed' in meals served in hotels, restaurants and clubs.[20] The food orders established minimum weights for loaves, which led bakers to increase the water content of the loaf. By the summer bread was frequently underbaked and soggy; and an outbreak of the bacterial infection 'rope' made some bread inedible. Once minimum weights were established the bakers raised the price of bread, so that loaves in the shops reached double their prewar prices late in 1917.

Discontent during 1917 led the War Emergency Workers National Committee to call for bread to be subsidized and the price reduced to 6d a quartern loaf. By the autumn, the War Cabinet accepted the Food Controller's proposal for a bread subsidy that would bring the price down to 9d a quartern from the 11½d or 1s 0d commonly charged. Problems of distribution from October onwards led to the appearance of queues at food shops, including bakeries. *The Times* reported queues in London forming from 5 a.m. on Saturdays – the peak shopping day for working-class housewives. On 20 December, it reported from Coventry that men in the munitions factories were leaving work to help their

<hr/>

[19] Peel, *How We Lived Then*, p. 91. See Barnett, *British Food Policy*, pp. 86–7 and ch. 6, 'Labour and the new consumerism' for a full account of the government's response to civilian discontent.

[20] *British Food Journal (BFJ)*, March 1917, p. 37; April 1917, p. 55. The peacetime extraction rate of flour had been about 72 to 73 per cent but in November 1916, the Wheat Commission raised it to 76 per cent. Many millers had ignored this order. Another aspect of the Food Orders restricted the use of grain to human consumption to prevent farmers from feeding grain to animals. Higher extraction rates brought shortages of animal feedstuffs and high prices.

wives by queuing.[21] The impact on morale could not be ignored and the government was forced to accept the need for general rationing of food in December 1917, though the introduction of livestock control regulations at the beginning of 1918 created a 'meat famine' for the civilian population. By February, queues had reached 'gigantic proportions', particularly for tea and margarine, and the news reached men at the front.[22] The censors in France became concerned at the tone of servicemen's letters home: 'We out here won't have our wives and children starving, War or no War, those at home have got to see our dependents get sufficient food', wrote one man. Another letter contained the view that: 'All the men's wives seem to tell their husbands about the trouble they have to get the food stuffs. You would think they would come to some terms when they see the country in that state.' The army command feared that food problems in Britain were causing defeatism to spread when the censor could read: 'It makes one think at this time that this was brought to an end.' The chief censor at Calais reported that 'the greatest effect appears to be produced by men returning from leave' and morale had suffered considerably in consequence. General Bonham Carter was sent in person by the army's general headquarters to see the Food Controller, Lord Rhondda, and his deputy Mr Clynes. In response the Ministry of Food sent lecturers to France – particularly men from the large industrial areas, such as Tyneside and Clydeside – and made a film showing conditions at home. Messages from Lord Rhondda and Mr Clynes were part of a special campaign in the British press called 'Smile across the Channel' to encourage families to send cheerful news to their men at the front.[23] None of this could disguise the fact that a major crisis in the distribution of foodstuffs was being experienced in the winter of 1917–18, which diverted the attention of the civilian population from the war. On her return from France in the spring of 1918, Vera Brittain noted: 'The agony of the last few weeks in France appeared not to interest London in comparison with the struggle to obtain sugar; the latter was discussed incessantly, but no one even wanted to hear about the former.'[24]

[21] Beveridge, *British Food Control*, p. 195.

[22] Ibid., pp. 201–2.

[23] PRO, MAF60/243. The effect of food queues at home on men at the front (Sydney Walton, 16 April 1918).

[24] Vera M. Brittain, *Testament of Youth* (1933), p. 430, cited by Dorothy F. Hollingsworth, 'Rationing and economic constraints on food consumption since the Second World War', in Oddy and Miller, *Diet and Health in Modern Britain*, pp. 255–73.

Plate 4.2 Men serving in the armed forces in the Great War were given priority in the allocation of food. Their rations exceeded 4,000kcal per day. Men 'at the front' were often unaware of food shortages at home. (Image courtesy of The Advertising Archives)

AN EAST END FOOD QUEUE

Plate 4.3 Rising food prices and problems of distribution led to extensive queuing for food in the final months of 1917. The government called for a reduction in food consumption yet delayed the introduction of rationing until 1918. (Reproduced by permission of the British Library, Shelfmark 09080.cc.16)

The failure of voluntary restraint, 1916–17

The National War Savings Committee formed in April 1916 was concerned not only with the selling of savings certificates but also with limiting civilian consumption generally. Its Women's Auxiliary War Savings Committee began to hold exhibitions for housewives to meet the rising cost and scarcity of food and fuel.[25] These activities became formalized once the Ministry of Food came into existence in December 1916. During 1917 its Local Authorities Division ran a series of propaganda campaigns. In September, Sir Arthur Yapp was brought in from the Young Men's Christian Association (YMCA) to organize The League of National Safety. The League claimed 'All Food Savers are Active Allies to the Men in the Trenches', though its propaganda campaign proved to be a conspicuous failure. At the beginning of 1917, the Ministry of Food announced 'voluntary rations' amounting to 4lb. breadstuffs, 0.75lb. sugar and 2.5lb. of meat per head per week, which it followed in February by publishing Lord Devonport's appeal to the nation, *A National Lent*: 'Let us proclaim during the war a NATIONAL

---

[25] Peel, *How We Lived Then*, pp. 72–3.

LENT. The nation will be better and stronger for it, mentally and morally as well as physically.'[26] The Ministry's *Food Economy Handbook*, which asserted that 'before the war the nation could have lived on the food it wasted', became a target for the Royal Society's Physiology (War) Committee. The scientists retorted that prewar consumption of bread and flour had averaged 5.25lb. per week among working-class families, and had already risen to 6lb. during the war. Since bread was a major source of energy, poorer families might eat 10lb. a head and male labourers up to 14lb. of bread a week.[27] Attempts by the government to restrict the consumption of carbohydrate foods were unrealistic but continued to reflect official thinking: on 15 March 1917, the War Cabinet decided that potatoes should be 'rationed' by limiting their use to 6oz. per head per day, with one potato-less day per week. Thus potato consumption was to be restricted to 36oz. (2lb. 4oz.) per week. The amount allocated to the army at home would be kept to the same limits. Such proposals took no account of their nutritional effects, a subject which the government was unwilling to consider. In April 1917, the Ministry of Food's new Director General of Food Economy asked for press support:

In view of the Food Economy Campaign which the War Savings Committees are about to undertake all over the country – The food difficulty – the only real difficulty – is that which is centred on the wheat supply. Potatoes, as you know, are practically exhausted, but man can live without potatoes – he cannot live without breadstuffs –

(1) Without great economy we cannot get through till the next harvest. We must reduce our present rate of consumption of bread and wheat flour.
(2) We can get through without distress to anybody if every person were to eat one pound less of bread per week than they normally consume.
Bread is the difficulty, and I am relying upon your help to direct all publicity in your paper.[28]

Nevertheless, on 30 May 1917 the conclusions of the War Cabinet were that 'compulsory rationing was undesirable at present'.[29] The propaganda campaign to reduce food consumption continued throughout the

[26] PRO, MAF60/52, Food Economy. The appeal was a direct quotation from Lloyd George's speech to the House of Commons on 19 December 1916. Hansard, Parliamentary Debates, 1916, House of Commons, col.1348.
[27] Beveridge, *British Food Control*, pp. 36–8; Barnett, *British Food Policy*, p. 108.
[28] PRO, MAF60/52, Food Economy. Draft letter by Mr Kennedy Jones, MP, 4 April 1917.
[29] PRO, MAF60/108, Cabinet Papers. Rationing: Memoranda and Decisions. War Cabinet, 334 Minutes, Wednesday, 30 January 1918. War Cabinet (151), 30 May 1917.

year by posters, leaflets and meetings addressed by a pool of speakers from the Ministry of Food. With such a negative message as 'we must eat less to maintain the stocks we have. Our men at the Front who are fighting for us must have full rations' the economy campaign relied heavily on a sense of patriotism. King George V followed up his earlier restrictions upon the consumption of alcohol in the Royal Household by a proclamation in the Eat less Bread campaign in May, which was read in churches and chapels on four consecutive Sundays.[30]

Leaflets such as *Thirty-four Ways of Using Potatoes; Carrot Cookery*; and *No Meat! Try these Substitute Dishes* were uninspiring reading, while *Christmas Dinner Recipes* featuring 'Poor Man's Goose' – made from slices of liver, onion and potatoes flavoured with sage – were a burden for housewives facing growing food queues. Unrealistic – and unscientific – slogans such as 'Eat slowly: you will need less food'[31] made a strange contrast to the appeals to maximize the output of munitions. The Ministry's speakers (among whom were Mrs Maud Pember Reeves and Mrs C. S. Peel) could be patronising and insensitive. On 10 November 1917, Mr H. G. Corner of the London Telephone Service wrote to the Ministry:

> I find there is a certain amount of feeling amongst some of our staff against the Food Economy Lectures . . . I find that the outstanding points are:–
>
> (1) The irritation produced amongst the people by inability to obtain certain essentials such as tea, butter, sugar and margarine.
>
> (2) The facts that prices are so high and their earnings and those of their families (who belong to what is usually known as the lower middle class) so low, produce the feeling that it is something like impertinence on the part of the people from a higher stratum of society to lecture them on food economy when perforce the most rigid economy is practised in their own families.
>
> (3) The lecturers are assumed to be coming from the wealthier and more comfortable classes and the girls allege that some of the ladies who addressed them on war savings said some rather tactless things, they (the lecturers) assuming that the girls had much more to spend and to waste than they actually had (I am bound to say that some of the lecturers on war savings did lay themselves open to this charge, not apparently realizing the position of their audience).[32]

---

[30] Peel, *How We Lived Then*, Appendix VI; Coller, *State Trading Adventure*, p. 40.
[31] Unfortunately, Mr Kennedy Jones was a Fletcherite! See M. Barnett, 'Fletcherism: the chew-chew fad of the Edwardian era', in D. F. Smith, ed., *Nutrition in Britain: Science, Scientists and Politics in the Twentieth Century* (1997), ch. 1.
[32] PRO, MAF60/52. Food Economy.

George R.I.

We, being persuaded that the abstention from all unnecessary consumption of grain will furnish the surest and most effectual means of defeating the devices of Our enemies, and thereby of bringing the War to a speedy and successful termination, and out of Our resolve to leave nothing undone which can contribute to these ends or to the welfare of Our people in these times of grave stress and anxiety, have thought fit, by and with the advice of Our Privy Council, to issue this Our Royal Proclamation, most earnestly exhorting and charging all those of Our loving subjects the men and women of Our realm who have the means of procuring articles of food other than wheaten corn as they tender their own immediate interests, and feel for the wants of others, especially to practise the greatest economy and frugality in the use of every species of grain, and We do for this purpose more particularly exhort and charge all heads of households

TO REDUCE THE CONSUMPTION OF BREAD IN THEIR RESPECTIVE FAMILIES BY AT LEAST ONE-FOURTH OF THE QUANTITY CONSUMED IN ORDINARY TIMES.

TO ABSTAIN FROM THE USE OF FLOUR IN PASTRY AND MOREOVER TO RESTRICT OR WHEREVER POSSIBLE TO ABANDON THE USE THEREOF IN ALL OTHER ARTICLES THAN BREAD.

Given at Our Court at Buckingham Palace this Second day of May in the Year of Our Lord 1917 in the Seventh Year of Our Reign

GOD SAVE THE KING

NOW WE THE UNDERSIGNED MEMBERS OF THIS HOUSEHOLD HEREBY PLEDGE OURSELVES ON OUR HONOUR TO RESPOND TO HIS MAJESTY'S APPEAL.

_____

_____

_____

The Ministry of Food pressed ahead with its national economy campaign. In the same month, it wrote to all local food economy committees: 'The Food Controller is anxious to have practical demonstrations of Economical Cookery held in every town and village in the country.' The Ministry hoped more people would join the League of National Safety and went on to remind the population that the 'voluntary' rations were maximum amounts and people should try to consume less.[33] Wartime recipes, however, faced much opposition. Housewives were suspicious of substitutes such as maize. Among the poorer classes limited resources – and husbands' attitudes – did not permit experiment: 'Give 'im beans, an' get a black eye for me pains!' was the response to one cookery demonstration.[34] Recipes using substitutes made sad reading: 'Mock Duck' made from lentils, rice or mashed potatoes required the cook 'to season well, shape as much like a duck as possible' or 'Scotch Trifle (can be made with cold porridge)'.[35] Recipes for 'Potato Butter', 'Cornflour Butter' or merely extending butter or margarine by blending with milk and gelatine reflected the fact that 'bread and scrape' was still a complete meal for the poor.

The final act of the food economy campaign was to invoke the Food Hoarding Order of April 1917. This gave power of entry to search for stocks of food and imposed fines on sellers as well as those found hoarding. The announcement of a 'Conscience Week' in February 1918 to allow hoarders to surrender their stocks provided an amnesty until 25 February 1918 – the day rationing began – to hand in food. Like so much of the campaign for voluntary restraint, it had little effect.[36]

Rationing, 1917 to 1920

Despite the public alarm caused by rising food prices, the Ministry of Food, riven by internal dispute and unsure as to what government policy was, made little progress in solving problems of food distribution. In April 1917, it requisitioned all the flourmills in the country.[37] Lord Devonport's illness led to his replacement by Lord Rhondda in June 1917. The Ministry's task had been formulated by the report of the Physiology (War) Committee of the Royal Society. This stressed the need

---

[33] PRO, MAF60/52. M.G. Food Economy 1, 11/1917.
[34] Peel, *How We Lived Then*, p. 91.
[35] Mrs C. S. Peel, *'Daily Mail' War Recipes* (1918), pp. 39, 56–7.
[36] Beveridge, *British Food Control*, pp. 239–40.
[37] R. J. Hammond, *Food: Volume I The Growth of Policy* (History of the Second World War, United Kingdom Civil Series) (1951), pp. 3–4; Barnett, *British Food Policy*, p. 126, notes that the mills were operated by the Wheat Commission.

YOU ARE
RESPECTFULLY
INVITED TO EAT
A LITTLE LESS.

BY REQUEST
A. YAPP.

THE GREAT UNCONTROLLED.

Lord Rhondda. "LOOK HERE, JOHN, ARE YOU GOING TO TIGHTEN THAT BELT, OR MUST I DO IT FOR YOU?"
John Bull. "YOU DO IT FOR ME. THAT'S WHAT YOU'RE THERE FOR."

Plate 4.4 Lord Rhondda, the second Food Controller, was in office from June 1917 until his death in July 1918. The 'poster' on the wall is based on Sir Arthur Yapp's 'League of National Safety' which began its food economy campaign using an anchor symbol in September 1917. Frank Coller in *A State Trading Venture* (Oxford, 1925) provided its epitaph: 'The brilliant success achieved by Sir Arthur in other spheres was not repeated in his new undertaking; over the ultimate fate of the millions of small badges reminding one of Alexandra Day and cards recalling Christmas, a veil is discreetly drawn.' (Reproduced by permission of the British Library, Shelfmark 5270)

to 'ensure the equitable distribution of the available food'. The best way to do so, in the Committee's view, was to maintain adequate supplies of bread, with the provisional warning that if rising prices meant that any part of the working class received less food 'its output of work will, of necessity, be reduced'.[38] While the scientists on the Physiology Committee continued to press their recommendations on the Ministry of Food throughout 1917, they felt that much of their advice was ignored. Instead, they turned to the War Cabinet secretariat as a means of trying to influence government policy.[39] Since the War Cabinet gave little sustained thought to the problem of the civilian population's food supply, neither the Cabinet nor the Ministry of Food took any decisions on principle that confirmed or contradicted the Physiology Committee's advice. Thus, while the scientists emphasized that a national food policy was necessary to maintain output, the rationing scheme was based on solving the problems of distributing food to shops. In the end the Ministry of Food's system of food rationing relied on the principle that bread would not be rationed but other foodstuffs that competed for space in ships and ports would. The quantities of the rations are shown in Table 4.1. It is likely that rationing had less effect upon the wartime consumption of food than the price controls that were introduced in 1917. More important still were the complex relationships established with the USA after it entered the war, which provided a framework for inter-allied credit and for purchases of American food.[40] This meant that by 1918, 52 per cent of the wheat and flour, nearly 84 per cent of the bacon and ham, over 31 per cent of the meat and almost 38 per cent of the dairy produce imported came from the USA.[41] While the U-boat campaigns were still a threat, the Dominions in the southern hemisphere were prevented from providing more of Britain's food by the length of the voyages, which would have tied up more shipping.

Confronted with growing discontent, the Ministry of Food seemed paralysed and unable to take the lead on food rationing. Rhondda and Clynes both opposed compulsory rationing in 1917.[42] Shortages, rising prices and endless queuing forced the Ministry to reassess its plans for national registration of consumers as food control committees began to operate local municipal rationing schemes. Late in December 1917, the Ministry issued an Order endorsing the local schemes already under way.

[38] *The Food Supply of the United Kingdom*, 1916, p. 18.
[39] For the limited effect of the scientists on food policy, see Barnett, *British Food Policy*, ch. 5.
[40] Ibid., ch. 7, for a detailed account of the negotiations and Herbert Hoover's role as the American Food Administrator.
[41] Ibid., p. 165.
[42] Ibid., pp. 146–7.

Table 4.1 Civilian food rations per head per week, 1917 to 1920

Date	Sugar	Jam	Tea	Bacon	Meat	Butter	Margarine	Lard
Dec 1917	8oz.	4oz.	2oz.	4oz.	1s.3d	Fats jointly = 4oz.		4oz.
May 1918	8oz.	4oz.	2oz.	8oz.	10d	Fats jointly = 4oz.		4oz.
June 1918	8oz.	4oz.	2oz.	8oz.	10d	Fats jointly = 5oz.		4oz.
July 1918	8oz.	4oz.	2oz.	16oz.	10d	Fats jointly = 5oz.		4oz.
				off ration				
Dec 1918	8oz.	4oz.	off ration		10d	Fats jointly = 5oz.		
Jan 1919	12oz.	4oz.			10d	Fats jointly = 5oz.		off ration
Feb 1919	8oz.	off ration			10d	1–2oz.	off ration	
Dec 1919	8oz.				off ration	1–2oz.		
May 1920	8oz.					off ration		
Nov 1920	16oz.							
	off ration							

Note: Sugar rations were reduced to 6oz. in 1919 during the rail strike and again from January to March 1920.

At the end of January 1918, the War Cabinet approved the principle of national compulsory rationing, and a system of general rationing for London and the Home Counties administered by the Ministry of Food came into operation on 25 February 1918.[43] The food queues, which in the preceding month had totalled half-a-million people in the Metropolitan Police District, began to shrink, though they were not eliminated until May. Scientific opposition to the Ministry's scheme was avoided by the fact that the Rationing Committee included Professor Noel Paton, the distinguished physiologist, and that the quantities of rationed foods appeared to be sufficient to allow the diets of adults to be within the range of 2,450 to 3,900kcal (10,250 to 16,320kj) per day. The system adopted involved food coupons being issued to consumers but, in order to control distribution, required consumers to be tied to particular retailers. This was not what the War Cabinet had expected and led to Beveridge's well-known conclusion: 'It is a sober statement of fact that the Ministry of Food made its own and much of Lord Rhondda's reputation by putting accidentally into practice one system of rationing while it was formally engaged in devising a different system.'[44] The meat crisis, however, continued even after livestock control regulations had been accepted by the trade. Mr Clynes explained the problem to the House of Commons:

> The meat problem in a nutshell is that we had to arrange that the required number of beasts and sheep should be killed in 14,000 slaughter-houses and delivered, together with their proportion of frozen meat, to 52,000 retailers' shops through 2,000 Local Food Committee areas, and that must be done at the right moment, or as near possible, in order to supply the demands of 40,000,000 consumers.[45]

The meat coupons issued were based on a money value, though the ration allowed was linked to a specific weight for bacon or ham. Its success depended upon national uniformity of meat prices being charged for standard cuts, a process only introduced into the wholesale trade at the end of 1917.[46] In May 1918, the meat ration would buy only 12oz. (including an 'average' amount of bone) though there was an additional 10oz. of bacon or ham. Finally, on Sunday, 14 July 1918, the first national, uniform system of food rationing came into operation. It was

[43] See Beveridge, *British Food Control*, pp. 204–5, 229, for the administrative confusion.

[44] Hammond, *Food, Vol. I*, pp. 4–7. For the debate and scheme in full, see Beveridge, *British Food Control*, particularly p. 229.

[45] E. M. H. Lloyd, *Experiments in State Control at the War Office and the Ministry of Food* (Oxford, 1924), pp. 162–3.

[46] Ibid., p. 172.

ironic that after only a fortnight, a glut of imported fatty American bacon arrived which enabled bacon to be derationed at the end of July.[47] Eating out whether in schools, factory canteens or restaurants required the consumer to hand over a meat coupon (or even half a coupon) for any meat portions supplied.[48] Otherwise food for caterers was controlled by the Public Meals Act, 1917, which had strange rules regarding the supply of sugar. In restaurants it could be used in cooking but was not on the table; in hotels it was on the table but for residents' use only. Railway buffets and teashops were fortunately exempt from such regulations. Food manufacturers found the regulations confusing and the Ministry's officials could be uncomprehending. Faced with an acute shortage of sugar, C. J. Wilkin of the jam firm in Tiptree, Essex went to London 'to see the Jam Controller in Park Lane. "Turned out to be a barrister. Very difficult to convince that 1lb. of sugar and 1lb. of fruit would not make 2lbs. of jam".'[49] Any national scheme of rationing required enforcement. During 1918 to 1919 there were over 50,000 prosecutions, running at a rate of a hundred a day from February 1918 until the Armistice in November.[50]

Health

The evidence assembled in Chapter 3 suggests that food consumption on the eve of the war among the working classes was based on a relatively narrow choice of foods. Some 6 to 7lb. of bread, a pound of sugar and 3 to 4lb. of potatoes per head per week were the principal items in the diet. Taken altogether, the foods eaten yielded an energy value of around 2,300 to 2,400kcal per head per day of which two-thirds came from carbohydrates. Wartime comparisons with prewar peacetime diets are not straightforward since there was no systematic monitoring of consumption during the war. Prewar energy intakes calculated from family budgets surveys were well below the contemporary estimates based on food supply statistics. However, they match quite well with energy intakes measured among a small number of Glasgow families surveyed by Dr Alice Ferguson between 1915 and 1918. Dr Ferguson's analysis calculated energy intakes at around 2,650kcal per 'man value'.[51]

[47] Beveridge, *British Food Control*, p. 217.
[48] Curtis-Bennett, *Food of the People*, p. 234.
[49] Maura Benham, *The Story of Tiptree Jam. The First Hundred Years 1885–1985* (Tiptree, 1985), p. 30.
[50] Beveridge, *British Food Control*, p. 235.
[51] Alice Ferguson, 'The family budgets and dietaries of forty labouring class families in Glasgow in war time', *Proceedings of the Royal Society of Edinburgh*, 37 (1916–17), pp. 117–36.

The effect of the war on working-class diets meant that by 1918 the rising cost of food had halved the consumption of sugar, butter and cheese, and had restricted the consumption of meat by one-third and lard by a quarter. More bread and potatoes were bought and there were also increases in the small amounts of bacon and margarine purchased. Offal, being unrationed meat, became a prize for which butchers' favours had to be sought. Eggs were regarded as a luxury food of limited nutritional value. Government restrictions on feed for hens drove the price of an egg up to 4d or 5d each.[52] In effect, price rises and scarcities during the war restored the restricted diet that had been commonly experienced by the working classes in the late Victorian and Edwardian times though rising prices had eliminated the prewar importance of sugar as a cheap source of energy. In June 1918, the Report of the Cost of Living Committee compared food consumption in a 'standard' family with that of July 1914. Ordinary people ate more bread and potatoes than before the war. They used more flour, rice, tapioca, oatmeal and milk but meat, bacon, lard, butter, cheese and sugar consumption had been reduced. While energy values in 1918 were only 3 per cent below prewar intakes, there was a qualitative deterioration in the working-class diet.[53]

The lack of nutritional evaluation of civilian diets during the war means that judgements regarding the state of the health of the civilian population depend upon epidemiological data. Although initially the war was held to be deleterious to health, one revisionist view suggested that infant mortality showed a marked decline and concluded that health in Britain improved during the war years.[54] While it is true that death rates fell, particularly the standardized death rate of females in England and Wales, the effect of the war on the health of children aged between 1 and 15 was less clear. The deaths of children under 15 from measles reached a peak in 1915 not seen since 1896. Tuberculosis also increased rising from 1.4 per thousand in 1914 to 1.57 in 1918. While young children aged under 5 were not affected, the death rates of those in the 5 to 14 age range showed significant increases. Professor J. R. Marrack concluded: 'It is remarkable that the relatively slight deterioration in the food supply in Britain should have had an indisputable effect on the health of children over five years old.'[55] A further insight came from two reports that examined the extent of rickets in the context of economic

[52] Peel, *How We Lived Then*, pp. 87, 92.
[53] *Report of the Working Classes Cost of Living Committee*, PP 1918 (Cd.8980), VII.
[54] J. M. Winter, 'The impact of the First World War on civilian health in Britain', *Economic History Review*, 2nd. ser., Vol.XXX, 3 (August 1977), pp. 487–507.
[55] Marrack, *Food and Planning*, pp. 209 12.

and social conditions. The Medical Research Committee (MRC), which had been established in 1913, funded investigations into nutritional deficiency diseases and into the nature of the 'accessory food factors' that Hopkins had identified in 1912.[56] In 1917, Dr Margaret Ferguson's assessment was that half the children in 'industrial populations' – that is, in cities where smoke and buildings obscured sunlight – were affected by rickets. A further study concluded that rickets had shown a considerable increase during the war.[57] Although the social gradient in British society meant that middle-class children were better fed than those in working-class families where incomes were limited, they were not immune to nutritional deficiencies. Normally, the stature of middle-class children reflected their better nutrition; and the clearest evidence for this was put before the National Service Medical Boards by Professor Arthur Keith in 1918.[58] However, during the war itself, some middle-class children suffered from food shortages more than those of other social classes, especially those shortages created artificially by the moral restraint campaign. At Christ's Hospital in Sussex, Dr Friend, the School Medical Officer, recorded an increase in defective physique among school entrants from 20 per cent before 1916 to 60 to 80 per cent between 1917 and 1921. Boys aged 16 to 17 showed lower weight gains, notably when bread was restricted during the food economy campaign. When margarine replaced butter in the school, a marked increase in the number of broken bones occurred between 1918 and 1922. Dr Friend's explanation in retrospect was that the school diet was deficient in vitamin D, which impaired calcium metabolism, and a mild form of rickets was present.[59]

---

[56] The Medical Research Committee was funded by the National Insurance Act, 1911, to investigate diseases from which the insured population suffered. It became the Medical Research Council in 1920. See A. Landsborough Thomson, *Half a Century of Medical Research, Volume One* (1973), ch. 2.

[57] M. Ferguson and L. Findlay, *A Study of Social and Economic Factors in the Causation of Rickets*, Medical Research Committee Special Report Series, No.20, 1918; H. C. C. Mann, *Rickets: the Relative Importance of Environment and Diet as Factors of Causation*, MRC Special Report Series, No.68, 1922.

[58] *Report upon the Physical Examination of Men of Military Age by National Service Medical Boards*, PP 1919 (Cmd.504), pp. 6, 23. Keith's standard physique was based upon 1,000 Cambridge students, whose mean height was 5ft. 9in. The mean height of Grade I men seen by the National Service Medical Boards was 5ft. 6in.

[59] Marrack, *Food and Planning*, p. 209; G. E. Friend, *The Schoolboy. A Study of his Nutrition, Physical Development and Health* (Cambridge, 1935), pp. 71–2.

Decontrol, 1918 to 1921

Rationing food improved distribution but not quality. By the spring of 1918, the extraction rate of flour from wheat had risen to 92 per cent. The admixture of other cereals was raised from 10 to 30 per cent and the Ministry of Food tried unsuccessfully to persuade bakers to use potato flour in bread. Neither the millers and bakers nor the consumers accepted these arrangements with any pleasure. However, by the summer of 1918, the Food Controller allowed some relaxation in restrictions as imports of American wheat began to increase. Bread made from 70 per cent government regulation flour and 30 per cent imported white flour was legalized. Once the Armistice was signed on 11 November regulations started to be dismantled. By the end of 1918, an extraction rate for wheat flour of 76 per cent was permitted and the requirement to use an admixture of other grains was abolished. The repeal of the Bread Order enabled the baking of cakes and biscuits with sugar and chocolate to be resumed. Even the final stages of control produced difficulties for food manufacturers. C. J. Wilkin of Tiptree noted:

> Company designated to preserve all Blackberries collected in greater part of Essex. School children given special holidays. Blackberries poured into Factory in truck loads from all parts. Chief jam-boiler working till 12 o'clock Saturday night and on Sunday morning. 258 tons Blackberry Jam made that year. Control shortly after discontinued. Large part of jam left on hand.[60]

Rationing survived beyond the end of hostilities: margarine was derationed in February 1919, meat in December 1919, but rationing of butter continued until May 1920 and sugar until November 1920.[61] The prolongation of restrictions on food after the war was commonly blamed as a source of the discontent experienced by many in the immediate postwar years:

> The demobilised men who are returning daily to find a miserably dull life in town and village are loud in their complaint and are asking if this is the 'freedom' they fought and suffered for. During the week-ends, when those who have been working throughout the week have a little time for rest and recreation, 90 per cent of the licensed houses are displaying cards indicating that they have no beer, the small quantity available during the week having been consumed by those who are living on the Government dole, provided by taxpayers, including the hard-working people who are deprived of legitimate refreshment on Saturday nights.[62]

---

[60] Benham, *The Story of Tiptree Jam*, p. 30.
[61] Curtis-Bennett, *Food of the People*, p. 236.
[62] Beveridge, *British Food Control*, June 1919, p. 54.

Rationing was seen as part of the emergency measures retained in place in case of unrest after the war. The Ministry of Food's organization for food distribution was utilized fully during the national rail strike of September 1919.[63] With retail food prices in January 1920 136 per cent higher than July 1914, there were strong political reasons to extend the life of the Ministry.[64] Strategic considerations meant that government support for food production was continued after the end of the war by the Agriculture Act, 1920. The 1920 Act extended the policy of minimum prices for wheat and oats and improved the security of tenure for tenant farmers.[65] The emphasis on stimulating food production continued as county agricultural executive committees began to bring land back under crops. Furthermore, the relocation of some ex-servicemen on horticultural smallholdings after the war through the auspices of the Land Settlement Association revived the concept of regenerating the countryside.[66] It was, however, a half-hearted measure: urban Britain no longer saw the countryside as central to food production. Rationing of food in 1918, by introducing the principle of tying consumers to retailers, had formalized the concept that urban consumers were dependent upon urban suppliers. For townspeople – over 80 per cent of the population – food came to Britain in ships and was bought from shops.

The immediate postwar market suffered from the success of the wartime regime. Over-production of foodstuffs by primary producers overseas meant cheap imports seeking markets in the United Kingdom until world cereal prices collapsed. This led to the repeal of price support for cereal production in 1921 and to the termination of the Ministry of Food in March 1921.[67] Strange as it may seem, the state costed its wartime activities in the case of the Wheat Commission, the Sugar Commission and the Ministry of Food. The final accounts for the Ministry of Food's operations from 1917 to 1921 showed a profit of £11.7M from food trading. Overall, when expenses, losses and interest on capital were taken into consideration, there still remained a considerable net profit of £6.39M.[68] However, economic thought was changing and the policies of free trade and non-intervention in markets

---

[63] Mowat, *Britain Between the Wars*, pp. 39–40.
[64] PRO, CAB27/106. Cabinet Committee on the De-Control of Food, pp. 80, 160.
[65] Pollard, *British Economy, 1914–67*, p. 134.
[66] Following the 1905 Royal Commission on the Supply of Food in Time of War, all County Councils had been required to make land available for smallholdings. By 1914 there were only 14,000 in existence. See W. Ashworth, *An Economic History of England 1870–1939* (1960), p. 64. In Scotland, the Board of Agriculture created a small number of crofts in the 1920s.
[67] Pollard, *British Economy, 1914–67*, p. 135; Barnett, *British Food Policy*, p. 212.
[68] Coller, *State Trading Adventure*, p. 346.

by the government began to be questioned.[69] The effect of the Great War had been to bring about government intervention into aspects of people's lives – such as the control of their food – to an extent that would have been unimaginable in 1913.

[69] See Lloyd, *Experiments in State Control*; Coller, *A State Trading Adventure*. A. J. P. Taylor, *English History 1914–45* (Harmondsworth, 1970), p. 113, refers to it as 'war socialism'.

5

FOOD AND FOOD TECHNOLOGY IN THE INTERWAR YEARS

> The armistice of 1918 meant that, sooner or later, the huge corn production
> and inflated costs of agriculture would have to be adjusted to the normal
> demand for a cheaper, more varied and more nutritious diet – the State did
> little to help with this painful task of readjustment.[1]

The necessity for some major readjustment in Britain's food supply was
aggravated by the postwar policy of the Coalition government. Seeking
to maintain high agricultural output at home for strategic reasons, the
Agriculture Act 1920 offered guaranteed prices for cereals and greater
security of tenure to tenant farmers. Faced with the collapse of wheat
prices from the high point of 1920, the government abolished the
Ministry of Food on 31 March 1921, and hurriedly introduced the Corn
Production (Repeal) Act, 1921, to remove price guarantees and reduce
agricultural wages. The Retail Food Prices Index, begun in July 1914 at
100, peaked at 256 in 1920. It fell to 229.5 in 1921 and to 176 in 1922
as arable land began to go out of production. From 12.4M acres in 1918,
the area of arable fell below 10M acres in 1929.[2] The 1920s therefore
began with falling food prices, a trend that continued for most of the
interwar period.[3] As the policy of free trade came under question,
the Linlithgow Committee carried out an extensive survey of the nation's
food supply.[4] A temporary sugar-beet subsidy was introduced in 1925[5]
and a system of distinguishing home-grown produce – the National
Mark Scheme – was tried. The campaign by the Empire Marketing
Board to stimulate milk consumption in the hope of improving markets
for dairy farmers was another attempt to stabilize agriculture. In spite of

[1] PRO, MAF152/168. Official History of the United Kingdom at War: 1939–1945
Food Production (unpublished volume by Edith H. Whetham, July 1946), p. 9.
[2] E. H. Whetham, *The Agrarian History of England and Wales, Volume VIII,
1914–1939* (Cambridge, 1978), pp. 139, 173.
[3] Pollard, *British Economy, 1914–1967*, pp. 134–5; Mowat, *Britain Between the
Wars*, pp. 250–8.
[4] *Final Report of the Departmental Committee on the Distribution and Prices of
Agricultural Produce*, 1924 (Cmd.2008)
[5] British Sugar Subsidy Act, 1925. See Whetham, *Agrarian History, Volume VIII,
1914–1939*, pp. 165–9, 244, for the increase in output and acreage.

these efforts, domestic agriculture faced collapse as Britain reverted to the pre-1914 pattern of importing a large part of its food supplies:

> In 1930, this country, with less than 3 per cent of the world's population, took about 99 per cent of the world's exports of bacon and hams, 96 per cent of the eggs, 59 per cent of the beef, 46 per cent of the cheese, 32 per cent of the wool, and 28 per cent of the wheat and wheat flour.[6]

In general, there was much surplus capacity in industry. The most notable example in food processing was flourmilling. The resumption of milling at inland sites during the First World War left the industry with surplus capacity, while the demand for flour was static. During the 1920s the closure of smaller mills and the re-establishment of the pre-1914 pattern of large mills at ports processing imported grain occurred. By the end of the 1930s, around two-thirds of Britain's flour was produced by three firms: Rank's, Spiller's and the Co-operative Wholesale Society. The 'rationalization' of the milling industry resulted in a strong trade organization – the Millers' Mutual Trade Association – whose quota and pricing systems remained a mystery to the Ministry of Food for much of the Second World War.[7]

Technology and food processing

Food processing benefited most from the introduction of new canning techniques brought from the USA. Britain's National Food Canning Council initially had six member firms in 1926 but by 1934 there were eighty canning factories in areas such as the Vale of Evesham for fruit and Lincolnshire for vegetables, principally peas.[8] Although condensed milk was the largest commodity produced during the interwar years, Table 5.1 shows how rapid was the growth of canned fruit and vegetables. Retained imports of tinned fruit increased at such a rate that domestic production amounted to only 10 per cent of imports in 1935. However, the marked growth of indigenous vegetable-canning brought output almost up to the level of retained imports by that time. Production of canned fish was limited by the acceptability of different varieties: Britain's pilchards and herrings were never as popular as imported sardines and Canadian salmon. As a result, retained imports of canned fish were eight to nine times greater than home output. On the

---

[6] K. A. H. Murray and R. L. Cohen, *The Planning of Britain's Food Imports* (Oxford, 1934), p. 5.
[7] Pollard, *British Economy, 1914–67*, pp. 107–8; see also PRO, MAF84/380.
[8] Pollard, *British Economy, 1914–67*, p. 108.

Table 5.1 Supply of canned foods in Britain, 1924 to 1935

Foodstuffs	1924		1930		1935	
	Output (tons)	Imports (tons)	Output (tons)	Imports (tons)	Output (tons)	Imports (tons)
Meat products[1]	8,600	48,300[2]	18,200	68,850	20,300	65,100
Fish	7,550	53,250	7,000	64,800	8,650	70,500
Vegetables	2,000	35,900	15,700[3]	37,550	60,650[3]	64,350
Fruit	5,850	105,000	15,750	139,100	23,300	234,350
Condensed milk	38,300	109,100	43,750	129,800	148,750	89,200

Source: Based on P. Johnston, 'The development of the food-canning industry in Britain during the inter-war years', in Oddy and Miller, *Modern British Diet*, pp. 173–85.

Notes
1 Including meat extracts.
2 Canned beefs only.
3 Includes a small amount of bottled vegetables.

other hand, the threefold growth of condensed milk production between 1930 and 1935 began to reverse market shares: imports, which had formed 75 per cent of Britain's supply in 1930, had fallen by 1935 to under 40 per cent. Prepared foods were also a growing market; tinned soup production increased from 6,500 tons in 1930 to 11,700 tons in 1935. Nevertheless, despite the growth of the domestic canned food industry, over 70 per cent of the total supply of canned foods in 1938 was still imported.[9]

Nutrition and food manufacture

Those food manufacturers in the field of special food supplements or 'patent foods' – most of which had developed from association with medical treatment and with recommended programmes of child-rearing – were boosted by new scientific knowledge regarding physiology and nutrition. In 1919 the MRC's *Report on the Present State of Knowledge Concerning Accessory Food Factors (Vitamins)*[10] became something of a bestseller. Its influence extended well beyond the scientific community into professional health circles and the food industry. It ran to a second

[9] See J. P. Johnston, 'The development of the food-canning industry in Britain during the inter-war years', in Oddy and Miller, *Modern British Diet*, pp. 173–85.
[10] MRC Report No.38 (1919). The term 'vitamines' was originally in use but the final 'e' was dropped at Drummond's suggestion. See Drummond, *Englishman's Food*, p. 424.

edition in 1924 following the report of Dr Harriet Chick's work in postwar Vienna which enabled the disease of rickets to be understood fully for the first time.[11] A third edition *Vitamins: a Survey of Present Knowledge* was published in 1932, by which time further discoveries had occurred and the commercial preparation of vitamins had begun.[12] By the late 1930s, the Technical Commission of the League of Nations had begun to publish recommended vitamin allowances. These new concepts were used by pharmaceutical companies to develop the manufacture of 'food' products while food manufacturers found 'health' to be an even stronger message for advertisements extolling the qualities of their products. Since not all vitamins were known – though it was realized that their absence led to deficiency diseases – there was an obvious opportunity to claim health-giving values for any new patent-food products. Even 'roughage' – more usually associated with the ideas of Denis Burkitt and Hugh Trowell in the 1970s – made its appearance in 1927 as important for a healthy diet.[13] The market for some of the nineteenth-century staples such as malt extract, cod-liver oil and dried milk produced by firms like Allen & Hanbury of Bethnal Green peaked early in the interwar years but declined later as new products entered the market. During the 1920s, Allen & Hanbury faced competition in the milk-food sector as Joseph Nathan & Co, importers of New Zealand frozen meat and butter, expanded their dried-skimmed-milk business. Nathan's had introduced a dried-milk baby food in 1908 under the name Glaxo, the 'Food that Builds Bonnie Babies',[14] and by 1921 the sales of Glaxo totalled £1.5M. Nathan's started a milk research department under Harry Jephcott in 1919. He was instrumental in Nathan's purchase of a licence to produce cod-liver oil containing concentrated vitamin D. In 1924, Nathan's began to promote Glaxo as 'The Sunshine Baby Food'. It contained, they claimed, 'sunshine vitamin D to build strong bones and teeth'. They also introduced Ostelin, the first vitamin concentrate produced commercially in Britain. Allen & Hanbury responded by adding supplements to their 'Allenbury's Food for Infants' and 'Allenbury's Malted Rusks' and advertised them as 'fully protective against rickets and allied disorders'.[15] As the milk-food business declined

---

[11] H. Chick *et al.*, MRC Special Report Series, No.77, *Studies of Rickets in Vienna* (1923).

[12] MRC Special Report, Series No.167 (1932).

[13] R. Graves and A. Hodge, *The Long Week-end* (Harmondsworth, 1971), pp. 185–6. For later views on fibre in the diet, see H. C. Trowell and D. P. Burkitt, eds, *Western Diseases, their Emergence and prevention* (1981).

[14] G. Tweedale, *At the Sign of the Plough: Allen and Hanbury and the British Pharmaceutical Industry, 1715–1990* (1990), p. 145; the quotation is from the company's *Daily Mail* advertisements.

[15] Tweedale, *Allen and Hanbury*, p. 148.

Plate 5.1 Dietary supplements began to be sold for their vitamin contents. Cod-liver oil was advertised as containing vitamins A and D from 1924 onwards. Its taste remained a problem for consumers until Allen and Hanbury's Haliborange was marketed in 1934. Imitations followed, such as Crookes Laboratories' Halycitrol in 1935, which contained orange juice and glucose. (Reproduced by permission of *The Chemist and Druggist* and the British Library BL Newspaper Library 316)

and new vitamin syntheses were achieved, Allen & Hanbury offset their declining fortunes by introducing Haliborange in 1934 as a means of removing the fishy taste of cod-liver oil and creating a dietary supplement containing vitamins A, C and D.[16] Dietary supplements and patent foods became big business in the 1930s with products such as Glaxo's Ostermilk being available at cut prices in infant welfare centres from 1932, a marketing ploy followed unwillingly by Allen & Hanbury for their Allenbury products in 1934. By 1935 the Glaxo brand had become so well known, and so important to Nathan's, that the vitamin and health-food business was organized into a separate subsidiary company, Glaxo Laboratories Ltd at Greenford, Middlesex. Other firms entered the market: Burroughs Wellcome began to supply Ryzamin-B, a 'rice polishings concentrate' which promised 'health and vitality', while Norwegian Cod Liver Oil offered 'the direct road to Nature's fount of health'. The fishy taste of cod-liver oil led Lecimel and SevenSeas to claim that their products were more palatable than their competitors'.[17] Even Cadbury's were attracted to health foods and began producing a diabetic chocolate in 1938.

Food retailing

For multiple retailers in the food trades, the interwar years were a time of expansion. They had begun largely as provision merchants but as they expanded the number of their shops and the range of their products, the former distinction between the provision merchant and the grocer who sold dry goods became blurred. Sainsbury's, for example, already had 123 branches in 1919 and expansion, particularly in the new suburban areas linked to London by the extension of the underground railway, came at a rate of three shops annually. Their organization was unaltered since before the outbreak of war. In a typical shop there were six departments: groceries, bacon and hams, cooked meats, fresh meat, dairy products, and poultry, game and rabbits. Even as late as the 1920s, the traditional trade of 'breaking bulk' was still important. Sainsbury's customers could expect to have their own containers filled with vinegar or mustard pickles; cheese and butter were still sold from the barrel and wrapped for each customer. Such practices made the retail market for food seem largely unchanged from pre-1914 days but Sainsbury's was by

[16] Ibid., pp. 151–3.
[17] *The Chemist and Druggist*, 6 January 1938. See S. M. Horrocks, 'Nutrition science and the food industry in Britain, 1920–1990', in A. P. den Hartog, ed., *Food Technology, Science and Marketing: European Diet in the Twentieth Century* (Phantassie, East Lothian, 1995), pp. 7–18.

no means typical of the shops to be found in urban industrial working-class areas in the Midlands or north of England or Scotland. A bigger chain than Sainsbury's was Lipton's, operating 460 shops in England and Wales and 100 in Scotland by the mid-1920s. The retail co-operative societies were also entrenched in working-class areas as competitors to the 'tea stores' and 'dairies' – the multiple-outlet provision merchants based on cheap tea and margarine. Built up by Thomas Lipton, George Watson (Maypole Dairies) and others, by 1914 they had largely become vehicles for the wholesale margarine trade of the Dutch producers Jurgens, who sold to the Home and Colonial Stores and Shepherd's Dairies, and Van den Bergh's, who supplied Pearks', Meadows' and Keeloma.[18] The biggest margarine vendor was Maypole Dairies, which bought its supplies from the Danish company, Monsted's. During the early 1920s, Maypole came close to collapse. It had restricted its retail trade to just four commodities and the weakness of the margarine market in Britain caused its downfall. Maypole's profits fell from over £1M in 1919 to £0.25M in 1924, at which point Sir George Watson, the principal shareholder, agreed to sell Maypole to the Home and Colonial Stores and thus, indirectly, to Anton Jurgens.[19] Lipton's, like Maypole, was also in difficulties: Thomas Lipton was ageing but refused to retire; in 1927, Van den Bergh's bought 25 per cent of Lipton's shares and control passed out of his hands.

This consolidation of the multiple retailers in the hands of the Dutch margarine producers meant that the housewife in the 1920s was almost certain to buy some of her provisions and groceries from them unless she shopped only at the Co-op. However, although the four big multiples, Maypole, Home and Colonial, Meadow's and Lipton's had some 43 per cent of the food market between them in 1921, by 1927 their market share was down to 20 per cent. Nevertheless, the Dutch margarine manu-facturers now had a better foothold in the British provisions market and were no longer reliant on one commodity only. This enabled them to manipulate prices. When Jurgens' and Van den Bergh's raised the mini-mum price of margarine to 8d per pound in the 1920s, they prevented a price war and protected the profits of the small shopkeeper at the housewife's expense. With the cheapest Australian butter retailing at 1s 8d per pound, margarine could no longer be undercut by cheap 'colonial butter' as it had been in the 1890s. In one sense, to call Jurgens and Van den Bergh 'Dutch manufacturers' ignores the local processing of edible

---

[18] See C. H. Wilson, *The History of Unilever*, Vol. II (1954), ch. VII, for the division of the market between Jurgens' and Van den Bergh's companies. Jurgens finally took over Home and Colonial in 1920. Van den Bergh's, technically a British company since 1896, also supplied margarine to Lipton's before 1914.
[19] Ibid., ch. XV.

oils. By the 1920s, Lever Brothers had a major plant at Bromborough in Cheshire, Maypole's supplies came from Monsted's factory at Southall in Middlesex, Jurgens was refining edible oil at the Olympia Mill, Selby, as well as Purfleet in Essex, and Van den Bergh, while still importing large quantities from the Netherlands, had a major oil refinery at Fulham. Another newcomer to the high street was MacFisheries, a chain of retail fishmongers created by W. H. Lever after the failure of his attempt to develop the economy of the Outer Hebrides. MacFisheries was backed by supplies from subsidiaries that Lever had bought, namely the Aberdeen Steam Trawling Company, Helford Oysterage and the fish-canning business of Angus Watson & Co, Newcastle.[20]

Public analysts continued to put pressure on retailers to reform their practices throughout the interwar period. The early food standards' legislation had been directed against the independent food retailer in British towns, particularly the small-scale trader. The proprietors of back-street and corner shops, market stallholders and retail dairymen found themselves before the magistrates for various offences generally associated with attempts to extend the amount or marketable life of various commodities. Although retail food marketing was being transformed by the chains of multiple retailers, in some trades – such as fishmongers and butchers – the traditional 'open shop' was still in use where food was displayed to passers-by without the protection of windows. While the public analysts mounted a campaign against the open shop during the 1920s, the grocery trade was characterized increasingly by the standardization and pre-packaging of commodities formerly sold loose, such as tea, sugar, butter and margarine. Branded food products had been advertised since the nineteenth century in newspapers, on billboards and at railway stations; in the twentieth century advertisements appeared in theatres and cinemas and on commercial radio stations. Branded food products were changing the nature of food retailing. The manufacturer's price had become more significant than any element of skill in presenting and selling goods that the shopkeeper might possess. Instead, the small shopkeeper had to accept that his most important attribute was to provide the variety of competing brands that consumers might demand in response to the food manufacturers' advertisements.

Packaging and new products

The growing sale of branded and pre-packed foods meant that the quality of food became the concern of the factory bakers, biscuit manu-

---

[20] Wilson, *Unilever*, Vol. I, pp. 261–2.

facturers, confectioners, suppliers of jams, pickles, sauces, relishes and condiments that appeared on the retailers' shelves. Food quality became associated with the trademarks of the leading brands – Cadbury, Rowntree, Huntley and Palmer, Tate & Lyle. For those supplying goods 'loose' or unwrapped, such as bakers and butchers, quality was more difficult. It was therefore the food manufacturer, rather than the individual retailer, who became involved with product standards. Once foods were sold wrapped, packaged, or supplied in containers such as bottles or cans, the manufacturers had some degree of control over the quality of their product as it reached the consumer. During the 1920s almost all canned foods were imported already canned, since the technology was predominantly American. Not until G. H. Williamson & Sons Ltd of Worcester installed American semi-automatic can-making machinery in 1927 did any significant production occur in Britain. Williamson's produced 4M cans in 1928 and their output had risen to 24M in 1930. Through a merger with the American company Continental Can in the same year, Metal Box began 'open-top' can-making and erected a new plant at Perrywood near Worcester. This 'open-top' production made containers to be filled and closed at the canneries.[21] During the 1930s the major buyers of cans were the large-scale processors of milk and cream, vegetables and fruit. United Dairies, the Co-operative Wholesale Society and General Milk Products (packers of Carnation Milk) were large customers of Metal Box. Vegetable-canning was limited mainly to processed peas developed by Batchelor's of Sheffield. Like the milk processors, Batchelor's, Lincolnshire Canners, Wisbech Produce, United Canners and Beaulah each spent more than £50,000 a year on open-top cans. Smaller purchases were made by Libby's, Chivers, Hartley, H. J. Heinz, Ambrosia, Express Dairy and Oxo.[22] The development of cellophane in the 1930s was also important as a new material for wrapping dry groceries and cigarettes.

The new products of the American firms that entered the British food market – including those from names like Heinz and Kellogg – accentuated the tendency to wrap or package food. Kellogg introduced Corn Flakes and All Bran to the British breakfast table in 1922. Rice Krispies followed in 1929 but it was not until 1938 that Kellogg began to manufacture its products at Trafford Park, Manchester. Other American firms had begun to manufacture in Britain earlier: Quaker opened a plant at Ware in Hertfordshire in 1920 and built a factory at Southall, Middlesex, in 1936. In 1925 a subsidiary of the Canadian Shredded Wheat Company began production of 'Welgar' shredded wheat at Welwyn Garden City. Weetabix Ltd began manufacturing at Burton Latimer,

[21] W. J. Reader, *Metal Box A History* (1976), pp. 45–59.
[22] Ibid., pp. 70–1.

Northamptonshire, in 1932.[23] Thus, by the 1930s, these American firms and a number of large British manufacturers – Associated Biscuit Manufacturers, United Biscuits, Nevill's, Garfield Weston, the British Sugar Corporation, Tate & Lyle, Unilever[24] and Vestey's – were becoming important suppliers to the food retailers. For bread, ready-to-eat breakfast cereals, biscuits, sugar, chocolate confectionery, margarine and frozen meat, the dominant position of a small number of firms had the effect of imposing rigidities upon the food market in much the same way as oligopolies developed generally in British industry during the interwar years. The new products were part of the symbiotic relationship between the food industry and the consumer. From the 'flapper', who 'loves chocolate creams and me' in the 1920s to new housewives eager to buy their food materials 'in the nearest possible stage to table-readiness', time-saving was the new attraction stressed by advertisers:

> the complicated processes of making custard caramel, blanc-mange, jelly, and other puddings and sweets, were reduced to a single short operation by the use of prepared powders. Porridge had once been the almost universal middle-class breakfast food. It now no longer took twenty minutes to cook. Quick Quaker Oats reducing the time to two: but even so, cereals in the American style, eaten with milk, began to challenge porridge and bacon and eggs in prosperous homes.

As the new food-processing factories proliferated in southern England in the 1930s – close to the areas of new housing and new industries, where the standard of living for the middle classes was rising – more new products appeared in the shops in bottles and especially in tins:

> almost every kind of domestic and foreign fruit, meat, game, fish, vegetable could be bought, even in country groceries. Foodstuffs that needed no tin-opener were also gradually standardized: eggs, milk, and butter were graded and guaranteed and greengrocers began selling branded oranges and bananas.[25]

One marked growth field was branded confectionery. Although Cadbury's Dairy Milk and Bournville plain chocolate bars originated before 1914, confectionery brands proliferated in the interwar years.

---

[23] See E. J. T. Collins, 'The "consumer revolution" and the growth of factory foods: changing patterns of bread and cereal-eating in Britain in the twentieth century', in Oddy and Miller, *Modern British Diet*, pp. 33–6.

[24] See Wilson, *Unilever*, Vol. II, Book III, ch. I. Unilever was created in 1929 from Lever Brothers and the Margarine Union (Margarine Unie N.V.) which had been formed by Anton Jurgens and Van den Bergh's Margarine Ltd.

[25] Graves and Hodge, *Long Week-end*, pp. 40, 171–2.

Cadbury's Milk Tray, which had been introduced in 1915 in bulk packages supplied to shopkeepers, became available in half-pound (227g) and pound (454g) boxes. In the 1920s and 1930s, Cadbury brought out its Flake (1920), Crème Eggs (1923), Fruit and Nut (1928), Crunchie (1929), Whole Nut (1933), and Roses Chocolates (1938). Cadbury Brothers merged with J. S. Fry & Sons, a Bristol chocolate producer whose product lines included Fry's Chocolate Cream and Fry's Turkish Delight. The falling costs of raw materials, transport and production in the interwar years coupled with extensive advertising brought prices down. Chocolate bars, chocolate biscuits and snack biscuits became generally available for eating on journeys, for picnics and on holidays – occasions when eating was for pleasure and enjoyment rather than of necessity – as well as special treats such as Christmas boxes of chocolates and Easter eggs.[26] The novelty and excitement prompted by these new foods were often related to successful marketing campaigns. The 1930s saw a battle between Cadbury's and Ovaltine for the bedtime drink market in which Wander Ltd, the producers of Ovaltine, skilfully exploited commercial radio advertising available in Britain through the powerful Radio Luxembourg transmitter and its Ovaltineys' club for children. Cadbury's produced a special cocoa tin for children containing miniature animals and backed by its Cococubs' club and magazine. It too sponsored radio programmes in the 1930s.[27] These and other business techniques developed by the best-run food manufacturers and catering firms were a significant aspect of the new technology in the food industry. Mass-production systems, including standardization through close attention to portion control, and cost reduction, were important in firms such as J. Lyons & Co which were engaged in the growing catering business and the leisure industry, and depended upon developing a mass market for their products. Catering for large events such as the British Empire Exhibition at Wembley in 1924, which 17M people visited, demonstrated the scale of Lyons' operations.

Commercial catering

As the interwar years began, the fish-and-chip shop was the most widespread catering outlet known to the public. Fish-and-chip shops remained small-scale undertakings; multiple branches did not develop in the interwar years. Despite the interwar depression in some manufacturing districts, fish-and-chip shops were seen as a lucrative venture

---

[26] Cadbury Ltd, *The Story of Cadbury Limited* (Birmingham, 1997).
[27] Communication from the Information and Library Service, Cadbury Trebor Bassett Ltd.

especially if located close to public houses or cinemas. Where seating was provided the eating-in trade was mainly at midday and during the early evenings. However, fish-and-chip shops also sold food wrapped in paper for consumption outside the shop, usually with an outer wrapping of newspaper for insulation. In poorer districts fish-and-chip shops catered only for a take-away trade. While purchases might be taken home to eat, much was eaten outdoors. Fish and chips were eaten in parks or at the seaside by holidaymakers, but in everyday life people ate from the open paper wrappings while walking along the street. After public houses closed at 10.30 p.m., there was a late demand for fish and chips to eat in the streets, particularly at weekends, though many shops closed on Sundays, due possibly to religious sentiment in some neighbourhoods, but supported by those fish friers who wanted to reduce their working hours. From 1937 all fish-and-chip shops were closed on Sundays except for those in holiday resorts during the summer season.[28]

Although fish and chips were attracting cinema-goers and motorists, as well as women shoppers in the 1930s, the teashop appealed to the more 'respectable' members of the working classes and lower-middle classes, who had grown up influenced by the temperance movement during the late Victorian period. By the 1920s, J. Lyons & Co had 250 teashops and three multi-floored Corner Houses in central London, which could each seat up to 3000 people.[29] Office workers took quick lunches at Lyons' or the ABC or Express Dairy teashops but it was also possible to eat breakfast or high tea in Lyons. The speed and efficiency of operations led Lyons' waitresses to be known as 'nippys'. Standardized portions, including cooked food, were supplied from a centralized base at Cadby Hall in Hammersmith, west London. Strict price and portion control meant that a lunch of roast beef and two vegetables was available for 10d (£0.04). At this price profits were almost negligible, and the profitability of Lyons' teashops declined during the 1930s. By 1939 food manufacturing – tea, coffee, bread, cakes, ice-cream and groceries – was more important than teashops.

Ice-cream and chilled milk

The First World War accelerated the decline of the natural ice trade and, despite a short recovery in the immediate postwar years, imports of natural ice had ceased by the end of the 1920s.[30] The extensive

[28] Walton, *Fish and Chips and the British Working Class*, pp. 84–6.
[29] See D. J. Richardson, 'J. Lyons and Co. Ltd: caterers and food manufacturers, 1894–1939', in Oddy and Miller, *Modern British Diet*, pp. 161–72.
[30] R. David, 'The Anglo-Norwegian ice trade', *Business History* (1995), p. 66, notes

growth of refrigeration capacity at sea and in the meat industry reduced the demand for natural ice. In the processed meat industry, Wall's, the sausage-makers, turned to ice-cream to make up for slack trade in sausages during the summer months. The mass production of ice-cream made it the first frozen food to enter working-class diets, following Wall's invention of the 'Stop-me-&-buy-one' tricycle early in the 1920s.[31] The limited extent to which electricity was available in working-class homes ruled out of the use of refrigerators, even if they could be afforded; any application of refrigeration in domestic kitchens was confined to the richest households. For ordinary people, the growth of entertainment outside the home in the interwar years, particularly at the cinemas, led to the expansion of ice-cream sales. Wall's began to supply refrigerators on hire to cinemas and sweet shops. By 1939, they supplied 15,000 shops and had a turnover of about £1.5M.[32] For home consumption, the firm operated 8,500 tricycles on the streets and had 136 depots all over the country to supply them. Prompted by the success of Wall's, Lyons entered the ice-cream trade. In the last peacetime year, Lyons produced 3.5M gallons (15.9M litres) of ice-cream for sale. On a smaller scale, the Forte family catering business began to open 'ice-cream parlours' in the 1930s. Following an initial success at Weston-super-Mare, they opened others at holiday centres in southern England – Weymouth, Bournemouth and Brighton. The promotional work of the Milk Marketing Board from 1933 onwards suggested other opportunities for leisure catering. The Board was under pressure from Walter Elliot, the Minister of Agriculture, to increase milk sales; his officials informed the Milk Marketing Board that

> he would welcome evidence that the Milk Board was trying to solve the problem of surplus milk in a manner which would, on the one hand, avoid expenditure from the Exchequer, and, on the other, involve no restrictions upon foreign and oversea (*sic*) Dominion supplies. . . . Because the present state of affairs in which thousands of infants are short of milk in a land flowing with milk is nothing short of a disgraceful cynical scandal.[33]

that the journal *Cold Storage and Produce Review* ceased to report on the natural ice trade from 1930.

[31] Wilson, *Unilever*, Vol. I, p. 5. W. J. Reader noted that the first tricycles were used in Acton in 1922 to distribute the output from a small ice-cream plant imported from the USA earlier that year. See Monopolies and Mergers Commission, *Ice Cream and Water Ices* (Cmnd. 7632, 1979), para. 63. The tricycles had an insulated box in front of the rider chilled by dry ice (solid CO_2).

[32] Monopolies and Mergers Commission (MMC), *Ice Cream and Water Ices*, para. 64.

[33] PRO, JV7/82 Milk Marketing Board, W. P. Hildred to S. Foster, General Manager, 17 July 1935

Plate 5.2 Street food-selling was modernized in the 1920s by the Wall's ice-cream tricycle, often ridden by an ex-serviceman complete with medals. It also provided home deliveries. (Reproduced by permission of Birds Eye Wall's Ltd. Image courtesy of The Advertising Archives)

In June 1935, the Board had written to the Town Clerks of all the major south coast resorts from Margate round to Weston-super-Mare in an attempt to promote summer milk consumption, suggesting that 'it is felt that the provision of milk bars in suitable places, would be of assistance'.[34] The initial success of Hugh Macintosh's first Black and White milk bar in Fleet Street led Charles Forte to open the Meadow Milk Bar in Regent Street, London in 1935 and Woolworth to install its first milk bar in its new Oxford Street store. London acquired its Moo Cows, its Laughing Cows and its City Milk Bars; Edinburgh had United Milk Bars and Liverpool its Milk Cocktail Bars. Department stores in the provinces were quick to follow. By the end of 1935 there were twenty-seven milk bars open in Britain, 587 by the end of 1936 and 1,010 by the end of 1937. London had the largest number – over 127 by the end of 1936 – followed by Lancashire and Yorkshire. Despite the prosperity of the Midlands' car towns, milk bars were not popular there. In Glasgow, the idea of children's milk bars was employed in 1937 to provide children between the ages of 2 and 15 with milk during the summer school holidays. After four were opened with remarkable initial success, all closed in September. The Scottish Milk Marketing Board described it as a 'costly' experiment and concluded that milk drinks were a drain on 'the meagre family purse'. Housewives' money could be better 'spent on more filling foods' – an echo of pre-1914 middle-class moralizing on the diets of the poor. At the outbreak of war in 1939, there were fourteen Black and Whites and five Forte's milk bars in London and southeast England,[35] but the biggest chain was in Woolworth's shops followed by British Home Stores. Marks and Spencer expressed interest but had only four milk bars open in August 1938. Initially, the Black and Whites were 'remarkably bare' and sold only milk drinks, ice-cream but 'no sundaes and no other food'. By contrast, Charles Forte's staff made soups and ice-cream, cut sandwiches and baked cakes in the basement of a warehouse in Percy Street, in London's West End, which supplied all his branches. By the end of 1937, there were 384 milk bars operating solely to sell milk products, to which the Milk Marketing Board supplied its 1938 recipes for Sicilian Shakes, Chocolate Banana Creams, Hollywood Shakes and Mint Juleps.

New low-temperature technology

Although milk bars provided a new market for Drikold, Imperial Chemical Industries' brand of dry ice, the interwar period saw little

---

[34] PRO, JV7/116, circular letter dated 7 June 1935.
[35] Charles Forte, *Forte: The Autobiography of Charles Forte* (1986), pp. 30–40; see also annual progress reports in the Milk Marketing Board's file JV7/116 at the PRO.

further use of refrigeration. During the 1930s, the initial use of blast-freezing by Smethurst's of Grimsby produced frozen fish for commercial caterers and institutions but Smethurst's did not attempt to enter the retail trade.[36] The limited development of frozen-food products in interwar Britain depended upon attempts to introduce the quick-freezing process which Clarence Birdseye had developed for the General Foods Corporation in the USA. General Foods had set up a subsidiary company called Frozen Foods Corporation Inc, which sold the new products under the brand name of Birds Eye. Although ICI had spent £10,000 trying out quick-freezing early in the 1930s, and Lever Brothers and Unilever's Board of Directors had discussed Birds Eye's products in 1933, only MacFisheries was interested.[37] Birds Eye products, therefore, were unknown in Britain until an American, Robert Ducas, chairman of Winget Ltd, a firm of engineers at Rochester, Kent, began to take an interest in them. In 1938, Ducas persuaded Chivers and Sons, the Cambridgeshire fruit-canners and jam-makers, to experiment with an American plate-freezer at their Huntingdon factory. Successful results led to the formation of Frosted Foods Ltd in June 1938, to develop Birds Eye frozen-food products in the United Kingdom.[38] General Foods owned most of the capital and the patents for the technology, but Robert Ducas was managing director, and Winget Ltd, guided by American engineers, began to make quick-freezing equipment. It was decided that the marketing of Birds Eye products would be a specialized operation and the responsibility of a separate company, jointly owned between Frosted Foods and Chivers. Birds Eye Foods Ltd was formed in August 1938 to market and distribute all goods under the Birds Eye brand name except fish which, in 1940, was allocated to MacFisheries on a royalty basis.[39]

Economic policy and international trade

Free trade was abandoned in 1931 when Britain left the gold standard. However, when protection finally came it excluded food, though the

[36] W. J. Reader, *Birds Eye: The Early Years* (Walton on Thames, 1963), pp. 2–3.
[37] Ibid., p. 4. Between 1929 and 1952, the full name of the company was Lever Brothers and Unilever Ltd. Thereafter, it became Unilever Ltd.
[38] C. Wilson, *Unilever, 1945–1965* (1968), p. 171. Although quick-freezing techniques pioneered by Clarence Birdseye in the 1920s and 1930s were expensive and still somewhat experimental, Unilever began discussing frozen foods with him as early as 1933. Dr Reader believed that the Directors might have been considering frozen foods as early as 1929.
[39] Reader, *Birds Eye*, pp. 5–6. Frosted Foods held 55 per cent of the capital and Chivers 40 per cent, with the remaining 5 per cent provided by outside sources.

Minister of Agriculture had powers under the Horticultural Products (Emergency Duties) Act, 1931, to restrict imports of fresh fruit, flowers and vegetables.[40] Nevertheless, wheat, maize, meat and animals were all free of tariffs under the Import Duties Act of 1932. Instead, the Agricultural Marketing Act, 1931, was used to create marketing boards for a range of home-grown produce, notably milk, bacon, potatoes and hops. A subsequent act, the Agricultural Marketing Act, 1933, allowed for quotas to be imposed on food imports. Some change in the source of imports resulted: less came from foreign countries and more from the British Empire. In 1933, 50 per cent of imports originated in the Empire compared with 38 per cent in 1927 to 1929.[41] Falling prices for agricultural produce in the early 1930s failed to stimulate agriculture into producing more of the nation's food. Although the Milk Marketing Boards (for England and Wales and Scotland) established milk prices at a level that encouraged output, it was difficult to increase consumption, even though subsidized school-milk schemes and low-priced milk for mothers in distressed areas were introduced.[42] Farmers along main roads were unable to resist the spread of housing during the building boom of the 1930s. By the late 1930s, the concept of creating a green belt around major urban areas was introduced. However, as suburban sprawl and ribbon development continued, the distinction between town and countryside became blurred, as building plots removed land from food production. Some additional stability to agriculture was given by the reorganization of the sugar industry in 1936, which extended the sugar-beet subsidy in arable areas, while a Wheat Commission and a Cattle (later Livestock) Commission were introduced to handle other subsidies.[43] The attempted organization of the agricultural industry was in line with the corporatism of the interwar years and, however limited its achievements in improving farmers' incomes, provided some framework for emergency planning. Despite the progress in food technology and food processing, the underlying reliance on food imports meant that governments in the late 1930s had no policy that prepared agriculture and the food industry for war. The Agriculture Act, 1937, envisaged the conversion of grassland to arable in the event of war but failed to

---

[40] Mowat, *Britain Between the Wars*, p. 415; see Murray and Cohen, *Britain's Food Imports*, Appendix II, for the full list of import regulations.

[41] Murray and Cohen, *Britain's Food Imports*, p. 92. The Empire included the Irish Free State.

[42] Mowat, *Britain Between the Wars*, pp. 438–9; Pollard, *British Economy, 1914–67*, pp. 139–41. The Agricultural Marketing Act, 1931 was followed by a Reorganization Commission for milk. The Milk Marketing Board was obliged to find a market for all milk offered for sale by producers. It was therefore required to engage in commercial enterprises. See the PRO Guide to Class JV.

[43] Winnifrith, *Ministry of Agriculture, Fisheries and Food*, pp. 25 6.

establish any policy of home food production. Moreover, the expression of confidence that Britain would not starve in the event of war made in Mr Chamberlain's speech at Kettering, in July 1938, put on one side any plans to increase home production of food until war should be declared.[44]

[44] See Whetham, *Agrarian History, 1914–1939*, p. 328; PRO, MAF152/168. Dr Edith Whetham's criticism of the Prime Minister was also apparent in her unpublished volume *Food Production*, completed in July 1946, for the Official History of the United Kingdom at War: 1939–1945. Marginal notes indicate that her critical views influenced the decision not to publish it as Volume III of the official *History of Food*.

6

THE QUESTION OF MALNUTRITION BETWEEN THE WARS

When T. S. Ashton wrote his essay 'The treatment of capitalism by historians' in Hayek's *Capitalism and the Historians*, he regarded the 'hungry thirties' as a novel and unwelcome epithet for the years before the Second World War.[1] Ashton's fears that the 1930s would become labelled in this way were borne out when Branson and Heinemann chose 'Eating or not Eating' as one of their themes and later when the *History Workshop Journal* took up the question in the 1980s.[2] However, this social concern about the diet of the 1930s has eluded close analysis. The purpose of this chapter is to attempt a quantitative evaluation using contemporary data, even though this raises problems of a conceptual nature. It is difficult today, let alone in the 1930s, to agree upon a standard by which health might be measured; in consequence, the use of the term 'malnutrition' is fraught with difficulties, since it may mean over-nutrition as well as under-nutrition, for which it is commonly used. When used in place of under-nutriton, it may mean a diet that failed to provide people with sufficient amounts of various foods to maintain normal levels of physical activity and, in addition, failed to provide normal patterns of development in children and young persons or the maintenance and repair of tissue in adults. This is not necessarily an extreme condition characterized by starvation or sterility or overt signs of ill-health. However, diets restricted in variety, as when the percentage of energy from carbohydrate sources such as starchy foods rises above 60 to 70 per cent of the total energy value, may be defective – even if only marginally so. Any search for malnutrition in interwar Britain has to be done against the background that the food supply appeared to provide adequate resources for the population in aggregate terms. Table

---

[1] T. S. Ashton, 'The treatment of capitalism by historians', in F. A. Hayek, *Capitalism and the Historians* (1954), p. 55.
[2] Noreen Branson and Margot Heinemann, *Britain in the Nineteen Thirties* (1971), ch. 14; see also *History Workshop Journal*, 13 (spring 1982), pp. 110–29 and 19, (spring 1985), pp. 105–27; and *Journal of Contemporary History*, 23 (1988), pp. 445–64.

Table 6.1 Estimates of Britain's food supply expressed as weekly food consumption per head of the population, 1920 to 1938

Date	Bread (lb.)	Potatoes (lb.)	Sugar (oz.)	Fats (oz.)	Meat (lb.)	Milk (pt.)
1920–23	5.8	4.0	23	13	2.0	3.3
1924–28	5.6	3.3	28	14	2.1	3.4
1929–33	5.8	3.3	27	15	2.2	3.3
1934–38	5.4	3.0	27	16	2.2	3.4

Table 6.2 Estimates of Britain's food supply expressed as daily nutrient intake available per head of the population, 1920 to 1938

Date	Energy value (kcal)	Energy value (kj)	Protein (g)	Fat (g)	CHO (g)	Iron (mg)	Calcium (g)
1920–23	2,905	12,155	87	107	398	13.8	0.57
1924–28	3,020	12,636	90	115	408	14.1	0.59
1929–33	3,115	13,033	93	122	415	14.5	0.60
1934–38	3,080	12,887	92	126	399	14.4	0.61

6.1 shows that supplies kept pace with population growth. Sugar, fats, meat and milk were all in excess of the levels of consumption before 1914, though the milk supply may not have been adequate. The nutrient analysis is shown in Table 6.2, and suggests that there was enough food available for an adequate diet to be eaten by everyone, though it should be noted that calcium levels were only marginally adequate. Faced with this evidence nutritionists found it difficult to impress on interwar governments that malnutrition could exist among the British people. It was even harder for politicians to accept. In his autobiography, John Boyd Orr wrote:

> Mr Kingsley Wood, the Minister of Health, asked me to come and see him. He wanted to know why I was making such a fuss about poverty when, with old age pensions and unemployment insurance, there was no poverty in the country. This extraordinary illusion was genuinely believed by Mr Wood who held the out-of-date opinion that if people were not actually dying of starvation there could be no food deficiencies.[3]

---

[3] Lord Boyd Orr, As I Recall (1966), p. 115.

Science with a social conscience

One factor that must be considered in this context is how the new knowledge of nutrition had developed in the interwar years. British scientists, notably Frederick Gowland Hopkins, Harriet Chick and Edward Mellanby, were among the leading workers in the discovery and synthesis of vitamins. By 1924, the Medical Research Council (MRC) had published enough evidence to show the role of vitamins in the diet.[4] Two years later, another MRC report by Dr H. Corry Mann, *Diets for Boys During the School Age*, showed publicly how the new advances in knowledge could be applied.[5] This created not only a climate of scientific excitement in the 1920s but also produced among socially conscious scientists – especially those who had served in the war – a concern that the new knowledge should be put to remedial use. Indeed, the 1920s began with a sense of hope that the limitations in the physique of the nation's manpower revealed by the Military Service Acts might be improved. Scientists felt that science had been of service to the state during the Great War.[6] It became accepted wisdom among scientists that their advice to plough up land for cereal production had been the correct policy. By contrast, it seemed that the German scientists' policy to concentrate on meat production had been a failure and left Germany short of food in 1918. The postwar conversion of the Medical Research Committee of the Department of Scientific and Industrial Research into the Medical Research Council, in 1920, seemed to present increased opportunities for scientists to diagnose ill-health and the effects of inadequacies in the nation's diet.[7] The creation of the Ministry of Health out of the Local Government Board appeared to offer the opportunity of a new administrative structure that could warn the government and alert Medical Officers of Health (MOHs) and general practitioners of dangers to public and personal health. George Newman, who in the years before 1914 had shown himself to be one of the outstanding epidemiologists of his generation, now held the key position of Chief Medical Officer to both the Board of Education and the Ministry of Health.[8]

---

[4] MRC, Special Report Series, No. 38, *Report on the Present State of Knowledge Concerning Accessory Food Factors (Vitamins)* (1919).
[5] MRC Special Report Series, No. 105 (1926). Dietary supplements of milk or butter at a boarding-school for boys produced the largest increments in growth.
[6] See *The Food Supply of the United Kingdom*, 1916; Ministry of Food, Committee on Rationing, 1917; Committee of Imperial Defence, Standing Sub-Committee on Manpower in a Future War.
[7] The Haldane Committee's report suggested that government policy should be informed by research. See Ministry of Reconstruction, *Report of the Machinery of Government Committee*, PP 1918 (Cd.9230), XII.
[8] See M. A. E. Hammer, 'The birth of a nation's health; the life and work of George

The governments of the 1920s and 1930s did not retain the crisis mentality that had developed during the First World War. Rising unemployment in the 1920s was accompanied by limitation on public expenditure. Scientists employed in Whitehall reported a brief flurry of activity in the autumn of 1921 in calculating the energy values of foodstuffs, but the lack of epidemiological work by the Ministry of Health led the MRC to establish a Nutrition Committee in 1922 with a view to undertaking a major dietary survey.[9] The progress of the MRC's plan was limited by the tightness of its budget and the fact that both the Council and its Secretary, Sir Walter Fletcher, regarded the commitment to vitamin research by its Accessory Food Factors Committee as sacrosanct. At the same time, cuts in public expenditure removed the pressure from Newman to undertake survey work. Indeed, Newman, with his new status, lacked his former enthusiasm for fieldwork.[10] In this he was aided by Fletcher's caution and, in 1924, by Treasury intervention to try to prevent a duplication of research outlets. By then, a 'Concordat' had been reached between the Ministry of Health and the MRC that gave the initiative in epidemiological work to the Ministry. As it had only a small research budget and its preoccupations were overwhelmingly in the fields of local government, housing, national insurance and the poor law, the effect of the Concordat was to prevent any major dietary surveys from being carried out in England and Wales for the greater part of the interwar period.[11]

Attempts by the MRC to stimulate the Ministry of Health's interest in nutrition, or the application of nutritional knowledge to the Ministry of Health's community medicine programmes, had little effect, and it was a sense of growing frustration which produced the revolutionary proposal from Professor Edward Mellanby in 1927 that an independent board of nutrition be established to advise the government.[12] This was a rational

---

Newman to 1921', Ph.D. thesis, Cambridge, 1995 for the politics of Newman's appointment. Newman was a protégé of Robert Morant (and the Webbs).

[9] PRO, FD1/4367 (originally MRC 2100, part 1), 30 October 1921, M. Greenwood to Sir Walter Fletcher.

[10] PRO, FD1/4367. Greenwood to Fletcher: 'Newman ... seems to regard everything as a stunt.'

[11] PRO, FD1/1374 (originally MRC 1190, part 1). The agreement was signed by Sir Walter Fletcher for the MRC and Sir George Newman for the Ministry on 22 January 1924. The Concordat did not apply to Scotland since the Board of Health for Scotland was not a party to it. The term 'Concordat' was used in 1928 in the Report of the Research Coordination Sub-Committee of the Committee of Civil Research, Section IV, pp. 43–4.

[12] See *BMJ*, 8 October 1927, pp. 633–6. As chairman of the MRC's Committee for Accessory Food Factors, Mellanby was a central figure in the rapidly developing field of vitamin knowledge. See MRC, Special Report Series No.167, *Vitamins: A*

suggestion since various policy-making bodies in the 1920s had drawn on outside experts for nutritional advice rather than on the Ministry of Health, whose remit extended only to England and Wales. The research bottleneck was solved by the formation of the Empire Marketing Board in 1926 with a budget of £1M, a quarter of which was assigned to research. With this new source of funding, nutrition surveys began in 1927. The Research Sub-Committee of the Empire Marketing Board, chaired by Walter Elliot,[13] made grants available for Dr John Boyd Orr, the Director of the Rowett Research Institute, Aberdeen, to carry out nutritional surveys in seven Scottish towns. In the same year, the MRC financed a much more limited inquiry in St Andrews. The weekly food consumption revealed by the Empire Marketing Board surveys is shown in Table 6.3. The key to the seven-town survey was milk. The Empire Marketing Board was anxious to use the findings of Dr Corry Mann on the nutritive value of milk to increase consumption and thus stimulate British agriculture. It needed research into the existing levels of milk consumption on which to base its publicity campaign. For Orr and other members of the MRC Nutrition Committee, who had given up plans for a national survey of diets in favour of the more limited seven-town survey in Scotland, milk promotion was merely a lever to get into working-class homes, even if they had to confine their activities to Scotland to utilize Elliot's support and to avoid the Concordat with the Ministry of Health. Until Mellanby's criticism of the Ministry of Health's inactivity in 1927, the Ministry had made regular and somewhat platitudinous statements about nutrition. The air of social commitment which characterized Newman's first postwar report as Chief Medical Officer of the Board of Education[14] gave way, by 1923, to comparing the number of deaths from starvation (16) with those from being struck by lightning (11) or homicide (18).[15] 'An appreciable amount of under-nutrition' did exist, admitted Newman, but 'in so far as this result is a consequence of poverty alone, it lies beyond my province to discuss it, and without doubt poverty is the principal factor involved.' The need for variety in the diet and the special value of milk,

---

Survey of Present Knowledge, HMSO, 1932. It was Mellanby's work in 1918 that identified an anti-rachitic factor, later known as vitamin D.

[13] Walter Elliot, Conservative MP for Kelvinside from 1924, was at that time Parliamentary Under-Secretary of State for Scotland and formerly Parliamentary Under-Secretary of State for Health for Scotland, 1923–24 and 1924–25.

[14] Board of Education, *Annual Report of the Chief Medical Officer for 1920*, PP 1921 (Cmd.1522), XL. Even so, Newman was already claiming that 'deficiency diseases and rickets in their grosser manifestations are now fortunately comparatively rare in this country'.

[15] Ministry of Health, Annual Report of the Chief Medical Officer for 1923, *On the State of the Public Health* (1924), para. 347, p. 132.

The King's Chef, Mr. Cédard, with
Their Majesties' gracious consent, has supplied
to the Empire Marketing Board
the following recipe for

An

Empire Christmas Pudding

1 lb. of sultanas	AUSTRALIA
1 „ „ currants	AUSTRALIA
1 „ „ stoned raisins	SOUTH AFRICA
6 ozs. „ minced apple	CANADA
1 lb. „ bread crumbs	UNITED KINGDOM
1 „ „ beef suet	NEW ZEALAND
6 ozs. „ cut candied peel	SOUTH AFRICA
8 „ „ flour	UNITED KINGDOM
8 „ „ demerara sugar	WEST INDIES
4 eggs	IRISH FREE STATE
½ oz. ground cinnamon	CEYLON
⅓ „ ground cloves	ZANZIBAR
⅓ „ ground nutmegs	STRAITS SETTLEMENTS
1 pinch pudding spice	INDIA
1 tablespoonful brandy	CYPRUS
2 tablespoonfuls rum	JAMAICA
1 pint old beer	ENGLAND

S.W.G.1. Issued by the Empire Marketing Board and Printed for H.M. Stationery Office by Waterlow & Sons Limited, London, Dunstable and Watford.

Plate 6.1 The Empire Marketing Board, established in 1926, promoted British and Empire produce in an attempt to stimulate British agriculture. (See S. Constantine, *Buy and Build The Advertising Posters of the Empire Marketing Board* (1986).) (Public Record Office CO 956/602)

Table 6.3 Weekly food consumption per head in Scottish urban working-class families, 1928 to 1933

Survey	Number of families	Bread (lb.)	Potatoes (lb.)	Sugar (oz.)	Fats (oz.)	Meat (lb.)	Milk (pt.)
Seven Towns (1928)							
Glasgow	57	5.7	3.8	14	8.8	1.1	2.6
Greenock	132	5.3	3.3	16	8.6	1.0	2.2
Paisley	31	7.0	3.3	15	8.1	1.3	2.4
Edinburgh	112	5.4	3.2	14	8.1	1.1	1.7
Dundee	37	5.3	3.1	13	7.2	1.2	1.6
Aberdeen	150	4.1	3.6	17	7.6	1.2	3.3
Peterhead	104	4.1	4.5	17	5.9	0.8	2.6
Depression (1933)							
Aberdeen	66	3.6	2.2	16	4.2	1.0	2.6
Peterhead	49	4.4	2.9	15	4.0	0.8	1.9

fruit and green vegetables was repeatedly stressed, as was the need to educate housewives. No attempt to cost these recommendations took place, although the annual report for 1926 noted that the high cost of milk and green vegetables partly explained the very low levels of consumption. By the end of the 1920s, Newman's report was stressing the value of 'accessory elements in nutrition', namely 'fresh air, exercise, rest and moderation in all things'[16] as a means of defusing the scientists' claims that he must take account of 'accessory food factors' as vitamins were still commonly known. Rising levels of unemployment began to challenge the Ministry of Health's position. Evidence of poor health among schoolchildren, reported initially in 1927, began to accumulate from 1930 onwards and, during the second Labour government, Arthur Greenwood, as Minister of Health, may have put pressure on his officials to take more positive action. The nutritional analysis of the Empire Marketing Board surveys shown in Table 6.4 suggests that these diets in the 1920s were significantly better than many before 1914 in terms of energy value and most nutrients but, armed with the new knowledge of vitamins, the scientists were prepared to press the case for inadequacy. Even in Scotland, where milk consumption was greater than in England, calcium intakes were low. Unquestionably, the Ministry of Health felt itself to be under attack.

[16] Ministry of Health, AR of the CMO for 1928, *On the State of the Public Health* (1929), p. 197.

Table 6.4 Daily nutrient intake per head in Scottish urban working-class families, 1928 to 1933

Survey	Energy value (kcal)	(kj)	Protein (g)	Fat (g)	CHO (g)	Iron (mg)	Calcium (g)
Seven Towns (1928)							
Glasgow	2,669	11,167	80	74	414	15.0	0.62
Greenock	2,495	10,439	75	67	399	13.5	0.55
Paisley	2,900	12,134	87	77	464	16.0	0.61
Edinburgh	2,545	10,648	76	68	407	14.0	0.61
Dundee	2,409	10,079	72	67	379	13.1	0.53
Aberdeen	3,030	12,678	91	88	470	16.0	1.38
Peterhead	3,002	12,560	90	77	488	16.3	1.31
Depression (1933)							
Aberdeen	1,926	8,058	67	49	303	11.6	0.48
Peterhead	2,118	8,862	69	47	355	12.2	0.40

From the civil servants' perspective, fears of proliferating consultative bodies began to arise. The Economic Advisory Council (EAC) provided an obvious and apparently expanding threat.[17] The personnel of its Dietetics Committee – Major Walter Elliot; Sir Frederick Gowland Hopkins (President of the Royal Society); Professor E. P. Cathcart (Glasgow); Sir Walter Fletcher; and Dr J. B. Orr – were all scientists committed to implementing the new knowledge of nutrition. Previously their connexions had been through the MRC but via the EAC their ideas could reach Cabinet level. The Ministry of Health's response was to establish its own Advisory Committee on Nutrition in January 1931 under a medical statistician, Professor Major Greenwood, and to take care that it incorporated Gowland Hopkins, Cathcart and Mellanby. Sir Walter Fletcher, strongly critical of the Ministry of Health's inactivity, was thus outflanked. In a letter to Lord Dawson of Penn, Fletcher wrote:

You asked me about the new Nutrition Committee at the Ministry of Health. All I know is that Robinson last December told me he was setting up a 'Food Advisory Committee', composed of Hopkins, Mellanby, Cathcart, Mottram, Greenwood and another. I said I was glad indeed they were getting forward in that line, but could not see the point of his appointing almost exactly the

[17] The Committee of Civil Research (CCR) was formed in 1925 and established a Committee on Dietetics, which began investigations into the deficiencies of colonial pasture land in East Africa. A sub-committee was appointed to consider the medical questions of human nutrition that emerged during its work in Kenya. The CCR's work was transferred later to the EAC in 1930.

MORE THAN HALF THE CATCH IS SOLD AS FRIED FISH

Plate 6.2 In the summer of 1931, the Empire Marketing Board ran a campaign to encourage the eating of fish, using the slogan 'There's All the Health of the Sea in Fish'. (See Constantine, *Buy and Build*.) (Public Record Office CO 956/310)

same Committee as we had systematically at work. My own view is that the medical administrators have delayed inexcusably to use the abundant new knowledge that has been pouring out of the laboratories in the past fifteen years.[18]

The Greenwood Committee's purpose became apparent quite soon. At its third meeting in November 1931, it discussed as a matter of urgency the charge that 'the Ministry of Health has taken no steps, whether by administrative action or propaganda to make this knowledge [i.e. vitamins] available for the public advantage'. By 1932 the Committee had published two memoranda, one on *Diets in Poor Law Children's Homes* and the second, *The Criticism and Improvement of Diets*, which was directed towards Medical Officers of Health and introduced recommended dietary standards.[19] It seems surprising that the Ministry

[18] PRO, FD1/4369 (formerly MRC 2100/1, part 3). Letter dated 15 April 1931. Lord Dawson had just been appointed a member of the MRC. 'Robinson' was Sir Arthur Robinson, Permanent Secretary to the Ministry of Health. Fletcher's anger at Newman's failure to act and the complacency of his annual reports may be found in FD1/1375 (MRC 1190, Part 2).
[19] PRO, MH56/11 and MH56/15.

did not see the implications of this step immediately but it no doubt assumed that publications of this kind were read by administrators and trained professional workers rather than the general public. Indeed, when the Greenwood Committee stated that it cost 4s 6d a week to feed a child in a poor law home and further, that an adult man in sedentary work needed 3,000kcal (12,550kj) per day and 37g of protein from animal sources, they had little inkling of where this would lead during a time of economic distress. Belatedly, in 1933, the Greenwood Committee began to discuss some kind of nutritional advice for the general public, but nothing came of it.

The Hungry England debate

Despite the levels to which unemployment had risen at the beginning of the 1930s, the press had not made much of the obvious connexion between being out of work and its effects on the nutritional status of men and their families, though the term 'Hungry England' began to be used in 1932.[20] Reports of 'hunger-marchers' and their arrival in London appeared in the autumn of 1932, but it was a coroner's inquest on the wife of an out-of-work bricklayer in January 1933, during a cold and snowy period of the winter, which finally brought the debate out into the open in sensational terms. The *Daily Herald* reported the woman's death from pneumonia with the headline 'Heroic Mother Starves in Silence' and the coroner's comment: 'I should call it starving to have to feed nine people on £2 8s and pay the rent.' The case was taken up in the letters column of *The Week-end Review* under the heading 'Hungry England', on 4 February 1933. The flood of subsequent correspondence led the *Week-end Review* to establish a 'Committee of Inquiry' on 11 March 1933, which included the veteran statistician A. L. Bowley and Professor V. H. Mottram, despite the fact that Mottram was still a member of the Ministry of Health's Advisory Committee on Nutrition.[21] When the Committee of Inquiry's report appeared in the *Week-end Review*, on 1 April 1933, it was very moderate in tone but concluded that in some cases it would not be possible to achieve the Advisory Committee's recommendations on dietary standards with Public Assistance Committee allowances.

The Ministry of Health did not ask its Advisory Committee to comment on the Hungry England report until the end of July 1933.

---

[20] See A. F. Brockway, *Hungry England* (1932).

[21] V. H. Mottram was Professor of Physiology at King's College School of Household Science in the University of London. He was the principal author drafting the two memoranda published by the Advisory Committee on Nutrition.

However, the debate intensified as articles on malnutrition, particularly among schoolchildren, appeared in the *Proceedings of the Royal Society of Medicine, the Medical Officer* and the *Lancet*. Between July and October, the Committee drafted various comments that accepted the adequacy of the Hungry England report's calculations for adults, although differences of opinion began to emerge on the subject of children's diets. Greenwood, faced with a surprising degree of intransigence by members of his committee to whose academic reputations he felt he must defer, wrote to the Ministry that:

> There is not at present sufficient agreement among those whose experience gives them the right of judgement for it to be possible to advise the Ministry upon many of the problems submitted.

The Ministry had been prepared for this from the outset. In 1930, when planning the membership of its Nutrition Committee, Newman had been advised:

> It would, indeed, be easy to select a Committee the elements of which would neutralize one another, so that in our selection we shall have to take the risk, or such little risk as there is, of coming down on the side of those with a positive policy.[22]

With the dispute in the Advisory Committee on Nutrition still unresolved, the report of a British Medical Association (BMA) Nutrition Committee was published in the *British Medical Journal* in November 1933. This recommended that an 'average' man required 3,400kcal (14,225kj) per day and 50g of 'first-class protein' from animal sources. From the Ministry's point of view the report's appearance was 'highly tactless and inopportune'.[23] It brought about an immediate denial by Mr Geoffrey Shakespeare, the Parliamentary Under-Secretary to the Ministry of Health, since it 'threw doubt on the contention by the Ministry of Health that distress and poverty, brought about by unemployment, had not resulted in malnutrition'.[24] Further comments in the press, questions in the House of Commons and discussion on a BBC radio programme intensified the embarrassment that the BMA report created.

In retaliation, the Ministry of Health sent out a circular to Medical Officers of Health reiterating the dietary standards of 3,000kcal (12,550kj) per day and 37g of first-class protein suggested in 1932 in *The Criticism and Improvement of Diets*. Although this should have constituted a rebuff to the BMA's committee on a professional level, the

---

[22] PRO, MH56/43. Dr Carnwarth to the Chief Medical Officer.
[23] PRO, MH56/40. Comment by Dr Magee.
[24] PRO, MH56/54.

heightened degree of sensitivity on both sides led Dr Anderson, Medical Secretary of the BMA, to send a public statement and letter to *The Times* in January 1934. A vigorous correspondence followed, which included the intimation of Professor Greenwood's resignation as Chairman of the Ministry's Advisory Committee, and led Lord Dawson to intervene to suggest a joint meeting of the two committees to examine their different recommendations. With hindsight, it might seem an inconsequential issue but the importance for the administrators in the 1930s was that the Ministry's standard for an adult male could be achieved for an outlay of 4s 10½d per week while that of the BMA required 5s 6d per week. After two joint meetings of the committees in February 1934, tempers had subsided enough for a jointly agreed sliding scale of energy requirements to be published. The scale ranged from 2,700 to 4,000kcal (11,295 to 16,735kj) per day, due to the insistence of Professor Cathcart who was eager to introduce a lower level of energy requirements. Reports in the press were generally critical, and on 11 July 1934 the Ministry of Health was pleased to accept Professor Greenwood's resignation. This seemed to be the best way of dissolving the Advisory Committee on Nutrition even though, on the preceding day – 10 July 1934 – the Permanent Secretary of the Ministry of Health, Sir Arthur Robinson, had received an advance copy of a Cabinet paper: 'The Need for Improved Nutrition of the People of Great Britain'. This was a report from the Economic Advisory Council's Sub-Committee on Scientific Research recommending that a new committee of the EAC should enquire into defective nutrition and poor physique, and discuss what form a national food policy should take. While the report originated from the MRC's concern at the lack of implementation of scientific research, it reflected Sir Maurice Hankey's fears that manpower resources in the armed services would be a problem if he succeeded in persuading the government to adopt rearmament policies.[25] Although Hankey obtained the support of Stanley Baldwin, then Lord President of the Council, Robinson and Newman were appalled at this new attack on the integrity of the Ministry of Health. They could obtain no support from Agriculture and Fisheries as the Minister, Walter Elliot, was strongly in favour of the EAC's policy. Only by prevailing upon Sir Warren Fisher at the Treasury that the EAC's proposed committee would mean duplication in government organization – a cardinal sin in the Civil Service's catechism – could they defend their position.[26] In doing so they were forced to establish a new Advisory Committee on Nutrition chaired by Lord Luke.

---

[25] PRO, CP131(34). Mellanby had become Secretary of the MRC in 1933 and Hankey was Cabinet Secretary. See S. W. Roskill, *Hankey Man of Secrets, Vol. III, 1931–1963* (1974), p. 92, for Hankey's contact with Mellanby.

[26] Despite the fact that Warren Fisher supported Hankey on rearmament, he would not flout Treasury policy on expenditure.

Food, health and income

The question of whether there was malnutrition in Britain in the 1930s is bound up with the publication of John Boyd Orr's *Food, Health and Income* in February 1936. When the book appeared it represented the frustrations of three men with radical views: Orr himself, E. M. H. Lloyd, a civil servant, and Walter Elliot, Minister of Agriculture and Fisheries. From his experience in carrying out nutrition surveys, Orr felt that sufficient evidence had been accumulated for the formulation of a government food policy. However, the events of 1933 to 1934 had tied Mellanby and Gowland Hopkins to the official viewpoint of the Ministry of Health while others who held positive views on the role of nutrition, such as Professor Mottram and Professor Crowden, had been denigrated through the Advisory Committee on Nutrition's dispute with the BMA's Nutrition Committee.[27] Orr's work in the 1920s had brought him into contact with E. M. H. Lloyd who, although a career civil servant, had avoided departmental ties and loyalties for most of the interwar period.[28] Lloyd became Secretary of the Empire Marketing Board's Research Committee in 1926 and, later, Secretary to the Market Supply Committee when it was formed after the Agricultural Marketing Act, 1933, came into operation. Lloyd's work made him aware of the problems faced by British agriculture during the final years of free trade and, once protection was adopted, led him to the view that governments rather than market forces must determine food supply.

From the late 1920s onwards, attempts to stimulate British agriculture concentrated on animal farming and, in particular, on the need for better marketing and distribution of milk. The milk promotion campaign of the late 1920s was limited in its effect and there remained the problem of disposing of surplus milk. To this end, Walter Elliot put the subsidized school milk scheme through the Cabinet in 1934 and allowed the Market Supply Committee to have almost complete independence. He permitted its work to expand beyond what had been originally envisaged under the Agricultural Marketing Act to include what both Lloyd and Orr believed to be necessary, namely a study in human food consumption.[29]

---

[27] Professor Crowden held a chair at the London School of Hygiene and Tropical Medicine.

[28] Lloyd's work in the First World War led him to publish *Experiments in State Control at the War Office and the Ministry of Food* in 1924.

[29] See Orr, *As I Recall*, p. 90. Elliot's contacts with Orr were much closer than is sometimes realized. They had been medical students at Glasgow University and first met (if Orr's memory is to be trusted) at an Officers' Training Corps camp organized by Professor E. P. Cathcart in 1908. After the war, Elliot had carried out research at the Rowett Research Institute in his parliamentary vacations and had been awarded

Thus, when the Ministry of Health's Advisory Committee on Nutrition was reconstructed in May 1935 under Lord Luke, the overlap with the Market Supply Committee's work was apparent at its first meeting in June. Lloyd was invited to join the Luke Committee and to chair a Food Consumption Statistics Sub-Committee. With remarkable speed, he drafted an interim report into food consumption at different income levels which the Luke Committee adopted in November 1935.[30] Opposition to this work began to develop within the Ministry of Health during the autumn and the decision was taken not to publish it. Despite that, once the General Election was over, Lloyd gave a paper summarizing the report to the Agricultural Economics Society in December 1935,[31] and a fuller version, complete with nutritional analysis, was published by Orr as *Food, Health and Income* in February 1936. Its impact had major repercussions.[32] Lloyd was transferred from the Market Supply Committee to the safer backwater of the Food (Defence Plans) Department of the Board of Trade[33] and from 1937 onwards both the Market Supply Committee and the Luke Advisory Committee on Nutrition became increasingly sterile bodies.

In other ways, *Food, Health and Income* forced the government's hand. Orr was able to obtain £15,000 for a much larger survey from the Carnegie Trust in which he could match food consumption patterns against clinical examination.[34] The case made by Orr was reinforced a few months later by the publication of Dr M'Gonigle's *Poverty and Public Health*.[35] Questions in the House of Commons led the Ministry of Labour to appoint its own Advisory Committee on Working-Class Expenditure in May 1936. Originally intended to acquire 'comprehensive data on the consumption of food by all sections of the working classes' for the use of the Ministry of Health, the Ministry of Labour took fright after *Food, Health and Income* appeared. They proposed to

a D.Sc. in 1922 for a 'Study in mineral metabolism with special reference to rickets and similar bone lesions in other animals and in the human'. During the later 1920s, Elliot helped Orr 's Directorship of the Rowett by personal gifts, by the introduction of potential sponsors and, as Chairman of the Empire Marketing Board's Research Committee, by providing grants for the Institute's work.

[30] PRO, MAF38/23, FCS 15, *Report of an Investigation into Food Consumption at Different Income Levels.*

[31] E. M. H. Lloyd, 'Food supplies and consumption at different income levels', *Journal of the Proceedings of the Agricultural Economics Society*, Vol. IV, 2 (April 1936).

[32] Its impact within government cannot be fully understood today as many of the Ministry of Health files have been weeded out.

[33] Lloyd's subsequent work was drawing up rationing schemes.

[34] See Rowett Research Institute, *Family Diet and Health in Pre-War Britain*, Carnegie UK Trust (Dunfermline, 1955), p. 10.

[35] G. C. M. M'Gonigle and J. Kirby, *Poverty and Public Health* (1936).

the Ministry of Health that the 'Advisory Committee [on Working-Class Expenditure] should not include any nutrition experts'.[36] Instead, in a memorandum to the Cabinet, they pointed out the need for a government inquiry:

> The results of various enquiries made by private investigators, however, applying to different periods and usually only to particular localities or selected sections of the working classes are already being utilized for the purposes of propaganda.[37]

In turn, the Ministry of Health finally decided to implement the Luke Committee's recommendation that an official dietary survey should be undertaken. Dissatisfied with the proposals of the Ministry of Labour's inquiry as being inadequate to permit a nutritional analysis, the Ministry of Health began a separate survey in 1937 to 1938.

Dietary surveys in the 1930s

The picture of working-class diet in Britain during the period of large-scale unemployment in the 1930s needs to be interpreted against this background of the changing knowledge of nutrition and the inertia of politicians and civil servants. Table 6.5 shows the weekly food consumption revealed by the various surveys, and Table 6.6 provides a daily nutritional analysis per head.

The 1,152 family budgets which formed the basis of *Food, Health and Income* were not part of a carefully collected survey but obtained in response to an enquiry 'from one of the main branches of the food industry'. The budgets were then arranged into six income groups of which 952 with incomes below £1 10s represented working-class families and 200 were from middle-class families. Orr's calculations of the nutritional value of the diets then formed the basis for his well-known conclusion that 'a diet completely adequate for health according to modern standards is reached only at an income level above that of 50 per cent of the population',[38] even though he found amongst the better-off working-class families diets with energy values of 2,900–3,100 kcals which were closely in accord with the Ministry of Health's recommended dietary standard of 3,000kcal per day. Additional evidence of the diets of the 1930s was provided by the later family

[36] PRO, MH79/345, 6 February 1936, Phillips (Ministry of Labour) to Chrystal (Ministry of Health).
[37] PRO, MH79/345.
[38] Orr, *Food, Health and Income* (2nd edn), p. 44.

Table 6.5 Weekly food consumption per head shown by dietary surveys in the 1930s

Survey	Number of families	Bread (lb.)	Potatoes (lb.)	Sugar (oz.)	Fats (oz.)	Meat (lb.)	Milk (pt.)
Food, Health & Income (1936)							
Middle class		3.4	2.3	18.0	13.1	1.6	5.0
English northern towns		5.3	2.4	15.3	11.5	1.5	2.4
Women's Co-op Guild		5.4	2.3	16.4	13.7	1.6	2.6
Mean	*1,152*	*5.1*	*3.1*	*17.8*	*13.7*	*1.6*	*3.1*
Carnegie sample (1937)							
Scotland	70	4.6	2.9	16.0	8.6	1.1	3.2
England	140	5.1	3.2	17.0	11.6	1.4	2.8
Ministry of Health (1937–38)							
Surrey	17	3.1	2.1	19.2	12.6	1.4	3.6
Essex	45	4.1	2.5	17.8	10.6	1.4	3.0
South Wales	68	2.2	2.9	17.5	12.6	1.0	2.4
Ely	26	3.6	2.1	18.8	13.8	1.2	2.2
Ministry of Labour (1937–38)							
Mean	75	5.5	3.7	21.6	15.3	2.0	3.2
Glossop, 1938	35	4.4	2.2	19.2	13.8	1.2	2.3
Working-class wives, 1939	2	2.9	1.1	10.9	5.9	0.4	1.2

budget surveys. The survey financed by the Carnegie Trust was the largest and comprised 1,046 families in England and 667 in Scotland. Orr chose a variety of locations in both countryside and towns and was careful to include families of the unemployed in his respondents. Later criticism of his work suggested that it was 'designed to study the effect on family diet and the health of children of economic depression, with low wages and widespread unemployment'.[39]

By the late 1930s both the Ministry of Health and the Ministry of Labour were committed to carrying out family budget surveys so that they would be in control of the data collected. The results of these

[39] A. H. Baines, D. F. Hollingsworth and I. Leitch, 'Diets of working-class families before and after the Second World War', *Nutrition Abstracts and Reviews*, 33 (1963), pp. 653–68. The figures for the Carnegie Survey in Tables 6.5 and 6.6 are based on a stratified sample designed to eliminate this bias.

Table 6.6 Daily nutrient intake per head shown by dietary surveys in the 1930s

Survey	Energy value		Protein	Fat	CHO	Iron	Calcium
	(kcal)	(kj)	(g)	(g)	(g)	(mg)	(g)
Food, Health and Income (1936)							
Middle class	2,775	11,611	77	111	361	13.2	0.98
English northern towns	2,400	10,042	73	81	345	12.6	0.48
Women's Co-op Guild	2,830	11,841	78	107	389	14.2	0.67
Mean	*2,960*	*12,385*	*84*	*112*	*388*	*11.2*	*0.67*
Carnegie sample (1937)							
Scotland	2,457	10,280	74	79	362	13.7	0.70
England	2,538	10,619	76	96	343	13.7	0.65
Ministry of Health (1937–38)							
Surrey	2,450	10,251	73	98	319	13.1	0.78
Essex	2,510	10,502	75	92	345	13.3	0.71
South Wales	2,260	9,456	61	83	322	10.8	0.61
Ely	2,460	10,293	68	101	326	11.7	0.75
Ministry of Labour (1937–38)							
Mean	*3,230*	*13,514*	*83*	*124*	*440*	*16.9*	*0.75*
Glossop, 1938	2,510	10,502	69	92	345	12.2	0.58
Working-class wives 1939	1,305	5,460	36	38	203	5.9	0.28

surveys appear in Tables 6.5 and 6.6. The collection of family budgets by the Ministry of Labour through Employment Exchanges and Women's Institutes produced over 12,000 responses, of which 10,762 families provided evidence for four separate weeks in October 1937 and January, April and July 1938. The size of the Ministry of Labour's survey reflected the interest stimulated by a broadcast by Ernest Brown, Minister of Labour, on 4 October 1937. The Ministry set an upper income limit of £250 per year for non-manual workers and completely excluded the unemployed. The results were heavily weighted towards London and the southeast, which provided 26 per cent of the budgets, compared with only 6 per cent from the north of England.[40] The

[40] Only ninety-nine returns have been preserved in the PRO. See LAB17/8–106. The figures in Tables 6.5 and 6.6 are based on an analysis of the seventy-five returns which are complete for the four weeks surveyed.

Ministry of Health, dissatisfied with the Ministry of Labour's approach, began to survey some 300 families, mainly among rural and lower-paid workers, which was completed in 1938 but never analysed.[41] The remaining examples in Tables 6.5 and 6.6 are diets based on a survey by the Medical Officer for Glossop in 1938 and also two budgets quoted by Margery Spring-Rice in *Working-Class Wives*.

The failure of policy

When the Carnegie Report was finally published in 1955, Professor A. F. Thomson wrote retrospectively of the 1930s:

> We had a population in which frank deficiency disease was rare but in which generalized malnutrition was undoubtedly widespread, manifested by imponderable but evident impairment of health and vitality and by easily measured defects of growth and form.[42]

The confident ring of this assessment owes much to the experience of wartime rationing and full employment in postwar Britain. However, during the 1930s, there was no political will to implement any solution to the problem of poor growth and health and, indeed, more energy was devoted to denying the existence of any problem than to its solution. After 1937, when the Ministry of Health's Second Nutrition Committee reported, government responsibility for 'feeding the nation' became a common figure of speech. Nevertheless, during the 1930s, no one was prepared to discuss the implementation of large-scale supplementary feeding programmes for children. The Ministry of Health felt justified in ignoring the claims of the pressure groups, such as the Children's Minimum Council, in view of the general opposition to family allowances. The introduction of the school-milk schemes in 1934, while satisfactory as an outcome of the Empire Marketing Board's campaigns, was no substitute for the failure of governments to integrate nutritional knowledge into social policy in the interwar years.[43]

---

[41] The Ministry of Health sent its survey to the Rowett Research Institute for processing but this was never done. The figures in Tables 6.5 and 6.6 are based on my calculations from some 150 returns that survived at the Rowett Research Institute for the four areas covered by the survey.

[42] Rowett, *Family Diet and Health in Pre-War Britain*, Appendix I, p. 70.

[43] In a lecture at the Royal Institution in 1940, Drummond claimed that he had persuaded the London County Council to introduce a 'health dinner' based on the 'Oslo breakfast' in a poor part of East London but that it ran for only one year before the evacuation of children at the outbreak of war stopped it. Royal Institution, *The Nation's Larder* (1940), pp. 15–16.

In evaluating the interwar family budget diets it should be noted, first, that this modern analysis of the data shows lower energy values than those suggested by the calculations carried out by Orr's team. Although the contemporary analysis seems to have overestimated energy values the revised figures suggested here do not necessarily place the families in these surveys into a danger zone of under-nutrition. Second, there is no evidence in the interwar years of any change in the distribution of food within families away from the nineteenth-century pattern in which adult males took a disproportionate share, particularly of food from animal sources. There remains the likelihood, therefore, that if adult wage-earners had satisfactory diets, nutritional problems were present for growing children, especially during adolescence, and for pregnant women or lactating mothers. Contemporary research provided evidence that this was the case. Dr Helen Mackay's investigations in East London revealed that though 'chlorosis' or 'green sickness' had disappeared since the First World War, infantile anaemia due to a shortage of iron in the diet was still widespread, and May Mellanby's work on dental caries in children showed the need for vitamin D in the diet.[44] Further confirmation that this was indeed so came from clinical examinations undertaken by the Ministry of Health during the Second World War.[45] In areas of long-term unemployment where economic distress was pronounced the evidence of under-nutrition was obvious. Despite the provision of economic aid for South Wales, in parts of northern and northeastern England and part of central Scotland under the Special Areas Acts of 1934 and 1936, under-nutrition among schoolchildren was visible at routine medical examinations. Assessments of nutritional status were cursory but Grade C 'Slightly subnormal' and Grade D 'Bad' suggested that between 11 and 12 per cent of all children medically examined in the 1930s were undernourished. Table 7.12 indicates that in some distressed areas the proportion was approximately double the national average. Nevertheless, the interwar years did see the beginnings of the secular trend in children's growth. Between 1920 and 1940, children of elementary school ages gained 2 to 3.5in. in height and 5 to 13.5lb. in weight, though this progress slowed during the depressions of the early 1920s and early 1930s.[46] Despite the concern with malnutrition that developed in areas where long-term unemployment became marked,

---

[44] See MRC Special Report Series Nos 157 (1931), 159 (1931) and 211 (1936).

[45] Ministry of Health, Report of the Chief Medical Officer of the Ministry of Health, *On the State of the Public Health during Six Years of War* (1946), p. 119.

[46] E. M. B. Clements, 'Changes in the mean stature and weight of British children over the past seventy years', *BMJ*, 24 October 1953, pp. 898–902, and J. B. de V. Weir, 'The assessment of the growth of schoolchildren with special reference to secular changes', *British Journal of Nutrition*, 6, 1 (1952), pp. 19–33.

school medical officers began to make some observations of improvements in children's growth.

The ossification of ideas at the Ministry of Health, together with the associated attempts to protect departmental integrity, led to a major failure in interwar social policy. The Ministry of Health's medical officers became highly resistant to the advances in science. The scientists overstated their case on the need for vitamins and calcium in the diet, undoubtedly; but the reaction in the Ministry – and particularly in the later reports of Sir George Newman – and the search for contradictions and inexactitudes which might be used to invalidate the scientists' recommendations and to prevent the publication of critical reports, was a direct cause of the rift between the Ministry and its advisers. In this, the publication of *Food, Health and Income* was a catalyst. However, the scientists' pressure on the government was never sufficiently united to overcome personal differences of opinion. Eventually, in 1937, Lord Luke's committee did recommend that the government should commit itself to a 'more extensive application of recent discoveries of nutrition', but this remained little more than a platitude in Whitehall until events forced action.[47]

[47] PRO, MH56/213, Ministry of Health, Advisory Committee on Nutrition, *First Report* (1937), Summary, iv, pp. 28–9. The Luke Committee's terms of reference (para. 5) had required it to consider whether the government should apply 'the lessons of recent nutritional science to the feeding of the nation'. Although, technically, this was the first national food policy for the United Kingdom, it was accepted by the Colonial Office only for application in dependent territories. Despite the publication of recommended allowances for nutrients by the Technical Commission of the League of Nations during the 1930s, the Ministry of Health had no published scale of recommended nutrient intakes before 1969.

7

THE SECOND WORLD WAR

The myth of a planned diet, 1939 to 1950

While it was generally accepted that the war 'might well be lost on the food front'[1] and despite the publication of the Luke Report in 1937, the government had no national food policy when war was declared in 1939, due largely to the political opposition to supplementary feeding programmes. The most important consideration for the people was the government's immediate assumption of responsibility for the supply and distribution of food. The politicization of the question of malnutrition in the 1930s meant there were many ready to advise the government of its responsibilities. Penguin Books published a Penguin Special in March 1939 by F. Le Gros Clark and R. M. Titmuss, *Our Food Problem*, and George Walworth put forward the case in favour of co-operative societies in *Feeding the Nation in Peace and War*. By 1940, these radical voices were joined by John Boyd Orr in *Feeding the People in War-Time*.[2] In the event, nutritional knowledge played remarkably little part in the planning of the food rationing scheme that was eventually adopted.

Food control

Fear of immediate air attack accelerated government action. Over the weekend of 2–3 September 1939, Smithfield and Billingsgate markets were moved out of central London and concern was expressed about holding stocks of food at ports.[3] In October 1939, the War Cabinet's Home Policy Committee formed a Sub-Committee on Rationing. The

---

[1] Ministry of Health, Report of the CMO, *State of the Public Health during Six Years of War* (1946), p. 114.
[2] F. Le Gros Clark and R. M. Titmuss, *Our Food Problem. A Study of National Security* (Harmondsworth, 1939); G. Walworth, *Feeding the Nation in Peace and War* (1940); John Boyd Orr and David Lubbock, *Feeding the People in War-Time* (1940). Another Penguin Special was Frank Wokes, *Food the Deciding Factor* (Harmondsworth, 1940). Among the many books offering postwar solutions was J. R. Marrack, *Food and Planning* (1942). Unpublished advice received by the Ministry of Food may be found in the PRO in MAF84/291.
[3] PRO, MAF152/44, *Five Years of Food Control* (typescript), p. 1.

discussion centred around meat and sugar, during which it became clear that shipping strategies and Britain's obligations to feed the armed forces and support France were dominant. Civilian food consumption in Britain was, in effect, residual.[4] Rationing was then discussed in the War Cabinet's Ministerial Sub-Committee on Food Control, which met from November 1939 onwards.[5] Its initial concern was with the supply of sugar. At the second meeting in December, the Committee noted that there had been considerable hoarding and sugar consumption was already approximately 20 per cent above the peacetime level. Sugar was regarded as a basic food during the war and an essential source of energy. In consequence, Walter Elliot, then Minister of Health, argued for as large a sugar ration as possible and proposed a ration of 1lb. per head per week before finally accepting 12oz. for domestic and 8oz. for manufacturing purposes.[6] Even so, Elliot returned to the same point later, claiming that since 'fuel foods were interchangeable', a smaller sugar ration meant more wheat would be required for human consumption.

Unlike pre-1914 assessments of Britain's food needs, defence plans in the later 1930s assumed that there would be a major shortage of shipping in which to carry imports. Any scarcities of food would bring about inflation similar to that between 1914 and 1918, the prevention of which was uppermost in the minds of the planners. Between 1938 and 1939, the Food (Defence Plans) Department of the Board of Trade was able to create some strategic reserves of food by buying whale oil, sugar and wheat in the open market.[7] The Ministry of Food, which absorbed the Food (Defence Plans) Department, was created by Order in Council on 8 September 1939. Its function as a ministry for the supply of food raised questions regarding its role in connexion with nutrition policy and, therefore, its relations with the Ministry of Health. Since the Food Policy Committee reported directly to the War Cabinet, departmental friction of the kind that persisted during the interwar years

[4] PRO, CAB75/27. See H.P. (R) (39), 5. This Ministry of Food memorandum set out the budget method of determining meat rations: food supply (home production of meat plus imports) less the requirements for the Allies (the French army) and British services left the amount available for civilian rations.

[5] PRO, CAB74/1, Home Policy Committee, p. 58. The Food Control Sub-Committee became an independent committee of the War Cabinet as the Food Policy Committee on 9 April 1940.

[6] PRO, CAB74/1, second meeting, 1 December 1939, pp. 15–16. See also Memorandum F.P. (M) (39), 2, dated 1 December 1939.

[7] R. J. Hammond, *Food: Volume I, The Growth of Policy* (1951), pp. 8, 20–3. Prewar purchases of frozen and canned meat were not delivered before the war began.

was limited.[8] Belatedly, the Ministry of Health formed a parallel Standing Committee on Medical and Nutritional Problems in 1941 and claimed the right to advise the government on nutrition policy.[9]

Although there were three Ministers of Food during the Second World War, the first, W. S. Morrison (1939–40), and the third, Colonel J. J. Llewellin (1943–5), have been largely forgotten. The Minister of Food, in the recollections of many after the war, was Lord Woolton, though in fact he was Minister from only April 1940 to November 1943. Woolton created a 'General Department' at the Ministry which, at least from 1941 onwards, attempted to formulate food policy, though the commodity supply divisions remained largely impervious to its influence. Despite Woolton's notable success with people's morale, even he found the commodity activities of the Ministry of Food hard to control. The Imported Cereals Committee, for example, was located in James Rank's house at Godstone, Surrey, throughout the war. Commodity supply schemes were often badly thought out and some inflicted unnecessary shortages on the public, such as the lack of fish in 1939 and again in 1941. Other examples were the disappearance of eggs from towns from 1940 to 1941, and the fiasco of the National Vegetable Marketing Company formed in 1941 to handle the distribution of carrots and onions.[10]

The scale of the problem faced by the government in supplying Britain with food was immense. The Ministry of Food's annual turnover of £1 billion made it the world's largest trading organization during the war years.[11] The stimulation of home food production was therefore essential. The Ministry of Agriculture acquired powers to control land use for cultivation and to direct food production by reviving the system of county war agricultural executive committees. By 1943–4, food production in the United Kingdom had expanded by some 25 per cent above prewar levels. In energy terms, the intensification was dramatic:

[8] Hammond, *Food: Volume I*, p. 59. In *The State of the Public Health during Six Years of War*, p. 7, the Chief Medical Officer of the Ministry of Health paid tribute to the 'close and friendly co-operation' between the Ministry of Food and the Ministry of Health.

[9] Ministry of Health, *The State of the Public Health during Six Years of War*, p. 114. The membership had the same departmental representation as the Food Policy Committee.

[10] Hammond, *Food: Volume I*, ch. XXIX; also R. J. Hammond, 'British wartime food control', *Food Research Institute Studies*, Vol.3, No. 3, 1962, Stanford and PRO, MAF152/164. Correspondence indicates that officials forced the removal of a chapter on the National Vegetable Marketing Company from Hammond's first volume; however, see *Food: Volume II, Studies in Administration and Control* (History of the Second World War, United Kingdom Civil Series) (1956), pp. 580–1.

[11] Winnifrith, *Ministry of Agriculture, Fisheries and Food*, p. 35.

By 1918/9, the peak of the effort resulting from the First World War, the net output of calories had been increased by about 24 per cent, compared with the years before the war; in the Second World War, the same increase had been achieved by the second harvest of the war and by 1943/4 this had been quadrupled.[12]

In the Great War, there had been no rationing before 1918, which meant that prices had risen, and prices rationed consumption. Planning for the Second World War began in 1937 on the basis that the system imposed in 1918 would be largely repeated: people would have ration books but they would not be free to use them anywhere; they must be 'registered' at specific shops for their rations. It was a scheme devised by the food merchants and manufacturers which required a huge administrative bureaucracy. The co-operative movement was its chief beneficiary: '28 per cent of the entire population (13.5 million people) registered with the Co-op for their supplies.'[13] The use of a money value for meat rationing was intended to limit consumption of the more expensive cuts by those who could afford them. Basic foods – bread, potatoes and other vegetables – were off ration with the view of allowing consumers to eat as much of them as they wanted, though the number of times that bread rationing was discussed during the war suggested that there was nothing sacred about these exclusions.[14] Later, the Ministry of Health had the audacity to claim that prewar nutritional knowledge had determined wartime policy: 'the knowledge available at its outbreak was sufficient to ensure that the general policy laid down was on sound lines and that the people's diet was not left to the dictates of taste, appetite, or chance.' This made 'it possible to arrange for a balanced diet for all'.[15] This statement is easily disproved. The Scientific Sub-Committee on Food Policy did not meet until June 1940, when the rationing scheme was already in place. Under the chairmanship of Sir William Bragg, it included some of the leading nutritionists of the day: Professor E. P. Cathcart (Glasgow), Professor Sir Edward Mellanby (Medical Research

---

[12] Sir Keith Murray, *Agriculture* (History of the Second World War, United Kingdom Civil Series) (1955), pp. 243–4, quoted in Winnifrith, *Ministry of Agriculture*, p. 29. Once the Second World War was over, increased agricultural output became a central concern for British governments wishing to limit hard currency expenditure on food imports from North America. The postwar Labour government sought to increase output by 50 per cent over prewar levels and the Conservative administration of the early 1960s sought to raise output to 60 per cent of prewar figures.

[13] J Birchall, *Co-op: The People's Business* (1994), p. 136.

[14] Rationing and the associated points allocation scheme is explained clearly in John Burnett, *Plenty and Want* (3rd edn), ch. 13.

[15] Ministry of Health, *The State of the Public Health during Six Years of War*, p. 115.

Council) and Sir John Orr (Rowett Research Institute), though the nutritionists were diluted heavily by scientists from the Agricultural Research Council.[16] It followed that the balance of the discussion was tilted towards food production, animal feeding policies and the reduction of waste, rather than the relationship between human consumption and health.[17] At the first meeting Cathcart, Mellanby and Orr were asked to draw up an agreed memorandum of 'the food requirements of man in biochemical terms and a translation of these into actual foodstuffs'. This resulted in Orr's 'Iron Ration', shown in Table 7.1, which consisted of six foods only: bread, fats, potatoes, oatmeal, vegetables (cabbages and/or kale; and roots, especially carrots and swedes) and milk. While this diet limited demands upon shipping, it was a pre-industrial diet, perhaps not strange to Orr, who had been born in rural Ayrshire in 1880, but long since vanished from urban areas of England. However, while the nutrient analysis in Table 7.2 shows that it yielded adequate amounts of minerals such as iron and calcium, the 'Iron Ration' was low in carbohydrates and fats and so offered insufficient energy for most normal activity. With the German advance in 1940 cutting off food imports from Denmark and the Netherlands, it looked as if the 'Iron Ration' might become a necessity when the Minister of Food reported to the War

Table 7.1 Orr's 'Iron Ration' per day

Bread (oz.)	Fats (oz.)	Potatoes (oz.)	Oatmeal (oz.)	Vegetables (oz.)	Milk (pt.)
11.8	1.5	16.0	2.0	6.0	0.6

Source: Scientific Food Committee, Memorandum SFC (40) 6.

Table 7.2 Daily nutrient analysis of Orr's 'Iron Ration'

Energy value (kcal)	(kj)	Protein (g)	Fat (g)	CHO (g)	Iron (mg)	Calcium (g)
1,920	8,101	56.9	60.6	306	10.4	0.88

Source: As Table 7.1.

[16] PRO, CAB74/11, First Meeting at The Royal Society, 7 June 1940. Professor J. C. Drummond, as Principal Scientific Adviser to the Ministry of Food, attended later meetings only as an observer. The agricultural membership of the Committee consisted of Professor A. W. Ashby (Aberystwyth), Professor F. L. Engledow (Cambridge), Professor J. A. Scott-Watson (Oxford) and Mr W. Gavin, Agricultural Adviser to the Ministry of Agriculture and Fisheries.
[17] See PRO, CAB74/11 and CAB74/12.

Cabinet that there was only twelve to fourteen weeks' supply of food in the country at the end of June. The Sub-Committee's fourth meeting was concerned with retail prices since Orr was 'perturbed at the consequences of rising price levels to the dietary of the poorer groups of consumers'. They 'should be informed by the Ministry of Health if any evidence of general malnutrition as a result of war time diets appeared in the population'. Cathcart also expressed concern that 'owing to the reduction in the meat ration the poorer families were faced with a shortage of animal protein'.[18] Nevertheless, no change in policy was envisaged: bread rationing 'would certainly be interpreted as the first sign of surrender'.[19]

Bread – the key to Britain's food policy

Bread was a central topic in the Scientific Sub-Committee's meetings, not only with regard to its possible inclusion in the rationing scheme but also in terms of raising the extraction rate of flour from the peacetime level of 73 per cent. Sir Henry French, Permanent Secretary at the Ministry of Food, thought 'bread rationing definitely inflicted privation on the poor' and wondered whether any major change in composition of the loaf was achievable. He doubted whether a flour of 80 per cent extraction, which would change the white loaf to a wheatmeal one, could be milled from home-produced wheat.[20] The Scientific Sub-Committee on Food Policy proved remarkably ineffective against the entrenched interests of the food industry, namely the Millers' Mutual Trade Association, which could rely on the backing of senior civil servants. The minutes of the second meeting in June 1940 reveal that pragmatism always overrode nutritional principles:

> The question of the percentage extraction rate of flour was discussed. There was agreement as to the physiological superiority of flour of high extraction, but the practical disadvantages of such flour, viz. that it soon degenerates on storage, that brown bread is wasteful because it soon becomes stale and is then very difficult to use up in the kitchen, and the evident preference of the population for white bread, led to the conclusion that the level of extraction should not be raised generally above the point where the flour ceases to produce white bread, but that arrangements be made by the Ministry of Food to place a brown bread made from flour of a high extraction on the market at the same price as white bread and emphasize its value in their propaganda.[21]

[18] PRO, CAB74/12, SFC (41), 4.
[19] PRO, MAF152/130. Policy of the Ministry of Food, 31 July 1940.
[20] PRO, CAB74/1, third meeting, 4 December 1939, pp. 21–5.
[21] PRO, CAB74/11, SFC (40) 2, 20 June 1940, p. 1.

By 1941, the Scientific Sub-Committee on Food Policy had achieved little. Bread quality had not changed and rising prices were causing hardship among the poorest groups in society. In January 1941, a proposal from the Ministry of Food for bread made from 85 per cent extraction flour was sent to the MRC's Accessory Food Factors Committee for comment. It was agreed that, as a result of Dr R. A. McCance's experiments, calcium should be added to white flour but 'ferrous salts' should not. No decision was reached on raising the extraction rate of flour.[22] At the third meeting of 1941, a loaf based on 85 per cent extraction flour was agreed but it was understood that milling machinery would require adjustment. Drummond was eager for the Ministry of Food to begin propaganda in favour of the 85 per cent extraction loaf but the subject was referred to the Cereals Division of the Ministry of Food for technical advice, which allowed the millers to delay its implementation even further.[23]

Additional opposition to bread from 85 per cent extraction flour came from an Interdepartmental Conference on Livestock Policy which feared that if feed stuffs were reduced, 1M animals would need to be slaughtered and there would be a threat to the milk supply. In April 1941, the Scientific Sub-Committee learned that National Wheatmeal flour was already on sale, though: 'it was doubtful whether it would make much headway against existing wholemeal flours and proprietary breads unless the production of these flours was prohibited. This would be particularly the case if the public became aware that Calcium Carbonate had been added to National Wholemeal Flour.' Moreover, 'the Minister of Food would be reluctant to compel the public to eat wholemeal bread until the shipping situation made such a course imperative.'[24]

The extraction rate of wheat flour remained around 73 to 76 per cent from 1939 until early in 1942 because the trade in offals was of value to the millers and animal feed suppliers. Eventually, with shipping losses increasing during the Battle of the Atlantic, the millers were forced to accept an extraction rate of 85 per cent in April 1942. This introduced

---

[22] PRO, CAB74/12, SFC (41) 1 and SFC (41) 2; MAF84/291. Proposals by the millers to add vitamin B1 in April 1940 were not implemented. By the time Roche Products Ltd, which held the patent for vitamin B_1, had built a factory at Welwyn Garden City, the extraction rate had been raised to 85 per cent.

[23] PRO, CAB74/12, SFC (41) 3; Sandra Hunt, 'The Second World War: bread under government control, 1939–56', unpublished Rank Prize Fund research paper. PRO, MAF84/380 shows that the millers had provided no accounts 'to show what kind of profits are being earned' as late as November 1942.

[24] PRO, CAB74/12, SFC (41) 5, 6, 7. Shortages of animal feed stuffs were also a threat to the meat ration, as no cattle could be imported from Eire, where there was foot and mouth disease.

National Flour and the National Loaf, and wartime bread became a standard commodity for the first time.[25] The decision was not based on the nutritional advice that the government had been receiving since 1940 but, as was later admitted, 'with the prime purpose of saving valuable shipping space'.[26] Despite the publicity attached to the launch of the National Loaf consumer resistance remained steadfast during 1942 and 1943. The main reasons given were that white bread was tastier, easier to digest and of a better consistency than National Wheatmeal bread. A further survey in 1944 indicated the decreasing popularity of National Wheatmeal bread.[27] Among a sample eating an average of 4lb. of bread per head per week, roughly half either disliked it or accepted it as a consequence of the war. Some two-thirds thought white bread was better and roughly three-quarters wanted National Wheatmeal bread discontinued at the end of the war. Although there were later reductions in the extraction rate, bread never regained its peacetime qualities until well after the war.

The persistence of inequalities in the diet

Much debate took place in the early years of the war without any evidence of how consumption had been affected by shortages and rationing or even, from 1940 onwards, by enemy air-raids. In London, there was an attempt to compare food consumption between February and July 1940 with that between February and May 1941. Tables 7.3 and 7.4 show, first, that inequalities in the diet persisted under rationing and, second, that changes in the rations were not reflected equally in the food consumption of different income groups. For example, the reduction in the sugar ration from 12oz. in 1940 to 8oz. in 1941 had the greatest effect among the poorest families in Group A and the least effect on the better-off families in Group D. Meal patterns were maintained but the poorer families increased their reliance on 'bread and spread', especially at breakfast. Suppers were most affected as food was taken to the air-raid shelters or light meals were prepared for an emergency. Meat sandwiches and cocoa or milk drinks replaced cooked meals (and 'bread and spread' meals) and tea-drinking at suppertime.

---

[25] 'The National Loaf', *BFJ*, April 1942, p. 31. Raising the extraction rate obviated the much-delayed plan to add vitamin B_1 (thiamine) to flour in addition to calcium.
[26] Hammond, *Food: Volume I*, pp. 259–61. It became effective on 6 April 1942. See the *BFJ*, April 1942, 31. Also PRO, MAF84/394, draft for the Minister of Food's press conference, 2 January 1945.
[27] PRO, RG23/61. Wartime Social Survey, New Series 49A, *National Wheatmeal Bread* by Gertrude Wagner, typescript, undated (possibly April 1944).

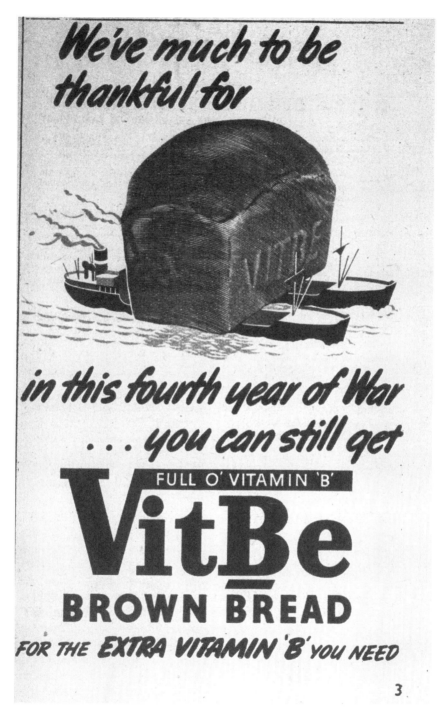

Plate 7.1 The introduction of the National Loaf in April 1942 made the remaining peacetime brands of brown bread more attractive. (Image courtesy of The Advertising Archives)

Table 7.3 Weekly food consumption per diet head in London between February and July 1940

Food expenditure group (sh/week)	No. of families	Bread (lb.)	Potatoes (lb.)	Sugar (oz.)	Fats (oz.)	Meat (oz.)	Milk (pt.)
A (<5/–)	24	2.71	3.15	12.9	7.0	18.5	1.0
B (5/ – 7/–)	24	4.69	3.16	14.4	6.6	25.4	1.7
C (7/ – 9/6)	25	3.88	3.38	14.4	8.6	30.6	2.3
D (>9/6)	27	3.52	3.94	15.8	11.3	37.7	3.4

Source: Scientific Committee on Food Policy, 1941, document 38.

Table 7.4 Weekly food consumption per diet head in London between February and May 1941

Food expenditure group (sh/week)	No. of families	Bread (lb.)	Potatoes (lb.)	Sugar (oz.)	Fats (oz.)	Meat (oz.)	Milk (pt.)
A (<5/–)	10	3.30	3.26	8.6	7.1	19.0	2.2
B (5/ – 7/–)	35	3.33	4.33	10.3	7.5	23.4	3.1
C (7/ – 9/6)	40	3.61	4.36	10.6	9.2	29.9	3.5
D (>9/6)	18	3.95	4.62	13.8	9.1	29.1	4.7

Source: as Table 7.3.

Tables 7.5 and 7.6 show little change in energy intakes as less fat in the diet was offset by an increase in carbohydrates. By 1941, margarine had been fortified with vitamins so that comparison with vitamin intakes in 1940 was difficult, but the report indicated that vitamin A deficiency still existed in the lowest expenditure group. What was clear was that whatever the increase in liquid milk consumption, all expenditure groups remained deficient in calcium.[28] Another survey of 843 working-class families in major cities in January 1941 suggested that the rise in liquid milk consumption under the National Milk Scheme occurred in part, at least, as a result of the 'greatly reduced' condensed milk supplies during 1940. The report concluded that between 1937 and 1938 and spring 1940, energy intakes had fallen by about 10 per cent and were showing a further reduction by January 1941. At the same time energy require-

[28] PRO, CAB74/12, SFC (41) 38 (1 September 1941), pp. 7–10.

Table 7.5 Daily nutrient intake per diet head in London in 1940

Food expenditure group (sh/week)	No. of families	Energy value (kcal)	Protein (g)	Fat (g)	CHO (g)	Iron (mg)	Calcium (g)
A (<5/–)	24	1,728	48	59	239	7.0	0.43
B (5/ – 7/–)	24	2,046	60	67	284	9.6	0.50
C (7/ – 9/6)	25	2,390	69	84	324	11.6	0.63
D (>9/6)	27	2,746	81	114	331	12.9	0.80

Source: as Table 7.3.

Table 7.6 Daily nutrient intake per diet head in London in 1941

Food expenditure group (sh/week)	No. of families	Energy value (kcal)	Protein (g)	Fat (g)	CHO (g)	Iron (mg)	Calcium (g)
A (<5/–)	10	1,740	49	57	248	7.5	0.37
B (5/ – 7/–)	35	2,090	59	75	280	9.3	0.51
C (7/ – 9/6)	40	2,405	70	94	303	12.0	0.60
D (>9/6)	18	2,747	79	105	352	12.1	0.77

Source: as Table 7.3.

ments were assumed to have risen through additional physical activity due to longer hours at work and also such extra activities as fire-watching and digging for victory. By January 1941, energy value differentials were as pronounced as in 1940, and lower income groups were assessed as being deficient in protein intake, vitamin B_1 and vitamin C.[29] These deficiencies, a year after rationing had begun, produced no remedial action even though the scientists were aware of them. At the December 1941 meeting of the Scientific Committee on Food policy, Professor Cathcart questioned the allocation of milk for children. He thought one pint per day for children under age 2 was inadequate: it should be two pints a day for the under-twos and there was no need for any priority milk for children over 12 years. Professor Drummond observed that in allocating milk the Ministry of Food had relied on 'the special Nutrition Committee of the Medical Research Council'. On the other hand, protein supplies for adolescents were thought to be dangerously low, which led

[29] PRO, CAB74/12, SFC (41) 35 (5 July 1941), pp. 2–5

Dr Magee to suggest: 'adolescents should be given priority in regard to milk supplies as the incidence of tuberculosis in this group had risen since the war.' Despite this, it was agreed 'that no action should be taken'.[30] For adults, however, the 'dip' in nutrient intakes during the years 1940 to 1941 suggested that 'there were indications that the actual intake of food was insufficient to supply the energy necessary for the long hours in factories'.[31]

Making-do in time of scarcity

It was some time before the civilian population felt the full force of food rationing. Although 'voluntary' restrictions were called for, those who could stocked up on tinned food and those people who remembered the First World War bought what sugar they could store before rationing started. Everyone thought it prudent to lay in some 'essential' foods. A Birmingham woman keeping a diary for Mass Observation noted: 'Friday, 1 September [1939] I bought quarter lb Bournville Cocoa 5d, 1 tin of chicken and ham roll 6d, quarter of tea 9d, 2lbs sugar 5d for the store cupboard today.'[32] The phrase 'there is a war on' rapidly became commonplace and heightened people's concerns about food supplies. The disruption caused by evacuation brought additional difficulties for women who found themselves uprooted from their homes: '29th [October 1939]. Three women said they were starving themselves in order to pay the fare home. . . . Other women said they found such difficulty in the country shops. Food was much dearer at the village grocer's. Nothing can be bought ready cooked and they did not understand the coal cooking ranges of the country.'[33] By December 1939, with Christmas approaching, shortages and uncertainties began to worry

---

[30] PRO, CAB74/12. SFC (41) 13, 3 December 1941, pp. 2–3. After 1941, the Scientific Sub-Committee on Food Policy's opinions seemed no longer to be required. It met only twice more, in February 1942 and February 1943. In 1943, the Scientific Sub-Committee on Food Policy met at the War Cabinet Rooms under Sir Henry Dale to receive new terms of reference and to consider a scheme for differential rationing of an important foodstuff. Their discussion was not recorded in the Scientific Sub-Committee's minutes. As the scheme was 'not likely to be introduced' the Scientific Sub-Committee's report would be agreed by correspondence - and there were no further meetings. [SFC (43) 1]. The subject discussed, however, was shown by Memorandum SFC (43) 1 to have been a further scheme by the Ministry of Food to ration bread.
[31] PRO, MAF152/144.
[32] Dorothy Sheridan, ed., *Wartime Women. An Anthology of Women's Wartime Writing for Mass Observation 1937–1945* (1991), p. 47.
[33] Sheridan, *Wartime Women*, p. 58.

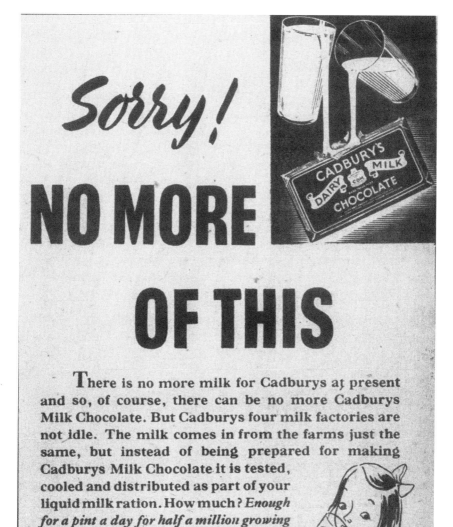

Plate 7.2 Wartime controls meant that many branded foods were unavailable. (Image courtesy of The Advertising Archives)

people: 'There was very little bacon in town today and women were anxiously asking each other if they knew of a shop which had any in.'[34] Not surprisingly, there were some sharp increases in food prices following the declaration of war. The Retail Food Index (RFI) had risen 14 per cent by April 1940 and was 23 per cent higher a year later. Prices of foods not in the RFI rose even more sharply, by 35 per cent up to April 1940 and, despite the introduction of controls on food prices in August 1940, to 47 per cent by April 1941.[35]

During the autumn of 1939, delays in decision-taking by the Cabinet, the registration of the population, the issuing of ration books by the Ministry of Food's local food offices and registration with retailers postponed the implementation of rationing.[36] Sugar, butter and bacon were rationed from 8 January 1940; other foods followed as control schemes were adopted. For well-off families, restrictions were not felt for some time:

> the baker's on the corner has in the window rather fewer cakes than pre-war days, but still plenty of biscuits, sweets and tinned fruits, and Wednesday's pork pies as usual. Food supplies are excellent. . . . Even with the meat ration of 1s. 10d. worth per person per week we do very well, for we can also buy fish, poultry and game, sausages and offal without coupons. Butter is also plentiful – the ration has been increased to ½lb per head per week, and bacon is also ½lb per head per week, which is as much as we require.[37]

In some country districts supplies were more erratic, though being in the country had its compensations:

> Jan 31st [1940] We have run out of coal. . . . We have had no meat this week, as the butcher has not come. He had hardly any last week. A customer brought us 2 rabbits on Monday, so we are not starving, but lots of people, my great aunt among them, have had no meat. Ever so many people have had no coal all the week. Arnold shot us 2 pigeons in the wood opposite.[38]

---

[34] See Richard Broad and Suzie Fleming, eds, *Nella Last's War* (Bristol, 1981), p. 24. Diary for Tuesday, 19 December 1940.

[35] PRO, CAB74/12, SFC (41) 38, Dietary Surveys, p. 2.

[36] See Hammond, *Food: Volume I*, ch. VIII.

[37] Peter Donnelly, ed., *Mrs Milburn's Diaries: An Englishwoman's Day-to-day Reflections 1939–1945* (1995), p. 30, entry for 3 April 1940.

[38] Sheridan, *Wartime Women*, p. 80, The diary of Muriel Green in a Norfolk village. The lack of meat was not necessarily due to scarcity but may have been disrupted by the rationalization of slaughtering policy. See Ministry of Health, *The State of the State of the Public Health During Six Years of War*, p. 124, which notes the closure of some 12,000 slaughterhouses and the concentration of the meat supply through 700 controlled slaughterhouses.

Some foods, such as cream, disappeared completely when its sale became prohibited in 1940. The growing scarcity of foods such as fish, offal, onions, lemons and tinned goods during 1940 and 1941 led to daily queues outside food shops:

> It's the custom for fish and fruit shops in Barrow to print their special lines on the outside window with a small brush dipped in whitening: '*SPECIAL!* RABBITS. CRABS.' The better-class shops *never* do, and I was really amused by one such shop today, for on both windows – it's on a corner – was printed neatly and in extra large letters: NO EGGS NO LEMONS NO ONIONS NO LEEKS NO PAPER BAGS. I wondered how many times Mrs. Jones had had to say those words before, in exasperation, she printed them on the window.[39]

There arose a queue culture among housewives. Place order was observed meticulously – though the posting of children as place-markers by women queuing at other shops was acceptable. Queuing became a feature of wartime life for housewives that continued throughout the war and well beyond, as long as restrictions on food availability continued.[40] For tinned goods, the introduction of the 'points' rationing scheme, in December 1941, allowed a fairer distribution of scarce items and was generally popular, though queues continued. Points were also required to buy biscuits, some dried fruits, syrup and breakfast cereals. From 1942 onwards, a further scheme of 'personal points' was applied to sweets.[41]

The effects of rationing

In general, rationing was applied to animal products and tropical or semi-tropical products. As food supplies fell in 1940 and 1941, despite the rationing scheme, in the early part of 1941 'there were indications of impaired health and working efficiency'.[42] Mrs Amy Briggs, a nurse in Leeds, visited her young daughter in hospital in Knaresborough: 'Sunday 2 November [1941] Find Anne playing about in ward but looking very pale and wan. Informed by sister-in-charge that we must

---

[39] Broad and Fleming, *Nella Last's War* (Friday, 8 November 1940), pp. 85–6.
[40] See N. Longmate, *How We Lived Then. A History of Everyday Life During the Second World War* (1977), ch. 13, 'The kitchen front', for experiences of food queues.
[41] Ministry of Health, *The State of the Public Health During Six Years of War*, pp. 115–16.
[42] *Food Consumption Levels in the United States, Canada and the United Kingdom*, 1944, quoted in the British Medical Association, Report of the Committee on Nutrition, BMA, 1950, para. 115, p. 41.

blame the wartime food for her condition – no eggs, no meat and nothing which goes to keep children strong.'[43] The wartime restrictions on foodstuffs were generally tolerated. A survey of consumers between February 1942 and October 1943[44] revealed that while people accepted rationing if they felt they were 'doing something to help the war' there was some dissatisfaction with the system. This was accentuated if it was suspected that some areas benefited more than others. Mrs Nella Last visited Blackpool in April 1942 and found a marked contrast with the closed and shuttered shops of Barrow-in-Furness:

> I cannot *possibly* find words to express my surprise at the lavish luxury of the shops. There was everything as in peacetime, and the only restrictions I saw were '7 coupons' etc., or the 'points' value on tinned goods. Tinned fruit, first-grade salmon, and every possible kind of lovely food on points. Whole roast chickens, potted herrings and cooked sausage ready for carrying away, plates of attractive salads, fried chicken – all coupon-free. And the cakes! Stacks of lovely cakes, pies, biscuits, tarts, gateaux, plate-pies, cream-cakes and fancy cakes of every kind. In Woolworth's, Marks and Spencer's, Hill's and Ledgerwood's, there were *hundreds* of pies and cakes – and as for the biscuits and ice-cream, I'd never seen more in peacetime.

She rationalized her surprise by noticing the 'obviously "city people"' and remembering 'all the civil servants who had been evacuated there'.[45] The administration of food rationing was generally unpopular: 'The Food Officials here simply will not help the matron [of a nursery] out of her dilemma, but pass her on from clerk to clerk, and the "boss" is unreachable.'[46] Men engaged in heavy work complained that the meat ration was inadequate and housewives that the fat ration was too small. It was generally accepted that the system was better than that in the First World War and that price control was an important element; over 80 per cent of respondents thought it should be continued after the war ended. The most unpopular scheme was the sale of oranges for the under-fives.

The categories and amounts of rationed foods set out in Table 7.7 show how similar amounts were to those introduced in 1918 when

---

[43] Sheridan, *Wartime Women*, pp. 141–2.

[44] PRO, RG23/9A. Wartime Social Survey, *Food During the War: A Summary of Studies on the Subject of Food made by the Wartime Social Survey Between February 1942 and October 1943*, by Gertrude Wagner, typescript, undated.

[45] Broad and Fleming, *Nella Last's War* (Monday, 27 April 1942), pp. 199–201. Parts of the Ministry of Agriculture had been evacuated to Lytham St Annes in June 1940.

[46] Sheridan, *Wartime Women*, pp. 145–6. Mrs Trowbridge, a volunteer worker in Bradford who billeted soldiers, was also critical of failures to provide rations for transient servicemen.

Table 7.7 Weekly food rations per head in the two World Wars

Date	Sugar	Tea	Bacon	Meat	Butter	Margarine	Lard
1918	8oz.	2oz.	4oz.	1s 3d	1oz.	4oz.	4oz.
June 1940	8oz.	2oz.	3oz.	1s 0d (*c.*14oz.)	6oz. together		1oz.
1945	8oz.	2.5oz.	4oz.	1s 2d (*c.*16oz.)	6oz. together		1oz.

Source: Ministry of Health, *The State of the Public Health during Six Years of War* (1946).

Note: Jam and preserves (2oz. in 1940 but 4oz. by 1945) were also rationed in both wars.
Cheese (1oz. in 1940 but 2oz. by 1945) and milk (2pt./head/week) were also rationed in the Second World War.

there was no pretence at nutritional planning. There was, of course, a difference between rations and actual consumption since food eaten out was off-the-ration. Table 7.8 shows weekly food consumption per head during the war and the postwar period of rationing. The effect of rationing may be seen in the reduction in sugar and fats consumed compared with the prewar Carnegie Survey figures from 1937, and the increased dependence on bread and potatoes. Meat consumption changed little from the prewar level but the rise in milk consumption was notable, despite its inclusion in the rationing scheme from November 1941 onwards and its rise in price.[47] Some of the growth in liquid milk consumption was undoubtedly due to the restriction placed upon the import of tinned milk, but the promotion of milk in the 1930s never had similar success in increasing consumption. Although Table 7.8 shows a remarkable degree of stability in the diet, there were some variations. Food consumption was at its lowest during the Battle of the Atlantic in 1942 and 1943 and, as can be seen in Table 7.9, the energy value of the diet in these years fell below 2,300kcal (9,500kj) per day. While Lend Lease imports from the USA brought in protein-rich foods – canned meat and fish, cheese and new dehydrated products such as dried eggs and dried milk – the politics of obtaining food imports required a permanent British Food Mission in Washington. When the USA entered the war after Pearl Harbor, the demands of US armed services and the home market led to a 'meat crisis' in 1943 as the US Department of Agriculture tried to reduce supplies to Britain. The meat ration of 1s 2d per week was maintained with difficulty.[48]

[47] See Hammond, *Food: Volume II*, Appendix, Table VI, p. 799. Table VII indicates that milk prices from 1941 to 1946 were around 30 per cent above prewar prices.
[48] PRO, MAF152/136.

Table 7.8 Weekly food consumption per head of the population, 1937 to 1950

Date	Bread[1] (lb.)	Potatoes (lb.)	Sugar (oz.)	Fats (oz.)	Meat (lb.)	Milk (pt.)
1937	3.8	3.2	17.3	11.6	1.4	2.8
1941	5.4	4.3	8.6	8.3	1.8	3.6
1942	5.1	4.3	8.4	8.7	1.6	3.8
1943	5.1	4.5	8.7	8.7	1.6	4.3
1944	5.2	4.5	9.0	9.2	1.8	4.4
1945	5.3	4.3	9.1	8.6	1.6	4.4
1946	4.3	4.4	15.0	8.2	1.7	4.0
1947	4.3	4.1	15.7	7.8	1.5	3.9
1948	4.7	3.7	16.4	8.9	1.5	4.0
1949	4.5	4.1	17.1	10.6	1.4	4.4
1950(a)	4.2	4.0	15.9	11.5	1.9	4.6
1950(b)	4.3	3.9	16.4	11.6	1.9	4.8

Source: 1937 = calculated mean of English families (1046) in the Carnegie Survey. For the 1940s see MAFF, Report of the National Food Survey Committee, 1951 (1952).

Notes
The amounts in these columns do not necessarily equate with the ration allowances since both 'visible' and 'invisible' sugars and fats are included.
[1] Includes flour and other cereals.
(a) The 1946–50 figures are for urban working-class households only.
(b) All households.

Many people were not completely dependent on the rations for their food. For some the 'black market' provided access to food 'under the counter';[49] while for those rich enough there were off-the-ration hotel and restaurant meals, capped in price at 5 shillings (25 pence):

Monday 24th November [1941] – to the Queen's Hotel [Birmingham] for lunch. It sounded so good. 'Hors-d'oeuvre,' said the foreign waiter, and when it came it looked quite attractive, though it was mostly the same old potato, cabbage, carrot, parsnip and beetroot with a nice fat sardine. Good thick soup next and then fish – which was not a good choice for us as we ought to have fish cakes at home this evening – followed by a chocolate mould. The first forkful or two were good, but it soon palled as it needed more sugar. This is a record of a 'five bob' war luncheon.[50]

[49] 'A black market in necessities hardly existed.' This view, expressed by the Ministry of Health, was at odds with the experience of many housewives. See Ministry of Health, The State of the Public Health During Six Years of War, p. 122.
[50] Donnelly, Mrs Milburn's Diaries, p. 116; Wartime Women, pp. 187–8. Joan Arkwright, a WAAF who kept a diary for Mass Observation, noted that the price of a meal did not include 'extras' which sometimes concealed higher prices – 'price 5/- plus 1/- house charge'.

Table 7.9 Daily nutrient intake per head of the population, 1937 to 1950

Date	Energy value (kcal)	(kj)	Protein (g)	Fat (g)	CHO (g)	Iron (mg)	Calcium (g)
1937	2,540	10,627	76	96	343	13.7	0.65
1941	2,340	9,791	73	n.k.	n.a.	12.4	0.61
1942	2,270	9,498	74	n.k.	n.a.	13.5	0.67
1943	2,270	9,498	73	86	n.a.	13.3	0.86
1944	2,390	10,000	73	94	n.a.	13.5	0.87
1945	2,375	9,937	76	92	n.a.	12.7	0.88
1946	2,305	9,644	78	86	n.a.	14.4	0.91
1947	2,310	9,665	77	82	n.a.	14.3	1.00
1948	2,390	10,000	77	88	n.a.	14.2	1.01
1949	2,425	10,146	76	95	n.a.	13.6	1.03
1950(a)	2,440	10,209	77	102	n.a.	13.5	1.04
1950(b)	2,475	10,355	78	101	n.a.	13.6	1.06

Sources and notes: as Table 7.8; n.a. = not available, n.k. = not known.

People with gardens or allotments could supplement the fruit and vegetables supplied by shops, though the seasonal nature of growth and harvest limited availability. The Ministry of Agriculture ran a 'Dig for Victory' campaign in support of gardeners and allotment holders, but access to any land provided an opportunity – even in towns – to breed rabbits for meat, or keep poultry to supplement the rations with eggs. By the autumn of 1942, 3.7M people keeping poultry had 'surrendered egg registrations' in favour of their own hen's eggs.[51] For a largely urban population whose rural roots were hazy, if not already forgotten, the Ministry of Agriculture's advice and propaganda was helpful but most people listened to Mr Middleton's gardening advice on the radio.[52] Further attempts to spread information came from the Ministry of Food's 'Kitchen Front' posters, radio broadcasts and the Food Leaders' scheme between 1942 and 1952.[53] From an initial meeting called by Dr Innes, the Chief Education Officer of Birmingham, to ask the WVS and other voluntary bodies to provide a street-by-street organization 'to stop

[51] PRO, MAF152/45.

[52] PRO, RG23/26. Wartime Social Survey, Report No.20, New Series, 'Dig for Victory' An Inquiry into the Effects of the 'Dig for Victory' Campaign made for the Ministry of Agriculture in August and September 1942, typescript, undated.

[53] Longmate, How We Lived Then, ch. 13; see also Children's Nutrition Council, 'The Food Leaders' Scheme', Wartime Nutrition Bulletin, 32. Few files have survived: see PRO, MAF900/154, 155 and 160. The Ministry of Food's Food Advice Division was not dissolved until 1 May 1952.

Plate 7.3 'Dig for Victory' campaigns were aimed primarily at reducing imports of food. (Image courtesy of The Advertising Archives)

false rumours concerned with food', the numbers of Food Leaders in the United Kingdom rose to over 22,000 in 1945–6. At times of emergency, such as the Coventry air-raid in November 1940, providing drinking-water and hot food, especially freshly baked bread, was as important as restoring gas, electricity and water supplies. During the latter part of the blitz, Queen's Messenger Convoys were introduced to do this work, which in London was carried out by the London County Council's Londoners' Meals Service.[54] Voluntary groups and charities also provided mobile canteens for demolition and rescue workers after air-raids. In November 1940, married women were driving mobile vans for the YMCA supplying tea, hot meat pies and cakes to bombsite workers. Similar vans and stalls were set up at railway stations: 'nothing hot was sold except tea – our only beverage. The food was all of the meat pie, sausage roll, bun, and jam-tart variety – with chocolate and cigarettes.'[55]

The Wartime Social Survey

Despite all improvisation, the wartime diet had its limitations. There was plenty of bread and potatoes but only meagre portions of anything else. The restrictions on the diet caused concern; how were women managing? During the period of 5–21 November 1942, twenty-four interviewers of the Wartime Social Survey obtained responses from 2,576 housewives, both urban and rural, in three main areas of England – the north, Midlands (and East Anglia), and the south to discuss cooking and serving methods.[56] 'Potatoes are served regularly by everybody, and green vegetables – cabbage, sprouts, cauliflower – by the great majority.' In the previous week, more than three-quarters (78 per cent) had 'used vegetables in "made-up" dishes'. In the main these were stews produced by two-thirds of the housewives, while less than a quarter (23 per cent) had made other dishes such as vegetable hotpot or cauliflower *au gratin*. Some regional variation was seen: more roots and fewer green vegetables in the north and more use of made-up dishes in the south. It seemed obvious that rural housewives served more vegetables than did urban housewives and that working women cooked fewer made-up dishes. Similarly, the better-off served a wider range of green vegetables, especially beans and more made-up dishes, while housewives in lower income groups served more roots.[57]

[54] See Hammond, *Food: Volume I*, p. 155–8; also *Food: Volume II*, chs XXI–XXII.
[55] Sheridan, *Wartime Women*, pp. 103–5.
[56] PRO, RG23/30, Central Office of Information, The Social Survey, *Investigation into Household Cooking Habits for Certain Vegetables*, New Series 27 (no date [October 1942]).
[57] Ibid., pp. 3–4.

When methods of preparation and cooking were discussed, 84 per cent of housewives peeled potatoes, though a distinct minority – mainly in the upper-income groups – cooked them in their skins.[58] Housewives were also questioned about chopping methods, steeping in water and whether hot or cold water was used to start the cooking process. With regard to cooking times for green vegetables, 60 per cent put them in for 20 to 30 minutes, about 20 per cent for less and some 15 per cent for over 30 minutes. Over 60 per cent used soda or bicarbonate of soda when cooking. Potatoes were generally cooked for 20 to 30 minutes (75 per cent) though some 12 per cent cooked for less and between 9 and 13 per cent for more. Most housewives cooked with the intention of serving immediately (74 per cent) but some food was reheated due to the absence of workers or schoolchildren, while 29 per cent cooked potatoes for more than one meal at one time. Potato water was used by 75 per cent to make stews or stocks and so on, and over a half (53 per cent) used cabbage water in the same way.[59]

Variety and palatability were the principal casualties in the diet. Housewives found themselves using less fried fish, biscuits, vinegar, bottled sauces, bought pickles, flavouring essences, bottled cordials and crystals. Foods used more frequently included sausages and sausage meat, meat pies, tinned soup, powdered soup, Bovril, meat and fish paste, and cocoa.[60] In brief, women had increased their use of meat substitutes and soup to offset the limited availability of meat. Although they had cut down on flavourings and appetizers that might make their families want to eat more, this was not a conscious response but rather reflected the fact that these items were in short supply and frequently not available in shops. However, the need to use substitute food materials made popular dishes unpalatable: 'toad-in-the-hole is *not* what it was. That lovely pork sausage in a yellow batter, shining with fat, has given place to a beef (save the mark) beast, flavourless and tough-skinned, in a heavy khaki batter made with milk powder.'[61] On the whole, the British housewife showed a limited wish to experiment with either the Ministry of Food's recipes or new foods that were offered, though most accepted 'Spam'[62] and learned to cope with dried egg and dried skimmed-milk powder, known as 'household milk'. In the autumn of

---

[58] Ibid., p. 5.

[59] Ibid., p. 11–14.

[60] PRO, RG23/31, Central Office of Information, The Social Survey, *Manufacturing Foods Inquiry, Part II*, New Series 31 (December 1942). Between 30 November and 18 December 1942, 4,760 housewives were interviewed on behalf of the Ministry of Food.

[61] Donnelly, *Mrs Milburn's Diaries*, p. 192.

[62] 'Spam' was a name derived from Spiced Ham. It was quite popular. Other brands of tinned meat were 'Prem', 'Tang' and 'Mor'.

1942, the Wartime Social Survey sent fifty interviewers to find out how important manufactured foods were to housewives and what changes in their use had occurred during the war. They interviewed 4,388 house-wives in England, Wales and Scotland concerning five categories of manufactured foods: breakfast cereals, prepared desserts (including custard powder), prepared baking mixtures, cakes and biscuits, and jam.[63] Breakfast cereals (including oatmeal) were served by 82 per cent of housewives. Cornflakes (as a generic group of flake cereals) were used by 39 per cent, 40 per cent used prepared oats and 12 per cent used oatmeal. Cornflakes were more popular in the south of England and oat-meal more in use in Scotland but, overall, there had been an increased use of cereals during the war 'to replace foods which are now unobtain-able, or of which the ration is very small, especially bacon and eggs'. The limiting factors in the consumption of breakfast cereals were insufficient milk, sugar and a shortage of points coupons. Porridge was thought to be the 'most important' cereal by 46 per cent and any shortage of oat products 'would cause hardship'. The cornflakes group was rated most important by 28 per cent of the housewives interviewed.[64]

Prepared desserts were served by 94 per cent of respondents, two-thirds of whom used custard powder. The use of prepared desserts was thought to have decreased either because they were unobtainable or because of the lack of sugar and milk required to make them. House-wives missed prepared desserts: we 'need them in wartime when we have no other things'. They made 'the pudding much more palatable, especially when we have no fruit'.[65] Baking mixtures (Yorkshire pudding, pudding and cake mixes) were also missed when not available; some 46 per cent of housewives used them but there was a wide regional variation. Consumption was highest in the Midlands (56 per cent) but only a minority used them in Scotland (27 per cent). Some were 'not in the shops' but if they were available usage was limited by shortages of sugar and fats. 'There are very few things to make puddings with which are not on points' was one comment. A baked pudding 'makes for variety' and 'helps out with dinners and meat ration' was another. One baking mixture had 'sugar in it, and so helps out with sugar ration' said a third.[66]

The consumption of jam (and marmalade) was almost universal: 94 per cent of housewives took the full jam ration. It had been served the previous week by 96 per cent of respondents. Two-thirds put jam or

[63] PRO, RG23/29, Central Office of Information, The Social Survey, New Series 29, *Manufactured Foods Investigation* (undated [October 1942]), p. 1.
[64] Ibid., pp. 2–3, and p. 6, Table 10.
[65] Ibid., pp. 14–15, 16.
[66] Ibid., pp. 22–3

Plate 7.4 Nutritional advice and recipes were offered by the Ministry of Food's Food Advice Division. (Public Record Office MAF102/15)

marmalade on the table for breakfast every day and just over half (55 per cent) for tea. It was used for cooking (52 per cent) and in packed meals (27 per cent), and those not taking it thought it of poor quality or too expensive. Some took sugar instead, if retailers allowed it, to make their own.[67] Jam-making was widespread. Two-thirds of the housewives made some. There were predicable variations: more was made in rural and less in urban areas; more by non-working than working housewives. Cakes and biscuits were bought by 92 per cent of housewives with some 37 per cent buying them more often than before the war. Life would be hard without them; there was a 'shortage of fat for home cooking' and the shop goods were a 'substitute of (*sic*) other foods we can't get'. The great advantage was 'we don't need points for cakes and they are cheap'. When interviewers asked housewives what they needed more of, 68 per cent said jam, 41 per cent custard powder, 33 per cent cornflour and blancmange, and 31 per cent breakfast cereals.[68]

Wartime recipes were not inspiring; 'Woolton Pie' and 'Turnip Top Salad' with 'Pathfinder Pudding' or 'Eggless Sponge Pudding' could not ease the difficulties of making the rations go farther. 'Stale breadcrumbs' was a frequent but hardly an attractive ingredient of many recipes. The Wartime Social Survey concluded in 1943 that 'the Kitchen Front and other Ministry of Food publicity had not so far been successful in persuading housewives to include "made-up" dishes more frequently in their menu', a view at odds with postwar recollections by some dieticians.[69] From a more down-to-earth postwar perspective, it seemed:

> The controls and queues of the past eleven years have confirmed and consolidated, I think, the conservatism of the British housewife in the matter of buying food. . . . Those who succumbed to the official boosting of whalemeat, snoek and brisling mostly wish they had not. Those who were adventurous enough to spend 5s. or 6s. on cans of imported food labelled – apparently with the Minister's approval – with the words 'Sausages in brine', discovered that they had about 11 ounces of sausages in a pint or more of salt water. Could anything be more destructive of willingness to try something new?[70]

Teenagers were some of the most conservative; the introduction of Namco (National Milk Cocoa) for young factory workers in their tea breaks was a notable failure.[71]

---

[67] Ibid., p. 26.
[68] Ibid., pp. 32–5.
[69] PRO, RG23/9A, Wartime Social Survey, *Food During the War*, p. 23. One aspect of the 'Kitchen Front' was a programme broadcast daily at 8.15 a.m. on weekdays by the BBC.
[70] *BFJ*, January 1951, p. 1. See also Longmate, *How We Lived Then*, ch. 13.
[71] Ministry of Health, *The State of the Public Health during Six Years of War*, p. 117, and BMA, *Committee on Nutrition*, 1950, para. 146, p. 50.

Eating outside the home

Communal eating in schools, works canteens and British Restaurants afforded other opportunities to have food off-the-ration. British Restaurants were intended to provide meals for workers for whom factory canteens were not available.[72] The expansion of food supplied at work during the war resulted from the Factory (Canteens) Order and from the provision of miners' canteens by the Miners' Welfare Commission.[73] By December 1944, 62.2M meals a week were served in canteens and over 0.5M a day in British Restaurants,[74] though, since works canteens were not universally available, there was on occasion a sense of unfairness about these provisions:

> People who feed in restaurants and canteens have their rationed food at home, and what they eat in restaurants and canteens is *extra*. This is absolutely unfair. For 7 or 8 months this year I, along with several other housewives, helped in a canteen, reserved for ARP workers and police – the staff of a Control Report Centre. We helpers were astounded and disgusted at the quantities of food which were always procurable, and for which they paid ridiculously low prices. They had cups of tea, with sugar, in season and out. After a jolly good dinner at midday, there were cups of tea again by 3 p. m., and from about 4.45 p. m. to 6.45 p. m. we were harried to death cooking and serving egg and chips, sausage and chips, fish and chips, and scones or biscuits, or jam tart. They turned up their noses at salad or sandwiches – they must have a cooked tea, and all this without tipping up any coupons. Our husbands, on the other hand, didn't see an egg in months at a time, nor a tomato, and we couldn't afford to buy such things as cucumbers.[75]

The war brought no major changes in people's eating habits and the meal patterns common in the 1930s were retained through the war years.[76] Rationing, for example, did not diminish the differences in food habits between Scotland and England. In February 1943, a survey

---

[72] See Hammond, *Food: Volume II*, chs XXIII–XXV. The Ministry encouraged the setting up of Communal Feeding Centres in November 1940 but Winston Churchill proposed the title 'British Restaurants' in March 1941. In 1943, the Factories (Canteens) Order required all places of manual work employing more than 250 people to provide a canteen selling hot meals.

[73] See Sir Noel Curtis-Bennett, *The Food of the People Being the History of Industrial Feeding* (1949), ch. IX.

[74] BMA, *Committee on Nutrition*, Table XXIV.

[75] Sheridan, *Wartime Women*, p. 148. Mrs Trowbridge, volunteer worker, Bradford, 10 October 1941. See Curtis-Bennett, p. 267, for the fact that miners' families were allowed to use the miners' canteens one night per week!

[76] For meal patterns in the 1930s, see Sir William Crawford, *The People's Food*, 1938.

showed that breakfasts, evening meals and late evening snacks were eaten at home and 42 per cent of the sample still took their midday meal at home. Although 22 per cent ate in canteens at midday, only 2 per cent used British Restaurants.[77] Cafeteria-style eating was still novel and unfamiliarity made it unpopular:

> All tables were reserved, so I tried the cafeteria – my first experience of this kind of meal. Even wartime difficulties did not make me enjoy this method of serving oneself: pick up the tray, slide it along the bars, receive a slop of meat (not *too* bad, but a bit grisly), far too much potato and gravy and masses of cabbage. Next three prunes and a half and not too bad custard. With these I paid the woman at the end, who spoke in whispers, and walked off to a table – to find I had forgotten my knife, fork, etc. – went back and got them and ate. The coffee was vile so I left it. Last week I had an excellent meal in the room below for a few coppers more![78]

The preference expressed by many respondents in the 1943 Wartime Social Survey for eating at home outweighed the advantages of getting food off-the-ration. However, home cooking placed the burden of providing acceptable meals on the resourcefulness of the housewife in the food queues, as well as in the kitchen.[79] Similar arguments were advanced for schoolchildren to eat at home rather than at school: 'the mother wants to see them, she needs company, nobody knows better than herself what is good for the child, and she cooks anyway, so why not cook for the one child more.'[80] British Restaurants were better patronized in London than elsewhere. A greater sense of self-sufficiency in Scotland meant that less use was made of British Restaurants there and fewer purchases were made of commercial products – meat and fish pastes, powdered and tinned soups, custard powders, bottled sauces and pickles.[81] Despite the rise in working-class incomes during the war, there were still poor people with inadequate diets; those who spent least on food were still dependent on 'bread and spread' rather than on cooked meals.[82]

---

[77] Wartime Social Survey, *Food During the War*, p. 12.
[78] Donnelly, *Mrs Milburn's Diaries*, pp. 176–7.
[79] Longmate, *How We Lived Then*, ch. 13, 'The Kitchen Front', discusses the frustrations experienced by housewives in connexion with food.
[80] PRO, RG23/47. Wartime Social Survey, Report No.33A, New Series, *School Meals in Scotland, August 1943*, typescript, undated, p. 9.
[81] PRO, RG23/9A. Wartime Social Survey, *Food During the War*, p. 13.
[82] BMA, *Committee on Nutrition*, para. 111, p. 40.

Food quality

The quality of wartime food was kept under close scrutiny, as the war brought fears of food contamination by enemy action, particularly gas attacks. During the interwar years, public analysts had been concerned with understanding the new work in biochemistry that accompanied the discovery of vitamins; but they also faced the increasing task of testing foods under the Preservatives in Food Regulations of 1926, and the codifying Sale of Food and Drugs Act, 1938. Soon after the outbreak of war food shortages brought a range of 'substitutes' into the shops. Public analysts faced baking powder coloured yellow claiming to be egg, various flour-based substances that were advertised as milk substitutes, and a range of liquids proclaimed their value as fruit drinks, lemon essences and tonic wines. The vitamin values of many foods became central to producers' advertising campaigns.[83]

The government issued a mountain of food orders of which the first, symbolically, was the Sausages (Maximum Prices) Order of 1940 in which the minimum meat content of that mysterious food was defined. There were also new food standards to be applied by public analysts as rationing brought concern over the nutritive values of foods and as prewar regulations banning food preservatives were relaxed. Borax and sulphur dioxide were once more permitted in margarine, bacon, jam and dehydrated vegetables; sodium nitrite was permitted in bacon and pickled meat, and diphenyl impregnated paper was used to wrap such oranges as arrived in Britain.[84] The fortification of some foods with vitamins and minerals was an additional complication but there was considerable evidence that the war brought a marked deterioration in quality and availability of some foods. Canned meat was of variable repute. The minimum meat content of processed meats such as 'luncheon sausage, breakfast sausage, meat galantine and polony' had been reduced to 30 per cent. During wartime, notified cases of food-poisoning rose, as Table 7.10 illustrates. Some of this was blamed on the great increase in communal feeding coupled with a shortage of trained kitchen staff. Almost 75 per cent of the cases resulted from fresh rather than tinned or bottled food. Of these, the largest group of outbreaks were from meat[85] and between 1941 and 1948, 47 per cent of all cases

---

[83] Ministry of Health, *The State of the Public Health During Six Years of War*, p. 125.

[84] Ibid., p. 126.

[85] Ibid., pp. 44–6. See also G. H. Walker, 'Food and its adulteration during the present war', the Chadwick Lecture, reprinted in the *British Food Journal*, January to April 1945.

Table 7.10 Outbreaks of food-poisoning in England and Wales, 1939 to 1944

Year	Total outbreaks	Salmonella outbreaks	Number of salmonella cases
1939	83	47	94
1940	47	8	60
1941	151	76	141
1942	241	64	476
1943	247	194	767
1944	550	503	1,006

Source: Ministry of Health, *The State of the Public Health During Six Years of War*, Table 1, p. 43.

resulted from made-up meat products.[86] Other foods involved were milk and eggs, including American dried eggs.

The quality of fish was a problem even for coastal towns when inshore fisheries were closed, and a zoning scheme for fish supplies was introduced in 1942. Although designed to save transport costs, it increased the staleness of fish in many areas:

> I bought some herrings, too – more like pilchards, for there were twelve to the pound. When I recall the days when our fish came from Fleetwood, our kippers from the Isle of Man, our lovely plaice, fluke, shrimps and shell fish from our own Morecambe Bay, I wonder what mighty brain put us in the Aberdeen zone. Barrow people have always been such big fish-eaters: I always bought fish four or five times a week when the boys were home.[87]

Stale fish was commonplace for inland towns where, in Magnus Pyke's view, the fish-and-chip industry 'might almost be said to have been created to overcome the poor quality fish caught by the modern fishing industry'. Consumer resistance to wartime salt cod, and for that matter postwar snoek, did not waver.[88] Cheese quality had also deteriorated and the variety of cheeses available had diminished markedly. This was less a result of wartime circumstances than the prewar changes in the liquid milk market during the 1930s. But rationing had accentuated the trend: if social justice was to be maintained, any commodity must be acceptable to the whole population: 'rationed cheese must not possess too pronounced a flavour.' This ruled out blue cheeses such as Stilton

[86] M. Pyke, *Townsman's Food* (1952), p. 63 (citing the Ministry of Food Statutory Instrument No. 1509 of 1948) and p. 196.
[87] Broad and Fleming, *Nella Last's War* (5 April 1943), pp. 246–7; PRO, MAF152/44, Five Years of Food Control (typescript), p. 4.
[88] Pyke, *Townsman's Food*, p. 67.

and reduced production to 'Cheddar-type' cheese.[89] The most dramatic effect on the food supply during the war, however, had been the almost complete removal of poultry from the diet on the grounds that they ate imported grain. In consequence, feed allocations to livestock farmers reflected government priorities: first, to feed cows for milk production; second, to feed sheep and beef cattle, and finally, pigs and poultry. By the mid-twentieth century, therefore: 'poultry has become a rarity on the urban dining table: its price puts it beyond the reach of the ordinary family – except on special occasions like Christmas Day.'[90]

Nutritional status and health

The Second World War has been seen as a period of improvement in nutritional standards in Britain. Although the government was concerned that the energy value of the rations should be adequate, the planning of the diet owed relatively little to the precepts of nutrition, despite the role of Professor J. C. Drummond as Scientific Adviser to the Ministry of Food or the postwar claims of the Ministry of Health.[91] Margarine was fortified with vitamins A and D in January 1940 but Drummond's recommendation that the extraction rate of flour should be raised was ignored. Similarly, the output of home-produced meat depended upon feed supplies determined by the Ministry of Agriculture rather than by nutritional advice.[92] What advice was accepted was obtained in a piecemeal way; for example, although Drummond was the Ministry of Food's Scientific Adviser, Sir John Orr was asked to calculate how much extra rations were necessary for workers performing heavy manual labour. Similarly, the Cabinet accepted advice based on the research of Dr R. A. McCance and Dr E. M. Widdowson, in 1941, to fortify flour with calcium.[93] In addition, mothers and young children were given

[89] Ibid., pp. 126–8.
[90] Ibid., pp. 81–4. Pyke offered calculations derived from the School of Agriculture, Cambridge and the Imperial Bureau of Animal Nutrition (Rowett Research Institute), Aberdeen, that from 100lb. of digestible feed, the dairy cow produced 35lb. of animal protein, the pig 20lb., the bullock and sheep 8–15lb., whereas hens laid 30lb of eggs and produced 20lb. of meat.
[91] See Drummond, *Englishman's Food*, pp. 448–54. Dorothy Hollingsworth omits Drummond's resignation over bread rationing. Unofficial advice, such as that offered by Sir John Orr and David Lubbock in *Feeding the People in War-Time*, was certainly ignored.
[92] See n. 90 above.
[93] See Margaret Ashwell, ed., *McCance & Widdowson* (1993), pp. 23–5. The experimental work on mineral metabolism was published by R. A. McCance and E. M. Widdowson, *Journal of Physiology*, 1942, 101, pp. 44–85.

dietary supplements. Pregnant and lactating mothers and pre-school children received extra milk, and infant welfare clinics supplied cod-liver oil, orange juice and rose-hip syrup, though 'the uptake of these vitamin supplements was, however, disappointing'.[94]

In 1938, only 150,000 or just over 4 per cent of elementary school-children received school dinners, the bulk of which (110,000) were given free at 'feeding centres'. The school milk scheme, implemented in 1935, was well established however. Already some 55 per cent of the school population in England and Wales, or 2.5M pupils in all, drank milk at school in 1938, as Table 7.11 shows. The initial effect of the war on school meals was disruptive. As the evacuation schemes came into operation, many centres for feeding children closed and there was a drop in milk consumption in schools. Table 7.11 shows the extent of the deterioration by July 1940, when special financial provisions were introduced. Further measures followed in 1941 to increase the palata-bility of school meals by raising the allowances of meat and sugar. Subsequently, uptake increased significantly and, by the end of the war, nearly 40 per cent of schoolchildren had school dinners and over 70 per cent drank school milk, though it is surprising that the number eating school dinners was not greater, given that the food was off-the-ration.[95] The increase in consumption of milk and meals at schools in prewar special areas was a significant factor in the levelling up of nutritional status among schoolchildren during the war.

Table 7.11 Numbers of children having school meals and milk in England and Wales during the Second World War

Date	Meals		Milk	
	Number (M)	Percentage	Number (M)	Percentage
1938–39	0.150	4.4	2.500	55.0
July 1940	0.130	3.5	2.100	n.k.
February 1941	0.279	6.5	2.479	57.6
February 1942	0.607	14.0	3.386	77.9
February 1943	1.048	23.5	3.371	76.8
February 1944	1.495	32.8	3.428	76.3
February 1945	1.650	36.3	3.265	73.0
October 1945	1.840	39.7	3.322	71.7

Source: Ministry of Education, The Health of the School Child 1939–45 (1947).
Note: n.k. = not known.

[94] BMA, Committee on Nutrition, para. 144, p. 49.
[95] Ministry of Education, The Health of the School Child 1939–45 (1947), pp. 23–4.

At the end of the war there were contrasting views about the success of the rationing scheme. The nutritionists and dieticians held that health standards had been improved by better distribution of food, increased milk consumption and extensive communal eating through school meals, factory canteens and British Restaurants. Rationing, it was believed, had levelled up the British diet by increasing the food consumption of the lowest income groups, though it was admitted that the diet had 'become duller and drier' and not very palatable.[96] According to Orr and Lubbock, prewar Britain had consisted of one-third well-fed, one-third adequately fed and one-third whose diet was deficient. Rationing raised the nutritional status of the latter group to the level of adequacy. Unfortunately, despite the introduction of a dietary survey in 1940, the data available were never sufficient to monitor the nutritional status of the population fully. The clinical surveys for nutritional deficiency diseases carried out by the Ministry of Health in 1942 found no deterioration due to the wartime diet but the evidence of prewar deprivation was still present:

> Their findings were unexpectedly satisfactory, for even although they paid most attention to poor areas they found surprisingly little evidence of undernourishment or malnutrition which could not be attributed to past shortages. In districts which before the war had been subject to long periods of unemployment, many of the adults and adolescents, and particularly the women, showed that they had suffered severely, but only occasionally could evidence of a present deficiency be found.[97]

The British Medical Association's Committee on Nutrition attempted to make 'a clinical assessment of the nation's health in terms of nutrition' during the latter part of the 1940s.[98] Certain general trends seemed clear: wartime Britain had experienced falls in mortality and morbidity that were as great or even greater than in the interwar period. But the poverty of data available presented the Committee with many problems in making precise judgements. What is surprising is the degree of caution expressed by the Committee in making its general conclusion that the health of the British people had been well maintained. Nutrition, during the war, in the Committee's judgement, was 'uneven'

---

[96] Ministry of Food, *How Britain Was Fed in War-Time Food Control, 1939–1945* (1946), p. 4.

[97] These surveys were carried out initially by an American clinician, Professor Sydenstricker, provided by the Rockefeller Foundation, and later by medical officers from the Colonial Service. See Ministry of Health, *The State of the Public Health during Six Years of War*, p. 119.

[98] BMA, *Committee on Nutrition*, para. 15, p. 9.

in respect of a number of nutrients, including protein, iron, ascorbic acid (vitamin C) and vitamin A. That of expectant mothers was undoubtedly better, but for young children both of pre-school and school age, mortality from respiratory tuberculosis gave rise to concern. Rickets was still present in infants and young children, though a marked fall in dental caries among primary schoolchildren in some areas was probably due to dietary change, principally the reduction in sugar consumption during the war.[99] Table 7.12 shows the reduction in the proportion of children in the prewar Special Areas placed in nutrition grade 'C' or 'fair' (the prewar designation had been 'slightly subnormal') together with the levels of school meals and milk consumption reached in the autumn of 1945. Grade 'D' (prewar 'bad') also fell overall from 0.5 per cent in 1938 to 0.3 per cent in 1945. Even in poor areas, grade 'D' had been almost eliminated by 1945: in Jarrow, it fell from 4.84 per cent of children in 1938 to 0.25 per cent in 1945; in Pontypridd, from 2.03 to

Table 7.12 Nutritional improvement in prewar Special Areas during the Second World War

Area	Proportion of school population having meals and milk (autumn 1945)		Grade C nutritional assessment at routine medical examinations	
	Meals (%)	Milk (%)	1938 (%)	Oct. 1945 (%)
Counties				
Durham	30.1	73.7	23.4	17.26
Glamorgan	40.4	61.2	22.1	10.45
Monmouth	43.8	72.9	14.6	9.84
County Boroughs				
Gateshead	32.4	56.7	29.7	25.47
Merthyr Tydfil	63.7	76.1	26.6	7.40
England and Wales	39.7	71.7	10.8	8.90

Source: Ministry of Education, *The Health of the School Child 1939–45* (1947).

[99] Ibid., para. 16, p. 9 and paras 225–32, pp. 89–91; for caries, see John Welshman, *Municipal Medicine Public Health in Twentieth-Century Britain* (Oxford, 2000), p. 193.

0.52 per cent.[100] In general, throughout Britain, the physique of children living at home continued to improve during the war, though there was some check in growth rates during the period of evacuation, particularly for those children sent to camp schools.[101] However, between 1945 and 1947, a setback in growth rates affected children at all ages between 5 and 15. This suggested that the nutritional status of the population was much closer to the limits of adequacy than has been generally assumed.[102] Even the Ministry of Health – noted for taking the most optimistic view – could not claim that children's nutrition approached the optimum for growth, nor that the social gradient of heights and weights had been eliminated by rationing.[103]

The aftermath of war

Rationing placed restrictions on food choice and inhibited dietary change during the 1940s. The stability of the diet may be seen in Tables 7.8 and 7.9, which emphasize the fact that rationing was fully maintained, even when victory was in sight, though from 1944 onwards occasions such as Christmas brought seasonal supplements of nuts and dried fruits into the shops. When not even the slightest relaxation in food rationing was offered to the British people once hostilities had ceased, the consensus which underwrote the government's wartime food policy began to erode. In September 1948, Mass Observation noted people's growing resentment at queuing and by the following spring the overwhelming proportion of the population expressed the view that their diet was worse than before the war.[104] Tables 7.8 and 7.9 also

[100] Ministry of Education, *The Health of the School Child 1939–45*, pp. 23–4.

[101] Ministry of Health, *The State of the Public Health During Six Years of War*, p. 120.

[102] PRO, RG23/151. Central Office of Information, The Social Survey, *Schoolboys' Diets by Audrey Beltram*, typescript, undated (1949), pp. 1–2. See Ministry of Agriculture Fisheries and Food, *Fifty Years of the National Food Survey 1940–1990* (1991), p. 21. In ch. 2, Arnold Baines wrote: 'Between 1945 and 1947 there was some loss of weight in adults and retardation of growth in children.' Dorothy Hollingsworth confirmed this point.

[103] Ministry of Health, *The State of the Public Health During Six Years of War*, p. 121.

[104] I. Zweiniger-Bargielowska, 'Consensus and consumption: rationing, austerity and controls after the War', in H. Jones and M. Kandiah, eds, *The Myth of Consensus: New Views on British History, 1945–64* (Basingstoke, 1996), pp. 89–90. See also I. Zweiniger-Bargielowska, *Austerity in Britain: Rationing, Controls, and Consumption, 1939–1955* (Oxford, 2000), esp. ch. 3 *passim*.

show that economic policy rather than nutritional status was the major determinant of consumption patterns. For example, the greatest restrictions on diet were not caused by wartime attacks on Britain's food supplies but occurred in the postwar years. In fact, for the first two postwar years – 1946 and 1947 – the diet provided people with lower energy intakes than during the war itself.

The Housewives' League argued that married women were put under enormous stress by the necessity of trying to maintain 'normal' meal patterns when the fat rations were so very small.[105] The British Medical Association's Committee on Nutrition agreed, concluding that 'since 1939 the diet of the nation has, on the average, deteriorated in variety and palatability'.[106] Food became a focus for opposition to the Labour government: by the Conservatives in Parliament; by consumer groups such as the Housewives' League; and by food trade and food manu-facturing interests. The return to prewar food standards, particularly in the case of white bread, remained long delayed, though, as time passed, fewer people remembered what prewar white bread had been like. Flour extraction rates had been brought down to 82.5 per cent in October 1944 and to 80 per cent in January 1945 to show that 'we are gradually improving the palatability of the bread without affecting its nutritional value'. Although additional imports of 80 per cent extraction-rate flour were required under the aid programmes from Canada and the USA, it was important to encourage people's expectations that peace-time would bring relaxation in food controls.[107] Unfortunately, bad postwar harvests and the immediate ending of American Lend Lease aid, following the defeat of Japan in August 1945, led to sharp falls in reserves of wheat. In May 1946, when stocks were down to nine weeks' consumption, the Minister of Food, Sir Ben Smith, was forced to raise the extraction rate to 90 per cent. Mr Attlee, the Prime Minister, replaced Smith by John Strachey, who had the mischance to begin his term of office with the announcement that bread would be rationed from July 1946 and it would be necessary to surrender bread units when bread was bought. This was the last straw for Drummond and Dr Moran, who both opposed bread rationing; it brought about their resignations as scientific advisers to the Ministry of Food, in June 1946. During the following winter of 1946 to 1947, exceptionally cold weather froze vegetables in the ground and coal could not be moved; in January 1947, wheat and flour reserves fell to less than six weeks' supply

---

[105] The Housewives' League would have been surprised to learn that Sir Jack Drummond opposed cuts in the rations in 1946 on the same grounds of palatability.
[106] BMA, *Committee on Nutrition*, para. 154, p. 52.
[107] PRO, MAF84/393. Imports of wheat and flour were allocated by the Combined Food Board in Washington on which American officials exercised a majority.

and potatoes were also rationed for the first time. Bread rationing ended in 1948, when it was clear that there had been no breakdown in distribution and that the bread unit scheme was being widely ignored. At last, in April 1949, the first step in easing wartime restrictions came when sweets were de-rationed. The subsequent rush to buy led to their disappearance 'under the counter' and rationing had to be reintroduced in July. Restrictions on milk, fish and those goods obtained in exchange for points were abandoned in 1950, sweets were de-rationed in time for the Coronation of Queen Elizabeth in 1952, and food rationing ended finally in 1954.

8

THE REVIVAL OF CHOICE

Food technology, retailing and eating in postwar Britain

At the point when rationing began to be eased, Dr Magnus Pyke reviewed the food of the British people – or at least the majority of them – in a book entitled *Townsman's Food*.[1] After ten years of rationing, the townsman – or, more especially, the urban housewife – was thinking wistfully of times of former plenty. The countryside was an important part of this yearning, for it symbolized the source of good food to the urban population. However, Magnus Pyke was uncompromisingly dismissive of nostalgia and feelings of 'romantic regret for the simple foods of earlier centuries'. Memories of prewar availability of food had been making the urban housewife with a tin-opener something of a figure of fun for cartoonists in the 1940s. However, from the pragmatic viewpoint as food scientist, Pyke applauded her search for variety in the diet. To do so, she needed a tin-opener, for few in 1950 could live without canned meat, fish or fruit.[2] As a guide to the diet in the year 1950, *Townsman's Food* concerned itself largely with a description of the sources of food materials, i.e. bread and baked goods, vegetables, meat, dairy produce and so on, rather than processed food products. It was published in an age when confidence in science was much higher than it is today. Pyke, whose popular reputation rested upon his creed of bringing science to the people, saw the food industry as providing a 'social service'; after all, he wrote: 'the food industry has to keep the community alive and in tolerable health'.[3] However, *Townsman's Food* was published at a time when many wartime regulations were still in place, so there is little on food marketing or presentation. Symbolic of the slowness by which controls were being relaxed was wrapped, sliced bread, which had only been permitted since 1949. Some food technology was important: Magnus Pyke referred to gas storage of fruit, and

---

[1] At the 1951 Census, 80 per cent of the population were classed as urban and 20 per cent as rural.
[2] Pyke, *Townsman's Food*, p. vii.
[3] Ibid., p. 11.

the use of sulphur dioxide as a preservative, but when he claimed that 'Today, foods "in season" have been abolished. In the modern world, we expect all foods always to be "in season"', it is clear that the effervescent optimism which endeared Pyke to radio and television audiences had carried him away.[4] In fact, the reality was far less congenial. Restriction of food consumption was central to the 'age of austerity' during the late 1940s. Although bread rationing ended in 1948, peacetime bread was still the wartime grey National Loaf and rationing of butter, margarine and meat came to an end only in July 1954, by which time dietary change had been delayed for almost a decade after the war. State control of the food supply had limited new developments of frozen or dehydrated foods. For housewives, the 1940s had been an age of deference to the shopkeeper necessarily linked to seeking favours, such as better cuts of meat or obtaining items in short supply normally kept 'under the counter'. Such attitudes continued well beyond rationing.

Commercial food processing in 1950 was not without problems. Freezing ruptured the cellular structure of food so that appearance and quality deteriorated; there was chemical change in fat which meant that food could suffer from 'freezer burn'. Chilling was still found to affect flavour adversely. Magnus Pyke's view of processed food was typified by his description of ice-cream, which, as an unrationed food, had an aura of luxury and indulgence at the end of the 1940s:

> Modern British ice cream, therefore, is in general, a wholesome food; but its nutritional value may vary greatly in proportion with, firstly, the amount of dried milk it contains and whether the dried milk is from full-cream milk or from skimmed milk. Secondly, it may contain much or little fat. If ice cream is poor in milk and poor in fat, it must contain some other ingredient. This other ingredient may be flour or another cereal product, in which case the nutritional value of the ice cream will more closely resemble custard-powder custard than ice cream (using the name literally). On the other hand, the alternative ingredient may be water. If it is, the ice cream will gradually sink below the category of a food, and will have to take its place among such dietetic anomalies as jelly, of which a plateful contains a pinch of solid matter.[5]

There you have it: the excitement that food brought to mind in the mid-twentieth century was limited to jelly and ice-cream. There were processed peas as well, dyed green and sterilized, but the new frozen vegetables were a 'luxury' and very limited in their availability. In fact, the foodstuffs entering the British diet in the 1950s had yet to experience

---

[4] Ibid., p. 127.
[5] Ibid., p. 125.

the growth of food technology that characterized the second half of the twentieth century, during which time the amount of processing food underwent and the number of stages in the food chain increased dramatically. Much change depended upon the intensification of agricultural output, particularly with regard to livestock. During the 1950s and early 1960s, 'battery' production of eggs, the rearing of calves and pigs in small pens, and chickens in large sheds became the means to increase supplies. Concern began to be expressed over the welfare of the animals and the ethics of such production systems, though a government inquiry endorsed the methods used provided minimum safeguards were met.[6]

Restrictions on consumer choice remained in force even after the Conservative government was formed following the 1951 election. Food subsidies and agricultural price support policies introduced by the Agriculture Act, 1947, controlled the domestic food market, and the Ministry of Food continued its work until April 1955 when it was merged with the Ministry of Agriculture and Fisheries.[7] The symbol of wartime control, the subsidized loaf made from National Flour, remained in the shops. Not until 1953 did the millers gain permission to produce white flour free from price control. To do so, they had to accept new requirements to fortify it with thiamine (vitamin B_1), nicotinic acid and iron, as well as the calcium that had been added since 1941. Thus it was August 1953, a full eight years after the war had ended, before white bread reappeared in the shops. Initially sales proved disappointing, since a large loaf of 1.75lb. cost 1s 0d, while the National Loaf was on sale at 7½d. In practice, bakers and millers had already begun to ignore the bread regulations and were putting whiter flour into the National Loaf even before National flour was abolished. The National Loaf ceased to be sold in October 1956.[8] However, fortification was retained: flour of whatever extraction rate was required to contain 0.24mg of thiamine, 1.60mg of nicotinic acid and 1.65mg of iron per 100g. When lower extraction-rate flour decreased the amounts of these nutrients – as with the 70 per cent flour the millers and bakers wanted – levels had to be made up by the addition of chemicals. Although fortification of flour aroused some opposition, the improved palatability of white bread attracted the majority of consumers. Any

---

[6] See M. Pyke, *Technological Eating. Where Does the Fish Finger Point?* (1972), pp. 65–6, citing the Brambell Committee, *Report of the Technical Committee to Enquire into the Welfare of Animals kept under Intensive Livestock Husbandry Systems* (1965).

[7] Winnifrith, *Ministry of Agriculture, Fisheries and Food*, p. 39. The Ministry of Food's functions in Scotland were taken over by the Department of Agriculture for Scotland.

[8] Sandra Hunt, 'The Second World War: bread under government control, 1939 56', unpublished Rank Prize Fund research paper.

opposition by nutritionists to the lower extraction rate was muted by evidence that, in a normal mixed diet, flour of low or high extraction rate made no difference to children's growth.[9]

As food began to be de-rationed at the end of the 1940s, a landmark in the return to peacetime ways was the Festival of Britain in 1951, where eating and drinking became part of the first major postwar leisure event. Catering concessions for visitors were awarded to ABC and Forte. The Milk Marketing Board installed a 'Dairy Bar' in the 'Country Pavilion' to sell milk in half-pint cartons.[10] Forte ran a cafeteria operation that could serve thirty-two people per minute with snack meals, soft drinks and beverages, and followed this by catering for the new leisure development in Battersea Park, though 'rowdies and Teddy boys' led to the termination of the licence after three years.[11] Although milk bars and the cafeterias that survived the war had begun to attract the new class of teenagers, milk bars struggled in the 1950s. Despite some attempts to redevelop them – Fortnum and Mason opened a milk bar and soda fountain in 1955 and the Duke of Marlborough obtained the services of 'Bon Viveur' of the *Daily Telegraph* to open another at Blenheim Palace – the milk bar was replaced by the coffee bar as the fashionable leisure centre in the high streets during the 1950s. Some, such as the 2i's Coffee Bar at 59 Old Compton Street in Soho, featured the music of Tommy Steele and Cliff Richard, but all had the attraction of large, hissing, Italian Gaggia coffee machines, little glass cups and saucers and an air of sophistication that attracted young people.[12] The revival of choice also saw the reawakening of interest in food among middle-class Francophiles and left-wing intellectuals. Raymond Postgate wrote articles on food for the *Leader* in 1950 including imagining a 'Society for Prevention of Cruelty to Food' and starting a 'Good Food Club'. The following year he published the first issue of the *Good Food Guide* which sold 5,000 copies.[13] The reopening by Rosemary Hume and Constance Spry of the Cordon Bleu cookery school and the publication by Elizabeth David of *Mediterranean Food* in 1950 and *French*

---

[9] S. Davidson, R. Passmore, J. F. Brock and A. S. Truswell, *Human Nutrition and Dietetics*, 6th edn (Edinburgh, 1975), p. 202. See *Lancet* (1956), 1, p. 901, for the Medical Research Council's 'Report by a Panel on the Composition and Nutritive Value of Flour'.

[10] PRO JV7/117. Milk Marketing Board files.

[11] Charles Forte, *Forte: the Autobiography of Charles Forte* (1986), pp. 68–70.

[12] Christina Hardyment, *Slice of Life. The British Way of Eating Since 1945* (1995), p. 80, puts the number of coffee bars at 500 in London and 2,000 nationwide in 1960.

[13] C. Driver, *The British at Table 1940–1980* (1983), pp. 49–51. Florence White, a cookery writer in the 1930s, had published several editions of her *Good Food Register*.

Country Cooking in 1951 stimulated appetites jaded by currency regulations limiting holiday expenditure in France. Elizabeth David's later *Italian Food* (1954) and *French Provincial Cooking* (1960), like *The Constance Spry Cookery Book*, became standard texts for any housewife seeking to entertain with style.

Freezing and packaging food

The development of refrigeration in the second half of the twentieth century was the major advance in food technology. During the War, the Ministry of Food controlled any expansion of cold storage capacity. It allocated 1,000 tons of capacity for quick-frozen foods and licensed the building of a new 500-ton cold store at Histon, in Cambridgeshire. However, for most of the war, apart from some experimental freezing of fish and poultry, state control of the food supply reduced any opportunity to develop frozen foods. Frosted Foods Ltd turned its attention to the possibilities of establishing Birds Eye products abroad,[14] and in the absence of any support from General Foods in the USA, Frosted Foods began negotiations with Lever Brothers in 1941. Lever bought 75 per cent of the shares of Frosted Foods and, in 1942, began to plan for the mass production of major lines in fruit and vegetables, fish and meat. In 1943, Chivers sold its interest in Frosted Foods to Lever.[15] However, by 1945, quick-frozen food production was limited to a small unit handling meat in Belfast, though licences to freeze vegetable had been granted to Bailey's of Ware, Birds Eye and Smedley's. Birds Eye began growing peas around Spalding in Lincolnshire to be frozen at Batchelor's in Sheffield and in Southall, Middlesex. Experiments in freezing herrings were tried but in 1945 MacFisheries, the owner of a cold storage plant in Great Yarmouth, began buying fruit and vegetables in East Anglia.[16] In 1946, the earliest contract farming for freezing began: Birds Eye supplied seed and timed the harvest; in effect, it hired the farmer's land and labour.

At the start of the postwar era conditions did not favour innovative consumption, however much people with money to spend yearned for novelty and a sense that peacetime choice was being restored. In 1946, only 100 shops stocked Birds Eye products; cold storage facilities were required and refrigerated transport was necessary to supply the

---

[14] Frosted Foods' main interests lay in South Africa, Canada and Switzerland. See Reader, *Birds Eye*, p. 8.

[15] Reader, *Birds Eye*, pp. 9–10.

[16] Wilson, *Unilever, 1945–1965*, p. 172; Batchelor's and MacFisheries were both wholly owned by Lever Brothers.

shops.[17] Turnover was only £59,000. By 1948, 900 shops stocked frozen foods and, despite bad harvests (1949), labour disputes and fears that there would be no breakthrough into the mass market, Unilever began to build new processing capacity. Factories were opened in 1951 in Yarmouth, Lowestoft and Kirby (near Liverpool), and turnover reached £1M. By 1963, Unilever had opened plants in Grimsby, Hull and Eastbourne, and the firm's storage capacity for frozen foods had reached 50,000 tons; one-third of all white fish landed in Britain went to the freezers and frozen peas had become a major vegetable in the diet. Unilever's success attracted competition. By the early 1950s, newcomers to the industry included Eskimo Foods, Fropax, J. Lyons & Co, Ross Group and, from 1959, the Swedish company Findus.[18]

The willingness of consumers in Britain to accept processed foods differed markedly from that in other European countries.[19] Rationing delayed the development of frozen food products and in consequence vegetables, which had never been rationed, were the first items available. Frozen peas appealed to consumers immediately and have remained a mainstay of the frozen food industry ever since. Birds Eye introduced the Fish Finger in 1955 and Steaklets during the late 1950s. The rapid expansion of products led Birds Eye to have sixty product lines by 1961, including Dairy Cream Sponges and Puff Pastry, both of which offered alternatives to housewives' own skills in the kitchen. The introduction of Dinners-for-One began the move towards fully prepared meals.[20] By the end of the 1950s, therefore, convenience foods had become established in the British diet.[21] Consumer enthusiasm for them led the large food-processing companies to begin producing a wide range of frozen fish,

[17] Birds Eye benefited from the existence of Lever Brothers' own transport subsidiary, SPD Ltd, which developed refrigerated insulated vehicles to carry frozen foods. Wilson, *Unilever, 1945–1965*, pp. 172–3. See also W. J. Reader, *Hard Roads and Highways: SPD 1918–68* (1969). SPD stood for Speedy Prompt Delivery!

[18] See MMC, *Frozen Foodstuffs*, BPP, 1975–76 (HC674), XXII, p. 527, paras 23–4. Eskimo was owned by Associated Fisheries Ltd and Fropax by Union International Co Ltd. In 1969, Ross Young was bought by Imperial Group and Nestlé completed its acquisition of Findus, so that in the 1970s, following a series of amalgamations, the industry comprised three main processors: Birds Eye, Ross Young and Findus.

[19] Wilson, *Unilever 1945–1965*, pp. 202–3; Reader, *Birds Eye*, p. 40. Birds Eye attempted to introduce frozen foods to the Netherlands in 1945 but, by 1949, had losses amounting to 1M guilders. Unilever withdrew from marketing frozen foods on the Continent until 1957, when it re-entered in partnership with Vita of Leiden, and began selling products under the Iglo brand name. Unilever's other route into frozen foods on the Continent was through its major share in the Nordsee fishing fleet company of Cuxhaven.

[20] Reader, *Birds Eye*, p. 44.

[21] Convenience foods have been defined by the National Food Committee as: 'Those processed foods for which the degree of preparation has been carried out to an

Plate 8.1 Birds Eye's Fish Finger, introduced in 1955, epitomized the growth of frozen-food technology in postwar Britain. (Image courtesy of The Advertising Archives)

meat portions (burgers) and prepared dishes notable, from the point of view of the manufacturer, for their added-value component. During the third quarter of the twentieth century, the large food-processing firms dominated the frozen foods market: they could satisfy diverse outlets by offering a variety of well-advertised lines to the small independent shop and could discount long runs of standardized products to the growing supermarket chains.

The postwar growth in the availability of electricity as a source of power made low-temperature technology possible both commercially and in the home. Refrigerators in shops were usually chests with insulated lids that often formed part of the shop counter and it was not possible for customers to see their contents until sliding glass lids were introduced. During the late 1940s both Smedley's and Wall's hired out refrigerators to shops to encourage shopkeepers to stock frozen foods. Birds Eye Foods did likewise until late in 1948, when they decided that shopkeepers should be encouraged to tie up their own capital by buying their refrigerated storage capacity. The Co-operative Wholesale Society already had 300 cabinets in the retail societies' shops in 1948.[22] In larger shops, refrigerators tended to be in storage areas and not visible to customers. Food that had to be kept cold was seldom laid out on view except in fishmongers where it was arranged on stone slabs or tiled surfaces and usually kept wet or covered with crushed ice. From the advent of self-service in the early 1950s, the presentation of food to the customer had to change and the refrigerated display cabinet became part of the shop fittings. As most customers had no refrigerators at home, refrigerated cabinets operated at around −1° to +1°C (28° to 34°F) and the food sold was intended for immediate consumption.

During the 1950s and 1960s other innovations in the form of powdered soups and freeze-dried vegetables began to be marketed. These processes allowed some early forms of ready-prepared meals to be sold for reconstitution, but unlike frozen foods they made no special demands for storage or presentation. However, powdered and freeze-dried foods did require new packaging materials, as did frozen foods. In

advanced stage by the manufacturer and which may be used as labour-saving alternatives to less highly processed products.' See the Glossary of Terms in MAFF, National Food Survey, *Household Food Consumption and Expenditure* (annual series) cited in B. Davis, *Food Commodities*, 2nd edn (1987), p. 193. Convenience foods are classified as falling within four product sectors: frozen, dehydrated, canned and prepared (and partly prepared). Low-temperature technology has been a major factor in their development.

[22] Key Note Publications, *Key Note Report, A Market Sector Overview: Frozen Foods* (Hampton, Middlesex, 1991), pp. 24–6. However, see MMC, *Frozen Food-stuffs*, para. 132. Birds Eye still had 130 frozen food cabinets on loan in 1974, which had cost the firm £25,000 when new.

the 1950s, ICI's chemical plant at Wilton on Teesside began large-scale production of polyethylene. Its suitability for wrapping food materials in the form of plastic film enabled a major change in hygienic food-handling methods to accompany the growth of self-service methods of retailing. Firms such as Metal Box were in a monopoly position regarding the supply of metal containers to the food industry, though some of their customers – Heinz, Nestlé, Co-operative Wholesale Society (CWS), Chivers of Histon and Maconochies of Aberdeen – made part of their own supply. During the 1950s, Metal Box acquired production facilities in the new food packaging materials based on plastics. Among several small producers were BZ Products Ltd, makers of polythene and polystyrene stoppers and closures, and Flexible Packaging Ltd of Portsmouth, processors of ICI's polythene flakes into film tubes that could be cut and sealed for food containers, and makers of polythene coatings for board, kraft paper and aluminium foil. Metal Box bought Flexible Packaging in 1954.[23] In 1959 Metal Box agreed with a Monsanto company, Plax, to make plastic bottles, and later, together with Waddington's, formed Liquid Packaging Ltd in 1961. Metal Box's 'Diolite' polythene-coated card, which could be machine-folded, was important for frozen food production lines; Birds Eye alone ordered 60M Diolok cartons in 1964. During the 1960s, with plentiful cheap raw materials available, small-scale producers of plastic goods offered new, and previously unheard of, opportunities for packaging food unfrozen, such as supplying washed new potatoes in plastic bags.[24] From the 1970s, coated paper containers such as the Tetra Pak carton for milk, and the Tetra Brik and 'gable-top' cartons for liquids, such as fruit juices, became widely used,[25] as did ring-pull openers for cans. Inventiveness seemed to know no bounds: by the 1990s, even the humble tea-bag was patented in round and triangular shapes.

Retailing and the rise of the supermarkets

The enforced relationship between food retailer and customer during the years 1940 to 1950 had been maintained in two ways. On the one hand, the rationing scheme tied the consumer to a particular retailer except for

[23] Until then Flexible Packaging was a subsidiary of the cellophane producers, Transparent Paper Ltd.
[24] *BFJ*, March 1958, p. 23. The *British Food Journal* was happy to endorse the new packaging as more hygienic but warned that the composition of plastic wrappers might contain toxic material; see Reader, *Metal Box*, pp. 152–65.
[25] Although Ruben Rausing's patents were registered in Britain from 1944 onwards, there was some delay before these containers became widely used.

unrationed foods, such as bread, vegetables and fish, while on the other, food subsidies and the agricultural price-support scheme restricted food-price movements. The dismantling of the rationing scheme in the early 1950s was the signal for consumers to demand more choice, though Resale Price Maintenance (RPM) and the agricultural price-support system limited any marked changes in prices. With customers free from formal ties, market stability ended and food retailers became eager to vary prices, to offer new products and cut rising costs. The outcry over bread and flour prices in 1956 when the market was finally freed showed how variations in price and quality had become alien to British consumers when shopping for food. While RPM remained in operation, brand images were important and advertising was essential in attracting customers. With the growing importance of television as an advertising medium for food manufacturers after 1955, retailers needed other means to create customer loyalties. Some retailers saw trading stamps as essential marketing tools.[26] By 1962, five years after its start, Green Shield claimed that 8,000 independent retailers were offering stamps to their customers. However, any advantage to the small-scale shopkeeper was short-lived. Once the multiple retailers began to adopt price-cutting policies in the late 1950s they came into conflict with RPM restrictions operated by their suppliers, the food manufacturers. Trading stamps provided the multiples with a weapon that could be used to attack manufacturers' prices.

As a consequence of the growth in sales volume following the introduction of self-service in the 1950s, the balance of market power began to shift from food manufacturers to multiple retailers.[27] Retailers sought better margins from food manufacturers and began to develop own-label brands. In addition, as fresh produce departments for fruit and vegetables were introduced, the multiples began to press agricultural suppliers to adopt new production techniques and new grading and packing procedures. The scale of their purchasing requirements meant they were successful in bypassing traditional wholesale markets and

---

[26] Tesco's (Green Shield), Pricerite and Fine Fare (Sperry and Hutchinson's pink stamps) all adopted trading stamps in October 1963. Sainsbury's promoted an anti-stamp campaign and launched its SuperSavers promotion in November 1963. See Bridget Williams, *The Best Butter in the World* (1994), pp. 151–2.

[27] Self-service stores appeared in the early 1950s. There have been claims that Romford Co-operative Society experimented with self-service in 1949 and that Portsmouth Co-operative Society opened the first self-service store in Britain in the late 1940s. Generally, the pioneering move is attributed to Sainsbury's, which adopted self-service in its Croydon branch in July 1950 and opened its first supermarket in Lewisham some three years later. With a floor area of 7,500 sq.ft. (700m²) Sainsbury's Lewisham branch was for some years the largest supermarket in Europe.

At Sainsbury's Self-service shopping is EASY and QUICK

1—As you go in you are given a special wire basket for your purchases.

'—The prices and weight of all goods are clearly marked. You just take what you want.

3—Are you a fast shopper or a slow? You can be either when you shop at Sainsbury's!

4—Dairy produce, cooked meats, pies, sausages, bacon, poultry, rabbits and cheese—all hygienically packed.

5—Meat is served from Sainsbury's special refrigerated counters. Or you can serve yourself from the cabinets.

6—Pay as you go out. The assistant puts what you have bought into your own basket and gives you a receipt.

Plate 8.2 Food shops adopting the 'American' self-service system in the early 1950s found it necessary to educate customers in its use. (Reproduced by permission of Sainsbury's Archives. Image courtesy of The Advertising Archives)

instead were able to develop their own distribution networks. This rapid growth in scale by the leading multiple retailers created market power – including the development of market segmentation through their own-brand products – which the food manufacturers could not resist. The success of own-brand marketing enabled retailers to determine what profit margins they were prepared to accept on any particular line and put pressure on suppliers to accept reductions on their margins. Furthermore, the own-brand lines developed by Sainsbury's and Marks and Spencer were seen by consumers as establishing quality standards. For example, Tesco realized in 1978 that less than 20 per cent of its food was sold under its own labels, compared to 56 per cent of Sainsbury's. This led Tesco to 'reposition' itself in the market during the rapid price inflation of the 1970s.[28] Rising prices eroded the value of trading stamps, until they began to lose their appeal for customers. In firms such as Tesco, which Jack Cohen had built up on a price-cutting philosophy, profits fell between 1973 and 1975. Tesco re-evaluated its position in the cut-price sector of the market and decided to give up Green Shield stamps. The change in Tesco that followed the decision amounted to a metamorphosis for the company.[29] Over the weekend of the Queen's Silver Jubilee celebrations, Tesco closed all its stores from Saturday, 4 June to Thursday, 9 June 1977, reopening in new trading colours and employing a much advertised new pricing policy, Operation Check-out. Customer response was immediately enthusiastic and on such a scale that Tesco's wholesale and transport facilities came near to collapse in its efforts to supply goods to the shops.[30] Its market share rose from 7.9 to 10.8 per cent, while that of all other major retailers fell, though Sainsbury's restored its lost share of the market through its response, Discount 78.

The implications of own-label trading were not lost on other firms including Safeway (formerly Argyll) and Gateway;[31] the result was that the supermarkets' own-label share of packaged grocery turnover rose from 23 per cent in 1978 to 30 per cent in 1985. The supermarkets' command over the market was demonstrated by their concentrated buying power. As early as 1970, 600 buying organizations made up of the multiple retailers, the food wholesalers and the co-operative societies

---

[28] Price inflation in the 1970s followed from currency decimalization, entry into the European Community and the rise in oil prices.

[29] This marked the end of Jack Cohen's influence on the firm's policies.

[30] This account is based on D. Powell, *Counter Revolution: The Tesco Story* (1991).

[31] Gateway grew by absorbing Carrefour, Fine Fare, International Stores and Key Market in the 1980s. It was bought by Isosceles plc in 1989, after which a number of stores were sold to Safeway and Kwik Save. Somerfield was established as a trading name for Gateway in 1989, followed by Food Giant in 1991. Somerfield was floated in 1996 and bought Kwik Save in 1998. See Somerfield plc, *The Somerfield Briefing Pack*, 1999, and *Report and Accounts 1997/98*.

bought approximately 70 per cent of the goods sold retail in the grocery market. By 1975, 75 per cent of the grocery trade was in the hands of 344 buyers and, by the end of the decade, ninety major buyers controlled two-thirds of the United Kingdom's grocery trade. In 1980, the total number of buying organizations had fallen to 275, while the proportion of the trade for which they bought had risen to 82 per cent of the grocery market. The six major multiples alone bought 43 per cent of the groceries sold in the United Kingdom.[32] Only in the field of frozen foods was there any check to the growth of supermarkets as the home-freezer boom began during the late 1960s and early 1970s. Rapid inflation during the 1970s led consumers to see the advantage of buying and storing perishable foods at home against future price rises. As home-storage capacity grew, people began to buy ready-frozen foods from the new freezer centres being developed by the bulk-purchase suppliers. While this development expanded the market for frozen foods, it limited the growth of the supermarkets. Freezer centres provided another outlet for the major food manufacturers to keep control of the retail market until challenged by a Monopolies and Mergers Commission inquiry in 1974. The Report concluded that Birds Eye was operating in a monopoly situation under the Fair Trading Act 1973 because the Unilever companies together supplied more than a quarter of the frozen food market.[33]

New technology, particularly electronic funds transfer, also became significant in the food market not merely as a system of payments but also as a record of consumer choice and an aid to stock control. By the mid-1980s some 28 per cent of payments in UK supermarkets had become non-cash transactions. Buying food on credit depended upon the acceptance of credit cards by UK consumers.[34] In the late 1980s credit cards were used more in Britain than in any other European Community country. Food multiples therefore began to accept credit cards in the mid-1980s (except Sainsbury's, which held out against them until 1991) though no food multiple issued its own retailer card, except for Marks and Spencer which introduced its Chargecard in April 1985.

[32] In 1980 these were Sainsbury's, Tesco, Gateway, Fine Fare, International Stores and the Co-op.
[33] See MMC, *Frozen Foodstuffs*, para. 292. Birds Eye was required to modify its reserve-space discounting policy, which attempted to control retailers' displays of goods (see para. 342).
[34] Credit cards were introduced into the UK in 1966 with the launch of Barclaycard. Access (MasterCard) followed in 1973. By 1986 more than 20M credit cards were in use in the UK, with Access having around 10M accounts, Barclaycard (Visa) a further 8.6M, plus other bank cards and travel cards such as Diners Club and American Express.

By the late 1980s, however, all the major multiples accepted payment by the clearing banks' debit cards.

Committing capital to these activities increased the costs of retailing food. In consequence, from 1993 onwards, retailers resorted to price competition to increase market share. The initial stages of the price war were largely cosmetic and it was later restricted to cutting prices on specific items, since market segmentation enabled firms to offer product lines in different price ranges. By the end of the 1990s Somerfield's, for example, offered goods at four 'price points': Somerfield Basics, own brand, branded goods and Gold Selection ready meals. General levels of prices in whole sectors of the supermarket trade remained high, particularly in fruit and vegetables. The major retail chains deflected price competition by adopting 'loyalty cards', reminiscent of the earlier reliance on trading stamps, but the prime function of loyalty cards was to keep prices at levels that ensured the retention of previous profit margins. Finally, faced with growing opposition to new edge-of-town site expansion and rising costs, food retailers began to concentrate on the sales/retail area ratio as an indicator of success. Tesco eyed Sainsbury's enviously until spring 1995, when its growth in market share succeeded in pushing Sainsbury's into second place. One solution for increasing sales was to lengthen shop-opening hours, including Sunday opening and twenty-four-hour shopping. It was Sunday opening in the run-up to Christmas 1991 – illegal in England and Wales before the passing of the Sunday Trading Act, 1994 – which gave a new meaning to G. K. Chesterton's line: 'God made the wicked Grocer'!

Demographic and social change

The acceptance of more complex food processing and new methods of retailing were part of the profound social transformation that began in the mid-1950s. An understanding of the demographic and social change was essential to the success of supermarkets: firms needed to grasp what factors affected their markets and how consumers' choice of foods and drinks was conditioned by variables such as age, gender and the family life cycle. Consumer activities, interests, values and lifestyles determined meal patterns and foods purchased. Table 8.1 shows how the size and composition of households changed from the 1960s onwards. Between 1961 and 2000, the average household size in Britain fell from 3.1 to 2.4 persons; while the small household of one or two people increased from 44 per cent of all households to 64 per cent.[35] This change was

[35] Central Statistical Office, *Social Trends 31*, Table 2.2.

Table 8.1 Change in household structure in Great Britain, 1961 to 2000

Date	Mean household size (persons)	One person (%)	Two persons (%)	Married couple with dependent children (%)	Lone parent with dependent children (%)	Total households (M)
1961	3.1	14	30	38	2	16.3
1971	2.9	18	32	35	3	18.6
1981	2.7	22	32	31	5	20.2
1991	2.5	27	34	25	6	22.4
2000	2.4	29	35	23	6	23.9

Source: Central Statistical Office, *Social Trends 31* (2001), Tables 2.1, 2.2 and 2.3.

paralleled by the decline in the 'nuclear' family consisting of married couples with dependent children. In 1961, some 38 per cent of Britons lived in such a family unit but by 2000 only 23 per cent did so. At the same time, the proportion of people living in families consisting of a lone parent with dependent children rose from 2.5 per cent in 1961 to 6 per cent in 2000. This growing number of small and asymmetrical families included many, such as pensioners and single parents in receipt of welfare benefits or child support services. Even these low-income households were targeted by the supermarkets, since among them were many people who found convenience foods attractive in terms of the variety they offered and the sense of social participation in a 'consumer lifestyle' they brought.

The initial demographic factor that precipitated change in eating habits resulted from the increasing number of women who continued working after marriage. Between 1951 and 1971, the number of married women working more than doubled from 2.7 to 5.8 millions. That increased family income and gave them more control of its disposal, though at the cost of less time to spend at home in the kitchen. The convenience offered by the range of frozen foods greatly attracted working housewives, so that the domestic refrigerator became an essential rather than a luxury item of kitchen equipment. The historian of Unilever concluded: 'unquestionably the refrigerator was an integral part of the process that made frozen food a feature of everyday life' but coupled it with the rapid rise in television advertising budgets. From 1956 onwards, social change 'sprang from a new technology of communication and the essence of this was that it was irresistible and all pervasive'.[36] Britain in the late 1950s and 1960s became home-centred. Table 8.2 shows that cinema-going – the vehicle for the consumption of

[36] Wilson, *Unilever 1945–1965*, pp. 18–19.

Table 8.2 Changing leisure patterns in Great Britain, 1950 to 1959

Date	Television licences (M)	Cinema admissions (Billions)
1950	0.344	1.396
1951	0.764	1.365
1952	1.449	1.312
1953	2.142	1.285
1954	3.249	1.276
1955	4.504	1.182
1956	5.739	1.101
1957	6.966	0.915
1958	8.089	0.755
1959	9.255	0.601

Source: CSO, *Annual Abstract of Statistics, No.96* (1959), Table 87; No. 97 (1960), Tables 89 and 260.

so much ice-cream – collapsed between 1956 and 1959 as the ownership of television sets grew.

Advertising programmes began to be transmitted by the new independent television stations in 1955. Although short advertising films had been shown previously in cinemas, the importance of television was that it provided the immediacy of contact with consumers in their homes. It formed part of the new freedom to choose that the British people were experiencing after so many years of government control. Television advertising accentuated the increasingly sedentary nature of life and led to changes in meal patterns, with TV dinners and suppers, and take-away meals, growing in popularity. Food and drink were major targets for advertisers, particularly those food products marketed by American firms which already had experience of running television commercials in the USA. Kellogg, for example, began advertising its Rice Krispies in 1955 and its cartoon characters Snap, Crackle and Pop entered children's culture. As soon as these changes began Birds Eye Foods carried out a planned campaign of introductory advertising directed towards retailers and housewives, extolling the uses of frozen foods. Their advertising budget rose from £30,000 in 1951 to £1.5M in 1961 and their sales expanded from £1m to £37.5M over the same period.[37] In 1959, convenience foods accounted for one-fifth of total household

[37] Reader, *Birds Eye*, p. 35. Frosted Foods Ltd changed its named to Birds Eye (Holdings) Ltd in 1947. Charles Wilson notes that the General Foods Corporation retained an interest in it until 1957, when it became wholly owned by Unilever. See Wilson, *Unilever, 1945–1965*, p. 104.

food expenditure in Great Britain and the market for frozen foods, including fish, meat, vegetables and cakes, increased tenfold from £7.5M in 1955 to £75M in 1963.[38]

With the confectionery market and sugar and sweets only recently de-rationed there was much competition to create brand loyalties. The Murray Mints' slogan 'Too good to hurry mints' was seen as early as 1955, Rowntree's Fruit Gums were advertised from 1956 onwards, Fry's Turkish Delight from 1957 and Cadbury's Flake in 1959. Nestlé's 'Milky Bar Kid' appeared in 1961 and ran for nearly twenty years. Even mundane commodities such as tea and flavourings became subjects of major television campaigns. Brooke Bond began advertising its PG Tips with chimpanzees' tea-parties in 1956, and Oxo's Katie and her family ('Oxo gives a meal man-appeal') ran from 1958 to 1999. Advertising clichés, both characters and slogans, became so much a part of life that they entered the language and became figures of speech: 'Go to work on an egg' (1966), 'Beanz Meanz Heinz' (1967), milk's 'Watch out there's a Humphrey about' (1975) and 'A Mars a day helps you work, rest and play' (1978). Unilever's Captain Birds Eye (1968) and Quaker Oats' Honey Monster (1976) appealed to children, while Rowntree's Yorkie Bar-eating lorry driver (1976) targeted an adult audience. British television screens even showed one of the first global food advertisements in 1971: Coca-Cola's 'I'd like to teach the world to sing'. New technology brought advertisements for tea-bags – Tetley, from 1973 – 'instant' potatoes like Cadbury's Smash, also in 1973 – and instant coffee – Nestlé's Gold Blend, in 1981. Advertisements for bread and flour, from Home Pride Flour in 1969 to Hovis in 1974, tried in vain to stem falling consumption. Lower calorie bread, such as Nimble in the 1970s, appealed to people who were dieting. Soft drinks' manufacturers' advertising ranged from Schweppes in 1963 to R. White's Lemonade and Tango. Alcoholic drinks also featured in advertising: in the 1970s, for example, Courage Best Bitter; from 1974 a Cointreau advertisement that ran for fourteen years; and in 1983 competing campaigns for Holsten Pils and Hoffmeister beer. There were series in the 1990s for Stella Artois, Boddington's draught beer and Guinness' stout but whisky was not advertised until 1995 because of an industry-wide agreement not to use the medium. The agreement was abandoned in view of falling consumption and a belief that a generation had been lost to whisky-drinking.[39]

[38] Wilson, *Unilever, 1945–1965*, p. 165.
[39] I am grateful to Dr R. B. Weir for permission to quote from his unpublished paper '"The Gentleman's Agreement" and "The Lost Generation" spirits advertising and television (1954–1995)' given at the Economic History Society conference, Birmingham, 2002.

Advertising put pressure on consumers to equip their homes to store the new food products. The ownership of domestic refrigerators began to grow in the late 1950s. By 1971, 69 per cent of households in the UK owned a refrigerator with or without a freezer compartment.[40] Ownership of a 'deep-freeze' or freezer was, however, still a novelty: there were only 36,000 in the UK in 1967 but by 1973 10.5 per cent of households had one.[41] The patterns of ownership varied by television-viewing areas: ownership was highest in the south and lowest in the north. Over 16 per cent of social classes ABC$_1$ owned a freezer compared with 5 per cent of social classes C$_2$DE. Chest freezers dominated the market (74 per cent) though upright freezers (26 per cent) were becoming more popular. Encouraged by inflation during the 1970s, consumers eagerly accepted the discounting of frozen foods through freezer centres.[42] It was also notable that domestic freezers were becoming an item of kitchen equipment rather than something kept in a garage or outhouse, a trend influenced without doubt by the smallness of many new houses built during and since the 1970s.[43] By 1985, 95 per cent of households owned a refrigerator and 66 per cent a freezer.[44] With 87 per cent of UK households owning a freezer by 1993, the market approached saturation.[45] Their contents became basic items in the British diet: in 1990, 81 per cent of housewives surveyed by the British Market Research Bureau used frozen peas. Other staples used by housewives included frozen poultry (73 per cent), frozen vegetables (72 per cent), frozen meat products, such as pies or sausage rolls (72 per cent). Frozen pizzas (49 per cent) were less popular lines while packaged and frozen ready meals were used by only 33 per cent of housewives.[46] On this evidence, the highest consumption of frozen foods occurred among child-rearing families in lower socio-economic households, with a tendency for older people to use less. Prepared meals tended to be more expensive and their use was greater among the more affluent socio-economic groups in southern areas of Britain.

Owning a freezer, initially as a status symbol but later as an important addition to food-storage capacity, may have encouraged some housewives to cook in bulk and, by storing seasonal surpluses from gardens,

[40] CSO, *Social Trends 1972* (1972), Table 55.

[41] See MMC, *Frozen Foodstuffs*, para. 30. Bejam opened the first freezer centre in 1968 and by 1974 there were around 1,000 freezer centres in the UK (paras 32, 64).

[42] I. J. Hunt, 'Developments in food distribution', in J. Burns, J. McInerney and A. Swinbank, eds, *The Food Industry* (1983), p. 138.

[43] Birds Eye Foods Ltd, *The Cold Rush 1974* (Walton-on-Thames, 1974), unpaginated.

[44] CSO, *Social Trends 1987*, Table 6.15.

[45] CSO, *Social Trends 24 1994 Edition* (1994), Table 6.7.

[46] *Key Note Report, Frozen Foods*, pp. 4–16.

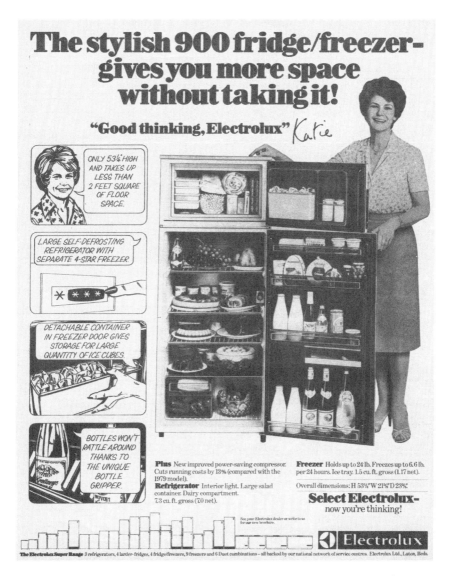

Plate 8.3 Oxo's Katie was pressed into service to advertise the advantages of domestic cold storage of food as purchases of fridge-freezers soared in the 1980s. (Image courtesy of The Advertising Archives)

to extend the availability of 'home cooking'. When freezer use began, housewives sought to make economies by holding large portions of food in store, though this brought the worry of possible mechanical breakdown, or worse, power cuts in the electricity supply. Peace of mind could be obtained by taking out an insurance policy, but even this did not alleviate the preparation problems that many began to shirk. The urban housewife found dealing with half a sheep inconvenient – even if the freezer centre had portioned it – and the number of occasions when meals merited large joints of meat scarcely justified their space in the freezer. Thus while chilled and frozen produce was instrumental in eliminating seasonality in food supply, it contributed to a large extent to the loss of many fundamental skills in preparing and cooking food. Housewives and numerous single-person households alike turned to the standardized products and ready-prepared meals sold by the multiple food retailers for the freezer and the microwave oven to which the freezer had become increasingly linked. Convenience and, for low-income families, participation in the consumer culture, outweighed the high costs of using manufacturers' products during periods of economic recession in the 1980s and 1990s. Novelty, regardless of the cultural boundaries of cuisine, led supermarkets to stock frozen portions of tikka masala pizza and curried chicken Kiev, truly British versions of 'fusion food'! Thus, low-temperature technology brought a dramatic increase in the variety of foods in British shops.

Technical and product developments in the later twentieth century

Frozen foods and the necessary storage equipment were adopted by the catering industry in each of its three market sectors: commercial, welfare and industrial. Caterers facing high labour costs and difficulties in attracting and retaining skilled labour found prepared frozen foods reduced wastage and preparation time. During the 1970s, Birds Eye claimed its catering products reduced unskilled labour costs by 40 per cent and food preparation areas by 30 per cent.[47] During the 1980s cook-freeze catering was developed whereby food frozen in a blast freezer within ninety minutes of preparation and stored at –18°C (0°F) could be transported frozen to be heated in convector ovens or microwave ovens twenty-five minutes before serving.[48] Although the application of this technique has been linked to developments in hospital catering,[49] most consumers became familiar with it in the guise of airline catering. Commercial catering firms' demand for frozen foods in the 1980s followed established lines; three-quarters of the frozen foods used by

---

[47] Birds Eye Foods Ltd, *Food Freezing* (Walton-on-Thames, 1975), p. 41.

[48] B. A. Fox and A. G. Cameron, *Food Science*, 4th edn (1982), p. 307; Davis, *Food Commodities*, p. 204. The earliest example of system catering originated in 1961 when the Top Tray range of prepared and quick-frozen meals in foil trays was produced to be 'end-cooked' in forced-air convector ovens. See National Catering Inquiry, *The British Eating Out at Work* (n.d. [1973]), p. 28.

[49] Any improvements were negated in the 1990s by outsourcing meal provision to contract caterers.

caterers were accounted for by potato chips and potato products (36 per cent), fish (21 per cent), and vegetables, other than potatoes (20 per cent). Meat products came to only 14 per cent with ready meals and desserts less than 10 per cent.[50] Frozen foods had replaced those raw foods that required intensive low-skill labour inputs in their preparation.

The creation of freezer centres as specialist retail outlets extended the market for frozen foods. Their importance must not be underestimated because many offered cut-price lines of domestic freezers through links with equipment manufacturers. In 1987, the strongest of these specialist frozen food retailers, Iceland Frozen Food Holdings,[51] acquired Igloo Frozen Foods in northeast England, the Freezeway chain in Scotland and Fulham Frozen Foods in Humberside. Two years later it bought its major rival, Bejam, and by the early 1990s Iceland was operating over 520 shops and accounted for some 13 per cent of the UK frozen food market. Although its stores were quite small with an average size of 5,000 sq. ft. (465m^2), Iceland was backed by a degree of vertical integration and grew on the basis that 65 per cent of its product range were own-label goods. Iceland claimed to be the largest retailer of domestic freezer equipment, having 20 per cent of all UK sales, together with significant sales of microwave ovens.[52] However, as Table 8.3 shows, freezer centres held only 15 per cent of the frozen food trade by value compared with the 70 per cent held by grocery multiples. In the early 1990s, the frozen food market was shared between two major processing firms, Unilever's Birds Eye and United Biscuits' Ross Young, with Nestlé's Findus a distant third. Own-brand lines retailed by grocery multiples held 35 per cent of the market in 1990, with smaller specialist producers obtaining the remaining 18 per cent.[53]

During the rapid inflation between 1974 and 1980, consumer expenditure on frozen foods increased annually by 24 per cent, but the large food-processing firms, facing rapidly rising costs, began to lose

---

[50] Cited in Davis, *Food Commodities*, p. 198.

[51] Later known as Iceland Group, of Deeside, Clwyd. In 1993, there were 299 freezer centres in England (of which only three were in Greater London), eight in Wales, four in Ulster but 178 in Scotland! See *Frozen and Chilled Foods Yearbook, 1993–1994*.

[52] N. Sanghari, P. Smith and G. Wills, *The Retail Reference Book 1992* (Manchester, 1992), pp. 27–8. Iceland owned Isle of Ely Farms Ltd, Super Value Packers Ltd and Milton Keynes Cold Storage Ltd, as well as 50 per cent of Au Gel, which operated a number of stores around Lille.

[53] *Key Note Report, Frozen Foods*, pp. 17 and 23. In 1994, the frozen food market, exclusive of ice-cream, was shared between: own brands 42.9 per cent; Birds Eye Wall's 19.8 per cent; United Biscuits (Ross Young) 9.2 per cent; McCain 3 per cent; Nestlé (Findus) 2.7 per cent; and others 22.6 per cent (personal communication, Birds Eye Wall's Ltd).

Table 8.3 The frozen-food market in Britain, 1990

By outlet	Percentage of market share by value
1 Retail distribution	
Grocery multiples	70
Freezer centres	15
Independent grocers	5
Others	10

By firm *2 Manufacturers' share*	Percentage of market share by value
Birds Eye Wall's	22
Ross Young/McVitie	20
Nestlé/Findus	5
Own label	35
Other	18

Source: *Key Note Report, Frozen Foods*, 1991.

control over their suppliers.[54] As interest rates rose, food manufacturers faced falling profits, but their attempts to put pressure on growers through tighter fixed-price contracts caused the latter to diversify. Growers began to establish their own freezer plants, facilitated by the services of the largest cold storage companies, Christian Salvesen, Union Cold Storage and Frigoscandia. Growers retained ownership of their crops until sold rather than selling at point of harvest, as under their former contracts with the food processors. By the late 1970s, such joint-venture contracts or market-linked contracts began to offer growers the opportunities to share profits, though at the cost of sharing risks.[55] In an attempt to sustain growth during the 1980s, frozen-food processors' media advertising expenditure rose from £37.7M in 1983 to £59.3M in 1989.[56] By 1990, Birds Eye's advertising budget for the press and television was in excess of £11.5M, while United Biscuits spent between

[54] Manufacturers' prices rose 13 per cent annually in the years 1974 to 1980 between the oil-price rises. As a result, the real value of frozen foods to consumers increased by nearly 10 per cent per year. Even over the longer period of 1970 to 1984, consumers' expenditure rose annually by just over 19 per cent. Averages calculated from the National Food Survey. See MAFF, National Food Survey, *Household Food Consumption and Expenditure* (annual series).
[55] J. Malcolm, 'Food and farming', in Burns *et al.*, *The Food Industry*, pp. 74–5. See also MMC, *Frozen Foodstuffs*, para. 51. In the mid-1970s there were some 100 cold storage companies owning about 134M cubic feet (379,000 cubic metres) of storage.
[56] *Key Note Report, Frozen Foods*, p. 32.

£5M and £6M advertising Ross Young's brands[57] and Findus between £13M and £14M. In part, this expenditure was a defence against new entrants in the frozen foods wholesale market offering specialized lines, such as Hillsdown in frozen poultry. The proliferation of firms weakened the position of the large manufacturers and brought the added problem of foreign competition attracted by the apparent sustained growth in the market. The American Campbell Soup Corporation bought Freshbake in 1988, Sara Lee Corporation began trading in Britain in the same year, and Heinz linked with Weight Watchers. The Canadian company McCain Inc, which had been retailing chipped potatoes and other potato products since 1968, also began a major diversification programme.[58] Newcomers from Denmark, France and Israel were also attracted to the market in the 1990s. However, in frozen foods, the large processing firms were able to protect their market against competition. Notwithstanding the large discounts they were forced to give to the major retail chains, they became subject to a Monopolies and Mergers Commission inquiry in 1974.[59] In the specialized field of ice-cream production, the producers defended their market with great success until 1979, when a Monopolies and Mergers Commission Report concluded that 'a monopoly situation as defined in . . . the Fair Trading Act 1973 existed'. Two firms, Wall's and Lyons Maid (then owned mainly by Glacier Foods with a minority stake from Nestlé), dominated the industry; a third, Treat's, based in Sheffield and Leeds, was, like Wall's, a wholly owned subsidiary of Unilever. The Report concluded that the restrictive practices of these firms operated against the public interest and forced the ending of their exclusive supply contracts.[60]

From the late 1970s, there was a major shift in the retailing of frozen produce, as open-top cabinets operating at −18°C (0°F) increasingly became standard fitments in supermarkets. Customers might then buy foods for long-term storage in home freezers as well as for immediate use. The expansion of frozen-food lines by the major multiple retailers

---

[57] United Biscuits bought Ross Young from Hanson Trust in 1988. *Key Note Report, Frozen Food*, p. 18.

[58] See company profiles in *Key Note Report, Frozen Foods*, pp. 42–9.

[59] See MMC, *Frozen Foodstuffs*, para. 292. The Report concluded that Birds Eye was operating in a monopoly situation under the Fair Trading Act 1973.

[60] See MMC, *Ice Cream and Water Ices* (Cmnd.7632), 1979, paras 6 and 429. The firms operated exclusive supply and retrospective discount policies. The Monopolies Commission required them to end their exclusive supply policies. In 1994, the take-home ice-cream market, i.e. that bought in supermarkets and shops (as distinct from the 'impulse' market of ice-cream bought in newsagents and places of entertainment), was divided between: own brands 44 per cent; Wall's 32 per cent; Lyons Maid (Nestlé) 4 per cent; and Mars 3 per cent. Others made up 17 per cent of the take-home market (personal communication, Birds Eye Wall's).

that followed began to put pressure on the smaller specialist frozen foods outlets, much as the supermarkets had earlier affected small-scale general grocers and independent retailers. Some major retailers initially began to operate their own freezer centres but later withdrew from such ventures, rather than operate two competing display systems. Instead the food retailers relied on the open-top display cabinets to make products more easily accessible to customers rather than the closed-top or closed-front cabinets commonly used in freezer centres. Chill cabinets began to be used to supply food at around 0°C (32°F) with short storage dates: in effect, for many product lines, 'chilled food' had become equivalent to fresh food. However, during the 1970s and 1980s, food-processing firms began to use freezing as an aid to develop the value-added component of their product lines and to satisfy consumer preference for fried foods. Meat and fish portions designed with breaded or battered coatings enabled the proportion of raw food material to be reduced while retaining the appearance of traditional fried foods. Some frozen processed-meat portions on sale in British supermarkets in the mid-1990s contained as little as 10 per cent meat, while some used 'reconstituted' or 'recovered' meat as part of their raw materials. By the 1990s, supermarkets offered frozen foods arranged in several major categories in their display cabinets: potatoes, mainly processed as chipped potatoes; meat, of which frozen poultry, both whole and by portions, formed the largest category; fish, notably as fish fingers; prepared foods such as burgers and pizzas; vegetables, of which peas remained dominant, though beans, broccoli and other vegetables commanded space in the cabinets; and, of course, ice-cream and various desserts. The minor categories of frozen foods included delicatessen, particularly seafood, pasta and rice prepared for microwave cookery and part-baked bread.

The recognition that demographic patterns were changing led supermarkets to develop small portions as stock-in-trade lines. As an encouragement to 'one-stop shopping' by their customers, supermarkets tried to out-flank freezer centres by producing individual dishes or meals that could be stored in domestic freezers before use. This brought low-temperature technology more fully into the home and new skills had to be learnt: which packaging materials were to be used in the freezer and which of them, if any, could be used in the microwave. This adoption of the microwave in Britain did not bring any reaction against frozen foods of the kind which market researchers claimed was developing in the USA in the 1990s. There, the use of frozen ready meals in microwaves had produced food textures when cooked which consumers found unpalatable and rejected in favour of fresh foods, or 'long life' microwave meals which need not be frozen.[61] Although long-life products arrived on

---

[61] *Key Note Report, Frozen Foods*, pp. 38–9.

supermarket shelves in Britain in the 1990s, they did not affect the demand for frozen foods and frozen ready meals.

Health and lifestyle marketing

From the 1960s onwards the health concerns regarding cardiovascular disease and obesity began to present retailers and food-processing firms alike with a marketing problem that marketing theory could not solve: namely how to encourage people to buy more but eat less. The super-markets' initial response was to encourage healthy eating and to develop a range of quality own brands. Further product development by food manufacturers during the 1980s led to small portion ready-made dishes, usually frozen for freeze-cook microwave technology – the one-person meals that reflected changing demographic trends and family structure and changing tastes. Manufacturers began to develop ranges of dishes such as Birds Eye's Menu Master or Findus' Dinner Supreme. Some low-calorie products such as Birds Eye's Healthy Options or Findus' Lean Cuisine targeted consumers with specific dietary or 'healthy lifestyle' interests, primarily body-weight loss. The increasing interest in vegetarianism provided an additional marketing focus for frozen food products. Another innovation was the introduction of 'ethnic' foods by supermarkets and their subsequent development as frozen food lines. In the 1990s, supermarkets offered frozen basic materials such as rice and noodles as well as prepared Chinese, Indian, Spanish, Italian, Greek and Mexican dishes. Ethnic recipes made a significant contribution to frozen ready meal ranges: in 1990, thirteen out of forty-one dishes in Birds Eye's Menu Master range were based on ethnic recipes, while the majority of dishes in Findus' Lean Cuisine and Dinner Supreme ranges used ethnic or pasta-based recipes.[62] Their acceptance by consumers altered the layout of British supermarkets radically. In the 1990s, frozen food display areas increased, together with the sales areas of other high valued-added foods and prepared dishes such as snack foods and delicatessen.

During the last quarter of the twentieth century, the success of the supermarkets seemed unstoppable: they adjusted their product ranges to match demographic changes, they incorporated new technology into their shop layouts and check-out procedures and they used market segmentation successfully to enhance their pricing policies. However, in the 1990s, the multiple retailers came face to face with the ultimate

---

[62] Ibid., p. 27. The trade journal *Frozen and Chilled Foods* held 2,200 product lines on their database in 1995.

and intractable problem of how to sell more food to people who wished to eat less. No supermarket chain wanted to acquire the sobriquet 'purveyors of obesity to the nation'; thus, increasing market share became crucial. The multiples concentrated on retaining consumers' loyalty by widening their range of services and ventured into the strange territories of petrol sales, clothing, DIY (do-it-yourself) supplies, and even banking and financial services. None of them, however, offered as completely comprehensive a service as that of H. J. Heinz. Consumers who bought Heinz's highly flavoured products found their energy intake rising and their waistlines expanding: those who became obese could try Heinz's low-calorie meals and, if all else failed, might turn for salvation to the slimming clubs run by that less well-known division of H. J. Heinz – Weight Watchers![63]

The changing pace and place of eating

Transatlantic innovations in catering found a receptive market in Britain. The earliest arrival in the high street was Wimpy, which opened its first franchise at the Lyons Corner House in Coventry Street, London, in 1954. Significantly, it was J. Lyons & Co Ltd that bought the UK franchise rights from Eddie Gold, Wimpy's American founder, to sell 2oz. (56g) hamburgers. The new concept of hamburger restaurants fitted in a Britain emerging from meat rationing, which had come into contact with many US servicemen during the 1940s.[64] For Lyons, it promised to be a development that might be more profitable than the traditional teashops. Lyons later sold Wimpy to United Biscuits, under whose management counter service was developed. In turn, United Biscuits sold Wimpy to Grand Metropolitan Hotels in 1989.[65] Over the thirty-year period from the 1950s to the 1980s, Wimpy had grown to more than 430 outlets, but a management buy-out retained 200 table-service restaurants and the trading name. By 1998, Wimpy's 200 franchisees were operating 280 counter-service outlets.[66] Wimpy was

[63] H. J. Heinz separated the Weight Watchers' slimming-clubs business from Weight Watchers' frozen foods in 1998. It sold the slimming clubs to Apax Partners in July 1999, but retained the Weight Watchers' frozen foods business.

[64] From 1942, the American Red Cross ran Rainbow Corner, the American Servicemen's Club in Shaftesbury Avenue, in a requisitioned Lyons teashop. See Forte, *Forte: The Autobiography*, pp. 57–8.

[65] '40th Anniversary for Wimpy', *Business Franchise*, no date, material supplied by Wimpy International Ltd.

[66] 'Wimpy develops new taste for acquisitions', *Franchise World*, July/August 1998, pp. 33–5.

followed by Kentucky Fried Chicken, which had nearly 400 outlets in 1987. More up-market, during the 1960s, were themed restaurants such as the Steak Houses.[67] The growth was not confined to meat products. Pizza Hut, a company formed in the USA in 1958, entered the UK market in 1973, opening its first outlet in Islington just before McDonald's started selling hamburgers in Woolwich in 1974. By 1986 Pizza Hut had 200 outlets and employed almost 15,000 workers. The total UK sales of fast-food meals in 1987 came to £1.5bn of which fish and chips was still the largest category. However, the sales of burgers, fried chicken, pizzas and so on, in total, were already greater than sales of fish and chips.[68] In 1998 there were 400 Pizza Huts employing 12,000 in the UK.[69] McDonald's growth from its first restaurant in 1974 was dramatic. At the end of 1999 it had over 1,000 outlets in the UK of which 302 were run by franchisees. McDonald's employed over 48,000; a further 16,500 worked in its franchises. The total sales from both its company-owned restaurants and its franchised outlets reached £400M and it catered for 2.5M people a day.[70] McDonald's logo was no longer confined to the high streets but extended to airports, cross-Channel ferries, leisure and retail parks.

The development of road transport during the 1950s led to a demand for roadside catering. As the motorway system evolved in the 1960s and motoring became an important aspect of holiday travel, the Ministry of Transport planned for service areas that would provide twenty-four-hour catering, including transport cafés selling at lower prices. The first two were established on the M1 when it opened in 1959. Forte's facilities became available in August 1960 at Newport Pagnell, and Watford Gap opened a month later, though sandwiches had been sold from specially installed 'garden sheds' earlier. Forte's later restaurants on the M6 in 1963 led to the brand of 'Motorchef' being adopted. Other leisure groups became interested with Top Rank Motor Inns opening on the M2 and M6 in 1963, Granada on the M1 (1965), M5 (1966) and M4 (1968) and Ross Group, the frozen foods producer, opening the last of the 'bridge restaurants' on the M1 in 1966. As sites proliferated, motorway service areas became 'part of the ritual of going away; for children a chance to have food and treats not normally allowed'.[71]

---

[67] See P. Bird, *The First Food Empire. A History of J. Lyons & Co* (Chichester, 2000), pp. 190, 196–9. London Steak Houses Ltd was a subsidiary of J. Lyons & Co.

[68] T. Lobstein, *Fast Food Facts* (1988), p. 78.

[69] In 1977, Pizza Hut was bought by PepsiCo. From 1982, Pizza Hut was operated jointly by PepsiCo and Whitbread. Since 1997, Tricorn Global Restaurants has operated Pizza Hut in conjunction with Whitbread plc.

[70] *McDonald's Fact File 2000*, pp. 5,10.

[71] D. Lawrence, *Always a Welcome* (Twickenham, 1999), pp. 19–32.

Additional facilities on other main roads were offered by Forte's Little Chef chain which grew from two sites in 1963 to forty-one in 1986, the year that Forte acquired the seventy-three-outlet chain of Happy Eater restaurants.[72]

Television advertising stimulated the demand for fast food from roadside catering outlets and high street chains. Within a year of its arrival in Britain, McDonald's was advertising in cinemas and a year later, in 1976, on television. This was aimed primarily at young people and especially children. Providing special menus for children, together with other facilities such as play areas, became standard practice among the roadside café chains and motorway service stations. Frozen food materials provide the complete basis of many 'children's menu' dishes – fish fingers or burgers, with peas and chips, followed by ice-cream – easily recognized and familiar presentation of food that would allay even the most suspicious juvenile palate. In the mid-1980s, the high street chains introduced various blandishments to attract parents holding children's parties. McDonald's offered personal appearances of the television advertisement character 'Ronald McDonald'; Kentucky Fried Chicken offered a 'Little Colonel's Meal' in a carton decorated with cartoons and puzzles; Pizza Hut provided a 'Care Bear Party' for special occasions, and Pizzaland's 'Party Time' included party hats, balloons and colouring sheets.[73]

The 1970s saw eating out in traditional institutional settings decline sharply in the face of commercialization. Fewer people ate in factory canteens and the consumption of school meals fell. By contrast, however, meals purchased in purely commercial settings – restaurants, public houses, sandwich bars, fast-food and ethnic food outlets, and fish-and-chip shops – showed an increase as luncheon vouchers came to be widely used, especially by city centre office workers.[74] Take-away meals grew from 14 per cent to 27 per cent of all meals eaten between 1975 and 1984: 'Amongst the lower social classes one in three purchase a take-away meal and eat it at home at least once a week, much of this being associated with watching videos.'[75] These changes were synonymous with the growth of 'a snacking lifestyle' in the last quarter of the

---

[72] Forte Holdings (formed in 1962) became Trusthouse Forte (THF) in 1971 by merging with Trust Houses Hotels. The purchase from Hanson of the Imperial Group's range of outlets (Welcome Break service areas, Happy Eaters and Harvester pub-restaurants) led to a major expansion in roadside sites which made Forte's Public Catering Division its fastest growth area in the 1980s.

[73] Lobstein, *Fast Food Facts*, p. 85.

[74] J. M. Pascoe, J. Dockerty and J. Ryley, 'Fast foods', in R. Cottrell, ed., *Nutrition in Catering* (Carnforth, 1987), p. 98. During the inflation of the 1970s, employers used luncheon vouchters to limit wage claims.

[75] G. Heald, 'Trends in eating out', in Cottrell, *Nutrition in Catering*, p. 75.

twentieth century. It reflected the increasing availability of sandwiches, confectionery and packaged drinks. Chocolate confectionery and snack foods became widely available in the 1990s, being sold in over 150,000 retail outlets in Britain. Sales occurred in supermarkets, retail confectioners and tobacconists – the 'corner shops' that were developing a much wider range of products in their attempt to compete with supermarkets – pubs, sports centres, petrol stations and motorway service areas. From the 1980s, extrusion technology made new products possible. Among its range of product lines, Cadbury produced snack foods such as Picnic (1958), Double Decker (1976), Wispa (1983), Boost (1985), Twirl (1987), Spira (1989) and Time Out (1992). Coupled with the intensive and compelling television advertising that began in the 1960s, confectionery became a growing market. Producers realized that 'Confectionery is half-way between food and fashion so innovation is the key to success, providing excitement and variety for consumers'. Total confectionery sales in Britain rose from 663,000 tons in 1981 to 803,000 tons in 1990 when sales of the leading chocolate brands – Rowntree's Kit Kat (acquired by Nestlé) and Mars Bars – were in excess of £100M each.[76] Snacks and sandwiches became an important part of the food industry. Sandwich bars proliferated in town centres and even supermarkets introduced sandwich cabinets into their stores; by 2000, the market for sandwiches in the United Kingdom was valued at £3 billion, while sales of soup totalled £65 million.[77]

The custom of 'eating out' in traditional restaurants also changed from the 1960s onwards and began increasingly to exhibit ethnic influences associated with immigrant cuisines. Until the end of the 1950s, the *Good Food Guide* primarily recommended restaurants practising European cooking, but with isolated examples of Chinese or Indian food. In its 1963 to 1964 edition, the *Good Food Guide* recommended eight Chinese and six Indian restaurants in London and a similar number in the provinces. The dramatic spread of Chinese and Indian restaurants from the late 1950s onwards was followed by Cypriot and Middle Eastern establishments. Higher priced and higher class restaurants still conformed to French style, though in London cuisines proliferated in the 1960s. A number of hotels achieved high standards of cooking – the

---

[76] Cadbury Ltd, *New Product Development* (Birmingham, 1997).

[77] *The Times*, 19 September 2000, p. 33. Prize Foods, the largest supplier of sandwiches to Sainsbury's, was formed in 1997 from a collection of businesses acquired in a management buy-out from Booker; *The Times*, 5 October 2000, p. 32, Snackhouse (formerly Benson's Crisps) expanded its range of snacks to reduce reliance on crisps. Snackhouse's product range comprised over 1,000 items, including low-fat ranges sold to chains such as Marks & Spencer. See also MSI, *Fast Food UK*, Chester, 2000.

Connaught was always in the *Good Food Guide* – but the new restaurant standards were set by French chefs become restaurateurs. The inception of what has been termed 'modern British cooking' possibly dates from the opening of Le Gavroche by Michel and Albert Roux in 1967. Raymond Blanc's Les Quat' Saisons followed, but the development of 'modern British cooking' in the 1970s owed much to British chefs and restaurateurs. A wider interest in cooking began to develop among the population at large as television brought cooking out of the women's magazines and placed it before a national audience. Early TV cooks such as Margaret Patten, Philip Harben and Fanny Cradock became widely known, and their eccentricities began to form part of national postwar culture. The development of colour TV transmissions suited food programmes and began the era of TV 'personality chefs' from Graham Kerr in the 1970s, Madhur Jaffrey in the 1980s creating interest in Asian herbs and spices, to Rick Stein in the 1990s. Long-running, more staid performers such as Delia Smith were unable to match the flamboyance of Keith Floyd or Jamie Oliver nor the technical performance of Gary Rhodes. However, in Britain, as in other countries, chefs in the late twentieth century began to create a new cuisine heavily dependent on the influence of cuisine minceur. They concentrated upon artistic plate presentation that televised well but had no roots in older style traditional cooking.

Drinking with meals

During the last two decades of the twentieth century, the British diet came to rely more and more upon the industrial concentration of food processing and manufacturing and the artifice of marketing. This concentration of ownership among food manufacturers and drink producers attracted the attention of regulatory authorities. In 2000, the European Commission forced Unilever to sell its Oxo and Batchelor soup brands as its purchase of Bestfoods brought with it ownership of Knorr soups and Hellmann's mayonnaise.[78] More dramatic still was the effect of the Monopolies and Mergers Commission's inquiry into the brewing industry in 1989, which destablized the marketing of alcoholic drinks. The subsequent Beer Orders forced brewers to sell off numbers

[78] *The Times*, 28 September 2000, pp. 27, 29. Bestfoods' Lesieur (mayonnaise) was seen as competing with Unilever's Amora Maille. Patience Wheatcroft wrote: 'No doubt Katie would shed a few tears at yesterday's news of another happy family being burst apart. She who believed that the secret of a contented home lay in the crumbling of an Oxo cube or two has long been banished from the TV screens, but Oxo remains one of Britain's better-known brands.'

of pubs, while between 1992 and 1994 over-capacity in brewing resulted in a price war. The consolidation in the industry that followed lowered costs and brewers found demand rising in a buoyant economy; their resulting hasty over-investment in pubs in 1996 and 1997 reduced returns. With earnings less than expectations in 1999 (World Cup football and Millennium sales proved poor) and the Office of Fair Trading reviewing the Beer Orders, brewers examined their assets with a view to disposing of their least profitable outlets. By 2000, the formerly highly fragmented UK beer market had become dominated by Interbrew of Belgium and Scottish and Newcastle Breweries, which owned Courage and the Kronenburg brands in the UK. However, with an ever-increasing share of the beer market in the hands of the multiple food retailers, brewers with large 'estates' of 'unbranded' public houses disposed of them. By the end of the twentieth century 'speciality' pubs owned by beer retailing chains often backed by venture capital were replacing the morose emptiness of brewers' tied houses – even those converted by 'exercises in Brewers Past' and decorated with:

> repro gasoliers, framed Edwardian photos, tennis rackets in wooden presses, dun canvas golf bags, a spot of canal-barge 'art'. It is meant to summon up some indefinable moment in Our Island Story. As indeed it does: it recalls the late Eighties when brewers' design departments were falling over each other in a pitifully unconvincing effort to make pubs appear old.[79]

The success of some chains seemed to depend upon bizarre, mock-traditional names. The Slug and Lettuce was developed by Sheila McKenzie as a 'female-friendly' pub chain.[80] Other such names included the Pitcher & Piano pubs owned by Wolverhampton & Dudley Breweries, and the Ha! Ha! Bars owned by the Yates Group. Successful firms providing alcoholic drinks included J. D. Wetherspoon, which had built up a chain of over 400 outlets by the end of the twentieth century. This firm claimed its success was based on creating pubs fitted to their locality, plus the selling of traditional cask ales. To encourage women drinkers, Wetherspoon's began selling California red and white wine at £4.99 a bottle.[81] The UK's biggest off-licence chain, First Quench, a joint venture between Whitbread and Punch Taverns, owners of Bottoms Up, Wine Rack, Threshers, Victoria Wine, and Hadows in Scotland, had

---

[79] Jonathan Meades, *The Times* Magazine, 30 September 2000, p. 66.
[80] *The Times*, 29 June 2000, p. 29. In 2000 it was bought for £31.6M by its rival, SFI Group, for development as a third brand alongside SFI's Litten Tree and Bar Med outlets.
[81] *Financial Times*, 9 September 2000, p. 17; *The Times*, 9 September 2000, p. 27.

2,500 outlets in the UK.[82] Town centre outlets for both drinks and food consumption changed and were modelled on fashionable crazes – some of which reflected manufacturers' attempts to extend their market. In the mid-1990s, drinks manufacturers tried to sell alcoholic drinks to under-age consumers through alcopops. Merrydown, the Sussex cider-maker (and producer of Shloer fruit juices), was at the forefront of the alcopops craze of 1995.[83]

Food in pubs also underwent change as the eating-out trend developed. Food provision was transformed by the introduction in the 1990s of open kitchens and blackboard menus. Some pubs developed speciality lines and The Eagle, in Clerkenwell, by offering such exotic items on its menu as Caldeira (Lisbon fish stew) in the early 1990s, gave rise to the term 'gastropub'. By the end of the 1990s, even suburban pubs offered food cooked before the customer by Thai or Mongolian cooks. Chains of low-budget food outlets, often referred to as 'family restaurants', were developed by the brewers who sought to dominate this sector of the market, for example, Whitbread's Beefeaters and Brewers Fayres which became numerous in the last quarter of the twentieth century. Their owners tried to differentiate them from the true 'fast-food' eating places. Ethnic cuisine was an important aspect of this development. In the year 2000, there were 8,500 Indian restaurants, a total which exceeded the number of fish-and-chip shops.[84] With holidays abroad popularizing food from the Mediterranean region, pizza chains developed during the 1970s and 1980s. By the end of the twentieth century, therefore, low-budget eating was dominated by ethnic cuisines. Thus the 'favourite meal' of the British when eating out which had retained a remarkable stability from the 1940s to the 1970s, based on tomato soup, chicken (or later steak) and trifle, passed into history.[85] The 'national dish' at the beginning of the twenty-first century was reported to have become 'chicken tikka masala'.

[82] *Financial Times*, 9 September 2000 p. 18. Nomura, the Japanese investment bank, bought First Quench for £225M in September 2000.
[83] Merrydown had obtained the UK rights to produce Two Dogs alcoholic lemonade (invented in Australia by Duncan MacGillivray).
[84] MSI, *Fast Food UK*, pp. 51, 61.
[85] See Burnett, *Plenty and Want*, 3rd edn, pp. 316–17.

9

FOOD CONSUMPTION, NUTRITION AND HEALTH SINCE THE SECOND WORLD WAR

Trends in food consumption

In the early postwar years there was a manifest desire to return to prewar patterns of food consumption and, indeed, the use of some foods recovered quickly from wartime constraints. Table 9.1 shows the trends in food consumption per head per week recorded by the National Food Survey, based on household consumption and excluding food and drink eaten outside the home.[1] As soon as restrictions were lifted, milk consumption rose to about 2.7 to 2.9 litres per head per week in the early 1950s. Similarly, cheese consumption recovered from below 60g per head per week in 1948 to around 80g per head per week by 1954. The use of eggs doubled to over four eggs per head per week by the mid-1950s and fruit consumption showed a similar increase from around 300g per head per week in 1946 to 600g ten years later. Biscuits, breakfast cereals, sugar and preserves began to re-enter the diet in larger amounts. Butter, so scarce during the war when rationed to about 2oz. per head per week (56g), was much in demand, with consumption rising to 127g by 1955 and reaching a peak of 175g per head per week in 1967. Lastly, purchases of meat and meat products recovered during the early 1950s and reached 955g per head per week by 1954. On the other hand, consumption of the wartime staples – bread and potatoes – fell from their peak levels in the late 1940s. Bread consumption, which had risen to 1.87kg per head per week in 1948, fell back to just under 1.6kg per head per week in 1954. Similarly, potato consumption fell from 2kg per head per week in 1946 to 1.76kg in 1954. For both foods this was merely the first phase of a downward trend that continued after the end of restrictions, until by the end of the twentieth century weekly bread consumption was less than 0.72kg per head and potato consumption down to 0.67kg in 1999. The shortage of sugar had also been a major problem during the Second World War, particularly when much emphasis was placed upon its importance as a source of energy in the diet. During the early 1950s,

---

[1] For its methodology, see MAFF, *Fifty Years of the National Food Survey* (1991).

Table 9.1 Weekly household food consumption in Great Britain, 1945 to 2000

Date	Milk and cream (ml)	Cheese (g)	Eggs (no)	Fruit (g)	Potatoes (g)	Other vegetables (g)	Bread and cereal products (g)	Sugar and preserves (g)	Beverages[a] (g)	Fish and fish products (g)	Fats[b] (g)	Meat and meat products[c] (g)
Second World War rationing												
1942	2,137	101	1	197	1,877	1,024	2,310	378	n.a.	187	245	746
1945	2,517	71	3	318	1,863	1,155	2,424	414	n.a.	261	245	746
The era of postwar rationing												
1946	2,449	72	3	302	1,999	1,155	2,339	425	n.a.	299	233	757
1950	2,938	72	4	513	1,759	1,039	2,315	466	77	188	329	846
1954	2,887	82	4	594	1,761	894	2,288	599	102	161	331	955
The return to free choice												
1955	2,892	80	4	621	1,698	905	2,269	616	100	169	337	976
1960	2,921	86	5	698	1,588	972	2,000	594	101	166	339	1,017
1965	2,949	91	5	725	1,509	987	1,880	583	98	164	336	1,066
1970	2,887	102	5	723	1,470	1,107	1,791	553	102	152	339	1,121
1975	2,913	107	4	676	1,243	1,134	1,624	388	88	127	315	1,054
1980	2,604	110	4	795	1,163	1,260	1,571	375	85	136	318	1,140
1985	2,348	111	3	766	1,162	1,246	1,526	291	77	139	286	1,042
1990	2,169	113	2	895	996	1,265	1,470	219	70	144	255	968
1995	2,170	108	2	996	803	1,258	1,468	175	63	144	218	945
2000	2,081	110	2	1,120	707	1,279	1,508	138	58	143	186	966

Source: DEFRA, National Food Survey.

Notes

n.a. = data not available

[a] Non-alcoholic beverages, principally tea and coffee.

[b] Fats = total visible fats, i.e.butter, margarine, lard, and vegetable oils and spreads.

[c] Total meat = beef and veal, mutton and lamb, pork, bacon and ham, poultry and sausages.

sugar consumption rose rapidly to over 500g per week in 1955 and remained above 500g per head per week until 1963. Even while the final phase of food restrictions was still in operation, new foods began to enter or re-enter the diet. Oranges, bananas and other fruit returned to the shops. Canned and frozen vegetables appeared. Among meat products, pork, bacon and ham recovered from the restrictions of rationing and poultry reappeared in the diet after the wartime constraints on poultry feed were lifted.

Once rationing ended, long-term change in the postwar diet began to be seen. There was a gradual rise in the consumption of liquid whole milk to 2.8 litres per head per week in 1962 and 1963, but this was followed by a decline to 2 litres in 1984 and 1.5 litres in 1988. During the 1990s, the consumption of liquid whole milk collapsed from 1.1 litre in 1991 to 0.63 litre in 1999. This change was offset by the rise in skimmed and semi-skimmed milk consumption from the 1980s onwards. Complementing this change was the rise in popularity of yoghurt and fromage frais, which grew from novelty-food status in the 1960s and early 1970s to a consumption of over 100g per head per week from 1993 onwards.

Although fresh green vegetables had been promoted heavily by Ministry of Food propaganda, wartime levels of consumption were not maintained once peacetime conditions prevailed in the food markets. Consumption had risen to 500g per head per week during the war but in the 1950s and early 1960s fell to 400g; it remained above 300g per head per week between 1966 and 1984 but from 1987 onwards fell further to under 250g per head per week during the 1990s. Consumption of other fresh vegetables – roots, tubers and bulbs – remained above 300g per head per week but from the late 1980s fell to under 250g per head per week during the 1990s. Some of the falling consumption of fresh vegetables was offset by the use of frozen vegetables, which amounted to more than 100g per head per week in 1977 and around 200g from 1991 onwards. It is interesting to note that from 1975 consumption of canned and frozen vegetables (that is, processed vegetables) exceeded the amounts of fresh green vegetables in the diet, presumably as home preparation of vegetables for cooking became less attractive.

The removal of some restrictions on food in 1950 saw flour consumption rise above 200g per head per week, a level it maintained during a home-baking boom in the 1950s. Flour consumption dropped below 200g in 1959 and fell steadily thereafter, apart from several years in the late 1970s at a time of rapid inflation; it was below 150g per head per week from 1982 onwards, below 100g from 1989 and by the late 1990s down to 60g per head per week. Like flour, the consumption of cakes and pastries was high in the 1950s and 1960s within the range of 150 to 190g per head per week. However, from 1965 consumption fell below 100g in 1974 but stabilized at between 70g and 90g per head per week for the rest of the twentieth century. As snack-food eating habits developed during and after the 1970s, there was no further reduction in the consumption of cakes and pastries. Similarly, postwar conditions brought an increase in biscuit eating to more than 100g per head per week in 1950 which then, after further growth, later stabilized at around 160 to 165g from 1959 to 1977. Consumption fell to around 150g per head per week during the 1980s and 135 to 140g in the 1990s. Breakfast cereals showed a continual rise from around 40g per head per week in the early 1950s to 100g after 1980. By the 1990s consumption of breakfast cereals ranged from 130 to 140g per head per week. Although sugar consumption had been above 500g per head per week in the late 1950s and early 1960s, it fell rapidly – despite the promotion of sugar as a loss-leader in supermarkets – to under 400g in 1973, 300g by 1982, under 200g by 1988, until at the end of the 1990s it was under 110g per head per week. Preserves – jams and honey – rose to almost 180g per head per week in the late 1940s but then began a decline, which matched the diminishing role of bread in the British diet. By 1958 the consumption of preserves had fallen below 100g per head per week; the decline continued to around 66g per week in the 1970s and to half that by the end of the twentieth century.

Health concerns undoubtedly had some effect upon the choice of foods in the last quarter of the twentieth century. Purchases of animal foods – meat, fish, eggs and fats – were all affected by consumer attitudes. Sugar consumption fell only gradually despite such assaults as John Yudkin's *Pure White and Deadly*.[2] Concern that diet could be a factor in coronary heart disease had more impact on fat consumption than sugar. Margarine, which had maintained and even increased its use while food restrictions were in operation until 1954, fell from over 100g per head per week in 1960 to 74g in 1975. During the rapid inflation of the late 1970s and the economic depression of the early 1980s margarine consumption rose to 100 to 120g per head per week. By 1993, it was back to 70g per week and as low as 20g per week in 1999. Formerly regarded as a classic 'inferior' food of which more is eaten in hard times and less in good, margarine consumption reflected the marked growth in the use of vegetable fats and oils and low-fat spreads to which consumers were turning as they sought to reduce the saturated fatty acid content of their diet. Taken together, the use of vegetable fats, oils and low-fat spreads increased fourfold from around 27 to 30g per head per week in the 1970s to 120 to 140g per week between 1994 and 2000. By contrast, lard, once the major cooking fat, had almost disappeared from the diet by the end of the century. A less marked change occurred regarding fish. In the late 1940s, while meat, cheese and fats were still rationed, 250 to

[2] John Yudkin, *Pure White and Deadly: The Problem of Sugar* (1972).

300g of fish per head per week was eaten, but this was followed by a decline in total fish consumption to a low point of around 120g per week in the mid-1970s. By the 1990s, consumption of fish had increased to around 145g per head per week. While some of this recovery was due to the growing popularity of seafood, such as scampi, a small part of it resulted from an increase in the consumption of oily fish such as tuna, mackerel and farmed salmon.

Specific health scares affected the consumption of eggs and meat. Egg consumption remained steady at four eggs per head per week until 1978. With growing concerns about salmonella, consumption fell to under three eggs per week in 1987 and, following the 1988 scare, under two eggs per week from 1993 onwards. Worries about the safety of meat caused a number of fluctuations in consumption, as shown by the reduction in beef and veal eaten following the Aberdeen typhoid outbreak in the mid-1960s. Nevertheless, the major trend in the consumption of beef and veal, apart from the short upsurge to almost 300g per head per week in 1957 following de-rationing, was steadily downwards. From the early 1980s, when reports about mechanically recovered meat began to be published, consumption of beef and veal fell below 200g per head per week. Accentuated by Bovine Spongiform Encephalopathy (BSE) and fears of its human variant Creutzfeld Jacob Disease (CJD), beef and veal consumption fell to around 110g per week in the late 1990s. Mutton and lamb consumption showed a similar surge in the late 1950s reaching almost 200g per head per week, but the decline that followed meant that by the late 1990s under 60g per head per week was being eaten. Sausages maintained their level of consumption during the period of food rationing at about 100g per head per week almost unchanged until the 1970s, though during the 1980s and 1990s consumption fell from over 90g to 60g per head per week.

The most successful sectors of the meat market were those discriminated against by government feed policies during the Second World War: pork, bacon and poultry. Then, the size of the bacon ration was a constant source of complaint and pork was scarce. In the late 1940s consumption of pork, bacon and ham was down to 60g per head per week but increased once restrictions were lifted, reached 260g per week in 1970 and again in the early 1980s. A decline then set in and the consumption of pork, bacon and ham was down to 180g per week at the end of the twentieth century. Chicken showed a remarkable and almost unchecked growth: in 1950, the British ate 10g per head per week; by the late 1990s this figure had risen to 250g and the substitution of poultry for red meat was a major change in the diet during the 1980s and 1990s. Despite the changes in different sectors of the market, overall meat consumption remained remarkably stable between 1956 and 1989 at over 1kg per head per week. Even during the 1990s, in the face of BSE and alarm at the growth of food poisoning, consumption remained at around 950g per head per week. By and large, most people in Britain were not sufficiently attracted by vegetarianism to make such a drastic change in their food choice.

The nutritional value of the diet

The nutritional analysis of household food consumption by the National Food Survey is summarized in Table 9.2. The mean values conceal variations in intakes by region or income and, in particular, do not allow the distribution of the food among members of the family to be known. The National Food Survey shows that energy intakes in the immediate postwar years had fallen below the wartime levels for 1944 to 1945 to just over 2,300kcal (9,625kj) per head per day. This resulted from the restrictions imposed on bread and potatoes which brought the intake from carbohydrates down to 305g per head per day in 1946. In the following year, fat intake was down to 82g per head per day, a level which triggered off protests against the government's continuation of rationing at wartime levels.[3] The relaxation of food rationing between 1950 and 1954 led to significant gains in energy intake which rose to 2,475kcal (10,355kj) per day in 1950 and to 2,641kcal (11,050kj) per day by 1955. These gains resulted principally from a rise in fat intake to 107g by 1955. Carbohydrate intake, similarly, reached a high point of 364g per head per day in 1956, a sure sign of a population wanting more food and more variety in the diet. On the other hand, protein intake changed little, though it was composed of more animal protein than vegetable protein by contrast to the wartime diet of more vegetable than animal protein. Indeed, protein intake remained stable at around 75g per head per day until 1968, after which it fell below 70g per day in 1983 and was generally below 65g per day from 1990 onwards. The highest energy intake of the postwar era occurred in 1963 when 2,650kcal (11,090kj) was recorded. By the 1960s, however, carbohydrate intake was already declining, falling below 300g per day for the first time in 1973 and below 250g per day in 1984. Although fat intake continued to rise, reaching 120g per head per day in 1969, it declined thereafter to less than 100g per day in 1984 and had fallen to under 75g per day by the end of the twentieth century, as people ate less butter, lard and less fatty meat. Falling intakes of fat and carbohydrate led to the energy value of the diet dropping below 2,500kcal (10,460kj) per day in 1971, below 2,000kcal (8,368kj) in 1984 and less than 1,800kcal (7,530kj) in 1997. Postwar affluence affected these trends in the sources

---

[3] Total fat intake includes not only visible fats (butter, margarine, lard and vegetable oils) but also fat contained in foods such as meat, dairy produce and fish.

Table 9.2 Daily nutrient intake in Great Britain, 1945 to 2000

Date	Energy value (kcal)	Energy value (kj)	Fat[a] (g)	Protein (g)	CHO[b] (g)	Energy from Fat (%)	Energy from Protein (%)	Energy from CHO (%)	Calcium (mg)	Iron (mg)	Vitamin C[c] (mg)	Vitamin A (mg)	Vitamin D (µg)
Second World War rationing													
1945	2,375	9,937	92	76.0	309	34.9	12.8	52.0	875	12.7	43	2,908	3.57
The era of postwar rationing													
1946	2,307	9,652	86	78.0	305	33.6	13.5	52.9	912	14.4	44	2,926	3.43
1950	2,474	10,351	101	78.0	314	36.7	12.6	50.7	1,066	13.6	[43]	3,536	4.30
1954	2,626	10,987	107	77.0	340	36.5	11.7	51.8	1,034	13.4	50	3,911	3.60
The return to free choice													
1955	2,641	11,050	107	77.0	342	36.6	11.6	51.7	1,044	13.5	51	4,199	3.60
1960	2,630	11,004	115	74.7	345	39.3	11.4	49.3	1,040	14.1	52	4,360	3.25
1965	2,590	10,837	116	75.2	332	40.4	11.6	47.9	1,020	13.9	52	4,370	3.13
1970	2,560	10,711	119	73.7	317	41.8	11.5	46.5	1,030	13.4	52	1,350	2.82
1975	2,290	9,581	107	72.0	275	42.2	12.6	45.2	1,010	11.6	51	1,370	2.63
1980	2,230	9,330	106	72.7	264	42.6	13.0	44.4	960	11.3	58	1,350	2.85
1985	2,020	8,452	96	67.4	238	42.6	13.3	44.1	850	10.8	52	1,370	2.96
1990	1,870	7,824	86	63.1	224	41.6	13.5	44.9	820	10.4	52	1,100	3.02
1995	1,780	7,448	78	63.0	218	39.8	14.2	46.0	810	9.5	52	1,010	2.96
1999	1,690	7,071	72	63.2	211	38.3	14.9	46.8	790	9.6	57	760	3.14
2000	1,750	7,322	74	66.3	218	38.2	15.2	46.7	860	10.1	59	780	3.29

Source: DEFRA, National Food Survey.

Notes

[a] Fat = total visible fats plus fat contained in other foods such as meat, dairy produce and fish.

[b] Carbohydrate (CHO) = available carbohydrate, calculated as monosaccharide.

[c] The vitamin C value in brackets is an estimate to include cooking losses.

of the energy value of the diet. During the rationing period, over 50 per cent of the energy value of the diet came from carbohydrates, some 35 per cent from fats and some 12 to 13 per cent from protein. When the postwar dollar-gap crisis restricted food imports, the percentage of energy from fat fell to 33 per cent in 1946 and 1948 – and even 32 per cent in 1947. The proportion of energy from fat then rose steadily to reach 42 per cent in 1969. It remained at that level until the mid-1990s before falling below 40 per cent during the final years of the twentieth century. As fat provided more energy, so carbohydrate and protein provided less. Energy from carbohydrate sources fell below 50 per cent of the total in 1960, while from 1968 to the end of the century it was between 44 and 47 per cent. Protein sources provided less than 12 per cent of the energy value of the diet from 1954 to 1972, after which a gradual increase led it to exceed 14 per cent from 1995 to the end of the century (see Figure 10.1).

Health

One sign of improving health during the second half of the twentieth century was the increasing longevity of the population. Life expectancy at birth had begun to rise from the 1890s when it was just over 43 years for males and just under 47 years for females. Even before the First World War, children born in England and Wales in 1911 had a life expectancy of 51.5 years for boys and 55.4 years for girls. The trend continued unabated as the century advanced, with life expectancy at birth for boys reaching 66.2 years in 1951, and 69 years in 1971. Girls' life expectancy made even greater progress, reaching 71.2 years in 1951 and 75.2 years by 1971.[4] At the end of the twentieth century boys' life expectancy had risen to 74.9 years and girls' to 79.8.[5] The proportion of elderly people in the population increased from 5.3 per cent over 65 years of age in 1911 to 7.4 per cent by 1931. In 1960, nearly 12 per cent of the United Kingdom's population were over 65 years, and this category of older people had expanded to 15 per cent of the population by 1981.[6]

Although the secular trend in physical development evident among schoolchildren in the interwar years continued in the postwar era, there were still signs of the long-term effects of a restricted diet on adult stature. When the British Medical Association's Committee on Nutrition calculated the energy needs of adults in the late 1940s, they took as

---

[4] CSO, *Annual Abstract of Statistics 1980* (1980), Table 2.33, and *Statistical Abstracts of the United Kingdom*.
[5] Office for National Statistics, *Social Trends 2001*, No. 31 (2001), Table 7.1.
[6] Ibid., Table 1.4.

standard a man of 5ft. 6½in. (168.5cm) weighing 143lb. (65kg) and a woman of 5ft. 2in. (157.5cm) weighing 123lb. (56kg).[7] Despite the setbacks in health in the 1940s, the physical development of school-children progressed. By 1954, the School Medical Officer of the London County Council noted that within his school population, local differences in height and weight had 'largely disappeared'.[8] However, despite its poor districts, London had never been noted for a high proportion of children with unsatisfactory nutrition. Before the war, less than 6 per cent of its children were graded C ('Slightly subnormal') or D ('Bad').[9] In the provinces and in Scotland, environmental differences still affected physical development after the War. Better growth by children in poorer areas in the postwar years did not eliminate the social gradient in heights and weights. In Liverpool, in 1949, children's weight differ-ences between 'good' schools and 'poor' schools was 2.3lb. at 5 years of age, 3lb. at 8 years and 4.6lb. at 12.[10] In other locations in the 1950s, notably Sheffield and Newcastle-upon-Tyne, the social gradient still showed that children from 'good' districts were taller and heavier than those from less satisfactory areas. By the age of 15 there could be nearly three inches' difference in height between Social Class I and Social Class V.[11] The secular trend in growth continued in the second half of the twentieth century. Children in the 1990s between the ages of 5 and 13 were taller even than children in Social Class I in the 1950s. They were also heavier: at 9 years boys were 1.7kg and girls 2.7kg heavier than children in Social Class I in the 1950s; at 13, they were respectively 4.3kg and 5.3kg heavier.[12] Putting on weight was not viewed as favourably as it had been earlier in the century: 25 per cent of girls aged 8 to 15 reported themselves as trying to lose weight. Within the age group 16 to 24, over 30 per cent of young women assessed themselves as overweight and almost 50 per cent as trying to lose weight.[13]

[7] British Medical Association, *Report of the Committee on Nutrition* (1950), para. 28, p. 12. In *Dietary Reference Values*, the Department of Health quoted OPCS data which suggested that in the 1980s a man's mean stature was 5ft. 9in. (175.3cm) tall, and a weight of 163.9lb. (74.5kgs), while the mean stature for women was just over 5ft. 3½in. (161.8cms), weighing 132lb. (60kgs).

[8] Cited in Ministry of Education, *The Health of the School Child 1954–55* (1956), p. 23.

[9] D. J. Oddy, 'The health of the people', in T. C. Barker and M. Drake, eds, *Population and Society in Britain 1850–1980* (1982), Table 4.

[10] Ministry of Education, *The Health of the School Child 1948–49* (1950), p. 9.

[11] See Ministry of Education, *The Health of the School Child 1958–59* (1960), p. 14.

[12] Patricia Prescott-Clarke and P. Primatesta, eds, *Health Survey for England: The Health of Young People '95–97*, Joint Health Surveys Unit (1998), Tables 3.2, 3.3.

[13] Ibid., p. 8.

Dietary change in the 1950s, notably the increase in sugar consumption, was accompanied by a rapid growth in the incidence of dental caries. Calls for the fluoridation of water became a contentious point for discussion. Peacetime food regulations had previously been framed with a view to obtaining 'pure' food by prohibiting additives but now it was proposed to supply the body with a chemical.[14] Fluoridation began, experimentally, in 1956, when water supplies in Anglesey, Kilmarnock and Watford were treated. Although it became Ministry of Health policy in 1962, numerous anti-fluoridation campaigns developed before it was generally accepted, and became widely used in toothpaste.[15] However, by the 1960s, the commonest nutritional disorder was obesity.[16] In the late 1940s, the BMA had expressed the opinion that in a normal healthy diet, fat (both visible and invisible) should provide at least 25 per cent of the energy value. Even so, such a diet might be 'bulky and unsatisfying', in which case it would be appropriate for fat to provide 35 per cent of the energy needs required by greater physical effort.[17] However, the diet in postwar Britain was marked not only by a rising proportion of energy from fat but also by a reduction in the physical effort required during normal everyday life. This began in the 1950s. A growing use of private motor vehicles and the increasingly sedentary nature of work were undoubtedly factors in the general rise in body weight in Britain. Consuming more food, particularly snacks including crisps, ice-cream, biscuits, cakes and pre-packed cereal foods, played a significant part.[18] As the crude death rate for coronary heart disease soared in the 1950s from 1,264 per million for men and 652 for women in 1948 to 2,208 and 1,226 respectively in 1958, it became accepted that 'cardio-vascular disease and material advancement go hand in hand'.[19] There was general agreement among the medical profession that the rising fat content of the diet was contributing to the increase in coronary disease, but a vigorous debate ensued regarding the relative importance of saturated fats, which were mainly of animal origin, and unsaturated fats, which were found in vegetable and fish oils. This became simplified into the idea that animal fats caused heart disease but vegetable fats did not. A titanic battle followed between the margarine producers, notably Unilever's subsidiaries Jurgens' and Van den Bergh's on the one hand,

---

[14] During the Second World War, calcium carbonate had been added to flour in 1941 and margarine had been fortified with vitamins A and D. Flour became permanently fortified in 1953 (see Chapter 8).

[15] *BFJ*, October 1963, 128.

[16] As defined when Body Mass Index (BMI) exceeds 30, based on the formula: BMI = weight (kg)/height (m^2).

[17] BMA, *Report of the Committee on Nutrition*, para. 40, p. 14.

[18] *BFJ*, January 1962, p. 2; September 1962, p. 107.

[19] *BFJ*, January 1962, p. 1.

and the National Dairy Council and the butter-makers on the other, over the relative merits of butter and margarine in the 'healthy' diet. Television advertising challenging consumers to tell the difference between Stork margarine and butter became a national catch-phrase. Once the National Food Survey began to show separate values for the fatty acid components of the fat intake in the diet, it became clearer to what extent the margarine advertisements had frightened people into believing that saturated fats clogged arteries. Until 1976, the fat intake in people's diets comprised nearly 50 per cent saturated fatty acids, or a total amount of 50g or more per day. By the end of the century this had dropped to 39 per cent, or less than 30g per day, from saturated fatty acids. In the 1960s and early 1970s polyunsaturated fatty acids had contributed about 10g per day or only 9 per cent of total fats. By the 1980s and 1990s unsaturated fatty acid intake averaged between 13 and 14g per day which comprised 18 per cent of total fat intake.

A population becoming overweight, and with degenerative heart disease increasingly common, was in sharp contrast with the youth culture and fashion image of Britain in the 1960s. The physique of fashion models led to so much emphasis on body shape for young women and teenage girls in the later years of the twentieth century that slimming became a craze from the 1970s and 1980s onwards. The use of the term 'slimming' led to the misrepresentation of some food products, such as 'starch-reduced' breads, as 'slimming' foods. The Food Standards Committee attempted to tighten food-labelling regulations throughout the 1960s in the face of statements of questionable meaning, for example, that a product must be 'part of a properly designed diet'.[20] Slimming created new categories of products: artificial sweeteners to be carried in pocket or handbag, and low-calorie biscuits and drinks used as meal substitutes. Some of the claims made by marketing men under the generic term 'health foods' brought them into conflict with the Medicines Act, 1968 though, surprisingly, the Labelling of Food Regulations of 1970 avoided making any reference to 'health foods'.

Associated psycho-nutritional disorders such as anorexia and bulimia became dietary problems among the young, though on a lesser scale than those connected with obesity. Slimming gave a new focus to the growing number of cookery books that appeared in bookshops and on library shelves in the second half of the twentieth century. Among the first of its kind was John Yudkin and Gweneth M. Chappell's *The Slimmer's Cook Book*, which was published in 1961 to follow the dietary principles John Yudkin had set out in *This Slimming Business*. Books such as Michele Evans' *Cuisine Minceur Cookbook* brought the ideas of the French chef Michel Guérard to the housewife in 1977. By

---

[20] *BFJ*, January/February 1975, p. 10.

the end of the 1970s, news spread to Britain of the 'success' of the Scarsdale diet. Claims that it was possible to 'Lose up to 20 pounds in 14 days!' made Tarnower and Baker's *The Complete Scarsdale Medical Diet* a paperback success in 1980, and interest in the Scarsdale diet was heightened a year later when Dr Tarnower was murdered by Mrs Jean Harris. As slimming became a more systematic business with magazines on bookstalls multiplying in numbers, Weight Watchers published their own *Fast and Fabulous Cookbook* in 1984.[21]

Slimming was the reaction of a society in which over-consumption was made possible by the benefits of full employment and rising incomes. Not only were the 1950s and 1960s a period of economic progress and rising living standards, but also one of advances in scientific knowledge, notably in organic chemistry and microbiology, which were applied to food technology. The effects upon the food supply were overwhelmingly positive and accepted unquestioningly by the British public. Between the Agriculture Act, 1947 and entry into the Common Market in 1973, the food sold in Britain was generally safe, clean and relatively cheap. Food allergies were rare. The third quarter of the twentieth century was a time that might be characterized as the high point of food safety. Within the context of the Food and Drugs legislation, the food in the British diet was 'pure' and unadulterated. During the 1960s, bovine tuberculosis was eliminated and pasteurization of milk became universal.[22] Nevertheless, within this 'golden age' of technological achievements, questions began to be asked regarding some effects of postwar food technology. While improvements in food handling were welcomed after the Second World War, some reports raised the issue of whether the new packaging materials might be a source of toxic contamination. Intensive farming, particularly as applied to livestock production, led to the reporting of infestation and concern over means of prevention, such as the use of pyrethrum sprays in buildings. The Cold War brought new concerns: a recurrent theme from 1959 onwards was the degree of radioactivity in food materials, particularly the presence of strontium 90.

Changing technology brought further worries. In 1961, it was reported that the injection of antibiotics into animals prior to slaughter was less to do with weight gain than in the hope that antibiotics would delay carcass deterioration. The growing use of chemicals – antibiotics, pesticides and anti-oxidants – gave rise to a BBC television programme

---

[21] See J. Yudkin, *This Slimming Business* (1958); J. Yudkin and G. M. Chappell, *The Slimmer's Cook Book* (1961); Michele Evans, *Cuisine Minceur Cookbook* (1978); H. Tarnower and S. S. Baker, *The Complete Scarsdale Medical Diet* (New York, 1980); Weight Watchers, *Fast and Fabulous Cookbook* (1984).

[22] *BFJ*, 100, 10/11 1998, p. 454.

A Suspicion of Poison in 1962.[23] The *British Food Journal* followed this up with a non-stop series of articles on hygiene problems in food production, which centred on outbreaks of food-poisoning. Paraguayan corned beef led to the Aberdeen typhoid (*S. typhi*) outbreak in 1964; in 1965, concern began to be expressed at hygiene in the foreign restaurants that were proliferating in British towns. In the same year, the editor began to warn against the effects of foreign travel.[24] This was borne out specifically by the incidence of 'Spanish tummy' in 1966 but, by the early 1970s, as foreign holidays became more extensive, infections acquired from the Eastern Mediterranean, North Africa and the Far East came under discussion. In the post-1945 period, the *British Food Journal* kept salmonella continually under scrutiny, its sources varying from duck eggs in 1951, to Chinese eggs in the 1960s and frozen chickens in the 1970s.[25] El Tor cholera was news in 1974 and canned salmon in Birmingham in 1978 led to an outbreak of botulism.[26] By 1980, the mechanical recovery of meat from bones was reported, though not even the *British Food Journal* under the far-sighted eye of Dr Martin's editorship could foresee the reaction against intensive animal husbandry and the growth of the 'organic farming' movement that was to follow when BSE was eventually reported.[27]

A dramatic rise in food-poisoning cases began during the 1980s, as shown in Table 9.3. Notifications of food poisoning had been dropping gradually from the late 1950s until, during the mid-1960s, they fell below 10,000 cases per year. There followed a slow but steady rise to the mid-1980s, after which notified cases increased rapidly to over 60,000 cases in 1992 and over 90,000 in the late 1990s.[28] While it may be that both the public and the medical profession developed a heightened awareness of food-poisoning after 1988, when salmonella contamination of eggs and broiler chickens reached crisis proportions and producers were forced into widespread destruction of both stock and produce, this pattern remains largely unexplained. Several interrelated factors need to be disaggregated. One notable change was the adoption

---

[23] *BFJ*, January 1963, p. 1.

[24] *BFJ*, February 1965, p. 15; July 1966, p. 89.

[25] *BFJ*, May/June 1969, p. 70.

[26] *BFJ*, January/February 1974, p. 16; November/December 1978, p. 184.

[27] *BFJ*, July/August 1984, p. 102; May/June 1980, p. 82.

[28] CSO, *Annual Abstract of Statistics* (1995), ONS, *Annual Abstract of Statistics* (2001), Table 9.5. The changing basis of notifications in Scotland in the mid-1990s prevents the series from being extended to cover Great Britain. This therefore omits the serious E. coli 0157 outbreak of 501 cases (including twenty deaths) at Wishaw, Lanarkshire, in 1996. See T. Hugh Pennington, 'BSE and E. coli food crises', in A. Fenton, ed., *Order and Disorder: The Health Implications of Eating and Drinking in the nineteenth and twentieth centuries* (Phantassie, East Lothian, 2000).

of low-temperature technology in the domestic kitchen. Although families were able to store food in a way that was never possible before the Second World War, the sudden and widespread growth of refrigeration late in the twentieth century raised several issues of how it was being used. The growth in ownership of freezers matched the trend in food-poisoning cases in Table 9.3 but the 1980s also marked the rapid growth in purchases of microwave ovens and 59 per cent of UK households possessed microwaves by 1992.[29] The trend in food-poisoning also correlated with the development of microwave oven cookery. Did it reflect worsening hygiene in domestic and catering establishments; was food handled differently in the kitchen; or was it the effect of increased levels of food processing, as manufacturers sought greater value-added components in the price of their products?

Despite the general economic progress of the 1950s and 1960s, concern began to be expressed during the inflation and depression of the 1970s that the standard of living of some groups in the population was falling behind, with possible detrimental effects on health. The Child Poverty Action Group emphasized this criticism by drawing attention to failings in the Welfare State. Continuing differentials in mortality and morbidity rates led to an investigation into inequalities in health, known generally as the Black Report.[30] One aspect of the inquiry related to the dietary needs of at-risk groups such as pre-school children. The Black Report recommended that the National Food Survey should be developed 'into a more effective instrument of nutritional surveillance in

Table 9.3 Notifiable diseases: food-poisoning, 1983 to 1999

Date	England and Wales	Date	England and Wales
1983	17,735	1992	63,347
1984	20,702	1993	65,587
1985	19,242	1994	81,833
1986	23,943	1995	82,041
1987	29,331	1996	83,233
1988	39,713	1997	93,901
1989	52,557	1998	93,932
1990	52,145	1999	86,316
1991	52,543		

Source: CSO, *Annual Abstract of Statistics*, 1995, *Annual Abstract of Statistics*, 2001.

[29] CSO, *Social Trends*, 1994, Table 6.7. See *Key Note Report, Frozen Foods*, p. 38. The growth in microwave ownership was unaffected by the scare in 1990 that some microwaves failed to heat food sufficiently to kill harmful bacteria.
[30] Department of Health and Social Security (The Black Report), *Report of the Working Group on Inequalities in Health* (1980).

relation to health'[31] and, in view of the low take-up of welfare food and milk for pre-school children in the 1970s, it suggested that a non-means-tested scheme of free or low-cost milk should be available to parents, coupled with better distribution of the national dried milk and vitamins supplied by the welfare services.[32] To this end a greatly increased provision of special welfare foods and an enhanced free school meals programme was proposed. The Black Report also recommended that the National Health Service should have goals that 'might encourage the desirable changes in people's diet, exercise, and smoking and drinking behaviour'.[33] In view of the rise in unemployment during the 1970s, the Report recommended that child benefit be enhanced to offset inflation and the withdrawal of free school milk and food subsidies; in respect of which it quoted from the Department of Health and Social Security's *Eating for Health* (1978) that 'If all were to enjoy the best possible diet, the variation in average height and weight of different socio-economic groups in the United Kingdom would probably be less marked.'[34] The Report took refuge in the lack of evidence for this assertion by quoting the claim from *Eating for Health* that wartime food rationing, subsidies and price controls success had levelled up nutritional status.

The Black Report made further quotations from a study of the nutrition of pre-school children, carried out in 1967 and 1968 by the Committee on Medical Aspects of Food Policy (COMA). Vitamin intake was said to decline both with an increase in family size and a fall in family income (and therefore a decline in social class), but there was 'no evidence that our pre-school children were underfed'.[35] In its search for evidence regarding the possible under-nutrition of children, the Black Report followed the pressure groups of the 1930s, such as the Children's Minimum Council. The erosion of welfare services had begun at the end of the 1960s; one-third of a pint (189ml) of milk had been available free to all schoolchildren from 1946 to 1968, the year in which it was withdrawn from secondary schools. In 1971, milk was no longer provided after the end of the school year when children reached age 7, unless requested by a school doctor. In the same year the price of school meals was also raised. Despite the monitoring of these changes, surveys in the 1970s suggested that the consumption of school milk had no significant effect on physical growth, particularly if milk was drunk regularly at home. However, household milk consumption was falling in the 1970s, and in this respect the Black Report was published at a turning point in

[31] Ibid., paras 7.41–7.42, p. 213.
[32] Ibid., para. 8.16, p. 239.
[33] Ibid., paras 8.101, p. 288, and 8.109, p. 292.
[34] Ibid., paras 9.24, p. 312, and 9.41, p. 321.
[35] Ibid., paras 9.44–9.45, p. 322.

British dietary trends. While the Milk Marketing Board's promotion of milk in the 1930s had been concerned to increase children's physical growth, falling consumption which began in the 1980s, from 3.25pts (1,844ml) per head per week in 1985 to 1.37pts (9,778ml) in 1995, produced no obvious detrimental effects on health.[36]

By 1980, school meal consumption was continuing to fall. Following the price rise in 1971, the total percentage of pupils having school meals – whether paid for or free – fell from 70 per cent in 1975 to 62 per cent in 1977. It was surprising that there was no increased take-up of free school meals among the poorer families whose children were entitled to them. Accordingly, the Black Report contained the radical proposal that local authorities should be required to provide 'nutritionally adequate meals' in all schools free to all pupils, a point which was reiterated in the Report's conclusions that 'provision of meals at school should be regarded as a right' and supplied without charge.[37] The publication of the Black Report soon after the new Conservative government headed by Mrs Thatcher had taken office ensured that its recommendations were ignored and the Report suppressed. In fact, dietary preferences were changing and, instead of eating cooked meals, children used 'tuck-shops' or the vending machines for crisps, snacks and packaged foods that were being installed in schools. Evidence since the 1980s suggested that under-nutrition was not a problem in Britain; on the contrary, a survey of primary school children over the years 1974 to 1994 found that the percentage of children who were overweight was rising significantly. From 1984 to 1994, the percentage of English boys who were overweight increased from 5.4 per cent to 9 per cent and of Scottish boys from 6.4 to 10 per cent. The percentage of overweight girls rose from 9.3 to 13.5 per cent in England and 10.4 to 15.8 per cent in Scotland over the same period.[38] Moreover, some evidence has suggested that there is an association between deprivation and obesity in childhood and that childhood status is a predictor of adult obesity and morbidity.[39]

---

36 Ibid., paras 9.49–9.51, pp. 323–5.
37 Ibid., paras 9.64–9.65, pp. 327–8 and para. 9.105, p. 349.
38 Susan Chinn and R. J. Rona, 'Prevalence and trends in overweight and obesity in three cross sectional studies of British children, 1974–1994', *BMJ*, 6 January 2001, pp. 322, 24–6.
39 S. Kinra, R. P. Nelder and G. J. Lewendon, 'Deprivation and childhood obesity: a cross sectional study of 20,973 children in Plymouth, United Kingdom', *Journal of Epidemiology and Community Health*, 2000, June, 54 (6), pp. 456–60; T. J. Parsons, C. Power, S. Logan and C. D. Summerbell, 'Childhood predictors of adult obesity: a systematic review', *International Journal of Obesity*, 1999, 23, Supplement 8.

The nutritional impact of eating out

One change in consumer behaviour that began to have a noticeable effect upon the health of the population was the growing consumption of fast food, which was a buoyant sector of the market during the 1980s and 1990s. At the same time, expenditure on all forms of eating out was increasing. By 1999, spending on eating out in Britain reached a total of £7.08 per person per week. Table 9.4 shows that consumption of foods remained more or less stable in the major categories, notably meat and meat products (109g per head per week), and potatoes (119g per head per week). Consumption of ethnic foods, mainly Indian and Chinese, continued to rise, totalling 46g per head per week in 1999. Rice, pasta and noodles showed a similar trend, reaching 28g per head per week in 1999.

The figures in Table 9.4 conceal a number of regional variations. Expenditure was highest in London and significantly lower in Scotland and Yorkshire and northeast England. In 1999, Londoners consumed more ethnic meals, fish, fruit, sandwiches, ice-cream, desserts, biscuits and cakes than any other region of Britain. Scotland consumed more soup, rolls, soft drinks, rice, pasta, noodles and bread than other areas of

Table 9.4 Weekly consumption per head of food and drink eaten outside the home, 1994 to 1999

Foods	Year					
	1994 (g)	1995 (g)	1996 (g)	1997 (g)	1998 (g)	1999 (g)
1. Meat and meat products	109	108	99	107	110	109
2. Fish and fish products	n.a.	n.a.	23	23	25	24
3. Potatoes	n.a.	n.a.	114	119	123	119
4. Vegetables and salads	n.a.	n.a.	82	95	95	96
5. Rice, pasta, noodles	20	18	24	27	27	28
6. Ethnic foods	28	26	32	38	41	46
7. Sandwiches, rolls, etc.	70	73	66	89	81	82
8. Ice-cream, desserts, confectionery	78	68	74	75	68	62
9. Biscuits, crisps, nuts	16	14	24	22	21	20
10. Beverages and soup (ml)	401	405	409	422	408	390
11. Soft drinks (including milk) (ml)	310	330	336	348	318	323
12. Alcoholic drinks (ml)	539	535	483	490	435	408

Note: n.a. = not available.

Source: based on Table 4.3, National Food Survey 1999.

Britain.[40] Eating out was most extensive in London, where average spending on food and drink was £10.34 per head per week in 1999. By contrast, the lowest expenditure was in the East Midlands (£6.03), Yorkshire and Humberside (£6.06) and Scotland (£6.08). London also showed the highest expenditure on alcoholic drinks (£1.94) compared with £1.17 per head per week in Scotland. Notable items of consumption in London were beverages (420ml) bought each week and of soft drinks, including milk (454ml). Consumption of ethnic meals reached 90g per week in London compared with only 17g in Yorkshire and Humberside. Londoners also consumed more meat products and potatoes than any other region. Eating out acquired greater significance as income rose. Income group A spent £17.01 per week compared to group D's expenditure of £3.97. The foods bought did not change from one income group to another. Better quality foods may have been introduced as expenditure rose, and the demand for snack foods, such as biscuits, crisps and nuts, slackened in the highest income group.

Age was a major factor in choice of foods eaten out. The eating of burgers and kebabs made the 15 to 24 years age group the highest consumers of meat and meat products, soft drinks and confectionery but the lowest eaters of fruit. The highest consumption of potatoes was by 5 to 14-year-olds, which reflected their liking for potato chips. The biggest consumers of sandwiches, rolls and beverages were the 25- to 54-year-olds, the main age groups of the working population. Beyond 55 years, the consumption of all food and drink eaten out tailed off; expenditure by pensioner age groups was limited. In families with four or more children or in single-parent households expenditure was also low, and the foods eaten out reflected those which satisfied children's tastes and demands – a high consumption of potatoes, meat products (especially burgers and sausages) and soft drinks.[41]

Food and drink eaten out contributed significantly to the daily intake of energy and nutrients, though expenditure in money made it a high-cost gain. As shown in Table 9.5, the energy value of food and drink taken outside the home was around 260kcal in the late 1990s or some 14 to 15 per cent of total daily energy intakes. Fat provided 40 per cent of the energy value and over 46 per cent of energy from food alone when drinks were excluded. This was higher than the proportion of energy from fat in household food consumption, which fell from 40 per cent to 38 per cent over the same period.[42] Of the energy obtained from food and drink eaten out, 82 per cent came from food (including beverages),

---

[40] MAFF, *National Food Survey 1999*, p. 41.
[41] Ibid., Table 4.6, also p. 44.
[42] MAFF, *National Food Survey 1997*, Table 3.2; MAFF, *National Food Survey 1999*, Table 3.2.

Table 9.5 Daily nutrient intake per head of food and drink eaten outside the home, 1995 to 1999

Nutrient values		Year				
		1995 (g)	1996 (g)	1997 (g)	1998 (g)	1999 (g)
Energy value of food	(kcal)	240	255	265	260	255
eaten out	(kj)	1,004	1,067	1,109	1,088	1,067
Protein	(g)	6.9	7.1	7.7	7.7	7.8
(% of energy value)		*20*	*18.7*	*19.3*	*18.9*	*18.8*
Fat	(g)	11	11	12	12	11
(% of energy value)		*41.8*	*40.3*	*39.7*	*40.1*	*40.3*
Carbohydrate	(g)	24	28	29	28	28
(% of energy value)		*38.2*	*41*	*41*	*41*	*40.9*
Total energy intake	(kcal)	1,778	1,852	1,778	1,736	1,693
at home	(kj)	7,439	7,749	7,439	7,263	7,084
Energy value of food eaten out as % of energy intake at home		*13.4*	*13.7*	*14.9*	*15*	*15.1*
Percentage of energy value from fat if all drinks excluded		*50.3*	*47.8*	*46.9*	*46.8*	*46.8*

Source: based on Table 4.9, National Food Survey 1999.

9 per cent from alcoholic drinks, and 9 per cent from confectionery and soft drinks.[43]

The energy and nutrient values of food and drink taken outside the home varied according to expenditure patterns. The highest energy intake, 330kcal per day, was obtained in London and the lowest in Yorkshire and Humberside (220kcal) and northwest England (225kcal). Food eaten out is generally high in fat and, in particular, in saturated fatty acids.

Differentiating intake by income groups as shown in Table 9.6 reveals that the higher the income group, the more energy, protein, fats and sugars was obtained. Conversely, alcohol provided more energy in the lower income groups. A comparison of males and females aged 11 years and over shows that men obtained considerably more energy, protein, fat and sugars than women. Age also brought a marked decline in intake

[43] MAFF, *National Food Survey 1999*, p. 49.

Table 9.6 Daily nutrient intake per head of food eaten out, by income and gender, 1999

| | | Income groups | | | | | Gender | | |
		A	B	C	D	OAP	Male	Female	All
Energy value	(kcal)	395	315	270	180	155	334	253	255
of food	(kj)	1,653	1,318	1,130	753	648	1,397	1,059	1,067
eaten out									
Protein	(g)	13.1	9.5	7.9	5.1	4.5	9.5	7.3	7.8
(% of energy value)		18.5	18.1	19.1	19.9	22.0	18.9	14.1	18.8
Fat	(g)	18.0	14.0	12.0	8.0	7.0	15.0	12.0	11.0
(% of energy value)		40.9	40.8	39.7	38.9	38.8	39.2	41.5	40.3
Total sugars	(g)	19.0	16.0	14.0	9.0	8.0	18.0	15.0	13.0
Alcohol (% of		5.3	6.1	8.7	6.9	7.3	10.0	2.9	6.6
energy value)									

Note: Under 'Gender', males and females are aged 11 and over. 'All' includes children under 11 years.
Source: data from the *National Food Survey 1999*, Tables 4.9, 4.11 and 4.13.

of energy, protein and sugars, though the proportions of energy derived from fat and alcohol remained high.

Until the eating-out survey began, the National Food Survey had been recording a steady decline in energy intakes from 2,600kcal (10,880kj) in 1970 to just under than 1,700 (7,110kj) in 1999, a fall of some 900kcal. These figures, shown in Table 9.7, are based on food and drink consumed in the home. However, such a trend in falling energy intake seems to be at odds with the general impression that body weights have been rising and obesity has become a discernible problem in Britain. While the additional information provided by the eating-out survey gave a more accurate picture of food consumption at the end of the twentieth century, adding 250 to 260kcal per day to the energy intakes in the National Food Survey, as shown in Figure 9.1, only partly modified the downward trend in energy values.[44] Thus, in 1999, energy intake per head was approximately 1,950kcal per day rather than just under 1,700. Thus there is a conundrum at the end of the 1990s: Britons have become increasingly overweight and even obese at a time when energy intake has been apparently falling. This cannot be explained unless daily energy expenditure has undergone a dramatic reduction.

---

[44] Energy values in the National Food Survey since 1995 do not include the energy values given in the eating-out survey.

Table 9.7 Daily nutrient intake per head of the population in Great Britain, 1970 to 1999

Date	Energy value (kcal)	(kj)	Protein (g)	Fat (g)	CHO (g)	Iron (mg)	Calcium (g)
1970	2,600	10,878	75	121	322	13.7	1.05
1974	2,360	9,874	70	110	288	12.5	1.01
1975	2,290	9,581	72	107	275	11.6	1.01
1980	2,230	9,330	73	106	264	11.3	0.96
1985	2,020	8,452	67	96	238	10.8	0.85
1990	1,872	7,832	63	86	224	10.4	0.82
1994	1,790	7,489	62	80	218	9.7	0.81
1995	1,778	7,439	68	78	218	9.5	0.81
1999	1,693	7,084	63	72	211	9.6	0.79

Source: MAFF, Annual Reports of the National Food Survey.

As Table 9.8 shows, a recent assessment put the proportion of obese men and women in England at 17 per cent and 21 per cent respectively in 1998.[45] The progressive rise in body weight that has taken place since 1980 has created a major health problem in society. When the government published its Green Paper *The Health of the Nation* in 1991, the first key area was 'to reduce level of ill-health and death caused by coronary heart disease and stroke and the risk factors associated with them'. As part of its programme towards attaining these goals, the Department of Health set a target for 2000 to reduce the percentages of obese persons aged 16 to 64 in England to the levels pertaining in 1980, namely 6 per cent of men and 8 per cent of women. It also sought to

Table 9.8 Percentage of population aged 16 to 64 defined as obese in England, 1980 to 1998

Date	Men (%)	Women (%)
1980	6	8
1986	7	12
1993	13	16
1998	17	21

Source: NAO, *Tackling Obesity in England*, 2001.

[45] National Audit Office, Report by the Comptroller and Auditor General, *Tackling Obesity in England*, HC220, Session 2000–1 (2001), Executive Summary, p. 1.

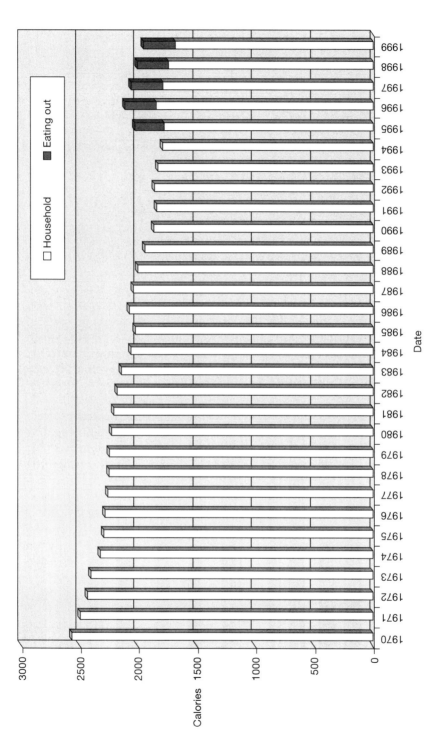

Figure 9.1 Daily energy intake per head in Great Britain, 1970 to 1999

reduce the proportion of energy intake derived from all sources of fats, and from saturated fatty acids in particular, to 35 per cent and 11 per cent respectively. By the time a strategy document – *Eat Well!* – was published in 1994, obesity levels were showing a marked increase, while the reduction in the total fat content and saturated fatty acid content of the diet was showing only a marginal decline.[46] Other goals concerned with consumption of food and drink, such as the aspiration to reduce levels of alcohol consumption in the population over the age of 18 years, were not met. More than a quarter of the male population in England consumed over twenty-one units of alcohol per week and the proportion of women consuming more than fourteen units of alcohol continued to rise to 13 per cent by 1994.[47] In 1997, faced with the evidence that obesity was still increasing and there was no fall in the consumption of alcohol by women, the House of Commons Public Accounts Committee asked the Department of Health to explain why it seemed unlikely that target reductions set for 2005 would be achieved. The Department of Health's anodyne response was that being obese or overweight depended on 'how much physical activity we take' and 'how much we eat and drink'. The trend:

> in our country and in a lot of other western countries was a long-term decline in the amount of physical activity we take on average. Although there was also a decline in the calories we actually consumed, there was a growing imbalance between what we expend in calories and what we take in.[48]

The Department was unable to explain how its targets for 2005 would be met, since the health education campaigns that were being undertaken had had a very limited effect. In spite of a developing epidemic of Type 2 diabetes associated with an overweight population, the Department of Health presumed that 'individuals had to make their own decisions at the end of the day on what they were going to eat and how physically active they were going to be in their lives'. In effect, the sedentary nature of life for many people meant that energy intake exceeded energy expenditure by a substantial amount, and their health and their waistlines showed it.

---

[46] NAO, Report by the Comptroller and Auditor General, *Health of the Nation: A Progress Report*, HC656, Session 1995–6 (1996) pp. 2–5, 8.

[47] Ibid., pp. 24–5.

[48] Committee of Public Accounts, Seventeenth Report 1996–7, *Health of the Nation: A Progress Report*, HC85 Session 1996–7 (1997), pp. 5–6.

10

OVERVIEW

Change in the twentieth century

From plain fare to fusion food summarizes the changes that occurred in the diet during the twentieth century, an era which began and ended with agriculture in crisis and the safety of food under scrutiny. For a small, over-populated island, Britain's policy of free trade before 1914 was necessary for the country to maintain itself by importing food, including much which could have been grown in the country. This left Britain open to 'starvation' campaigns during both World Wars. In 1917, and again in 1943, the worst years for submarine warfare, there were times when it appeared as if such campaigns might succeed. Rising food prices in the First World War caused great discontent in the absence of a fair system of distribution until the last few months of the war. The dissatisfaction of consumers in the food queues was never matched in the Second World War, when the distribution of food appeared to be more equitable. The reliance on imports for the bulk of the food supply continued until the last quarter of the century, even though trade policy changed, notably in 1931, when free trade was abandoned; in 1947, when wartime price support for agriculture was extended; and more recently, in 1973, when Britain entered the Common Market. In the years following the Second World War, food imports remained significant despite the stimulus of price support policies for agriculture. Table 10.1 shows that home production of food was still inadequate, and Britain relied upon imports for half its food supply during the 1960s and 1970s.[1] The use of express transport to meet the demand for increased variety – even to the extent of importing fresh food by air freight from the USA and African countries – maintained imports at a significant level during the later years of the century. From 1973, food supplies became subject to the European Commission's Common Agricultural Policy which introduced quotas, including taking land out of production ('set-aside') in order to maintain agricultural prices and incomes. This dismantled the international trading system involving the Commonwealth and other food producers that had created price stability in the British market. It also brought

---

[1] See chapters on agriculture, fisheries and forestry in Central Office of Information, *Britain 1965*, and *Britain 1975*.

Table 10.1 Percentage of total food supplies produced in the United Kingdom

Food product	1934–38 (%)	1951 (%)	1956 (%)	1964 (%)	1973 (%)
Wheat	23	33	20	47	57
Oils and fats	16	10	16	10	15
Sugar (refined)	17	23	22	27	30
Carcass meat	51	65	62	69	75
Bacon and ham	32	49	42	38	45
Butter	9	4	9	6	22
Cheese	24	18	43	42	57
Milk (liquid)	100	100	100	100	100
Eggs	71	86	96	98	98
Potatoes	96	98	93	95	94

Source: MAFF statistics summarized in CSO, *Britain* (annual series).

Note: Wheat includes flour as wheat equivalent; production of some foods (milk, potatoes) are the totals for human consumption.

about an end to the agricultural price support system operating during the 1950s and 1960s, so that food prices in shops rose rapidly during the 1970s. In addition to the repercussions of currency decimalization in 1971, the effects of the Common Agricultural Policy meant that by 1974 the index of retail food prices had risen almost 55 per cent over a matter of four years as Britain passed from a cheap to a dear food economy.[2] Despite the fact that the output of some home-produced food had increased considerably, by the end of the century one-third of all the food consumed in the United Kingdom was imported and even one-fifth of indigenous foods came from abroad.[3]

The era of plain fare, which lasted for the first seventy-five years of the twentieth century, was – at least until the Second World War – a period of low wages and under-consumption. Since purchasing power determines food consumption, full employment, as between 1915 and 1921 and from 1940 to 1967, marked advances in consumption that were never totally lost when economic downturns occurred. In brief, the twentieth century was a period of gradual transition from under-consumption of food to over-consumption. Fundamental to that change was the rise in purchasing power. The first Cost of Living Index in 1913 indicated that 60 per cent of income went on food. That fell below 30 per cent of income in 1951, was down to 20 per cent in 1971 and to 17 per cent in 1999.

[2] CSO, *Social Trends 5 1974* (1974), Table 84.
[3] DEFRA, *Agriculture in the United Kingdom, 2000* (2001), Table 2.1.

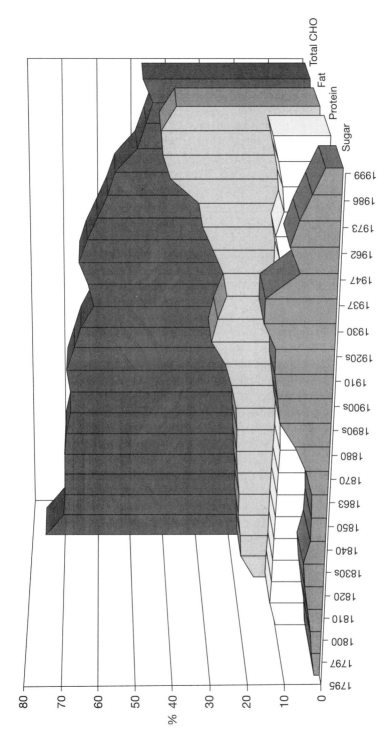

Figure 10.1 Energy sources of the British diet, 1795 to 1999

The twentieth century was not only a period when the population in general acquired the means to eat more – at least in the second half of the century – but also one when a greater variety of more palatable foods entered the diet. The dietary difference between rich and poor countries is that in countries where income is greater, people will obtain a higher proportion of the energy value of their diet from foods that contain more fats, more sugar and more protein from animal sources than will be the case in poor countries. If income is low, the diet will depend on starchy carbohydrate foods; and sugar, fats and protein will make only a small contribution to the energy value. Any country experiencing a rise in incomes over time will experience similar changes in the sources of energy in the diet. In Britain, data allow a long-term comparison over the nineteenth and twentieth centuries, which indicates how profoundly the diet has changed.

Figure 10.1 is based on family budget evidence up to 1940 and National Food Survey data from then on. It shows that during the nineteenth century starchy carbohydrate foods supplied approximately 70 per cent of the energy value of the diet – plain fare indeed! Fats provided about 20 per cent and protein 10 to 11 per cent of the energy value. By 1900, sugar supplied 13 to 14 per cent and fats 27 to 28 per cent of energy. Thus the reliance on starchy carbohydrate foods was beginning to decline and with it the monotony of the traditional cereal-based diet. By the 1930s, fats supplied over 30 per cent and sugar 18 per cent of energy. In the postwar diet, consumption of fats continued to rise until they provided 42 per cent of energy by the early 1980s, almost as much as the 44 per cent obtained from carbohydrates. At the end of the century, health concerns were bringing about some reversal in this trend, so that 38 per cent of energy came from fats and 46 per cent from carbohydrates, a level previously not known since the early 1970s.

There is little doubt that people before 1914 ate restricted diets and many lived in poor environmental conditions. The assessment by Sir Jack Drummond that there was malnutrition in Britain before the First World War seems to be unchallengeable. It was not just the poorer classes who ate restricted diets: the family budget evidence shows how widespread this was. The nutritional effects extended to anyone in regular employment up to an income of 30s a week (£1.50).[4] The negative consequences for health and physique were recorded by the military service tribunals following the imposition of conscription in 1916. In civilian life, full employment during the First World War was instrumental in breaking the pattern of restricted diets that had been a threat to health and growth

---

[4] In 1911, 75 per cent of the employed population in Britain were manual workers and 19 per cent in white-collar occupations. An income of £75 per year was common in both categories of employment.

in the nineteenth century. Although the collapse of the postwar economic boom in 1921 led to high levels of unemployment during the 1920s and 1930s, particularly in the older urban industrial areas, not all the gains were lost after the war. Some dietary change may be seen from the higher levels of sugar and fat consumption in Figure 10.1. This, and the growing purchases of commercial products such as packaged groceries, allowed meals in the interwar years to become more elaborate. Areas of poverty still existed, where diets as restricted as any in the nineteenth century were the norm, notably in northern English towns, in Scotland and the Rhondda mining community.[5] All the surveys made in the 1930s indicated higher protein and fat intakes than was common in the nineteenth century but the lack of any further gain in energy levels was due largely to falling carbohydrate intake. Iron and calcium intakes were improving, but in the northern towns in England the calcium level – the target of the Empire Marketing Board's milk campaign – was still far too low for health and growth. Despite the improved knowledge of nutrition there was a marked failure of social policy to rectify any problems.

There were many people, therefore, who experienced no great deprivation under wartime rationing in the 1940s, though the strain on many housewives' ability to make do was considerable. Wartime Britain maintained a good deal of its prewar class differentials in food consumption, as in other aspects of life, and in the early stages of the war the disruption and shortages meant that some people's diets were as inadequate as those common before 1914. For others, such as the armed forces and civil defence (including the police, fire brigades, air-raid personnel, as well as some civil servants) and those men engaged in heavy work, there was often more food available than had been their normal experience in peacetime. It was notable that consumers responded to any change in rations along social class lines; cuts in rations had more effect on the poor than the rich. Consequently, any evaluation of diets during the Second World War must discount much of the mythology of the beneficial nature of rationing. For practical reasons the population rejected much of the Ministry of Food's propaganda put out by the Food Advice Division. Moreover, the official history of the Ministry of Food almost completely ignored the black market in food – though it did admit that a ration book was said to have a value of £5.[6] While the black market was not a dominant aspect of wartime food supply, its presence was pervasive and affected all levels of society from the 'little extras' that shopkeepers provided for favoured customers, to the smuggling of food between Eire and Ulster. It even extended to the

---

[5] Orr, *Food, Health and Income*, 2nd edn (1937), p. 44 (and Foreword to the 1st edn).

[6] Hammond, *Food: Volume II*, p. 512.

amounts of sugar 'mislaid' in areas of the West Coast of Scotland where illicit distilling of whisky continued.[7] Other official views, such as those produced by the Ministry of Health, must be discounted as having the prime function of enhancing the Ministry's role, in view of its lack of control over food supply. Furthermore, the Ministry of Health was attempting to recover from the inadequacies of its policies and its unrealistic stand on malnutrition in the interwar years. On the other hand, the Ministry of Food was prepared to give credit to Orr's findings in the 1930s, elevating them to the status of a 'first national dietary survey' and vindicating Orr's assessment of the prewar standards of nutrition:

> The diet was generally deficient in calcium, vitamin A, vitamin B_1 and vitamin C. A considerable proportion of the population was also short of animal protein and iron. Correlation of diet with income indicated that this malnutrition was due chiefly to poverty, though in part to poor selection and purchase of food.[8]

Accepting that before the War 'much preventable ill-health was due to malnutrition' allowed officialdom to bolster its role in the Second World War, though the myth of the wartime diet as scientifically planned for health did not finally become established until later when Lord Woolton's *Memoirs* were published and the realities of rationing had been largely forgotten.[9] In this, the role of Sir Jack Drummond, as scientific adviser to the Ministry of Food, became embellished not only by Lord Woolton but also by Dorothy Hollingsworth in her revision of *The Englishman's Food*. In fact, science had little more influence on food policy during the war than it did in the 1930s. The vitamin B_1 fiasco in the early part of the war was such an example. The resistance of the millers, and the demand from the Ministry of Agriculture for grain 'offals' as animal feed, prevented the rise in the flour extraction rate that Drummond requested until the 1942 crisis in the Battle of the Atlantic.[10] Similarly, the fortification of flour with calcium, and of margarine with

---

[7] Ibid., p. 641.

[8] Ministry of Food, *How Britain Was Fed in War-Time*, paras 144–5, p. 45.

[9] F. Marquis (Lord Woolton), *The Memoirs of the Rt. Hon. The Earl of Woolton* (1959), p. 193. The Ministry had established the legend of its nutritional role as early as 1952, when its Food Advice Division closed down. In *The Times*, 11 August 1952, Sir Wilson Jameson asserted: 'During the late war the Ministry of Health was responsible for advising the Government on nutritional policy; the task of giving practical effect to such advice was a burden borne largely by the Ministry of Food.' See PRO, MAF256/4.

[10] PRO, MAF84/291, Cereal Products Division; also CAB74/12, Scientific Committee on Food Policy Minutes, 1941–43. SFC(41)6: 'With regard to the

vitamins A and D, which followed from the 'dip' in standards of nutrition between 1940 and 1941, was accepted for fear of possible losses of output in the war-production industries. In these matters, as in the postwar rationing of bread and potatoes, over which Drummond resigned in protest, economic constraints determined changes to food policy. The difference the war brought in levelling up the diet of the poorest one-third of the population who prewar were on 'bread and spread' was full employment, better wages and little else in the shops to buy. People were able to take up their rations without being short of money for other items in the household budget. Even so, for the civilian population in World War II, there was only enough to go round if women concentrated on feeding the men and children in their families rather than sit down at table with them.

The immediate postwar years left people longing for variety and freedom of choice. They were far from understanding the retailing revolution in foodstuffs that was to come, but no view of 1984 put before them by George Orwell could have prepared them for the social change of the second half of the twentieth century. To begin with, confidence and expectations were high. The general perception of food between 1950 and 1970 was that it was pure, unadulterated and safe to eat. The fortunate combination of full employment and rising wages presented the opportunity to consume more of the 'protective' animal foods – meat, fish, eggs and dairy produce – that had always been recommended for health in former times when under-nutrition and diseases such as tuberculosis had been widespread. By the mid-1950s, food in shops, whether from Britain or from trading partners in the Sterling Area, particularly the Commonwealth countries, was plentiful and relatively cheap. Yet urban consumers in Britain gradually became aware of dissonant and unwelcome voices. During the 1950s the worrying increase in cardiovascular disease raised dietary awareness. The implication of fats in this increase began a retreat from 'rich' diets of red meat and dairy products which, when played on by the marketing departments of the margarine companies, reversed the age-old premise that health was the outcome of eating well. There was also a fear that modern farming was losing its traditional relationship with the land and was becoming 'agribusiness', an ugly word that raised questions about

Committee's recommendations that only flour of 85% extraction should be milled in the United Kingdom, the Ministry of Food would be reluctant to compel the public to eat wholemeal bread until the shipping situation made such a course imperative.' It confirmed this at a press conference early in 1945. See drafts in MAF84/394: 'In March 1942, with the prime purpose of saving valuable shipping space, the milling ratio of wheat – that is, the extraction rate – was increased from 75% to 85%. This involved the disappearance of the white loaf.'

the nature of profits and the ethics of food production. The first use of the term in North America in the 1950s had no immediate impact in Britain,[11] but it was followed early in the 1960s by Rachel Carson's *Silent Spring*, which was widely available in Britain from 1965.[12] Her account of the widespread commercial use of pesticides, fungicides and herbicides, particularly chlorinated hydrocarbons such as DDT, in crop production in the USA, caused alarm. It helped focus concern in Britain following the 'fox death' phenomenon in 1959 and reports of dying birds in the spring of 1961. The alarm was a precursor to a number of dietary phobias fostered by reports of antibiotics and hormones (bovine somatotropin) injected into livestock to promote growth and milk yields. Food additives, particularly dyes, became a subject for discussion which raised fears of their carcinogenic properties. By the 1970s the public's confidence in its food was shaken.

From the late 1960s or early 1970s, livestock husbandry began to adopt recycling processes that led into uncharted waters. Recycling chicken protein into feed ensured the persistence of salmonella. Rendering animal carcass waste into animal feed 'concentrates' or meat-and-bone meal (MBM) raised the question of whether all organisms would be destroyed by rendering plants. The disease BSE first appeared about 1986. By 1990, there were 14,000 cases a year; beef consumption fell significantly and exports of British beef collapsed.[13] In the late 1980s, with chickens and eggs infected with salmonella, unpasteurized milk products and cook-chill meals contaminated by listeria, outbreaks of botulism, cattle infected with BSE and fears that the 1986 Chernobyl nuclear disaster had contaminated Welsh lamb, Britain's food supply was beset by problems that neither George Orwell nor even Magnus Pyke could have contemplated. During the 1990s, one in twenty of the United Kingdom's population consulted their medical practitioners annually with gastric disorders and growing numbers of food allergies began to be reported.

It would have been impossible for anyone in early postwar Britain to imagine the extent to which the countryside would be perceived as a source of danger by the late twentieth century. Traditionally the symbol of good-quality food, the countryside had become the producer of foods associated with obesity and heart disease eschewed by the health-obsessed. Yet the symbolic image of good food from the country had an

---

[11] The term was coined at Harvard Business School in 1955. See J. H. Davis and R. A. Goldberg, *A Concept of Agribusiness* (Boston, MA, 1957).
[12] Rachel Carson, *Silent Spring* (Harmondsworth, 1965). Her work was published in the USA in 1962 or 1963. Her death in 1964 led to a number of later editions.
[13] See R. W. Lacey, *Hard to Swallow* (Cambridge, 1994), and Pennington, 'BSE and E. coli food crises', in Fenton, *Order and Disorder*, pp. 1–9

irresistible appeal: in December 1999, the Ministry of Agriculture, Fisheries and Food produced a consultation document called *A New Direction for UK Agriculture* as a background for discussion of the European Union's possible Common Agricultural Policy reform. It proposed 'a farming industry that is vibrant, competitive and sustainable, producing quality food in accordance with high environmental and welfare standards'.[14] Such sentiments were incontrovertible: consumers expected food to have nutritious, wholesome and health-giving properties; but sentiments were overtaken by events when foot-and-mouth disease closed the countryside as the twenty-first century began.

The period from the 1890s to the 1970s had been one of relative stability in the diet when tastes had changed only slightly. There followed in the last quarter of the twentieth century a combination of circumstances – the experience of foreign travel, an awareness of ethnic cuisine due to immigration, television, technological innovation and sedentary lifestyles – that changed Britain's eating behaviour markedly. For some, meal patterns were modified: snack eating in the streets, on public transport and in the workplace led to 'grazing' rather than daily set meals. The advances in food processing, packaging and presentation, and the provision of places to eat and drink out were major influences on dietary habits. One example was instant coffee: the rapid growth in its consumption threatened tea for the title of Britain's national drink. Nowhere did technology have a greater impact than in the development of frozen foods. Home storage of frozen foods did not develop until the 1970s but, when it did, it fundamentally changed traditional cooking practices. No longer was it necessary or normal to buy large amounts of meat or poultry and cook the whole lot in one go, so that the remainder of the week was spent using up leftovers. Instead, cooking as demonstrated by the TV chefs of the 1980s and 1990s concentrated on the use of fresh materials (even if chilled or frozen in the shop) for each dish or meal. The viewer was not so much learning to cook as being programmed to heat up in a microwave oven what had been brought home from the shop or taken out of the freezer to eat while watching television. Cooking had become part of the leisure and entertainment industry rather than a practical necessity. Moreover, the TV chefs, on the whole, showed little interest in 'plain fare'. What they offered as 'modern British cooking' was not based on traditional family dishes but rather on an invented, plate-decorative cooking drawn from restaurant practice, and quite unlike the traditional roasts and pies for which Britain was famous.

Consumers' receptivity enabled food manufacturers to develop novelties to excite potential buyers. In the process, it was easy to make

---

[14] MAFF (DEFRA), *A New Direction for UK Agriculture*, December 1999, Agenda 2000, CAP Reform.

the consumer overlook the cultural background of the British diet. Although 'fusion food' as a term originated on the West Coast of the USA, food manufacturers in Britain eagerly adapted it to develop products with an international market that crossed culinary boundaries. Consumers were presented with mixtures of Pacific, Indian and European dishes. By the end of the twentieth century these and similar products could be found in the chilled cabinets of British supermarkets. In such product development, the 'value-added' component increased dramatically in the latter part of the twentieth century whether in the supermarket or corner shop. Consumers bought packaging, designer artwork, printing, aluminium foil, plastic and, when that was removed, they found food bulked out with water, extenders, colourings, phosphates and other additives.

In effect, the food industry – both manufacturing and retailing – changed the British diet dramatically in the last quarter of the twentieth century; as a result, many of the skills required to handle and prepare raw ingredients have been lost, as has knowledge of cooking methods. Yet newspapers offered readers new diets to try, healthy eating patterns to follow, and news-stalls carried a wide range of food magazines. Television programmes showed graphically the successes and failures of slimming programmes. By the 1990s British consumers faced the ultimate confidence trick of modern society: the global food manufacturers that sold food and then tried to help successful consumers, their best customers, in effect, to lose weight. However, although the food-marketing men had become well aware that the British were addicted to the stimulation of flavours and textures of food, even at the cost of becoming overweight to the point of obesity, the ultimate marketing concept – and the latest project of the food technologists – food with no nutritive value – was not yet available at the end of the twentieth century.[15]

This account of the food and diet of the people has concentrated upon mainstream changes. At the end of the twentieth century that approach may now be open to question. In the early and mid-twentieth century there was considerable conformity in meal patterns, cooking and choice of foods. Many of the influences on food consumption originated in the USA. The Americanization of the British diet began with American technology in the food-processing industry. It translated directly into new food commodities on sale in Britain; breakfast cereals, canned foods, soft drinks; even packaging, presentation, advertising and retailing techniques emanated from across the Atlantic Ocean. Consumer preferences,

[15] Food with no nutritive value may be created from non-absorbable fats and carbohydrates such as sucrose polyesters, with added extenders and flavourings, and can be made using the snack food industry's extrusion technology.

particularly in the age of mass cinema-going from the 1920s to the 1950s, sought to emulate American fashions. Even after Britain's entry into the Common Market, the USA remained a source of innovation for the food, drink and leisure industries. Since the 1970s, however, a number of factors have operated to reduce the normative elements of dietary behaviour and food consumption. Meals have changed. The 'full English breakfast' became a meal to be eaten on holiday in hotels that were re-inventing it as part of Britain's 'heritage', complete with a variety of dishes never previously seen on domestic breakfast tables. Furthermore, a snacking lifestyle meant that sitting down to eat meals as a family at home is no longer as 'normal' as it once was. Early in the 1970s, Magnus Pyke saw the possibility of an increasingly dysfunctional society developing as the practice of eating family meals declined:

> Teenage youths roam the streets – in Manchester and Manhattan, Tokyo, Moscow and Marseilles, or for that matter, in Mombassa or Lagos – and magistrates complain that their parents exert too little influence over their behaviour. The marvel of food technology makes it unnecessary for them to go home for their meals.[16]

These aspects of change led food consumption into an increasingly 'high-tech' mode delineated by lack of seasonality, a wide variety of processed foods from cuisines across the world, ready-prepared meals, and heating rather than cooking by way of preparation; and accompanied by continuing high levels of food-poisoning.[17]

Britain has been divided into the majority for whom a high-tech diet is acceptable and a growing minority who have sought alternatives; objections to intensive livestock husbandry, crop production, genetically modified food materials and chlorinated tap water have turned some consumers to 'organic' foods and bottled drinking-water. This demand for alternatives has become more than a mere crank fad, as the increasing allocation of shelf space for organically produced foods in supermarkets has demonstrated. However, at the end of the 1990s consumers have, as yet, shown less enthusiasm for the latest arrivals on supermarket shelves, 'functional foods'.[18] These nutritionally enhanced

---

[16] Pyke, *Technological Eating*, p. 96.

[17] The creation of a Food Standards Agency in 2000 has had no impact on food-poisoning.

[18] The British Nutrition Foundation's definition of a functional food is 'one with health promoting benefits and/or disease preventing properties over and above the usual nutritional value'. See http://www.nutrition.org.uk/conferences/keyfacts/functional; http://www.nutrition.org.uk/conferences/keyfacts/functional foods.htm or *Key Note, Functional Foods 2001 Market Assessment*, ed. Julia Keys (2nd edn), (2001).

products – breakfast cereals, 'cholesterol lowering' margarines, 'omega 3' eggs, fruit juices fortified with fibre or minerals, yoghurts and 'pro-biotic' fermented milk drinks – have been developed by international food firms as high-priced lines, and accepted by the major retailers as an additional opportunity for market segmentation.[19] By the end of the twentieth century it seems that people's eating habits are in flux, as offers to 'lead a happier, healthier life for much longer'[20] create further demand for alternative products and a continuing commitment to consumption. Thus the twentieth century, which began with plain fare, food adulteration and dietary deficiencies, ended with fusion foods, functional foods and an increasingly overweight population.

[19] For example, Unilever, General Mills, Kellogg, Quaker Oats, Danone and Pepsico, plus pharamceutical companies such as Novartis or Johnson and Johnson's McNeil Consumer Nutritionals. Nestleé's LC1 range of functional foods, introduced in 1999, was withdrawn from the UK market in 2000. The technology was developed in Finland by Raisio and in Canada by Forbes MediTech.
[20] Syn-Tech Nutriceuticals at http://www.syntechnutrition.com/intro/html

APPENDIX A

Quantitative food consumption and daily nutrient intake tables

A1	Weekly food consumption per head in family budget surveys, 1887 to 1913	237
A2	Daily nutrient intake per head in family budget surveys, 1887 to 1913	238
A3	Weekly food consumption per head in family budget surveys, 1920 to 1939	239
A4	Daily nutrient intake per head in family budget surveys, 1920 to 1939	241
A5	Weekly household food consumption per head in Great Britain, 1940 to 2000	243
A6	Household daily nutrient intake per head in Great Britain, 1940 to 2000	244

Table A1 Weekly food consumption per head in family budget surveys, 1887 to 1913

Survey	Date	Families	Milk and cream	Cheese	Eggs	Fruit	Potatoes	Other vegetables	Bread and cereal products	Sugar and preserves	Fish and fish products	Fats	Meat and meat products
			(ml)	(g)	(no.)	(g)	(g)	(g)	(g)	(g)	(g)	(g)	(g)
Board of Trade	1887	34	852	0	0	0	726	369	3,513	511	85	139	636
Booth	1889	30	795	0	0	114	953	398	2,996	398	199	111	726
Economy Club	1891–94	36	738	0	1	227	499	199	3,229	483	114	162	636
Oliver	1894	31	909	114	3	0	1,634	0	2,653	480	142	148	1,453
Schulze	1895	7	909	57	2	0	1,044	284	3,465	625	28	287	545
Mean		*138*	*852*	*28*	*1*	*84*	*937*	*243*	*3,128*	*477*	*127*	*148*	*834*
Rowntree	1899–1901	26	852	28	2	114	908	170	3,138	454	57	148	681
Paton	1900	16	909	28	2	341	545	398	2,317	426	199	119	545
England (rural)	1902	114	454	85	0	0	1,771	0	3,320	511	0	154	499
Scotland (rural)	1904	97	2,101	57	2	0	2,134	0	2,922	454	142	139	318
Ireland	1904	37	1,818	9	2	0	3,178	0	2,207	341	0	85	272
UK (urban)	1904	1,944	966	85	2	170	1,317	909	3,178	568	227	230	590
Mean		*2,234*	*1,022*	*82*	*2*	*152*	*1,396*	*794*	*3,148*	*553*	*206*	*218*	*569*
Dundee	1906	14	1,647	20	2	57	1,271	312	2,741	483	142	139	227
Bell	1906	6	341	0	1	9	817	199	4,408	596	0	204	454
Davies	1906	11	454	114	0	28	0	0	2,565	383	85	210	726
Women	1910	8	1,363	57	3	398	1,362	1,590	3,283	738	284	273	817
Rowntree	1912–13	42	454	20	0	57	908	540	3,260	398	28	162	318
Lindsay	1913	59	1,136	28	2	14	1,271	511	2,494	482	227	162	681
Mean		*140*	*908*	*31*	*1*	*54*	*1,048*	*507*	*2,881*	*468*	*141*	*172*	*528*

Table A2 Daily nutrient intake per head in family budget surveys, 1887 to 1913

Survey	Date	Families	Energy value (kcal)	Energy value (kj)	Fat (g)	Protein (g)	CHO (g)	Energy from Fat (%)	Protein (%)	CHO (%)	Calcium (mg)	Iron (mg)
Board of Trade	1887	34	2,240	9,372	57	59	372	23.0	10.5	66.4	310	10.3
Booth	1889	30	2,020	8,452	57	61	315	25.6	12.1	62.3	280	10.6
Economy Club	1891–94	36	2,091	8,749	60	54	335	25.7	10.3	64.0	270	9.1
Oliver	1894	31	2,799	11,711	114	93	366	36.0	12.5	51.5	500	15.5
Schulze	1895	7	2,454	10,268	75	61	384	27.6	9.9	62.5	360	10.9
Mean		*138*	*2,290*	*9,580*	*72*	*66*	*349*	*27.4*	*11.2*	*61.3*	*340*	*11.3*
Rowntree	1899–1901	26	2,069	8,657	59	57	328	25.6	10.9	63.4	310	10.1
Paton	1900	16	1,784	7,464	52	54	276	26.0	12.2	61.9	380	10.1
England (rural)	1902	114	2,148	8,987	55	51	362	23.1	9.6	67.3	280	9.2
Scotland (rural)	1904	97	2,365	9,895	59	67	391	22.6	11.3	66.1	620	13.3
Ireland	1904	37	2,150	8,996	40	58	390	16.6	10.8	72.5	480	13.3
UK (urban)	1904	1,944	2,443	10,222	74	67	378	27.3	10.8	61.9	470	12.3
Mean		*2,234*	*2,411*	*10,086*	*71*	*66*	*377*	*26.7*	*10.8*	*62.6*	*460*	*12.2*
Dundee	1906	14	1,968	8,234	64	64	345	18.9	11.1	70.0	580	10.2
Bell	1906	6	2,443	10,222	51	51	431	20.8	8.8	70.5	190	9.3
Davies	1906	11	1,790	7,489	79	79	243	34.8	11.1	54.2	300	7.2
Women	1910	8	2,551	10,673	79	73	383	28.3	11.7	60.2	630	13.1
Rowntree	1912–13	42	1,889	7,904	38	46	340	18.9	9.8	71.3	270	9.4
Lindsay	1913	59	2,131	8,916	62	64	330	26.0	12.0	62.0	580	11.2
Mean		*140*	*2,053*	*8,588*	*54*	*57*	*335*	*23.8*	*11.0*	*65.6*	*450*	*10.3*

Table A3 Weekly food consumption per head in family budget surveys, 1920 to 1939

Survey	Date	No.	Milk and cream (ml)	Cheese (g)	Eggs (no)	Fruit (g)	Potatoes (g)	Other vegetables (g)	Bread and cereal products (g)	Sugar and preserves (g)	Beverages (g)	Fish and fish products (g)	Fats (g)	Meat and meat products (g)
Dockers	1920	6	749			19	1,358	518	2,474	202			273	693
PO workers	1926	26	1,561			147	924	630	2,203	455			294	721
Bankers	1926	7	1,429			439	732	771	1,120	189			212	658
St Andrews	1927	7	1,748			788	471	712	811	222			192	526
Glasgow	1928	57	1,477			238	1,725	672	2,588	397			249	499
Greenock	1928	132	1,250			175	1,498	707	2,714	454			244	454
Paisley	1928	31	1,363			357	1,498	441	3,594	425			230	590
Edinburgh	1928	108	965			404	1,452	1,005	2,762	397			230	499
Dundee	1928	37	908			203	1,407	455	2,715	369			204	545
Aberdeen	1928	150	1,874			294	1,634	966	2,084	482			215	545
Peterhead	1928	104	1,477			189	1,816	889	2,082	482			167	363
Cardiff/Reading	1928	5	920			188	760	484	1,500	320			223	409
East Ldn Adv	1930	1	994			133	1,757	2,037	2,213	679			343	1,050
London	1931	5	1,057			392	1,505	798	1,855	392			203	791
LSE	1932	10	2,828			903	1,064	1,323	1,747	511			371	228
Newcastle	1933	6	532			105	833	308	2,945	378			238	350
N. England	1932–34	9	1,351			392	1,092	623	2,387	434			329	700
Peterhead	1933	66	1,092			56	1,337	315	2,257	413			112	364
Aberdeen	1933	49	1,456			84	1,001	343	1,854	448			119	469
Wmn's Co-op	1935	7	1,505			623	1,372	875	2,452	518			399	686

continued

Table A3 (continued)

Survey	Date	No.	Milk and cream (ml)	Cheese (g)	Eggs (no)	Fruit (g)	Potatoes (g)	Other vegetables (g)	Bread and cereal products (g)	Sugar and preserves (g)	Beverages (g)	Fish and fish products (g)	Fats (g)	Meat and meat products (g)
FHI I-IV	1932-35	952	1,079				1,498		2,452	456			349	590
FHI V-VI	1932-35	200	2,670				1,180		2,043	530			417	772
FHI Mean	1935	1,152	1,761				1,407		2,315	505			388	726
W/c wives	1934-48	2	686			56	490	196	1,498	308			168	182
Rowntree	1936	4	1,309			175	1,400	576	2,134	343			301	602
Ipswich	1937	11	826			119	1,120	875	2,927	469			187	497
Carnegie (E)	1937	140*	1,590			441	1,453	654	2,315	482			329	636
Carnegie (S)	1937	70*	1,818			484	1,317	220	2,088	454			244	499
MLab1	1937	75	1,818				1,680		2,498	612			434	908
MH1 (Surrey)	1937-38	17	2,045			924	953	644	1,517	544			357	636
MH2 (Essex)	1937-38	45	1,704			469	1,135	616	1,989	505			301	636
MH3 (SWales)	1937-38	68	1,363			294	1,317	609	1,951	496			357	454
MH4 (Ely)	1937-38	26	1,250			581	953	483	1,803	533			391	545
Glossop	1938	35	1,306			497	999	511	2,218	544			391	545

Note: *The Carnegie Survey figures are based on a stratified sample of the surviving returns.

Table A4 Daily nutrient intake per head in family budget surveys, 1920 to 1939

Survey	Date	No.	Energy value (kcal)	(kj)	Fat (g)	Protein (g)	CHO (g)	Energy from Fat (%)	Protein (%)	CHO (%)	Calcium (mg)	Iron (mg)
Dockers	1920	6	2,188	9,155	73	77	312	30	14	57	440	11.5
P.O. workers	1926	26	2,602	10,887	93	78	358	32	12	55	597	15.6
Bankers	1926	7	3,258	13,631	127	106	415	35	13	51	1,160	23.4
St Andrews	1927	7	1,918	8,025	70	62	259	33	13	54	760	11.4
Glasgow	1928	57	2,669	11,167	74	80	414	25	12	62	620	15.0
Greenock	1928	132	2,495	10,439	66	75	399	24	12	64	550	13.5
Paisley	1928	31	2,900	12,134	77	87	464	24	12	64	610	16.0
Edinburgh	1928	108	2,545	10,648	68	76	407	24	12	64	610	14.0
Dundee	1928	37	2,409	10,079	67	72	379	25	12	63	530	13.1
Aberdeen	1928	150	3,030	12,678	88	91	470	26	12	62	1,380	16.0
Peterhead	1928	104	3,002	12,560	77	90	488	23	12	65	1,310	16.3
Cardiff/Reading	1928	5	1,945	8,138	63	58	287	29	12	59	500	10.3
East Ldn Ad	1930	1	2,959	12,380	105	89	414	32	12	56	780	20.5
London	1931	5	2,173	9,092	75	71	310	31	13	57	510	12.6
LSE	1932	10	2,776	11,615	111	76	361	36	11	52	980	13.2
Newcastle	1933	6	3,035	12,698	57	99	539	17	13	71	380	15.6
N. England	1932–34	9	2,398	10,033	77	74	354	29	12	59	480	12.6
Peterhead	1933	66	2,118	8,862	47	69	355	20	13	67	400	12.2
Aberdeen	1933	49	1,926	8,058	49	67	303	23	14	63	480	11.6
Wmn's Co-op	1935	7	2,886	12,075	106	79	404	33	11	56	670	15.6

continued

241

Table A4 (*continued*)

Survey	Date	No.	Energy value (kcal)	(kj)	Fat (g)	Protein (g)	CHO (g)	Energy from Fat (%)	Protein (%)	CHO (%)	Calcium (mg)	Iron (mg)
FHI I-IV	1932–35	952	2,790	11,673	100	78	382	33	11	55	550	10.2
FHI V-VI	1932–35	200	3,290	13,765	136	96	401	38	12	49	890	13.2
FHI Mean	1935	1,152	2,960	12,385	112	84	388	35	12	52	670	11.2
W/c wives	1934–38	2	1,301	5,443	39	36	202	27	11	62	280	5.9
Rowntree	1936	4	2,245	9,393	80	67	320	32	12	57	470	12.6
Ipswich	1937	11	2,259	9,452	53	73	373	21	13	66	470	13.2
Carnegie (E)	1937	140*	2,538	10,619	96	76	343	34	12	54	650	13.6
Carnegie (S)	1937	70*	2,457	10,280	79	74	362	29	12	59	700	12.7
MLab1	1937	75	3,230	13,514	124	83	440	36	11	53	720	16.5
MH1(Surrey)	1937–38	17	2,453	10,263	98	74	319	36	12	52	780	13.1
MH2(Essex)	1937–38	45	2,509	10,498	92	75	345	33	12	55	710	13.3
MH3(SWales)	1937–38	68	2,263	9,468	83	62	322	33	11	57	610	10.7
MH4(Ely)	1937–38	26	2,461	10,297	101	68	326	37	11	53	750	11.7
Glossop	1938	35	2,513	10,514	92	69	346	33	11	55	580	12.2

Note: *The Carnegie Survey figures are based on a stratified sample of the surviving returns.

242

Table A5 Weekly household food consumption per head in Great Britain, 1940 to 2000

Date	Milk and cream (ml)	Cheese (g)	Eggs (no)	Fruit (g)	Potatoes (g)	Other vegetables (g)	Bread and cereal products (g)	Sugar and preserves (g)	Beverages (g)	Fish and fish products (g)	Fats (g)	Meat and meat products (g)
1942	2,137	101	1.40	197	1,877	450	2,310	378	n.a.	187	245	746
1945	2,517	71	3.01	318	1,863	1,155	2,424	414	n.a.	261	245	746
1950	2,938	72	3.50	513	1,759	1,039	2,315	466	77	188	329	846
1955	2,892	80	4.19	621	1,698	905	2,269	616	100	169	337	976
1960	2,921	86	4.64	698	1,588	972	2,000	594	101	166	339	1,017
1965	2,949	91	4.78	725	1,509	987	1,880	583	98	164	336	1,066
1970	2,887	102	4.66	723	1,470	1,107	1,791	553	102	152	339	1,121
1975	2,913	107	4.14	676	1,243	1,134	1,624	388	88	127	315	1,054
1980	2,604	110	3.69	795	1,163	1,260	1,571	375	85	136	318	1,140
1985	2,348	111	3.15	766	1,162	1,246	1,526	291	77	139	286	1,042
1990	2,169	113	2.20	895	996	1,265	1,470	219	70	144	255	968
1995	2,170	108	1.85	996	803	1,258	1,468	175	63	144	218	945
2000	2,081	110	1.75	1,120	707	1,279	1,508	138	58	143	186	966

Source: DEFRA, National Food Survey.
Note: n.a. = not available.

Table A6 Household daily nutrient intake per head in Great Britain, 1940 to 2000

Date	Energy value (kcal)	Energy value (kj)	Fat[a] (g)	Protein (g)	CHO[b] (g)	Energy from Fat (%)	Energy from Protein (%)	Energy from CHO (%)	Calcium (mg)	Iron (mg)	Vitamin C[c] (mg)	Vitamin A (mg)	Vitamin D (µg)
1940	2,355	9,853	n.a.	n.a.	n.a.	n.a.	13.1	n.a.	614	12.8	[51]	n.a.	2.93
1945	2,375	9,937	92	76.0	309	34.9	12.8	52.0	875	12.7	43	2,908	3.57
1950	2,474	10,351	101	78.0	314	36.7	12.6	50.7	1,066	13.6	[43]	3,536	4.30
1955	2,641	11,050	107	77.0	342	36.6	11.6	51.7	1,044	13.5	51	4,199	3.60
1960	2,630	11,004	115	74.7	345	39.3	11.4	49.3	1,040	14.1	52	4,360	3.25
1965	2,590	10,837	116	75.2	332	40.4	11.6	47.9	1,020	13.9	52	4,370	3.13
1970	2,560	10,711	119	73.7	317	41.8	11.5	46.5	1,030	13.4	52	1,350	2.82
1975	2,290	9,581	107	72.0	275	42.2	12.6	45.2	1,010	11.6	51	1,370	2.63
1980	2,230	9,330	106	72.7	264	42.6	13.0	44.4	960	11.3	58	1,350	2.85
1985	2,020	8,452	96	67.4	238	42.6	13.3	44.1	850	10.8	52	1,370	2.96
1990	1,870	7,824	86	63.1	224	41.6	13.5	44.9	820	10.4	52	1,100	3.02
1995	1,780	7,448	78	63.0	218	39.8	14.2	46.0	810	9.5	52	1,010	2.96
1999	1,690	7,071	72	63.2	211	38.3	14.9	46.8	790	9.6	57	760	3.14
2000	1,750	7,322	74	66.3	218	38.2	15.2	46.7	860	10.1	59	780	3.29

Source: DEFRA, National Food Survey.

Notes:

[a] Fat = total visible fats plus fat contained in other foods such as meat, dairy produce and fish.

[b] Carbohydrate (CHO) = available carbohydrate, calculated as monosaccharide.

[c] The vitamin C value in brackets is an estimate to include cooking losses.

n.a. = not available.

Sources of Tables A1 to A6

Pre-1914 family budget surveys

Board of Trade, *Returns of Expenditure by Working Men* PP 1889 (C.5861), LXXXIV.

Booth, C., *Life and Labour of the People*, Vol. I (London, 1889).

Economic Club, *Family Budgets: Being the Income and Expense of Twenty-eight British Households, 1891–1894* [attributed to Miss E. Collett and Miss Roberston] (London, 1896).

Oliver, T., 'The diet of toil', *Lancet*, 1895, I, 1629–1635.

Paton, D. N., Dunlop, J. C. and Inglis, E. *On the Dietaries of the Labouring Classes of the City of Edinburgh* (Edinburgh, 1901).

Rowntree, B.S., *Poverty: A Study of Town Life* (London, 1901).

Schulze-Gaevernitz, G. von, *The Cotton Trade in England and on the Continent* (1895).

England (rural): Board of Agriculture, *Consumption of Food and Cost of Living of the Working Classes in the United Kingdom and Certain Foreign Countries*, PP 1903 (Cd.1761), LXVII.

Scotland (rural) and Ireland: Board of Agriculture, *Second Report by Mr Wilson Fox on the Wages, Earnings, and Conditions of Employment of Agricultural Labourers in the United Kingdom*, PP 1905 (Cd.2376), XCVII.

UK (urban): *Second Series of Memoranda, Statistical Tables and Charts*, PP 1905 (Cd.2337), LXXXIV.

Dundee Social Union, *Report on Housing and Industrial Conditions and Medical Inspection of School Children* (Dundee, 1905).

Bell, Lady F., *At the Works: A Study of a Manufacturing Town* (London, 1907).

Davies, M. F., *Life in an English Village* (London, 1909).

Board of Trade, *Accounts of Expenditure of Wage-earning Women and Girls* PP 1911 (Cd.5963), LXXXIX.

Lindsay, D. E., *Report Upon a Study of the Diet of the Labouring Classes in the City of Glasgow* (Glasgow, 1913).

Rowntree, B. S. and Kendall, M. *How the Labourer Lives* (London, 1913).

Interwar surveys

Dockers, *Wages and Conditions of Employment*, PP 1920 (Cmd.936–7), XXIV

Post Office workers, Wage claims by manipulative grades. Evidence of Union of Post Office Workers, 1927

Bankers, Summary material at the Rowett Research Institute

St Andrew's, Returns at the Rowett Research Institute
Glasgow, Returns at the Rowett Research Institute
Greenock, Returns at the Rowett Research Institute
Paisley, Returns at the Rowett Research Institute
Edinburgh, Returns at the Rowett Research Institute
Dundee, Returns at the Rowett Research Institute
Aberdeen, Returns at the Rowett Research Institute
Peterhead, Returns at the Rowett Research Institute
Cardiff/Reading, Summary material at the Rowett Research Institute
East London Advertiser
London, Summary material at the Rowett Research Institute
LSE, Summary material at the Rowett Research Institute
Newcastle, Returns at the Rowett Research Institute
Northern England, Returns at the Rowett Research Institute
Peterhead, Returns at the Rowett Research Institute
Aberdeen, Returns at the Rowett Research Institute
Women's Co-operative Guild, Returns at the Rowett Research Institute
Food Health and Income, Summary material at the Rowett Research Institute
Working-class wives, Margery Spring Rice, *Working-class Wives, Their Health and Conditions* (Harmondsworth, 1939)
Rowntree, B. S., *Poverty and Progress. A Second Survey of York done in 1935* (London, 1941)
Carnegie Survey, Sample based on returns at the Rowett Research Institute
Ministry of Labour, Unpublished Returns in PRO, LAB17/8-LAB17/106
Ministry of Health, Unpublished Returns at the Rowett Research Institute
Glossop, Annual Report of the School Medical Officer, Education Committee, 1940

Second World War and after

Ministry of Agriculture, Fisheries and Food (now Department of the Environment, Food and Rural Affairs), *Reports of the National Food Survey* (annual series).

APPENDIX B

Method of analysing family budget and dietary surveys

Family budget surveys presented much information about food consumption, though it had seldom been collected in a form intended for nutritional analysis. Standardization was necessary before subjecting survey material to a computer-assisted process of analysis.[1] Total amounts of food recorded in historical material were assumed to be weights or quantities as bought. Source data were standardized as weights in grams by converting them from imperial weights or quantities. Data originally measured by monetary values were converted by drawing up a table of standard prices for the period of the survey and applying them to give food weights. These were divided by the duration of time over which the food was consumed (i.e. day, week, month or year), and also by the number of persons in the household. Expressing the results per head may be criticized, but since the recommended daily intakes of energy and nutrients in the United Kingdom for children of age 7 and over were broadly the same as for any adult in a sedentary life, the artificial 'man-value' scales commonly used in interwar analyses were rejected. R. A. McCance and E. M. Widdowson's *The Composition of Foods*, 3rd edn (1960) provided the database for the analysis. Foods were analysed as raw weights if there was no wastage in their preparation but wastage allowances as given in McCance and Widdowson were deducted. Otherwise, cooked values of foods were used; but raw foods were used when possible to avoid variation in cooking practices. Any foods fortified, such as bread and margarine, were replaced by equivalent quantities of flour and butter. If composition varied, as with different cuts of meat, qualities were assigned to foods which accorded with contemporary evidence.

Food intake per head per day was given by a food category programme which sorted foods into ten groups: flour, bread, potatoes, sugar, fats, meat, vegetables, fruit, milk and fish. The nutrient analysis programme expressed the diet as energy value, protein, fat, carbohydrate, sucrose and various minerals, particularly calcium and iron. Vitamins were not included in the nutrient analysis since it was concluded that problems of stability and losses in storage and preparation of foods would make the results meaningless.

[1] The computer program was designed in the Department of Nutrition, Queen Elizabeth College, by D. S. Miller and Pamela Mumford.

BIBLIOGRAPHY

Manuscript sources

Public Record Office

Ministry of Agriculture and Fisheries (MAF)
Board of Trade (BT)
Cabinet papers (CAB)
Medical Research Council (FD)
Milk Marketing Board (JV)
Ministry of Food (MAF)
Ministry of Health (MH)
Ministry of Labour (LAB)
Registrar General (RG)

Rowett Research Institute, Bucksburn, Aberdeen

Surviving manuscript returns from the:

Scottish Seven Towns inquiry
Summary material used in *Food, Health and Income*
The Carnegie Survey (1937)
Ministry of Health Family Budget Inquiry (1937–38)

Published works

(The place of publication is London unless otherwise stated)

Contemporary

Atwater, W. O., *Methods and Results of Investigations on the Chemistry and Economy of Food* (Washington, DC, 1895).
Bell, Lady F., *At the Works: A Study of a Manufacturing Town* (1907).
Beveridge, W. H., *British Food Control* (Oxford, 1928).
Booth, C., *Life and Labour of the People*, Vol. I (1889).
Booth, C., *Life and Labour*, second series, Vol. 5 (1903).
Bowley, A. L. and Burnett-Hurst, A. R. *Livelihood and Poverty* (1915).
British Medical Association, *The Doctors' Cookery Book* (1st edn, 1935: *Family Meals and Catering*) (1938).

British Medical Association, *Report of the Committee on Nutrition* (1950).

Brockway, A. F., *Hungry England* (1932).

Bulkley, M. E., *The Feeding of School Children* (1914).

Chittenden, R. H., *Physiological Economy of Nutrition* (New York, 1904).

Chittenden, R. H., *The Nutrition of Man* (1907).

Clark, F. Le Gros and Titmuss, R. M. *Our Food Problem. A Study of National Security* (Harmondsworth, 1939).

Clemesha, H. W., *Food Control in the North-West Division* (Manchester, 1922).

Cobbett, W., *Cottage Economy* (1822).

Crawford, Sir W., *The People's Food* (1938).

Critchell, J. T. and Raymond, J. *A History of the Frozen Meat Trade* (1912).

Crichton-Browne, Sir J., *Some Food Dangers* (1903).

Crichton-Browne, Sir J., *Parcimony* (sic) *in Nutrition* (1909).

Davies, M. F., *Life in an English Village* (1909).

Dundee Social Union, *Report on Housing and Industrial Conditions and Medical Inspection of School Children* (Dundee, 1905).

Economic Club, *Family Budgets: Being the Income and Expense of Twenty-eight British Households, 1891–1894* [attributed to Miss E. Collett and Miss Roberston] (1896).

Eden, Sir F. M., *The State of the Poor* (1797, facsimile edn, 1966).

Encyclopaedia Britannica, 11th edn (1910–11).

Friend, G. E., *The Schoolboy. A Study of his Nutrition Physical Development and Health* (Cambridge, 1935).

Good Things Made, Said and Done for every Home & Household, 34th edn (Leeds, 1896).

Hammond, R. J., *Food: Volume I The Growth of Policy*, History of the Second World War, United Kingdom Civil Series (1951).

Hammond, R. J., *Food: Volume II. Studies in Adminstration and Control*, History of the Second World War, United Kingdom Civil Series (1956).

Hampson, J., *The English at Table*, Britain in Pictures series (1944).

Hehner, O. and Angell, A., *Butter: Its Analysis and Adulteration*, 2nd edn (1877).

Jones, Sir Thomas G., *The Unbroken Front* (1944).

Leighton, G. R. and Douglas, L. M., *The Meat Industry and Meat Inspection* (5 vols) (1910).

Lewer, S. H. (ed.), *Wright's Book of Poultry* (1910).

Lindsay, D. E., *Report Upon a Study of the Diet of the Labouring Classes in the City of Glasgow* (Glasgow, 1913).

Liverpool Economic and Statistical Society, *How the Casual Labourer Lives* (Liverpool, 1909).

Lloyd, E. M. H., *Experiments in State Control at the War Office and the Ministry of Food* (Oxford, 1924).

M'Gonigle, G. C. M. and Kirby, J., *Poverty and Public Health* (1936).

Marrack, J. R., *Food and Planning* (1942, 1946).

Murray, K. A. H., and Cohen, R. L. *The Planning of Britain's Food Imports* (Oxford, 1934).

Murray, Sir K., *Agriculture*. History of the Second World War, United Kingdom Civil Series (1955).

Newman, G., *Report on the Milk Supply of Finsbury* (1903).

Newman, G., *The Control of the Milk Supply* (1904).

Newsholme, Sir A., *Fifty Years in Public Health* (1935).

Norwich, *The Destitute of Norwich and How They Live* (1910).

Orr, J. B., *Food, Health and Income*, 2nd edn (1937).

Orr, J. B. and Lubbock, D. *Feeding the People in War-Time* (1940).

Pankhurst, E. S., *The Home Front* (1932).

Paton, D. N., Dunlop, J. C. and Inglis, E., *On the Dietaries of the Labouring Classes of the City of Edinburgh* (Edinburgh, 1901).

Pavy, F. W., *A Treatise on Food and Dietetics*, 2nd edn (1875).

Peel, Mrs C. S., *'Daily Mail' War Recipes* (1918).

Peel, Mrs C. S., *How We Lived Then 1914–1918* (1929).

Reeves, M. S. P., *Round About a Pound a Week* (1915).

Rice, M. Spring, *Working-Class Wives* (Harmondsworth, 1939).

Rowett Research Institute, *Family Diet and Health in Pre-War Britain*, Carnegie UK Trust (Dunfermline, 1955).

Rowntree, B. S., *Poverty. A Study of Town Life* (1901).

Rowntree, B. S. and Kendall, M., *How the Labourer Lives* (1913).

Royal Institution, *The Nation's Larder* (1940).

Walworth, G., *Feeding the Nation in Peace and War* (1940).

Warren, G. C. (ed.), *The Foods We Eat* (1958).

Wokes, F., *Food: The Deciding Factor* (Harmondsworth, 1940).

Wright, L., *The New Book of Poultry* (1902).

Secondary

Ashwell, M., ed., *McCance & Widdowson* (1993).

Ashworth, W., *An Economic History of England 1870–1939* (1960).

Barker, T. C. and Drake, M., eds, *Population and Society in Britain 1850–1980* (1982).

Barker, T.C. and Harris, J. R., *A Merseyside Town in the Industrial Revolution* (1959).

Barker, T. C. and Savage, C. I., *An Economic History of Transport in Britain*, 3rd (revised) edn (1974).

Barker, T. C., McKenzie, J. C. and Yudkin, J. eds, *Our Changing Fare* (1966).

Barker, T.C., Oddy, D. J. and Yudkin, J., *The Dietary Surveys of Dr Edward Smith* (1970).

Barnett, L. M., *British Food Policy during the First World War* (1985).

Benham, M., *The Story of Tiptree Jam. The First Hundred Years 1885–1985* (Tiptree, 1985).

Birchall, J., *Co-op: The People's Business* (Manchester, 1994).

Bird, P., *The First Food Empire. A History of J. Lyons & Co* (Chichester, 2000).

Birds Eye Foods Ltd, *The Cold Rush* (Walton-on-Thames, 1974).

Birds Eye Foods Ltd, *Food Freezing* (Walton-on-Thames, 1975).

Black, M., *Food and Cooking in 19th Century Britain: History and Recipes*, Historic Buildings and Monuments Commission for England (1985).

Branson, N. and Heinemann, M., *Britain in the Nineteen Thirties* (1971).

Broad, R. and Fleming, S., eds, *Nella Last's War* (Bristol, 1981).

Burnett, J., *Plenty and Want*, 3rd edn (1989).

Burnett, J., *Liquid Pleasures. A Social History of Drinks in Modern Britain* (1999).

Burns, J., McInerney, J. and Swinbank, A., eds, *The Food Industry* (1983).

Cadbury Ltd, *New Product Development* (Birmingham, 1997).

Cadbury Ltd, *The Story of Cadbury Limited* (Birmingham, 1997).

Carson, R., *Silent Spring* (Harmondsworth, 1965).

Chaloner, W. H., *Social and Economic Development of Crewe, 1730–1923* (Manchester, 1950).

Cheke, V. E., *The Story of Cheese-making in Britain* (1959).

Cohen, R. L., *The History of Milk Prices*, University of Oxford Institute for Research in Agricultural Economics (Oxford, 1936).

Constantine, S., *Buy and Build The Advertising Posters of the Empire Marketing Board* (1986).

Cottrell, R., ed., *Nutrition in Catering* (Carnforth, 1987).

Court, W. H. B., *British Economic History 1870–1914, Commentary and Documents* (Cambridge, 1965).

Curtis-Bennett, Sir N., *The Food of the People Being the History of Industrial Feeding* (1949).

Davenport-Hines, R. P. T., ed., *Markets and Bagmen: Studies in the History of Marketing and British Industrial Performance 1830–1939* (1986).

David, E., *Harvest of the Cold Months* (1994).

Davidson, S. and Passmore, R., *Human Nutrition and Dietetics*, 4th edn (Edinburgh, 1969).

Davidson, S., Passmore, R., Brock, J. F. and Truswell, A. S., *Human Nutrition and Dietetics*, 6th edn (Edinburgh, 1975).

Davies, P. N., *Fyffes and the Banana: Musa Sapientum: A Centenary History 1888–1988* (1990).

Davis, B., *Food Commodities*, 2nd edn (1987).

Davis, J. H. and Goldberg, R. A., *A Concept of Agribusiness* (Boston, MA, 1957).

Donnelly, P., ed., *Mrs Milburn's Diaries: An Englishwoman's Day-to-day Reflections 1939–1945* (1995).

Driver, C., *The British at Table 1940–1980* (1983).

Drummond, J. C. and Wilbraham, A., *The Englishman's Food*, revised edn by D. F. Hollingsworth (1957).

Dyos, H. J., *Victorian Suburb: Study of the Growth of Camberwell* (Leicester, 1961).

Ensor, R. C. K., *England 1870–1914* (Oxford, 1936).

Evans, M., *Cuisine Minceur Cookbook* (1978).

Fenton, A., ed., *Order and Disorder: The Health Implications of Eating and Drinking in the Nineteenth and Twentieth Centuries* (Phantassie, East Lothian, 2000).

Floud, R. and McCloskey, D., *The Economic History of Britain since 1700*, Vol.2 (Cambridge, 1981).

Floud, R., Wachter, K. and Gregory, A., *Height, Health and History. Nutritional Status in the United Kingdom, 1750–1980* (Cambridge, 1990).

Forte, C., *Forte: The Autobiography of Charles Forte* (1986).

Fox, B. A. and Cameron, A. G., *Food Science*, 4th edn (1982).

Fraser, W. H., *The Coming of the Mass Market 1850–1914* (1981).

French, M. and Phillips, J., *Cheated not Poisoned? Food Regulation in the United Kingdom, 1875–1938* (Manchester, 2000).

Frozen and Chilled Foods Yearbook, 1993–1994 (Redhill, 1994).

Geissler, C. A. and Oddy, D. J., eds, *Food, Diet and Economic Change Past and Present* (Leicester, 1993).

Gourvish, T. R. and Wilson, R. G., *The British Brewing Industry, 1830–1980* (Cambridge, 1994).

Graves, R. and Hodge, A., The Long Week-end (Harmondsworth, 1971).

Hardyment, C., *Slice of Life The British Way of Eating Since 1945* (1995).

Hartog, A. P. den, ed., *Food Technology, Science and Marketing: European Diet in the Twentieth Century* (Phantassie, East Lothian, 1995).

Hayek, F. A., *Capitalism and the Historians* (1954).

James, R. R., *Henry Wellcome* (1994).

Jefferys, J. B., *Retail Trading in Britain 1850–1950* (Cambridge, 1954).

Jones, H. and Kandiah, M., eds, *The Myth of Consensus: New Views on British History, 1945–64* (Basingstoke, 1996).

Key Note Ltd, *Functional Foods 2001 Market Assessment*, ed. J. Keys, 2nd edn (Hampton, Middlesex, 2001).

Key Note Publications, *Key Note Report, A Market Sector Overview: Frozen Foods* (Hampton, Middlesex, 1991).

Lacey, R. W., *Hard to Swallow* (Cambridge, 1994).

Lawrence, D., *Always a Welcome* (Twickenham, 1999).

Lobstein, T., *Fast Food Facts* (1988).

Longmate, N., *How We Lived Then. A History of Everyday Life During the Second World War* (1977).

McDonald's Fact File 2000, McDonald's Restaurants Ltd (2000).

Marquis, F. (Lord Woolton), *The Memoirs of the Rt. Hon. The Earl of Woolton* (1959).

Mathew, W. M., *Keiller's of Dundee. The Rise of the Marmalade Dynasty 1800–1879* (Dundee, 1998).

Mathias, P., *Retailing Revolution. A History of Multiple Retailing in the Food Trades Based upon the Allied Suppliers Group of Companies* (1967).

Mennell, S., *All Manners of Food* (Oxford, 1985).

Minns, R., *Bombers and Mash* (1980).

Mitchell, B. R. and Deane, P., *Abstract of Historical Statistics* (Cambridge, 1962).

Mottram, V. H., *Human Nutrition*, 2nd edn (1963).

Mowat, C. L., *Britain Between the Wars, 1918–1940* (Cambridge, 1968).

MSI, Fast Food UK. Report by MSI Marketing Research for Industry Ltd (Chester, 2000).

National Catering Inquiry, *The British Eating Out at Work* (n. d. [1973]).

Oddy, D. J. and Miller, D. S., eds, *Diet and Health in Modern Britain* (1985).

Oddy, D. J. and Miller, D. S., eds, *The Making of the Modern British Diet* (1976).

Olsen, D. J., *The Growth of Victorian London* (Harmondsworth, 1979).

Orr, Lord Boyd, *As I Recall* (1966).

Orwell, G. (Eric Blair), *1984: A Novel* (1948).

Pelling, H. *A History of British Trade Unionism* (Harmondsworth, 1963).

Perry, P. J., ed., *British Agriculture 1875–1914* (1973).

Perren, R., *The Meat Trade in Britain 1840–1914* (1978).

Pfiffner, A., *Henri Nestlé from Pharmacist's Assistant to Founder of the World's Largest Food Company* (translated from the German by David Pulman) (Vevey, Switzeland, 1995).

Pollard, S., *The Development of the British Economy, 1914–1967*, 2nd edn (1969).

Powell, D., *Counter Revolution: The Tesco Story* (1991).

Pyke, M. A., *Technological Eating; Or Where does the Fish Finger Point?* (1972).

Pyke, M. A., *Townsman's Food* (1952).

Reader, W. J., *Birds Eye: The Early Years* (Walton-on-Thames, 1963).

Reader, W. J., *Hard Roads and Highways: SPD 1918–68* (1969).

Reader, W. J., *Metal Box: A History* (1976).

Rees, J. F., *Short Fiscal and Financial History of England 1815–1918* (1921).

Roskill, S. W., *Hankey Man of Secrets, Vol. III 1931–1963* (1972).

Sanghari, N., Smith, P. and Wills, G., *The Retail Reference Book 1992*, Centre for Business Research, Manchester Business School (Manchester, 1992).

Sheridan, D., ed., *Wartime Women. An Anthology of Women's Wartime Writing for Mass Observation 1937–1945* (1991).

Singer, C., Holmyard, E. J., Hall, A. R. and Williams, T. I., *A History of Technology*, Vol. V (Oxford, 1958).

Smith, D. F., ed., *Nutrition in Britain. Science, Scientists and Politics in the Twentieth Century* (1997).

Tarnower, H. and Baker, S. S., *The Complete Scarsdale Medical Diet* (New York, 1980).

Taylor, A. J. P., *English History 1914–45* (Harmondsworth, 1970).

Thomson, A., *Half a Century of Medical Research*, Vol. 1 (1973).

Thompson, F., *Larkrise to Candleford* (Oxford, 1954).

Trowell, H. C. and Burkitt, D. P. eds, *Western Diseases, Their Emergence and Prevention* (1981).

Tweedale, G., *At the Sign of the Plough: Allen and Hanbury and the British Pharmaceutical Industry, 1715–1990* (1990).

Walker, C. and Cannon, G., *The Food Scandal* (1984).

Walton, J. K., *Fish and Chips and the British Working Class, 1870–1940* (Leicester, 1992).

Warde, A. and Martens, L., *Eating Out: Social Differentiation, Consumption and Pleasure* (Cambridge, 2000).

Weight Watchers, Fast and Fabulous Cookbook (Sevenoaks, 1984).

Welshman, J., *Municipal Medicine. Public Health in Twentieth-Century Britain* (Oxford, 2000).

Whetham, E. H., *The Agrarian History of England and Wales, Volume VIII 1914–1939* (Cambridge, 1978).

Williams, B., *The Best Butter in the World* (1994).

Wilson, C. H., *The History of Unilever*, Vol. II (1954).

Wilson, C. H., *Unilever, 1945–1965* (1968).

Winnifrith, Sir J., *The Ministry of Agriculture, Fisheries and Food* (London, 1962).

Winstanley, M. J., *The Shopkeeper's World 1830–1914* (Manchester, 1983).

Wood, R. C., *The Sociology of the Meal* (Edinburgh, 1995).

Woodforde, J., *The Diary of a Country Parson 1758–1802*, selected and edited by John Beresford (Oxford, 1978).

Yesterday's *Shopping, Gamages General Catalogue 1914* (Ware, 1994).

Yudkin, J., *This Slimming Business* (1958).

Yudkin, J., *Pure White and Deadly: The Problem of Sugar* (1972).

Yudkin, J. and Chappell, G. M., *The Slimmer's Cook Book* (1961).

Zweiniger-Bargielowska, I., *Austerity in Britain: Rationing, Controls, and Consumption, 1939–1955* (Oxford, 2000).

Articles in journals

Baines, A. H., Hollingsworth, D. F. and Leitch, I., 'Diets of working-class families before and after the Second World War', *Nutrition Abstracts and Reviews*, 33 (1963), pp. 653–68.

Brown, E., 'The British egg supply', *Journal of the Royal Agricultural Society of England*, 61 (1900), pp. 605–45.

Children's Nutrition Council, 'The food leaders' scheme', *Wartime Nutrition Bulletin* (October/November 1944), p. 32.

Chinn, S. and Rona, R. J., 'Prevalence and trends in overweight and obesity in three cross sectional studies of British children, 1974–1994', *British Medical Journal*, 6 January 2001, p. 322.

Clements, E. M. B., 'Changes in the mean stature and weight of British children over the past seventy years', *British Medical Journal* (1953), pp. 898–902.

Ferguson, A., 'The family budgets and dietaries of forty labouring class families in Glasgow in war time', *Proceedings of the Royal Society of Edinburgh*, 37 (1916–17), pp. 117–36.

Hopkins, F. G., 'Feeding experiments illustrating the importance of accessory factors in normal dietaries', *Journal of Physiology*, 44 (1912), p. 425.

Kinra, S., Nelder, R. P. and Lewendon, G. J., 'Deprivation and childhood obesity: a cross sectional study of 20,973 children in Plymouth, United Kingdom', *Journal of Epidemiology and Community Health*, 54 (6) (2000), pp. 456–60.

Lloyd, E. M. H., 'Food supplies and consumption at different income levels', *Journal of the Proceedings of the Agricultural Economics Society*, 4 (2) (April 1936), pp. 89–110.

McCance, R. A. and Widdowson, E. M., 'Mineral metabolism of healthy adults on white and brown bread diets', *Journal of Physiology*, 101 (1942), pp. 44–85.

Mayhew, M., 'The 1930s nutrition controversy', *Journal of Contemporary History*, 23 (1988), pp. 445–64.

Medical Research Council, 'Report by a panel on the composition and nutritive value of flour', *Lancet*, 1 (1956), p. 901.

Mitchell, M., 'The effects of unemployment on the social conditions of women and children in the 1930s', *History Workshop Journal*, 19 (spring 1985), pp. 105–27.

Oddy, D. J., 'Urban famine in nineteenth-century Britain; the effect of the Lancashire cotton famine on working-class diet and health', *Economic History Review*, 2nd ser., Vol. 36, 1 (February 1983).

Oliver, T., 'The diet of toil', *Lancet*, 1 (1895), pp. 1629–35.

Parsons, T. J., Power, C., Logan, S. and Summerbell, C. D., 'Childhood predictors of adult obesity: a systematic review', *International Journal of Obesity*, 23 (1999), Supplement 8.

Pemberton, J. 'The Boyd Orr Survey of the nutrition of children in Great Britain 1937–9', *History Workshop Journal*, 50 (autumn 2000), pp. 207–29.

Rew, R. H., 'An inquiry into the statistics of the production and consumption of milk and milk products in Great Britain', *Journal of the Royal Statistical Society*, 60 (1892), pp. 244–78.

Walker, G. H., 'Food and its adulteration during the present war', the Chadwick Lecture, reprinted in the *British Food Journal* (January to April 1945), pp. 1–2, 11–12, 21–3, 32–4.

Webster, C., 'Healthy or hungry thirties?', *History Workshop Journal*, 13 (spring 1982), pp. 110–29.

Weir, J. B. de V., 'The assessment of the growth of schoolchildren with special reference to secular changes', *British Journal of Nutrition*, 6 (1) (1952), pp. 19–33.

Official publications

Parliamentary papers (in chronological order)

1864   *Sixth Report of the Medical Officer to the Committee of the Privy Council*, XXVIII.

1867   *Report to the Poor Law Board on the Uniformity of Workhouse Dietaries*, LX.

1883   *Report to the Board of Trade on the System of Deep Sea Trawl Fishing*, XVIII.

1884–85   *Report of the Royal Commission on Trawl Net and Beam Trawl Fishing* (C.4328), XVI.

1887   *Report of the Select Committee on Butter Substitutes Bill*, IX.

1887   Local Government Board, *Sixteenth Annual Report* (C.5131), XXXVI.

1893–94   *Report of the Select Committee on Sea Fisheries*, XV.

1893–94   *Report from the Select Committee on Marking Foreign Meat*, XII.

1896   *Report of the Select Committee on Food Products Adulteration*, 1894–96, IX.

1897   Local Government Board, *Twenty-Sixth Annual Report* (C.8583), XXXVI.

1900   *Report of the Select Committee on the Sea Fisheries Bill*, VIII.

1901   *Report of the Departmental Committee on Preservatives and Colouring Matter in Food* (Cd.833), XXXIV.

1903   *Census of England and Wales. 1901. Summary Tables* (Cd.1523), LXXXIV.

1903   Board of Agriculture, *Consumption of Food and Cost of Living of the Working Classes in the United Kingdom and Certain Foreign Countries* (Cd.1761), LXVII

1904   *Report of the Inter-Departmental Committee on Physical Deterioration* (Cd.2175), XXXII.

1904   *Report of the Inter-Departmental Committee on Physical Deterioration, Evidence* (Cd.2210), XXXII.

1905   *Report of the Departmental Committee on the Fruit Industry of Great Britain* (Cd.2589), XX.

1905   *Report of the Royal Commission on the Supply of Food and Raw Materials in Time of War* (Cd.2643), XXXIX.

1906   *Report of the Inter-Departmental Committee on Medical Inspection and Feeding of Children Attending Public Elementary Schools* (Cd.2779), XLVII.

1906   Fishery Board for Scotland, *Twenty-fourth Annual Report* (Cd.2986), XVII.

1906   *Report of the Inter-Departmental Committee on Medical Inspection and Feeding of Children* (Cd.2779), XLVII.

1907   Local Government Board, *Thirty-Sixth Annual Report* (Cd.3665), XXVI.

1909   *Report of the Departmental Committee on Combinations in the Meat Trade* (Cd.4643), XV.

1910   Local Government Board, *Thirty-Ninth Annual Report, Supplement. Report on Infant Mortality* (Cd.5263), XXXIX.

1910   Local Government Board, *Thirty-Ninth Annual Report, Report of the Medical Officer* (Cd.5312), XXXIX.

1911   Board of Education, *Annual Report of the Chief Medical Officer for 1910* (Cd.5925), XVII.

1911   *Accounts of Expenditure of Wage-earning Women and Girls* (Cd.5963), LXXXIX.

1912–13   Board of Trade, *Report of an Enquiry by the Board of Trade*

	into the Earnings and Hours of Labour of Workpeople of the United Kingdom (Cd.6053), CVIII.
1912–13	*The Agricultural Output of Great Britain* (Cd.6277), X.
1913	Local Government Board, *Forty-Second Annual Report. Supplement. Second Report on Infant Mortality* (Cd.6909), XXXII.
1913	*Report of an Enquiry by the Board of Trade into Working-class Rents and Retail Prices* (Cd.6955), LXVI.
1914	*Annual Report on Sea Fisheries for 1913* (Cd.7449), XXX.
1914	Local Government Board, *Forty-Third Annual Report. Supplement. Third Report on Infant Mortality (Lancashire)* (Cd.7511), XXXIX.
1914	Local Government Board, *Forty-Third Annual Report. Report of the Medical Officer for 1913–14* (Cd.7612), XXXIX.
1914	*Return on Water Undertakings (England and Wales)*, LXXIX.
1916	Board of Trade, *Report of the Physiology (War) Committee of the Royal Society on the Food Supply of the United Kingdom* (Cd.8421), IX.
1917–18	*Census of England and Wales. 1911. General Report* (Cd.8491), XXXV.
1917–18	Local Government Board, *Forty-Fifth Annual Report. Supplement. Report on Child Mortality* (Cd.8496), XVI.
1917–18	*First (Interim) Report of the Royal Commission on Sugar Supply* (Cd.8728), XVIII.
1917–18	*Second Interim Report of the Committee on the Production and Distribution of Milk* (Cd.8886), XVI.
1918	*Report of the Working Classes Cost of Living Committee* (Cd. 8980), VII.
1918	Ministry of Reconstruction, *Report of the Machinery of Government Committee* (Cd.9230), XII.
1919	*Report of the Travelling Commission of Enquiry into the Cost of Production of Milk* (Cmd.233), XXV.
1919	*Report upon the Physical Examination of Men of Military Age by National Service Medical Boards* (Cmd.504), XXVI.
1920	*Wages and Conditions of Employment of Dock and Waterside Labourers* (Cmd.936–7), XXIV.
1921	Board of Education, *Annual Report of the Chief Medical Officer for 1920* (Cmd.1522), XL.
1923	*Interim Report on Milk and Milk Products* (Linlithgow Committee) (Cmd.1854), IX.
1924	*Final Report of the Departmental Committee on the Distribution and Prices of Agricultural Produce* (Linlithgow Committee) (Cmd.2008), VII.

1975–76   Monopolies and Mergers Commission, *Frozen Foodstuffs*, HC674, XXII.

1979–80   Monopolies and Mergers Commission, *Ice Cream and Water Ices* (Cmnd.7632).

1995–96   National Audit Office, Report by the Comptroller and Auditor General, *Health of the Nation: A Progress Report*, HC656.

1996–97   Committee of Public Accounts, Seventeenth Report, *Health of the Nation: A Progress Report*.

2000–1   National Audit Office, Report by the Comptroller and Auditor General, *Tackling Obesity in England*, HC220.

Non-parliamentary papers

(Published by HMSO, or the Stationery Office, London, unless otherwise stated)

Agriculture and Fisheries, Ministry of, Economic Series:
  No. 10 *Report on Egg Marketing in England and Wales*, 1926.
  No.22 *Report on the Marketing of Dairy Produce in England and Wales. Part I. Cheese*, 1930.

Agriculture, Fisheries and Food, Ministry of, *Household Food Consumption and Expenditure* (annual series).

Agriculture, Fisheries and Food, Ministry of, *Fifty Years of the National Food Survey 1940–1990*, ed. J. M. Slater (1991).

Agriculture, Fisheries and Food, Ministry of, *National Food Survey 1999* (2000).

Education, Board (later Ministry) of, Annual Report of the Chief Medical Officer, *The Health of the School Child* (annual series).

Environment, Food and Rural Affairs, Department of, *Agriculture in the United Kingdom, 2000* (2001).

Food, Ministry of, *How Britain Was Fed in War-Time Food Control, 1939–1945* (1946).

Health, Ministry of, Annual Report of the Chief Medical Officer, *On the State of the Public Health* (annual series from 1921).

Health, Ministry of, Advisory Committee on Nutrition: *First Report* (1937).

Health, Ministry of, Report of the Chief Medical Officer, *On the State of the Public Health during Six Years of War* (1946).

Health and Social Security, Department of, *Recommended Intakes of Nutrients for the United Kingdom*, Reports on Public Health and Medical Subjects No. 120 (1969).

Health and Social Security, Department of, *Report of the Working Group on Inequalities in Health* [The Black Report], (1980).

Health, Department of, *Dietary Reference Values for Food Energy and*

Nutrients for the United Kingdom, Report on Health and Social Subjects No. 41 (1991).

Information, Central Office of, *Britain: An Official Handbook* (annual series).

Information, Central Office of, The Social Survey:

Investigation into Household Cooking Habits for Certain Vegetables, New Series 27 (no date [October 1942]).

Manufacturing Foods Investigation, New Series 29 (undated [October 1942]).

Manufacturing Foods Inquiry, Part II, New Series 31 (December 1942).

Schoolboys' Diets by Audrey Beltram, typescript (1949).

Information, Central Office of, Wartime Social Survey:

Report No.3, New Series, The *Kitchen Front* broadcast programme *A Survey among Housewives Conducted for the Ministry of Food*, typescript, 29 November 1941.

Report No.20, New Series, 'Dig for Victory', *An Inquiry into the Effects of the 'Dig for Victory' Campaign made for the Ministry of Agriculture in August and September 1942*, typescript, undated.

Food During the War: A Summary of Studies on the subject of Food made by the Wartime Social Survey between February 1942 and October 1943, by Gertrude Wagner, typescript, undated.

Report No.33A, New Series, *School Meals in Scotland, August 1943*, typescript, undated.

New Series 49A, *National Wheatmeal Bread* by Gertrude Wagner, typescript, undated (possibly April 1944).

Medical Research Committee (later Medical Research Council) Special Report Series:

No.20, Ferguson, Margaret and Findlay, L., *A Study of Social and Economic Factors in the Causation of Rickets*, 1918.

No.38, *Report on the Present State of Knowledge Concerning Accessory Food Factors (Vitamins)*, 1919.

No.68, Mann, H. C. C., *Rickets: The Relative Importance of Environment and Diet as Factors of Causation*, 1922.

No.77, Chick, H. *et al.*, *Studies of Rickets in Vienna*, 1923.

No.105, Mann, H. C. C., *Diets for Boys During the School Age*, 1926.

No.151, Cathcart, E. P. and Murray, A. M. T., *A Study in Nutrition. An Inquiry into the Diet of 154 Families of St Andrews*, 1931.

No.157, Mackay, Helen M. M., *Nutritional Anaemia in Infancy*, 1931.

No.159, Committee on Dental Disease, *The Influence of Diet on Caries in Children's Teeth*, 1931.

No.165, Cathcart, E. P. and Murray, A. M. T., *Studies in Nutrition. An Inquiry into the Diets of Families in Cardiff and Reading*, 1932.

No.167, *Vitamins: A Survey of Present Knowledge*, 1932.

No.211, Committee on Dental Disease, *The Influence of Diet on Caries in Children's Teeth (Final Report)*, 1936.

No.297, McCance, R. A. and Widdowson, E. M., *The Composition of Foods*, 1960.

Statistical Office, Central, *Annual Abstract of Statistics; previously Statistical Abstracts of the United Kingdom* (annual series).

Statistical Office, Central, *Social Trends* (annual series).

United Nations, World Health Organization, Technical Report Series, 1966, No.340 (New York, 1966).

Journals and periodicals

Baker and Confectioner.
Baker's Magazine.
Baker's Quarterly Magazine.
Baker's Record.
British Food Journal.
British Medical Journal.
Chemist and Druggist.
Fish Trades Gazette.
Fruit Grower Fruiterer Florist and Market Gardener.
Fruit, Flower and Vegetable Trades' Journal.
Good Food Guide.
Greengrocer, Fruiterer and Market Gardener.
Grocery.
Grocers' Journal.
Lancet.
Meat Trades Journal.
School Board Chronicle.

Theses

Hammer, M A E., 'The birth of a nation's health; the life and work of George Newman to 1921', University of Cambridge Ph.D. thesis (1995).

Oddy, D. J., 'The working-class diet, 1886–1914', University of London Ph.D. thesis (1971).

INDEX

abattoirs, 16–17, 88, 146n
accessory food factors, see nutrition, vitamins
Acts of Parliament:
  Agriculture Acts, 1920–47, 93, 95, 111–12, 171
  Agriculture Marketing Acts, 1931–3, 111, 125
  Contagious Diseases Acts, 1878–96, 18
  Corn Production Act, 1917, 75
  Education (Provision of Meals) Act, 1906, 63
  Fair Trading Act, 1973, 181, 191
  Import Duties Act, 1932, 111
  Margarine Acts, 1887, 1907, 26, 31–2
  Medicines Act, 1968, 211
  Midwives Act, 1902, 47
  Notification of Births Act, 1907, 1915, 47
  Public Meals Act, 1917, 89
  Sale of Food and Drugs Acts, 1875, 1899, 1938, 31, 160
  Smoke Nuisance Act, 1853, 14
  Special Areas Acts, 1934–6, 131
  Sunday Trading Act, 1994, 182
  Trade Marks Act, 1875, 8
adulteration, 2, 10, 23, 30–2, 235
advertisements, 8, 37, 98–9, 102, 105, 160, 183–6, 190–1, 196
age of austerity, 166–8, 170
Agriculture, Ministry of (later Agriculture, Fisheries and Food), 111, 151–2, 171, 232
alcoholic drinks, 39–40, 75–6, 82, 92, 185, 198–200, 218–20, 223
  alcopops, 200
  beer, 1–4, 39, 76, 92, 185, 199
  whisky, 185
Allen & Hanbury, 98–100

Americanization of the diet, 103–4, 184, 191, 194, 233–4
Atwater, W. O., 41

bacon, 1, 3, 17, 35, 54, 59, 62, 68, 71, 86–90, 96, 111, 146, 155, 160, 203, 205
bacteriology, 15, 77
Barnett, Dr Margaret, 77n, 82n, 84n, 86n
Battle of the Atlantic, 139–40, 229
Beer Orders (see also public houses), 198–9
Beeton, Mrs Isabella, 5
Bell, Lady Florence, 51
Beveridge, W. H., 76, 88
Birds Eye Foods (see also food manufacturers, Wall's), 110, 173–7, 184, 188–90
Birdseye, Dr Clarence, 110
biscuits, cakes and pastries, 7, 16, 36–8, 77, 92, 104–6, 109, 146–8, 153, 155, 157, 185, 201, 203–4, 210, 217–18
Black Report (*Inequalities in Health*), 214–16
blitz, 140, 142, 153
body mass index (BMI), 210n
Bovril, 154
bread, 1–4, 6, 12–16, 32, 34–5, 37, 50–1, 53–60, 62, 67–9, 71, 74, 77, 80–3, 86, 90–1, 106, 114, 119, 128, 136–42, 149–50, 153, 159, 169–71, 178, 185, 201–2, 204, 206, 230
  breadstuffs policy, 75, 77, 86, 136, 138
breakfast cereals, 35–6, 68, 103–4, 147, 155, 157, 184, 201, 204, 235
British Empire Exhibition, 105

British Food Journal, 31–2, 160n,
177n, 213
British Home Stores, 109
British Medical Association (BMA),
123–5, 164, 167, 208–10
British Restaurants, 158–9, 164
BSE (Bovine Spongiform
Encephalopathy), 205, 231
Burnett, Professor John, xi, 5, 68
butter, 1, 6, 21–2, 25–6, 62, 87,
90–2, 101–2, 146, 149, 201,
206, 211

cafés, x, 23, 38, 76, 195
cafeterias, 159, 172
canned food, 9, 96–7, 103, 147, 149,
154, 159–60, 169, 203, 233
cardiovascular disease, 210, 221, 230
Carnegie Survey, 128, 130, 149
Carnegie Trust, 126, 128
Carson, Rachel, 231
caterers:
Aerated Bread Company (ABC), 38,
106, 172
Express Dairy, 38, 106
Lyons, 38, 105–6
catering, 38, 105–6, 188–9, 194–6
railway, 10
roadside and motorway, 195–6
Cathcart, Professor E. P., 120, 124,
136–7, 143
cheese, 1, 3–4, 22–5, 56, 71, 90, 96,
100, 149, 161–2, 201–2, 204
chefs, 5, 198, 232
Chernobyl, 231
Chick, Dr Harriet, xi, 98, 115
Child Poverty Action Group, 214
Chittenden, Professor R. H., 42
CJD (Creutzfeld Jacob Disease), 205
Cobbett, William, 4, 27
cocoa, 9, 140, 144, 157
coffee, 106, 185, 232
coffee bars, 172
Cold War, 212
COMA (Committee on Medical
Aspects of Food Policy), 215
confectioners:
Cadbury Ltd, 9, 36, 100, 103–5,
185, 197

Fry & Co Ltd, Bristol, 9, 105, 185
Rowntree's, 9, 36, 185, 197
confectionery, 103–5, 153, 185, 197,
217, 219
convenience foods, 174, 183–5
cookery, 2–4, 50–4, 59, 82, 84, 153–7,
172–3, 186–8, 203, 211–12, 214,
232
Cordon Bleu, 172
utensils, 37
wartime, meatless, 82, 84, 156
coronary heart disease, 210, 221
cost-of-living index, 55, 57, 90, 225

dairy produce, 1, 3–4, 7, 11, 21–6,
31–2, 60, 86, 230
Davies, Maud F., 50
demographic indicators, 47–9, 90,
182–3, 192, 208, 218
censuses 30, 45
child mortality rate, 48–9
death rates, 90
household size, 183, 218
infant mortality rate, 47–8
life expectancy, 70, 208
dental caries, 131, 165, 210
Devonport, Lord, Food Controller,
72–3, 80, 84
dietary behaviour, 4–6, 32–4, 50–4,
60–3, 68, 201–6, 211–12, 230–5
Fletcherism, 82n
food allergies, xi, 231
slimming, 194, 209, 211–12, 233
slimming foods, 211
snack foods, 196–7, 204, 210,
217–18, 232
vegetarianism, xi, 206
dieting, Scarsdale Diet, 212
Dig for Victory, 143, 151–2
Drummond, Professor J. C., xi, 30, 43,
57, 70, 97n, 137n, 139, 143,
162, 167, 227, 229–30

eating out, 76, 194–8, 200, 217–20
Economic Advisory Council, 120, 124
eggs, 7, 26–8, 57, 59, 61, 90, 96, 135,
148–9, 151, 155, 160–1, 171,
201–2, 204–5, 213, 235
Elliot, Dr Walter, 107, 117, 120, 134

Empire Marketing Board, 95, 117–19, 125, 130, 228
England:
  London, 49–51, 53–4, 65, 75, 109, 129, 140, 142–3, 153, 159, 197, 209, 217–19
  Midlands, 45, 65, 109, 153
  northern England, 3–4, 6, 55, 65, 109, 129, 153, 209, 217–19, 228
  rural, 57, 63, 65, 67
  southern England, 3, 104, 107, 109
environmental conditions, 43–54, 227
ethnic meals, 193, 196–7, 200, 217, 232
European Union (Common Market), 212, 224, 234
  Common Agricultural Policy, 224–5, 232
  European Commission, 198, 224

family-budget surveys:
  dietary analysis, 63–70, 227
  restricted diets, 130–2, 227–8
fast food catering, 38, 109, 172, 194–6
fats, 4, 25–6, 71, 114, 137, 142, 204, 206, 210–11
Festival of Britain, 1951, 172
fish, 1, 5–6, 19–21, 36, 51, 54, 56–7, 61, 67–8, 71, 96–7, 121, 135, 147–50, 154, 158, 161, 169, 173–6, 178, 185, 189, 192, 202, 204–5, 230
fish and chips, 6, 38–9, 76, 105–6, 161, 195–6, 200
Fletcher, Sir Walter, 116, 120
flour, 3, 12–13, 15, 35, 55, 77, 86, 92, 96, 138–40, 171–2, 185, 203, 229
fluoridation, 210
food additives, 212–13, 231
food contamination, 31, 160, 212
Food, Health and Income, 125–9, 132
food manufacturers, 8, 16, 102–5, 178, 180, 188, 190–1, 193, 198, 232–3
  Associated Biscuits, 104
  British Sugar Corporation, 104
  Co-operative Wholesale Society, 7, 37, 96, 176–7

Heinz, 103, 185, 194
Huntley & Palmer, 36, 103
Jurgens, 35, 101–2, 210
Kellogg, 103, 184
Lyons, J., & Co Ltd, 105–7, 174, 194
MacFisheries (see also Unilever), 102, 110, 173
Monsted, 101
Nestlé, 9, 185, 189, 191, 197
Quaker Oats, 103–4, 185
Tate & Lyle Ltd, 104
Unilever plc (Lever Bros), 101–2, 173–4, 183, 189, 198, 210
Van den Bergh, 35, 101–2, 210
Wall's, 107–8, 176
Food, Ministry of:
  Great War, 72, 80–9, 92–4, 95
  World War II, 96, 134–5, 137–8, 146, 171, 203, 228–9
  Food Advice Division, 156, 228
food palatability, 36, 52, 161, 164, 167, 171, 227
food poisoning, 31, 160–1, 205, 213–14, 231
food preservatives, 31, 160, 170, 212
food processing, 1, 7–8, 12–30, 77, 92, 96, 102–5, 111, 170–1, 198, 232
food production, 72, 75, 93, 95, 111–12, 115, 125, 135–6, 224–5, 230–1
food quality, 102–3, 160–2, 231–2
food queues, 77–8, 80, 86, 88, 147
food rationing, 72, 80, 86–9, 92–4, 133–8, 146–53, 158–9, 164, 166–8, 169–71, 206, 228
food retailing, 8–9, 30, 34–8, 100–2, 177–82
  life-style products, 193–4
  own-brand sales, 180–1
  self-service, 178–9
  Sunday opening in England and Wales, 182
  supermarkets, x, 177–83, 191–4, 199, 204, 233–4
  trading stamps, 178, 180
Food Standards Agency, 234n
food supply, 1–2, 6–10, 57, 162, 224–5
food technology, 3, 7, 96–100, 105,

111, 169–71, 173–7, 197, 212, 232–3
baking, 14–16
brewing, 3, 31, 198–9
fish fingers, 174–5, 192, 196
freeze dried products, 176
long life products, 192–3
milling, 12–13, 84, 96, 139
food transport by rail, 6–7, 22
fortification of foods, 139, 142, 162, 171, 229–30
freezers, 181, 186–9, 191–2, 214
frozen food, 170, 173–7, 181, 183–6, 188–93, 203, 232
fruit, 7–8, 28–30, 57, 61, 68, 89, 96–7, 103, 119, 147–8, 151, 155, 169, 173, 177, 203, 218
functional foods, 234–5
fusion foods, x, 188, 224, 233, 235

Glaxo Laboratories, 98, 100
Good Food Guide, 172–3, 197–8
Great War (World War I), 23–4, 28, 34, 43–4, 71–94, 96, 106, 115, 136, 144, 224, 227
    Food Controller, 72, 75–8, 92
    food coupons, 88–9
    food economy campaign, 77, 80–4
Greenwood, Professor Major, 120, 123–4
groceries, 8, 35–6, 100, 102–4, 106, 154–5, 160, 180–1, 204, 228

Hankey, Sir Maurice (later Lord), 124
health, 89–91, 163–6, 208, 211, 214–16, 227
    health scares, 205, 211–13, 231
    Physical Deterioration, Inter-Departmental Committee on, 1904, 45, 54, 62
    stature (physical development), 70, 113, 166, 208–9, 210–11, 216
health foods, 211
Health, Ministry of, 115–32, 134–6, 138, 162, 164, 166, 229
    Advisory Committee on Nutrition: Greenwood Committee, 120–4
    Luke Committee 124, 132, 133
    Concordat with MRC, 116

Health and Social Security, Department of, 215, 221, 223
Hollingsworth, Dorothy, xi, 162n, 229
Hopkins, Sir Frederick Gowland, 43, 91, 115, 120, 125
Housewives' League, 167
Hungry England debate, 122–4
hungry gap, 1
hungry thirties, 113

ice, 7–8, 106–7, 176
ice cream, 8, 106–9, 170, 184, 191–2, 210, 217
indigestion, 33–4
industrialization, 1–2
international trade, 10, 71, 86, 93, 96, 110–12, 224–5
Ireland:
    diet in, 2, 56–7, 64–5
    food supplies from, 13, 17–18, 25–6, 139n

jam, 8, 36, 55, 57, 87, 89, 92, 157, 204
jelly, 8, 68, 104, 170

kitchen equipment, 36–7, 181, 183, 186–9, 192, 214, 232

Labour, Ministry of, 126–30
League of National Safety (see also Yapp), 80, 85
League of Nations, x, 98, 132n
Lend-Lease Aid, 149, 167
Lipton, Sir Thomas, 38, 101
Lloyd, E. M. H., 125–6
Lloyd George, David, 72, 75
luncheon vouchers, 196
Lyons' Corner House, 38, 106, 194

McCance, Dr R. A., 139, 163, 247
Mann, Dr H. Corry, 115, 117
margarine, 7, 26, 35, 56, 78, 87, 90, 92, 101–2, 142, 149, 204, 230, 235
Mass Observation, 144, 150n, 166
meal patterns, 4–6, 50–4, 140, 142, 150–1, 159–60, 184, 196–7, 200, 232–4
    favourite meal, 200

meat, 1, 3–7, 11, 16–19, 36–7, 52, 54, 56, 58–62, 67–9, 71, 74, 77–8, 80, 86–90, 92, 96–7, 111, 114, 119, 128, 134, 142, 148–51, 154, 159–61, 169, 176, 185, 189, 192, 194, 204–6, 213, 217–18, 230–1
  meat products, 97, 153–4, 161, 186, 192, 194–5, 202–3, 205, 217–18
  sausages, 7, 154, 158, 160, 205, 218
Medical Research Council (MRC), 91, 97–8, 115–17
  Accessory Food Factors Committee, 116, 139
Mellanby, Sir Edward, 115–17, 120, 136–7
Mellanby, Dr May, 131
Metal Box Company, 103, 177
microwave ovens, 188–9, 192–3, 214, 232
milk, 4, 9, 21–3, 32, 49–50, 56–62, 64–5, 103, 111, 114, 117, 119, 128, 137, 142–5, 149, 161, 172, 185, 201–3, 215–16, 228
milk bars, 109, 172
milk, condensed, 9, 23, 71, 97, 142
Milk Marketing Board, 107, 109, 111, 172, 216
milk pasteurization, 22, 212
milk sterilization, 22
Miller, D. S., xi, 247n
Millers Mutual Trade Association, 96, 138–9
Monopolies and Mergers Commission, 181, 191, 198–9
Mottram, Professor V. H., 41, 122, 125

National Food Survey, 201, 206, 211, 214, 220, 227
National Kitchens, 76
National Wheatmeal Bread (National Loaf), 139–40, 170–1
Newman, Sir George, 44, 115–17, 119, 132
Newsholme, Sir Arthur, 44, 47
nutrition:
  calcium intake, 64, 66–9, 91, 114, 119–20, 129, 132, 137, 142–3, 151, 228
  carbohydrate intake, 56, 63–9, 113–14, 120, 129, 137, 143, 151, 206–8, 227–8
  deficiencies:
    anaemia, 43, 65, 131
    restricted growth, 70, 131
    rickets, 43, 90–1
    scurvy, 43
    vitamin deficiencies, 43, 63, 91, 142–3
  dietary policy, see fortification of foods
  dietary supplements and welfare foods, 32, 98–100, 163, 214–15
  energy values of diets, 4, 41–2, 63–70, 88–9, 114, 120, 129, 137, 142–3, 151, 206–8, 219–21, 227
  fats, intake of, 42, 56–7, 63–7, 69, 114, 120, 129, 143, 151, 206–8, 210, 219–21, 227–8
  iron, intake of, 64–9, 114, 120, 129, 137, 143, 206, 228
  malnutrition, 70, 113, 131, 227, 229
  protein intake, 42, 63–4, 66–7, 69–70, 114, 122, 129, 137, 143, 151, 206–8, 219–21, 227–8
  under-nutrition, 67, 117, 131, 216, 230
  vitamins, 43, 63, 97–100, 115, 131–2, 142–3, 160, 162, 165, 171, 206, 215, 229–30

oatmeal, 3–4, 55–6, 61, 137, 155
obesity, 194, 210, 220–1, 223, 231, 233
Oliver, Dr Thomas, 61–2, 66
Orr, Dr J. B. (later Sir John, then Lord Boyd Orr), 114, 117, 120, 126–7, 131, 133, 136–7, 163–4, 229
Orwell, George (Eric Blair), 230–1

packaging and containers, 31, 36–7, 96–7, 102–4, 169, 176–7, 197, 212, 233
Pankhurst, E. Sylvia, 74
pasta, 193, 217

patent medicines (see also indigestion), 9, 33–4
Physical Deterioration, see health
pizza, 186, 188, 192, 195, 200
porridge, 3, 84, 155
Postgate, Raymond, 172
potatoes, 2–4, 28, 50–3, 55–9, 62, 65, 67, 69, 71, 77, 81–2, 90, 111, 114, 119, 128, 136–7, 142, 149–50, 153, 168, 177, 189, 191–2, 201–2, 206, 218, 230
public houses, 39–40, 92, 196, 199–200
  gastropubs, 200
  pub chains, 199–200
puddings and pies, 7–8, 37, 59, 63, 104, 148, 155, 157, 232
Pyke, Dr Magnus, 161–2, 169–70, 231, 234

railways, 9–10, 93
Reeves, Mrs M. A. Pember, 50–2, 54, 62, 82
refrigeration, 7–8, 17–19, 21–2, 24, 29, 107–10, 173–7, 186–93
refrigerators, 8, 37, 183, 186
resale price maintenance (RPM), 178
restaurants, 23, 76, 194, 197, 200
  dining rooms, 9, 38
  ethnic restaurants, 197, 200
  Steak Houses, 195
Retail Food Index, 95, 146, 225
retailers, multiple:
  Co-operative Retail Societies, 35, 37, 101, 136, 178n
  Home and Colonial Stores, 35, 101
  Iceland (Big Food Group), 189
  Lipton's Stores, 35, 101
  Marks and Spencer, 109, 180, 181
  Maypole Dairies, 35, 101
  Sainsbury, J., & Co, 100–1, 179–82
  Tesco, 180, 182
Rhondda, Lord, Food Controller, 72, 78, 84–6, 88
Rowett Research Institute, xii, 117, 125n, 130n
Royal Commission on Arsenical Poisoning, 1903, 31

Royal Commission on Sugar, 1914, 71, 93
Royal Commission on the Supply of Food, 1905, 12, 57
Royal Commission on Wheat, 1916, 72, 93
Royal Society, 75, 81, 84, 86
Runciman, Walter, President of the Board of Trade, 71

sandwich bars, 196–7
school meals, 62–3, 163, 165, 196, 215–16
school milk, 111, 125, 130, 163, 165, 215
Scotland, 2–4, 6, 20, 55–7, 63–5, 117, 119–20, 128, 131, 159–60, 189, 216–18
Sinclair, Upton, 31
slimming, see dietary behaviour
Smith, Sir Ben, 167
Smith, Dr Edward, 41n, 54, 60
snack foods, see dietary behaviour
social investigators, ix
  Booth, Charles, ix, 39, 53–4, 57–60, 62
  Rowntree, B. S., ix, 22, 30n, 39, 41, 52, 57–62, 65, 67–9
Strachey, John, 167
submarine warfare (see also Battle of the Atlantic), 71–2, 224
  U-boats, 72, 86
sugar, 4, 8, 12, 52, 58–9, 62, 68–9, 71, 74, 77–8, 80, 87, 89–90, 92, 114, 119, 128, 134, 140, 142, 144, 146, 149–50, 157, 201–4, 210, 228–9
supermarkets, see food retailing

tea, 2–3, 6, 9, 35–6, 38, 51, 54, 66, 74, 78, 87, 102, 106, 142, 144, 149, 153, 158, 185, 232
tea shops, 38, 106, 194
television, 183–5, 196, 232–3
temperance, 9, 38, 76
Thompson, Flora, 29–30

urbanization, 7, 27–8, 38, 44–5, 111

utilities:
    cooking by gas, 37, 50
    gas supply, 37, 50
    sanitation, 45–7
    water supply, 46

vegetables, 1–2, 7, 11, 28, 30, 57, 59,
    96–7, 103, 119, 135–7, 151,
    153–4, 167, 170, 173–4, 185–6,
    192, 202–3
vegetarianism, see dietary behaviour
vitamins, see nutrition

War Cabinet, 72, 77, 81, 86, 88,
    133–4, 137
    Scientific Sub-Committee on Food
      Policy, 136–9, 143
    Sub-Committee on Rationing, 133
Weight Watchers, 191, 194
Widdowson, Dr Elsie M., 163, 247
Women's Voluntary Service (WVS),
    151
Woolton, Lord, Minister of Food, 135,
    229
Woolworth, F. W., & Co Ltd, 109, 148

World Health Organization, 48–9
World War I, see Great War
World War II, 131, 133–66, 201, 205,
    212, 214, 224–5, 228
    black market, 150, 228–9
    coupons, 146, 148, 158
    diarists:
      Mrs Nella Last, 146–8, 161
      Mrs Milburn, 146, 159
    dried egg, 149, 155, 161
    food substitutes, 160–1
    Kitchen Front, 154, 157
    points coupons 147–8, 155, 157
    ration books, 136, 146, 228
    rationing, 133–4, 136–8, 140, 144,
      146–50, 155, 167–8, 170–2, 203,
      228
    recipes, 156–7
    Spam, 154
    sweet coupons (personal points),
      147
    Wartime Social Survey, 153–9

Yapp, Sir Arthur, 80, 85
Yudkin, Professor John, xi, 52n, 204